The Growth and Management
of the Japanese Urban System

STUDIES IN URBAN ECONOMICS

Under the Editorship of

Edwin S. Mills
Princeton University

Norman J. Glickman. ECONOMETRIC ANALYSIS OF REGIONAL SYSTEMS: Explorations in Model Building and Policy Analysis

J. Vernon Henderson. ECONOMIC THEORY AND THE CITIES

Norman J. Glickman. THE GROWTH AND MANAGEMENT OF THE JAPANESE URBAN SYSTEM

In Preparation

George S. Tolley, Philip E. Graves, and John L. Gardner. URBAN GROWTH POLICY IN A MARKET ECONOMY

The Growth and Management of the Japanese Urban System

NORMAN J. GLICKMAN
Departments of City and Regional Planning and Regional Science
University of Pennsylvania
Philadelphia, Pennsylvania

ACADEMIC PRESS
New York San Francisco London 1979
A Subsidiary of Harcourt Brace Jovanovich, Publishers

ACADEMIC PRESS, INC.
111 Fifth Avenue, New York, New York 10003

United Kingdom Edition published by
ACADEMIC PRESS, INC. (LONDON) LTD.
24/28 Oval Road, London NW1 7DX

Library of Congress Cataloging in Publication Data

Glickman, Norman J
    The growth and management of the Japanese urban
system.

    (Studies in urban economics)
    Includes bibliographical references.
    1. Cities and towns––Japan––Growth. 2. Urbanization
––Japan. 3. Urban economics––Case studies. I. Title.
II. Series.
HT147.J3G55   301.36'0951   78–8831
ISBN 0–12–286950–8

Contents

3

Growth and Change in the Japanese Urban System: The Experience of the 1970s

4

Migration and Urban Economic Development

5

The Spatial Structure of Japanese Cities

6

The Management of the Japanese Urban System: Regional Development and Regional Planning in Postwar Japan

7

Financing the Japanese Urban System: Local Public Finance and Intergovernmental Revenues

8

The Growth and Management of the Japanese Urban System

Preface

In the past 30 years, there has been a tremendous growth of Japanese cities, with the urbanization rate nearly doubling between 1950 and 1970. This trend, a continuation of prewar activity, has been accompanied by

A concentration of population and economic enterprise in the Tokaido megalopolis—the area along the Pacific coast between Tokyo and Osaka

Rural out-migration to Tokaido during the 1950s and 1960s, followed by relative out-migration from large centers in the 1970s

Significant suburbanization of population and jobs in the areas surrounding the largest metropolises

Problems of congestion and pollution in large cities

These phenomena have brought forth a series of public debates about the role of urbanization in Japanese life. Large cities have been praised as being spatially efficient by some observers and decried as congested, polluted, and of being contributors to the disintegration of social life by others.

Urban and regional policies formulated on all governmental levels have attempted to control and manage this urban growth. Several kinds of public policies have been followed. Among them are

Regional plans to coordinate regional development efforts of several national government ministries

Growth pole policies to bolster lagging rural regions during the 1950s and 1960s

Land use controls to contain the development of highly dense urban areas
Tax and transfer policies to redistribute income and tax monies from
    richer to poorer regions

This volume attempts to analyze Japanese urban and regional growth
processes and to provide a better understanding of government policies
aimed at managing growth. I have attempted to bring together a data base
which encompasses the major elements of the Japanese urban system—
those cities, towns, and villages whose citizens interact on a daily basis to
form the core of Japanese urban life. One should look at the entire
system—not just Tokyo and other large cities, as others have done—to fully
understand the nature of urban development.

I have taken a largely empirical and economic analysis approach in
doing so. Moreover, since the processes and policies which I have noted
above are common to other industrialized nations, I have adopted an international comparative perspective as well.

Chapter 1 provides the reader with an overview of the economic and
urban growth processes and outlines regional policies fostered during the
postwar period. In Chapter 2, I introduce a concept called the "Regional
Economic Cluster," or REC. RECs have been defined as the "functional
economic regions" or labor market areas which make up the Japanese
landscape. That is, the RECs attempt to coalesce all cities, towns, and
villages which form the daily commuting systems of metropolitan areas.
Such data have not been previously aggregated, and I argue that this is a more
meaningful way to interpret economic and social development than by using
individual cities or prefectures. The REC is the analogue to the American
Standard Metropolitan Statistical Area (SMSA), and the definition of the
REC makes comparisons with the United States and other countries more
easily managed. The time-consuming and difficult conceptualization and
collection of this data set leads to an analysis in Chapter 2 of the regional
development during the 1950s and 1960s, a period of very high economic
growth nationally. I view the relative centralization of the Japanese urban
system during that period, using the REC data base. Additionally, I present
regional development trends in other developed and less developed countries during the same period.

In Chapter 3, I extend the analysis to the 1970s and see a change in
migration and regional development patterns during a period of lower economic growth. I also present some migration analysis for 1954–1975 for
Japan and make use of migration data for other countries for similar periods.
I discuss the transition of regional development patterns from one in which
rural regions were drained of population to one in which some of the more
urbanized regions began to lose population.

Next, in Chapter 4, I delve more deeply into migration trends with an analysis of the relationship between migration and employment growth. I employ regression techniques here (as elsewhere in the volume) to draw some inferences about this relationship.

The internal structure of Japanese cities is the principal subject of Chapter 5. After viewing the spatial distribution of population and land prices, I construct an econometric model of Japanese land markets. This model forecasts the major determinants of cities' spatial arrangements. Comparisons to land use patterns in other countries concludes Chapter 5.

I look at regional planning in relation to regional development in Chapter 6, the first of two chapters on urban and regional public policy. Regional plans were formulated during the 1950s and 1960s to combat interregional imbalances in production, income, and population. I review these plans—again in an international context—and evaluate their effectiveness in bringing about the desired changes. Chapter 7 looks at a complimentary set of policies: intergovernmental taxes and transfers which aimed at the distribution of resources from rich to poor regions. I argue that it is important to look at these two sets of policies—regional planning and the intergovernmental tax system—as components of an overall regional policy. Finally, in Chapter 8, I present an overview of the findings of the study.

I have written this book to try to appeal to a wide audience. Although the book is highly empirical, most of the material will be understandable to the noneconomist. I have extensively used statistical methods such as regression analysis and shift-share to illustrate points which I hope are clearly made in a nonmathematical manner. In addition to economists, Japan area specialists, geographers, and those interested in political economy and urban planning will find this book of use in their work. I have written a reasonably analytical volume which I hope will fill a void in the analysis of Japanese urbanism. It does not cover all aspects of Japanese urban life, but goes deeply into regional development, migration, land use, and regional public policy.

Acknowledgments

My work on Japanese urban development could not have been carried out without the help of many people in Japan and this country. I came to this project with no formal training in Japan area study and, with no working knowledge of Japanese, depended upon others for explanations, language help, and encouragement. I take this opportunity to thank some of these people. A complete list would probably double this volume's length.

I first went to Japan in 1971 as a guest of the Japan Center for Area Development Research (JCADR). The invitation came from President Eiichi Isomura of Toyo University (who was then associated with the JCADR) through President Martin Meyerson of the University of Pennsylvania. Through Professor Isomura, who early on taught me that "social relations are more important than social science in Japan," I became enchanted by Japanese society and interested in urban problems there. The aid of Professor Isomura and Mr. Meyerson was critical at early stages of this research, and I thank them both.

This volume has grown out of 4 years (1974–1978) of research, which was predominantly funded by the Ford Foundation. At Ford, I am particularly indebted to William C. Pendleton who had the confidence in me to sponsor the early research which led to this volume. Others within the Ford Foundation who were helpful include John Bresnan, Carl Green, John Newmann, and Louis Winnick. Additional research funds were kindly made available to me through a Japan Foundation Fellowship which allowed me to go to Japan and work on Chapters 3 and 6 in 1976. Kichimasa Soda, head of the Exchange of Persons Department at the Japan Foundation, and his staff, made my stay productive.

Several research assistants and translators were of great help to me in my research. Yukio Oguri was responsible for collecting the data in the City Data Bank (see Chapter 7) and was an able and patient translator in Japan and co-worker in Philadelphia. Much of Chapter 5 is due to his efforts on an earlier jointly written article. I am deeply indebted to him as I am to Yoshitsugu Kanemoto, Toshinori Nozu, Taro Ochiai, Atsuyuki, and Kayo Okabe (who helped to define the Regional Economic Clusters in Chapters 2 and 3), Akihiko Tani, and Masafumi Tanifuji. In Philadelphia, I also worked closely with W. Warren McHone on an earlier version of Chapter 4 and with Erhan Gencer on a previous draft of Chapter 7.

My principal Japanese collaborator was Dr. Tatsuhiko Kawashima of Gakushuin University. He oversaw the development of the Regional Data Bank used extensively in Chapters 2 and 3 and was a perceptive critic of a draft of Chapter 6. I thank Tats Kawashima for his constant help and for sharing the hospitality of his family on my trips to Japan.

Other Japanese scholars who helped me greatly were Ikumi Hoshino, Noboru Sakashita, and Masahiko Honjo. I was the guest of public officials and scholars at several institutions, including the National Land Agency, the Bureau of Statistics of the Prime Minister's Office, the Economic Planning Agency, the Ministry of Home Affairs, Tokyo University, and Gakushuin University. Gakushuin's Economic Department graciously provided me with office space in 1974 and 1976, and its members were kind to me. I am grateful to the Japan Center for Area Development Research which provided me with my initial experiences in Japan and with the infrastructure for the early empirical research. I thank, in particular, Toshiyuki Yoshida, formerly of the JCADR, for his kindness during several visits to Japan between 1971 and 1974. I also thank the staff of the International House of Japan where I lived during my visits to Japan; collectively the staff members made each visit comfortable.

I was a visiting scholar at the International Institute for Applied Systems Analysis during 1977, where Chapters 2, 3, 6, and 7 were drafted and appeared originally as IIASA Research Memoranda. I extend thanks to Niles M. Hansen, Andrei Rogers, Koren Sherrill, and the staff of the Human Settlements and Services group at IIASA.

Several people provided detailed comments on drafts of this volume. David Kornhauser's reading of most of this volume was very helpful. I also received comments on individual chapters from Ronald Aqua, Bennett Harrison, Alain Plaud, Jean-Louis Sarbib, Daniel R. Vining, Jr., and Michelle White.

Efficient typing was done by Mary Blue, Lucy Holley, Susan Long, and Norie de Sanchez at the University of Pennsylvania, and by Annemarie Bütikofer at IIASA. I thank them all.

I wish to thank *Environment and Planning*, the *Journal of Regional Science,* the *Journal of Urban Economics,* and *Regional Studies* for permission to reprint material which originally appeared in their pages.

The facilities of the University of Pennsylvania were used for most of the research. I would particularly like to thank the Departments of City and Regional Planning and Regional Science, with which I am affiliated.

Any errors or misinterpretations which remain are, of course, my responsibility.

Mr. Masaru Harada did the calligraphy which appears on the dust jacket.

Finally, I thank Michèle H. Richman for her love, encouragement, and understanding throughout this project. It is to Michèle that this book is dedicated.

Some Dimensions of Japanese Urban Development

1

1 Introduction

In viewing postwar Japanese society, one is struck by many elements.[1] There is, for instance, the dynamism of its economic life as measured by the growth of industrial output and foreign trade. One also observes great advances in the standard of living and with it, alas, unfortunate levels of environmental disruption (what the Japanese call *kogai*). There is a social system and culture that rewards achievement and hard work; this fact is not so visible to the foreign observer, but is certainly present. There is an (underfunded) educational system that forms the framework for a system of meritocracy in business and government. And, fundamentally, there are bustling, overcrowded, large industrial cities existing adjacent to small towns with predominantly agricultural bases. This last aspect of Japanese life is the primary subject of this volume: the growth of the system of Japanese cities and the attempts to manage and orient this growth by government at various levels.

Chapter 1 serves as an introduction to the remainder of the book. Here I focus on some of the dimensions of Japanese economic and urban development, primarily since 1945. These aspects include metropolitan growth and

[1] For major studies of various aspects of Japanese society, see Allinson (1975), Benedict (1946), Burks (1972), Doi (1971), Dore (1958, 1959), Gibney (1975), Hall, J. N. (1970), Hall, R. B. (1976), Halloran (1969), Hane (1972), Ishida (1971), Kosaka (1972), Lockwood (1965), McNelly (1972), Nakane (1970), Okita (1975), Patrick and Rosovsky (1976a), Reischauer (1974, 1977), Stockwin (1975), Takahashi (1968), Thayer (1971), Tsuru (1958), Vogel (1975), and Ward (1967).

development, urban spatial structure and suburbanization, land use in cities, and migration among regions. At the same time, I also wish to look at the overall picture of economic development during the postwar period and to view urban development in that context. Finally, I want to introduce some notions concerning the management and the planning of Japanese cities and regions.

In Section 2, I observe the pattern of economic development of the national economy and its dynamic change over time. I do this in an international framework, comparing Japan to other nations as I shall do elsewhere in this volume. In Section 3, the dimensions of urban development are discussed using conventional data sources. Finding these units of observations lacking, I introduce a new data-collection scheme, the Regional Economic Cluster (REC), in Section 4. The REC is a functional urban region in which a central city of a region is linked in a systematic way with its surrounding suburbs via commuting patterns and other criteria. The REC data set is used extensively in my analyses in Chapters 2 and 3 as well as in other portions of the book. I conclude Section 4 with an introduction to the remaining material in this volume.

2 Postwar Economic Growth in Japan

2.1 Introduction

In this section, I outline the dimensions and sources of postwar economic growth in Japan in preparation for the discussion of urban and regional development in Section 3. During the period under study, expansion of the economy was rapid and sustained and was accompanied by growth-oriented government policies; these policies are part of the subject of Chapter 6 and will not be discussed here. My emphasis throughout this study will be on the relationship between increases in economic performance and changes in cities, and this section begins this set of discussions that will occupy us further in later chapters. In Section 2.2, I note the nature of Japanese economic development, followed by an effort to explain the sources of growth in Section 2.3. In Section 2.4, I discuss the consequences of economic growth on Japanese society.

2.2 Nature of Economic Growth

Patrick and Rosovsky (1976b) and Denison and Chung (1976) provide data and analyses of Japanese economic performance in the postwar period. They, and other commentators, show that economic growth in Japan was spectacular and was accompanied by vast economic and social change (which many have said was structural in nature) and massive urbanization; Table 1.1 highlights the growth of the Japanese economy and compares it to that of other industrial powers. According to Denison and Chung, the real increase of national income was 8.77% per year between 1953 and 1971.[2] Over the 20-year period 1952–1972 current value Gross National Product (GNP) per capita increased fifteenfold (from $182 to $2,823), and real wages (money wages deflated by the consumer price index) increased by a factor of three.

The strength of Japanese growth relative to other countries can be seen in Denison and Chung, where growth rates for 11 industrial countries are calculated and comparisons with Japan undertaken. For Japan, after standardization is made for national income accounting practices, the 1953–1971 average annual GNP growth rate was 9.17%. This can be compared to 3.85% per year for the United States (1948–1969), 2.29% for the United Kingdom (1950–1962), and 7.26% for West Germany (1950–1962). For further analysis and comparison, see Denison and Chung (1976, pp. 95–100). For the time period 1960–1975, Organization for Economic Cooperation and Development (OECD) (1976) data show Japan's real annual rate of GNP growth at 8.9% compared to 3.2% for the United States, 2.4% for the United Kingdom, and 5.2% for France.

Japan's real GNP growth rate from 1955 to 1976 is shown in Figure 1.1. One sees growth rates of 10% or more for several years during the 1960s. There was only 1 year (1974) in which there was an absolute decline in GNP. Figure 1.1 also shows GNP growth rates for the U.S. economy. There is only 1 year (1965) in which U.S. growth was faster than Japan's.

Although there has been a decline in growth in the 1970s, especially after the so-called "oil shock" of 1973, Japanese growth rates continued to be higher than those of the most advanced capitalist nations. Full employment has been the norm for Japan, with unemployment at essentially frictional levels, ranging between 1 and 1.8% between 1960 and 1974. However, growth was accompanied by considerable price inflation, which averaged 5.2% per year from 1963 to 1972 (Table 1.1) and which was much higher in the mid-1970s. Inflation was not as burdensome to Japan, however, as to other countries since the real rate of growth was so high. Particularly, there was a very rapid increase in the price of land during that time span. Between 1952 and 1975, the price index of urban land went up by a factor of 58. That index increased by 30% in 1973 alone; for further analyses of Japanese land prices and land use, see Chapter 5, Glickman and Oguri (1978), and Japan National Land Agency (1976).

---

[2] For the subset years of 1953–1961 and 1961–1971, average annual growth rates were 8.13 and 9.20%, respectively.

TABLE 1.1
Japan's Economic Growth in an International Perspective

	Japan	United States	France	West Germany	United Kingdom
Gross Domestic Product (GDP) per capita,[a] 1973	3,760	6,170	4,900	5,600	3,100
Average annual growth rates of GDP, 1968–1973[b] (percentage)	9.5	3.6	6.0	5.1	2.8
Gross fixed investment as a percentage of GDP, 1968–1972 average	38.7	17.0	26.3	25.9	19.6
Gross savings as a percentage of GDP, 1968–1972 (average)	39.3	17.5	26.8	27.5	19.2
General government revenue as a percentage of GDP, 1973	22.4	30.2	38.0	41.0	37.9
Government transfer payments as a percentage of GDP	5.7	9.9	20.8	16.6	14.8
Average annual growth rate of prices, 1963–1972					
Wholesale Price Index	1.3	2.6	3.2	1.6	3.7
Consumer Price Index	5.2	3.5	4.3	3.3	5.2

Employment by industrial sector as percentage of total employment, 1973 (percentage)					
Agriculture	13.4	4.1	12.2	7.5	3.0
Industry	37.2	31.7	39.3	49.5	42.3
Other	49.4	64.7	48.5	43.0	54.7
Share of world trade (percentage)					
1952	2.2	17.1	5.4	5.2	11.0
1972	6.2	12.5	6.3	10.2	6.2
Indicators of living standards					
Private consumption per capita, 1973[a]	1,910	3,840	2,913	3,000	1,960
Percentage of GDP spent on education, 1970	4.1	5.4	4.7	4.0	5.5
Dwellings completed per 1,000 inhabitants, 1970	16.8	11.3	10.5	10.7	6.1
Television sets per 1,000 inhabitants, 1972	225	474	237	293	305
Doctors per 1,000 inhabitants, 1971	1.15	1.57	1.38	1.71	1.29

Source: OECD (1975, 1977), Patrick and Rosovsky (1976b), and Denison and Chung (1976).
[a] GDP in producers' values in U.S. dollars at current prices and exchange rates.
[b] In 1970 prices.
[c] Standardized by Denison and Chung (1976; Table 2-12) for following years: Japan (1953–1971), United States (1948–1969), France (1950–1962), West Germany (1950–1962), and United Kingdom (1950–1962). See Denison and Chung for a discussion of standardization procedures.

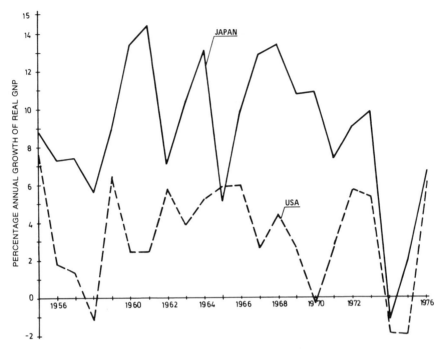

Figure 1.1. Average annual growth of Gross National Product for Japan and the United States, 1955–1976.

2.3   Sources of Economic Growth

The sources of long-term economic growth in Japan were many and have been reviewed extensively by several authors. Most have argued that there have been several elements in the dynamic change that occurred within the Japanese economy.

First, Japan has possessed a well-trained and hard-working labor force that was significantly underemployed in low-productivity efforts, particularly in the primary sector. Over the postwar period, labor was shifted from these low-productivity jobs to those in higher productivity areas, particularly manufacturing.

A second source of growth has been the tremendous increase in the physical stock of capital. There has been a very high rate of investment in plant and equipment, with the capital stock increasing faster than the growth of the labor force.[3] This high investment rate has been made possible by a

---

[3] Investment in plant and equipment in the private business sector increased at an average annual rate of 14.4% between 1952 and 1973; the labor force increased by only 1.49% per year over roughly the same period.

very high rate of personal savings among Japanese families and a high level of reinvestment by Japanese firms. For example, gross private investment as a percentage of GNP increased from 17.2% in 1952–1954 to 38.7% in 1968–1972. Gross private savings rose dramatically[4] over the same time span—from 16.5 to 39.3%; the latter figure is roughly twice the level for the United States; see Denison and Chung (1976, pp. 116–119) and Table 1.1 for comparative data concerning investment and savings. Thus, one of the reasons for low labor productivity—the low level of capital per worker—dramatically changed in the course of the 1960s and 1970s with the robust capital stock growth.

A third major source of growth has been technological change in Japanese industry. Some of this technology has been imported from foreign sources, but much was developed through research and development efforts of the Japanese themselves.

Fourth, the government has been supportive of growth and has fostered growth-oriented policies. The Liberal Democratic party, which has governed Japan since 1955, has been responsive to demands of its major financial backer, the business community,[5] in providing a variety of supportive policies such as subsidies, import protection, and related items for the purpose of stimulating private business growth.

There are, of course, other reasons for Japanese economic growth, among them the liberalization of foreign trade, which has led to an increase in Japan's share of world trade, from 2.2% in 1952 to 6.2% in 1972. Table 1.1 shows that over the same period much of this increase came at the expense of the shares of the United States and the United Kingdom. Other important growth inducers were greater economies of scale in industry, the procurement from American military installations (especially during the Korean War), and the very low level of nonproductive defense expenditures.

An important aspect of the growth process has been the relative neglect of the public sector for the sake of private-sector activity. This is manifested in data on the public sector, both in terms of comparisons to other Japanese economic aggregates and with respect to the public sectors of other nations. Thus, government consumption grew at an average annual rate (in current *yen* terms) of 14.8% between 1955 and 1974, whereas private-sector activity grew faster. For instance, gross domestic fixed capital formation (*GDFCF*) grew by 17.6% and exports by 16.1%. Government consumption as a percentage of GNP was relatively stable between 1955 and 1974, at around 9%. At the same time, *GDFCF* increased from 20.1% of GNP in 1955 to 35.0% in

---

[4] Among the reasons given for the high savings rate in Japan have been the low level of retirement benefits and support for the aged and the culture that encourages hard work and savings.

[5] For a Marxist analysis of this, see Halliday (1975). For a discussion about government–business relations, see Vogel (1978).

1970 and 33.1% in 1974.[6] Therefore, it appears that private-sector investment and export growth—the explicit objects of public policy—were achieved, in part, at the expense of the public sector.

Table 1.1 also shows that there was relatively little money devoted to the public sector compared with other countries. Government spending in 1973 was 22.4% of Gross Domestic Product (*GDP*) in Japan, whereas it was 30.2% in the United States and 41.0% in West Germany.

The major share of public capital was devoted to business-oriented infrastructure investments, such as for ports, sewers, land reclamation, and roads. Relatively little money was spent on social programs, such as public housing and education (see Table 1.1). As Patrick and Rosovsky (1976b, p. 44) say, "Government social overhead investments in roads, sewage systems, water supplies, and public housing was relatively neglected as were welfare and social insurance programs, and defense expenditures were kept below 1 percent of GNP."

For instance, according to the Japan Economic Planning Agency (EPA) (1975), industry-related public investment was 57% of total investment between 1959 and 1966; it fell to 51% by 1973, in part under the impact of protest by citizens who demanded more social (or "life-related") public spending. In Table 1.1, we see that Japan spent relatively little on social transfer payments.

Private consumption per capita in Japan was $1,910 in 1973, a figure that was below each of the other countries. In relation to GDP per capita, consumption was even lower: It was 50.8% of GDP, whereas comparative figures for the United States, France, and the United Kingdom are approximately 60%. This is another reflection of the high savings rate in Japan. Additionally, growth was accompanied by a fall in the share of Gross National Expenditures (*GNE*) going to private consumption. According to EPA data cited by the Japan Economic Research Center (1975), the rates of private consumption expenditures to *GNE* fell from 64.1% (1955) to 51.1% (1973).

Finally, Japan ranks high in the number of houses completed (a reflection of its attempt to raise previously low housing standards), high relative to income in the ownership of television sets, and low in the number of doctors per capita. I return to more observations on living standards in Section 2.4.

The picture that emerges from this discussion is one of a country with rapid economic growth that has been accompanied by high levels of savings and investment, a growing share of world trade, and a relatively resource-scarce public sector. Denison and Chung, in analyzing the growth of the Japanese economy during the period 1961–1971, divide the components of the growth process in the following way: Additional capital represented a 26.9% contribution to that decade's growth rate, advances in knowledge

---

[6] See Japan Bureau of Statistics, Office of the Prime Minister (1976a).

represented 25.4%, and economies of scale were responsible for 20.5%. Elements pertaining to the labor force were responsible for 28.0% of the growth rate, divided among greater man-hours, a more efficient allocation of labor among sectors, and a greater labor productivity due to educational factors.

I discuss some of the ramifications of these growth patterns next.

2.4 Consequences of Economic Growth

The growth that occurred in postwar Japan was accompanied by a dramatic structural shift in the organization of the economy and the spatial distribution of population and employment. Patrick and Rosovsky (1976b) indicate this through their analysis of the change in the proportions of the labor force and *GDP* by sector. There was a shift from primary industry to the secondary and the tertiary sectors. For instance, between 1956 and 1971, the share of labor in the primary sector fell from 41.9 to 17.4%.[7] Concomitantly, the labor force proportion in manufacturing rose from 17.7 to 27.2% and the tertiary sector increased from 34.1 to 47.2% during the same period. Within these broad categories one also sees interesting changes. For instance, there was a decline in labor-intensive light industries (such as textiles) and an increase in activity in electrical machinery (especially consumer electronics), transport, and equipment. There was, therefore, a shift from backward, low-productivity industry to more modern higher technology sectors.[8]

Another ramification of postwar growth and development was the rapid change in the spatial distribution of people and jobs within Japan. As has been shown in Glickman (1976) and will be discussed further in Chapters 2 and 3, there was an increasing concentration of economic activity along the Tokaido belt, especially in the heavy manufacturing industry. Table 1.2 shows the relative growth rates of production for the major regions from 1955 to 1972. There we see that in the early postwar period, production increases were greatest in the Coastal Kanto (Tokyo), Tokai (Nagoya), and Coastal Kinki (Osaka) regions. The rural regions (with the exception of Chugoku in 1955–1959) grew relatively slowly in comparison to the national average, although production growth rates did increase, especially in the late 1960s. The faster economic growth in the urban regions led to great disparities in incomes. In 1965, the per capita income of an average Tokyo resident was more than twice that for someone living in Kagoshima.

---

[7] We show the results of these patterns in Table 1.1 where the proportion of employment in agriculture is 13.4% in 1973. However, Japan still has relatively more agricultural workers than the other countries noted there.

[8] As Bieda (1970) and others have indicated, the Japanese economy continues to be highly dualistic, with a large-scale, high-technology sector operating beside a more primitive, low-technology sector.

TABLE 1.2
Relative Growth Rates of Total Production for Major Regions, 1955–1972

Region	1955–1959	1960–1964	1965–1970	1971–1972
Japan	1.00	1.00	1.00	1.00
Hokkaido	1.00	.71	.83	.95
Tohoku	.87	.78	.78	.95
Inland Kanto	.91	.91	.98	.89
Coastal Kanto	1.26	1.27	1.15	.96
Tokai	1.23	1.05	1.16	1.00
Hokuriku	1.01	.80	.87	.84
Inland Kinki	.97	.88	1.02	1.47
Coastal Kinki	1.46	1.14	1.00	.93
Chugoku	1.54	.93	1.00	.96
Shikoku	.79	.81	.90	.76
Kyushu	.78	.70	.81	1.48
Metropolitan areas	1.29	1.18	1.09	.96
Periphery of metropolitan areas	.94	.90	.99	1.00
Other areas	.86	.78	.85	1.06

Source: Japan Economic Planning Agency (1975).

The growth of job opportunities and the advantages of higher incomes produced tremendous increases in migration to the major metropolitan centers—Tokyo, Osaka, and Nagoya—during the 1950s and 1960s. This concentration reflected a desire for economically efficient spatial allocation of production. Firms that located in the Tokaido area were able to take advantage of agglomeration economies and to have access to both foreign and domestic markets. Although there was some spatial deconcentration beginning in the late 1960s, the period of highest economic growth (1955–1969) saw population increasingly clustered in a small number of large metropolitan areas. This resulted in many urban and social problems that have been associated with high-density living; these, of course, included pollution, congestion, social alienation, and high and rising land prices. Such problems were heightened by the low levels of public infrastructure devoted to social problems. Section 3 returns to the impact of structural changes on cities.

The ramifications of social priorities that fostered economic growth on the quality of life can be seen by comparing changes of important social indicators with the growth of the economy. Patrick and Rosovsky (1976b, pp. 28–35) report a set of social indicators for Japan, including those for safety, health, residential environment, education and culture, work and safety, and environmental pollution. The growth rate of these indicators is shown in Table 1.3 and compared them to changes in economic variables. The indicators of social well-being grew at approximately 5% per year during the 1960s. This was less than half of the economic growth rate. It can be

TABLE 1.3
Average Annual Growth Rates of Major Economic and Social Indicators, 1960–1970

Gross National Expenditures (constant prices)	11.1
Private business investment	15.4
Safety	5.0
Health	2.3
Residential environment	6.0
Work and social welfare[a]	5.5
Education[b]	3.4
Enviromental pollution[a]	.4

Source: Patrick and Rosovsky (1976b, Table 1-4) and Japan Economic Research Center (1975), citing data from Japan Economic Planning Agency *Annual Report on National Income Statistics*.

[a] For 1960–1969.

[b] University, college, and high school students per age group and pupils per teacher in elementary and secondary schools.

argued, therefore, that governmental (and societal) priorities with respect to growth resulted in relatively slow increases in nonincome components of the quality of life. This has resulted in a great amount of citizen protest over social conditions during the 1970s; on this, see Glickman (1972).

Therefore, we see that a great economic transformation took place in Japan after World War II. An economy that had substantial numbers of workers in agriculture and mining in 1940 became manufacturing- and service-based by the 1970s. Spatial change accompanied these events as people left farms for a small number of cities where they found higher paying jobs but often less than adequate social service levels. It is to a discussion of Japanese cities that I now turn.

3 Urban and Regional Development in Japan

3.1 Some Definitions

The nature and change in postwar Japanese cities and regions is the subject of this section. Under the impact of rapid economic growth, there were remarkable changes in the spatial distribution of people and jobs: There was great concentration in a relatively few cities and regions and depopulation in most others; these changes are the focus of Chapters 2 and 3 and have already been mentioned briefly in Section 2.4. Here, I set out some of the overall dimensions of this change in order to provide background for the material in the following chapters.

Before discussing the elements of urban and regional change, I shall give some definitions of the units to be used in this and later chapters. Most data are collected on the basis of political units on different geographical

TABLE 1.4
Japanese Major Regions

1. HOKKAIDO	17. Ishikawa	32. Shimane
TOHOKU	18. Fukui	33. Okayama
2. Aomori	CHUBU (Tosun)	34. Hiroshima
3. Iwate	19. Yamanashi	35. Yamaguchi
4. Miyagi	20. Nagano	SHIKOKU
5. Akita	21. Gifu	36. Tokushima
6. Yamagata	CHUBU (Tokai)	37. Kagawa
7. Fukushima	22. Shizuoka	38. Ehime
KANTO	23. Aichi	39. Kochi
8. Ibaragi	KINKI	KYUSHU
9. Tochigi	24. Mie	40. Fukuoka
10. Gumma	25. Shiga	41. Saga
11. Saitama	26. Kyoto	42. Nagasaki
12. Chiba	27. Osaka	43. Kumamoto
13. Tokyo	28. Hyogo	44. Oita
14. Kanagawa	29. Nara	45. Miyazaki
CHUBU (Hokuriku)	30. Wakayama	46. Kagoshima
15. Niigata	CHUGOKU	47. OKINAWA
16. Toyama	31. Tottori	

levels. First, there are a set of 47[9] prefectures of which 42 are called *ken*. Of the remaining prefectures, Osaka and Kyoto are urban prefectures (called *fu*), there is one metropolitan prefecture, Tokyo—*to,* and the circuit prefecture of Hokkaido (called *do*). The prefectures are mapped in Figures 1.4–1.7. These prefectures are, in turn, grouped into major regions that are listed in Table 1.4. Some of my later discussion is in terms of these major regions.

Second, there are a set of municipalities consisting of cities (*shi*), towns (*cho* or *machi*), and villages (*son* or *mura*). The major cities are shown in Figure 1.2. Within the municipalities are Densely Inhabited Districts (DIDs) that bring forth another view of urban concentration. These consist of clusters of enumeration districts[10] within cities, towns, and villages with a population of 4,000 inhabitants per square kilometer (km²) and a total population of 5,000 persons.

Finally, there is a set of rather indefinite clusters of cities, towns, and villages that, according to Kornhauser (1976, pp. 30–31), form other regions. These include regions such as *Kansai (Kinki* or *Kinai)*, the region around Osaka, although the definitions are often idiosyncratic and vary with the user

---

[9] This includes Okinawa, which reverted to Japan in 1972. Much of the discussion of urban change in this and later sections include discussions based on 46 prefectures, excluding Okinawa.

[10] Enumeration Districts (*ED*s) are the basic areal units for data collection in national census surveys. Most *ED*s consist of approximately 50 households, with nearly 580,000 for all of Japan. For further information see Japan Bureau of Statistics, Office of the Prime Minister (1975, p. 724).

Figure 1.2. Japanese cities.

and the purpose of the study. I shall use each of these definitions in the remainder of this section as a preview of my own set of regional definitions given in Chapter 2.

3.2 Long-Term Urbanization and Urban Change

There has been rapid urbanization throughout the twentieth century, although this urbanization (defined as the percentage of total population in cities) has often been mischaracterized as a postwar phenomenon. Some of the dimensions of this urbanization are given in Figure 1.3. In 1920, the first year for which good, comparable census data are available, about 18% of the Japanese populution lived in cities. However, this proportion doubled (to 37.9%) by 1940, and then doubled again to 72.2% by 1970. Therefore, the urbanization phenomenon that is often attributed to postwar development is really a continuation of prewar trends.

The increasing concentration of population in large cities is shown in Table 1.5 as well as in Figure 1.3. The proportion of population in cities of greater than 500,000 persons doubled from 1920 to 1970, from 11.9 to 24.5%. The number of cities in that category also increased dramatically. It is not commonly appreciated, however, that there was significant concentration in large cities even before the war: Nearly 20% of the 1940 population was in 6 large cities. There was considerable deconcentration during the war (due to the bombing-related evacuations), but the movement to large cities resumed after the war. However, Table 1.5 reveals that after 1950, the number of large cities increased greatly: Those with populations above 500,000, for

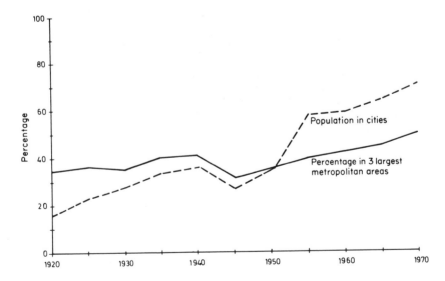

Figure 1.3 Urbanization in Japan, 1920–1970.

TABLE 1.5

Number of Municipalities and Percentage of Population by Size Class of Municipality, 1920–1970

Population size	Number of municipalities				Percentage of Japanese population			
	1970	1960	1950	1920	1970	1960	1950	1920
1,000,000 or more	8	6	4	2	20.1	17.9	11.4	7.1
500,000–999,999	7	3	2	4	4.4	1.9	2.1	4.8
300,000–499,999	21	12	18[a]	3[a]	7.6	4.6	5.7[a]	1.1[a]
200,000–299,999	41	21			9.5	5.5		
100,000–199,999	73	71	40	23	10.0	10.6	6.5	5.0
50,000– 99,999	182	160	91	64	11.9	11.5	7.6	6.8
50,000–or less	2,944	3,238	10,259	11,711	36.5	48.1	66.8	75.2
All Japan	3,276	3,511	10,414	11,807	100.0	100.0	100.0	100.0

Source: Japan Bureau of Statistics, Office of the Prime Minister 1970 Population Census (Vol. 1, Table 12) (Tokyo: Japan Bureau of Statistics, Office of the Prime Minister).

[a] 200,000–499,999 size class in 1920 and 1950.

example, increased from 6 to 15. There were almost three times as many cities in the 200,000–400,000 range as well. Therefore, there was dispersion of population down the city hierarchy[11] to medium-sized cities, a subject to which I shall return in Chapters 2, 3, and 8. Figure 1.3 also indicates the high concentration in three metropolitan areas of Tokyo, Osaka, and Nagoya that has been a feature of Japanese urban development throughout the period under study. About 38% of the population lived in these regions in 1920, compared with about 42% in 1970. As I shall note in greater detail in Chapter 3, there was some relative deconcentration from these and other large cities in the 1970s.[12]

What have these long-term trends meant for the interregional distribution of population? The long-term patterns of population growth by large region is depicted in Table 1.6, in which the nation has been divided into six regions and the proportion of total population in each is charted. The first three regions are the highly urbanized ones of Tokyo, Osaka, and Nagoya. Together, they had 33.6% of the nation's people in 1920; this figure increased to 36.56% by 1940. However, after World War II, the relative increase in concentration of the metropolitan regions increased greatly. Between 1950 and 1970 the proportion went from 35 to 46%; it increased again, but at a

[11] Also clear from Table 1.5 is the fall in the number of people living in a smaller number of cities below 50,000 population. Although 75.2% of the population lived in 11,711 such municipalities in 1920, these figures fell to 36.5% and 2,944 by 1970. Most of the decline in the number of municipalities occurred during the wave of municipal amalgamations in the 1950s.

[12] We can also look at changes in the DID population. The proportion of the population living in these areas increased greatly during the 1960s. In 1960, 43.7% of the population (40.8 million people) lived in DIDs compared to 53.5% (55.5 million) 10 years later. Thus, DID population increased by 14.7 million while the rest of Japan lost 4.4 million during the decade.

TABLE 1.6
Population Shares for Major Regions, 1920–1975

	1920	1930	1940	1950	1955	1960	1965	1970	1975
Capitol region[a]	13.86	14.50	17.56	15.69	17.27	19.12	21.93	23.26	24.15
Osaka–Kobe–Kyoto region[b]	12.17	13.05	11.04	11.74	12.27	13.04	14.14	14.78	14.98
Nagoya region[c]	7.61	7.67	7.96	7.69	7.66	7.85	8.15	8.30	8.41
Three metropolitan areas	33.66	35.22	36.56	35.12	37.20	40.01	44.22	46.34	47.54
Tohoku[d]	10.46	9.58	9.88	10.84	10.46	9.98	9.27	8.71	8.25
Kyushu[e]	14.73	13.87	13.70	14.55	14.49	13.81	12.59	11.63	11.09
Other[f]	41.15	41.33	39.86	39.49	37.85	36.20	33.92	33.32	33.12

Source: Japan Bureau of Statistics, Office of the Prime Minister (1971, 1976b).
[a] Tokyo, Saitama, Chiba, and Kanagawa prefectures.
[b] Osaka, Hyogo, Kyoto and Nara prefectures.
[c] Aichi, Gifu, and Mie prefectures.
[d] Aomori, Iwate, Miyagi, Akita, Yamagata, and Fukushima prefectures.
[e] Fukouka, Saga, Nagaski, Kumamoto, Oita, Miyazaki, and Kagoshima prefectures.
[f] All other prefectures.

slower rate between 1970 and 1975. The pattern for the rural regions, of course, is the mirror image of urban regions. There was great out-migration from 1920 on, which has only slowed down in the 1970s. I shall discuss this further in Section 3.3 and Chapter 3.

3.3   Migration Patterns

The metropolitan development noted in Section 3.2 was primarily a product of migration trends that swept people out of the countryside and into the cities. From 1920 on, there was a loss of migrants in the vast majority of Japanese prefectures. In the 1920–1925 period, for instance, 39 of Japan's prefectures had net out-migration. This polarization continued until 1970, when 34 prefectures lost migrants. For the postwar period, Figures 1.4–1.7 give the destination of these migrants. The prefectures marked in black had net in-migration, and there is striking concentration in the net destinations of the migrants. For 1950–1955 (Figure 1.4), one sees net out-migration from the nonmetropolitan prefectures (except Hokkaido) to the metropolitan prefectures around Tokyo, Nagoya, Osaka, and Fukuoka–Kitakyushu. Figure 1.5 shows even more concentration for 1955–1960: Only the three major metropolitan areas were net receivers of migrants. Also note in Figure 1.5 the beginnings of suburbanization, as prefectures such as Chiba (near Tokyo) had positive in-migration. This metropolitan decentralization continued in 1960–1965 (Figure 1.6) as Tokyo prefecture lost migrants for the first time and Kyoto, Nara, and Hyogo (all near Osaka) became net attracters of population. Additionally, Hiroshima and Shizuoka showed faster growth than previously. Finally, Osaka *fu* lost migrants in 1965–1970 (Figure 1.7), and there were further movements to regions lower down the urban hierar-

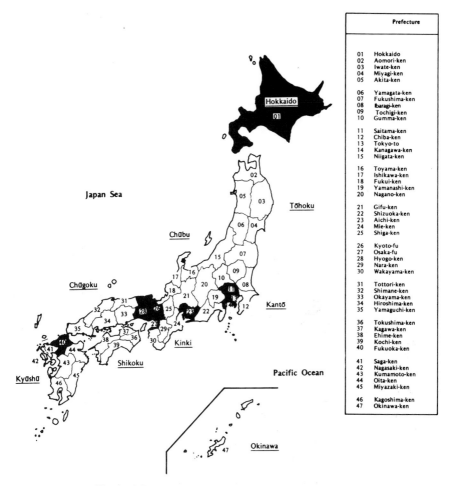

	Prefecture
01	Hokkaido
02	Aomori-ken
03	Iwate-ken
04	Miyagi-ken
05	Akita-ken
06	Yamagata-ken
07	Fukushima-ken
08	Ibaragi-ken
09	Tochigi-ken
10	Gumma-ken
11	Saitama-ken
12	Chiba-ken
13	Tokyo-to
14	Kanagawa-ken
15	Niigata-ken
16	Toyama-ken
17	Ishikawa-ken
18	Fukui-ken
19	Yamanashi-ken
20	Nagano-ken
21	Gifu-ken
22	Shizuoka-ken
23	Aichi-ken
24	Mie-ken
25	Shiga-ken
26	Kyoto-fu
27	Osaka-fu
28	Hyogo-ken
29	Nara-ken
30	Wakayama-ken
31	Tottori-ken
32	Shimane-ken
33	Okayama-ken
34	Hiroshima-ken
35	Yamaguchi-ken
36	Tokushima-ken
37	Kagawa-ken
38	Ehime-ken
39	Kochi-ken
40	Fukuoka-ken
41	Saga-ken
42	Nagasaki-ken
43	Kumamoto-ken
44	Oita-ken
45	Miyazaki-ken
46	Kagoshima-ken
47	Okinawa-ken

Figure 1.4. Net migration for prefectures, 1950–1955.

chy, as Okayama gained migrants.[13] As I note in Chapter 3, the process of urban concentration abated somewhat in the 1970s. Growth became concentrated in middle-sized regions, whereas the large ones saw relative (and, in some cases, absolute) decline.

The overall effect of these migration and urban growth patterns was one of high concentration in a few urban regions and considerable depopulation in most rural ones. Figure 1.8 shows the areas deemed depopulated by the National Land Agency. These areas cover most of the country; only the

[13] Not only were urban prefectures beginning to experience net out-migration, but their central cities were feeling such patterns. Of Japan's seven largest cities, all had positive in-migration in 1959. By 1965, three (Tokyo, Osaka, and Kitakyushu) were experiencing net out-migration. By 1971, only Yokohama and Kobe continued to be net receivers of migrants.

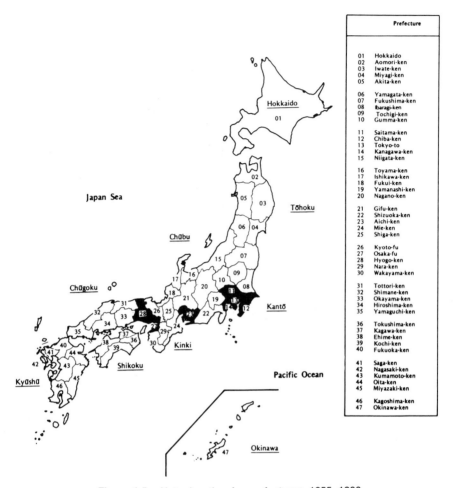

	Prefecture
01	Hokkaido
02	Aomori-ken
03	Iwate-ken
04	Miyagi-ken
05	Akita-ken
06	Yamagata-ken
07	Fukushima-ken
08	Ibaragi-ken
09	Tochigi-ken
10	Gumma-ken
11	Saitama-ken
12	Chiba-ken
13	Tokyo-to
14	Kanagawa-ken
15	Niigata-ken
16	Toyama-ken
17	Ishikawa-ken
18	Fukui-ken
19	Yamanashi-ken
20	Nagano-ken
21	Gifu-ken
22	Shizuoka-ken
23	Aichi-ken
24	Mie-ken
25	Shiga-ken
26	Kyoto-fu
27	Osaka-fu
28	Hyogo-ken
29	Nara-ken
30	Wakayama-ken
31	Tottori-ken
32	Shimane-ken
33	Okayama-ken
34	Hiroshima-ken
35	Yamaguchi-ken
36	Tokushima-ken
37	Kagawa-ken
38	Ehime-ken
39	Kochi-ken
40	Fukuoka-ken
41	Saga-ken
42	Nagasaki-ken
43	Kumamoto-ken
44	Oita-ken
45	Miyazaki-ken
46	Kagoshima-ken
47	Okinawa-ken

Figure 1.5. Net migration for prefectures, 1955–1960.

Tokaido region along the Pacific belt and scattered areas elsewhere in the country had major concentrations of population. These trends are discussed further in Chapters 2, 3, and 4. The policies to handle the dual problems of urban overconcentration and rural deconcentration are the subjects of Chapters 6 and 7.

3.4 Metropolitan Spatial Structure

As I have shown in Section 3.3, metropolitan decentralization—at least for the large regions—began to occur in the 1960s. I now take a closer look at this process. Table 1.7 indicates some of the spatial change that occurred within the three major metropolitan areas for the periods 1955–1960 and 1965–1970. Several patterns seem clear. First, there was a continuing de-

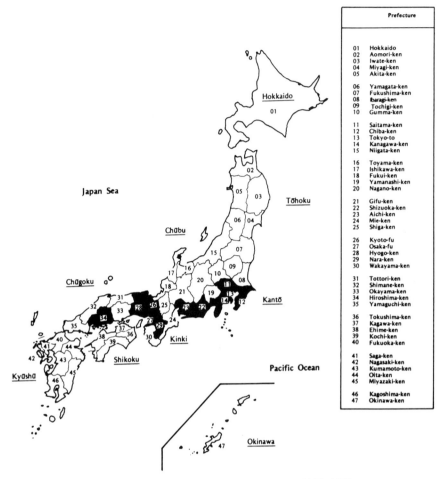

Figure 1.6. Net migration for prefectures, 1960–1965.

cline in the growth rates of the central portions (those within 10 km of the centers) of these regions; Tokyo's most central area was losing population absolutely after 1960. Even the area 10–20 km from the core showed declining population growth rates. Second, there was a "layering" effect as the outer subregions began to grow successively more quickly as time passed. For example, Tokyo's highest growth area was in the 10–20-km band in 1955–1960; the fastest growth was recorded in the 20–30- and 30–40-km areas in the succeeding time periods. Similar patterns also hold for the other regions. Third, the areas at the periphery showed rapidly increasing growth rates with time. Thus, Nagoya's subregion 40–50 km from the core lost 1.0% of its population during 1955–1960, but had a 12.4% increase in the late 1960s.

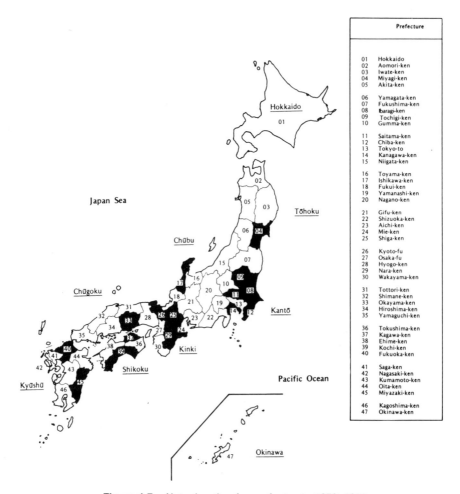

	Prefecture
01	Hokkaido
02	Aomori-ken
03	Iwate-ken
04	Miyagi-ken
05	Akita-ken
06	Yamagata-ken
07	Fukushima-ken
08	Ibaragi-ken
09	Tochigi-ken
10	Gumma-ken
11	Saitama-ken
12	Chiba-ken
13	Tokyo-to
14	Kanagawa-ken
15	Niigata-ken
16	Toyama-ken
17	Ishikawa-ken
18	Fukui-ken
19	Yamanashi-ken
20	Nagano-ken
21	Gifu-ken
22	Shizuoka-ken
23	Aichi-ken
24	Mie-ken
25	Shiga-ken
26	Kyoto-fu
27	Osaka-fu
28	Hyogo-ken
29	Nara-ken
30	Wakayama-ken
31	Tottori-ken
32	Shimane-ken
33	Okayama-ken
34	Hiroshima-ken
35	Yamaguchi-ken
36	Tokushima-ken
37	Kagawa-ken
38	Ehime-ken
39	Kochi-ken
40	Fukuoka-ken
41	Saga-ken
42	Nagasaki-ken
43	Kumamoto-ken
44	Oita-ken
45	Miyazaki-ken
46	Kagoshima-ken
47	Okinawa-ken

Figure 1.7. Net migration for prefectures, 1970–1975.

Table 1.8 shows similar out-migration trends from the core for the period 1967–1972. The table divides migration into central city and suburban components for the three largest metropolitan regions. Three important trends emerge from an examination of Table 1.8. First, total net migration to the regions as a whole declined with time. This is due principally to a decline of in-migration from nonmetropolitan regions and is consistent with the findings of Section 3.3 and Chapter 3. Additionally, however, Osaka and Nagoya began to lose migrants to other (mostly smaller) metropolitan centers by 1970. Second, out-migration from the central cities increased dramatically. This can be accounted for by more suburban-destination moves as there continued to be net in-migration from nonmetropolitan areas. Thus, the Tokyo *ku* area had out-migration of 99,900 persons in 1972 because of a

Figure 1.8. Depopulated regions (■) of Japan. [From Japan National Land Agency (1974).]

206,200-person out-migration to its suburbs; it had positive in-migration from nonmetropolitan and other metropolitan regions. This is also true for Nagoya. Third, net migration to suburban Tokyo and Osaka declined over time. This, too, is an indication of the lower growth of metropolitan regions in the 1970s.

4 Urban Growth and Change in Postwar Japan

4.1 A Review

In Section 3, I outlined some of the major features of Japanese urban development. The process of population concentration in the large metropolitan regions began prior to World War II but continued at even faster rates afterward. This was, in part, due to rapid economic development of the

TABLE 1.7

Metropolitan Spatial Change in the Tokyo, Osaka, and Nagoya Regions, 1955–1970

Distance from center (in kilometers)	Change in population (in thousands)			Percentage change in population		
	1955–1960	1960–1965	1965–1970	1955–1960	1960–1965	1965–1970
TOKYO						
0–10	549	−63	−296	13.4	−1.4	−6.5
10–20	1,213	1,337	791	29.8	25.3	12.0
20–30	387	846	1,017	22.7	40.4	34.6
30–40	259	717	1,119	15.4	36.9	42.1
40–50	55	274	423	3.1	15.0	20.1
Within 50 km, total	2,463	3,110	3,056	18.5	19.7	16.2
OSAKA						
0–10	680	489	273	20.7	12.3	6.1
10–20	269	681	530	19.5	41.3	22.7
20–30	137	243	354	13.3	20.7	25.0
30–40	130	252	316	7.8	14.0	15.4
40–50	32	78	105	1.9	4.5	5.8
Within 50 km, total	1,249	1,741	1,579	13.8	16.9	13.1
NAGOYA						
0–10	280	240	125	19.1	13.8	6.3
10–20	100	220	216	12.4	24.3	19.1
20–30	56	109	189	7.8	14.0	21.2
30–40	98	123	83	7.4	8.6	5.3
40–50	−5	5	67	−1.0	1.0	12.4
Within 50 km, total	529	698	678	10.9	12.9	11.1

Source: 1970 Population Census of Japan.

national economy and the fact that so much economic activity was centered in the Tokaido megalopolis. Thus, rural migrants were attracted to Tokyo and other large centers by high-paying jobs and the concomitant decline of agriculture in their home regions. Then, centrifugal forces began to send jobs and people to suburban portions of these regions. These trends were related to movements in jobs—first to large cities, later to the suburbs—and with significant interregional differences in income disparities. In order to manage and control the distribution of population among regions, to redirect employment locations, and to reduce income differentials, the government (at various levels) undertook several policies. These included regional development plans (especially for backward areas), tax and subsidy schemes to influence employment location, and many other programs. These planning laws, which were passed beginning in the early postwar years, were aimed at greater efficiency in an economywide sense. Plans were supplemented by a tax system that attempted to reduce income differences.

TABLE 1.8
Intraregional Net Migration for Major Metropolitan Areas, 1967–1972 (in thousands)

	Tokyo[a]		Osaka[b]		Nagoya[c]	
	1967	1972	1967	1972	1967	1972
Total net migration	280.4	180.5	107.1	29.4	25.8	17.3
Other metropolitan areas	40.2	29.2	2.2	−11.9	−11.0	−4.7
Nonmetropolitan areas	240.2	151.4	104.9	41.3	36.7	22.0
Central area	−10.4	−99.9	−67.3	−89.3	1.8	−16.9
Other metropolitan areas	24.4	19.7	−0.8	−3.9	.7	1.3
Nonmetropolitan areas	146.7	86.5	44.8	14.5	12.1	8.7
Suburbs	−181.5	−206.2	−111.3	−99.9	−11.0	−26.9
Suburbs	290.0	280.4	174.4	118.7	24.0	34.2
Other metropolitan areas	15.9	9.4	3.0	−8.0	−11.6	−6.0
Nonmetropolitan areas	93.5	64.8	60.1	26.8	24.7	13.3
Central area	181.5	206.2	111.3	99.9	11.0	26.9
Migration within central area	578.1	651.4	230.3	203.0	87.0	84.4
Migration within suburbs	429.5	588.3	347.7	451.5	197.2	224.6

[a] Keihin metropolitan area: The central area is defined as the Tokyo *ku* area, Yokohama, and Kawasaki *shi*.

[b] Hanshin metropolitan area: The central area is defined as Kyoto, Osaka, Sakai, Higashiosaka, Kobe, and Amagasaki *shi*.

[c] Chukyo metropolitan area: The central area is defined as Nagoya *shi*.

4.2 Outline of the Remainder of This Volume

The capsule summary of urban development and policy given in Section 4.1 sets the stage for the remainder of this volume, in which I shall attempt to elucidate these patterns more fully. The rest of this section previews the topics of Chapters 2–8.

One of the major problems facing an economist (or other social scientist) in analyzing urban problems is the data base to be used. The preceding sections presented an outline of urban development trends to the 1970s from standard statistical sources. However, this is not a comprehensive view of Japanese urban development because several elements are missing. For the most part, the data are based upon information collected for individual cities and prefectures. As a result, one cannot understand with any precision the relationship *among* cities. For instance, one should be able to see movements between central cities and their related suburban areas and movements among regions. In Section 3.4 we summarized some limited data for the three largest metropolitan regions. Unfortunately, we have little information on metropolitan regions other than the largest seven. Furthermore, the data for even these seven regions are extremely limited in both scope and time: Few variables are collected and for only a short time period. Moreover, the methods used for defining these regions are limited to arbitrary political (usually prefecture-based) boundaries. Ideally, I wanted to have regionalizations based upon economic, social, and other patterns that are more flexible than prefecture definitions. Such is not the case for the regional data generally available from the census. Also, it is important to know activity in smaller regions. Certainly, Akita's or Hakodate's urban patterns must be known if there is to be a comprehensive understanding of Japanese urban development. Knowing about Tokyo is simply not enough. Given current census data-collection efforts, it is not possible to analyze regional development in the small metropolitan centers.

It is with these problems in mind that I have defined a comprehensive set of *functional urban regions* that relate central cities and their surrounding subregions. I call these *Regional Economic Clusters* (RECs), and much of the rest of this volume uses a data base centered on the RECs. There are 80 such regions in Japan that, in total, have two-thirds of the national population residing within their boundaries. They have been defined on the basis of several criteria, including commuting patterns, level of urbanization, and employment distribution. These regions cut across prefectures and are similar to the American Standard Metropolitan Statistical Areas,[14] which also use commuting data to define functional urban regions. I believe that the RECs will allow a better unit of analysis with which to consider the major aspects of the development of the Japanese urban system than is otherwise possible.

In Chapters 2 and 3 I make direct use of the REC data as I summarize trends from 1950 to 1975. Chapter 2 views the period of rapid economic development (1950–1970) and employs the REC data set to chart population and employment shifts. After defining the RECs and describing my data-collection efforts, I proceed to look at interregional and intraregional shifts; in doing so, I make use of regression, shift-share, and other analytic techniques. Then I turn to a comparison between urban development patterns in Japan and other countries, concentrating on Western Europe, North America, and Asia. My purpose is to see how Japan's development was similar to other countries with regard to urbanization levels, the development of large cities, spatial structure, and regional development. Four appendices give more complete documentation of our techniques and data.

Chapter 3 extends the analysis given in Chapter 2 in at least two ways. First, it considers a time period, 1970–1975, in which economic growth slowed in comparison to the previous 20 years. It is important to understand what happened to the Japanese urban system under the economic conditions of the 1970s. Second, I consider additional data on urban change. The REC data are collected from census sources that are generally available every 5 years. Here, I analyze annual data for interprefectural migration to supplement the basic data set and examine in greater detail the interregional migration trends that occurred during the 1960s and 1970s. Furthermore, I return to my international perspective, considering migration patterns in

---

[14] See my discussion of this concept in Chapter 2, Section 2.1.

several industrialized countries. The purpose of this set of comparisons is to consider the problem of declining, highly urbanized regions around the world.

Migration patterns and employment growth among cities within the Japanese urban system are the subjects of Chapter 4. I use a regression model that relates employment growth by industrial sector to labor force migration, intracity employment shifts among industries, and changes in labor force participation rates. I therefore extend the analyses of Chapters 2 and 3 by explaining the employment growth previously examined, although with a more concentrated focus.

Chapter 5 concludes my consideration of the development of the Japanese urban system with some analysis of the spatial *form* of Japanese cities. I concentrate on patterns of population density and land prices using regression analysis of negative exponential and other functions; in doing so, I build upon some work by Mills and Ohta (1976) and others on this subject. I then analyze patterns by means of an econometric model of land use for 71 cities. The model is used to predict the central density and slope of the density functions, analogous variables for land price functions, and other variables. Last, I compare land use patterns in Japan with those of the United States, the United Kingdom, and West Germany.

Therefore, Chapters 2–5 catalogue the dimensions of many of the characteristics of the Japanese urban system. Although there are elements that I do not discuss, I attempt to detail the major trends. I show, as already noted, that there was increasing concentration within the Tokaido megapolis with high-density living, high land prices, and serious pollution and congestion.

Chapters 6 and 7 discuss governmental attempts to manage the growth of the urban system during the postwar period. Chapter 6 contains an analysis of national and regional economic planning, with particular emphasis on the latter. National planning is discussed in relation to other economic policies employed to increase economic growth, particularly monetary and fiscal policy. The focus then shifts to regional planning efforts, most of which were offshoots of national planning. I look at the effectiveness of regional planning in attempting to redress regional imbalances in income, production, and employment. Particularly, I examine attempts by the Japanese to use growth poles to increase economic activity in less developed regions. Finally, I examine parallel regional planning efforts in other industrialized countries that were faced with similar regional problems to see how approaches and techniques differed.

An important component of Japan's fiscal system, local government finance, is discussed in Chapter 7. I discuss the set of local government units and intergovernmental relations and undertake regression analyses of the determinants of local revenue patterns during the 1960s. Because the fiscal system is supposed to redistribute revenues from rich to poor regions, I examine the extent to which this goal was achieved. I view this redistribution through the tax system as an adjunct to the planning efforts discussed in Chapter 6; where public investment remained highly centralized in rich, urbanized regions (through the planning apparatus), the tax system has helped poorer regions and has helped to reduce interregional income disparities. Therefore, Chapters 6 and 7 should be viewed as attempts to explain the management of the urban system.

Finally, I tie together some of the highlights of this volume in Chapter 8, which synthesizes the findings on growth and development from Chapters 2 and 3, the migration discussions of Chapters 3 and 4, and considerations of spatial structure from Chapters 2, 3, and 5. Finally, I look at the policy responses to these phenomena, integrating the planning and tax system analyses of Chapters 6 and 7.

References

Allinson, G. D. (1975). *Japanese Urbanism: Industry and Politics in Kariya, 1872–1972*. University of California Press, Berkeley, California.

Benedict, R. (1946). *The Chrysanthemum and the Sword: Patterns of Japanese Culture*. Meridian, New York.

Bieda, K. (1970). *The Structure and Operation of the Japanese Economy*. John Wiley and Sons Australasia Pty. Ltd., Sidney, Australia.

Burks, A. W. (1972). *The Government of Japan*. Crowell, New York.

Denison, E. F. and W. H. Chung (1976). *Economic growth and its sources*, in H. Patrick and H. Rosovsky, eds., *Asia's New Giant: How the Japanese Economy Works*. The Brookings Institution, Washington, D. C. Pp. 63–151.

Doi, T. (1971). *The Anatomy of Dependence*. Kodansha, Tokyo.

Dore, R. P. (1958). *City Life in Japan: A Study of a Tokyo Ward*. University of California Press, Berkeley, California.

Dore, R. P. (1959). *Land Reform in Japan*. Oxford University Press, London.

Gibney, F. (1975). *Japan: The Fragile Superpower*. Norton, New York.

Glickman, N. J. (1976). On the Japanese urban system. *Journal of Regional Science, 16*, 317–336.

Glickman, N. J. (1972). Conflict over public facility location in Japan. *Area Development in Japan, 6*, 20–43.

Glickman, N. J. and Y. Oguri (1978). Modelling the urban land market: The case of Japan. *Journal of Urban Economics, 5*, Forthcoming.

Hall, J. W. (1970). *Japan: From Prehistory to Modern Times*. Delacorte, New York.

Hall, R. B. (1976). *Japan: Industrial Power of Asia*. Van Nostrand, New York.

Halliday, J. (1975). *A Political History of Japanese Capitalism*. Pantheon Books, New York.

Halloran, R. (1969). *Japan: Images and Reality*. Knopf, New York.

Hane, M. (1972). *Japan: A Historical Survey*. Scribners, New York.

Ishida, T. (1971). *Japanese Society*. Random House, New York.

Japan Bureau of Statistics, Office of the Prime Minister (1971). *1970 Population Census of Japan: Volume 1, Total Population*. Japan Bureau of Statistics, Office of the Prime Minister, Tokyo.

Japan Bureau of Statistics, Office of the Prime Minister (1975). *Population of Japan: Summary Results of 1970 Population Census of Japan*. Japan Bureau of Statistics, Office of the Prime Minister, Tokyo.

Japan Bureau of Statistics, Office of the Prime Minister (1976a). *Japan Statistical Yearbook, 1976*. Japan Bureau of Statistics, Office of the Prime Minister, Tokyo.

Japan Bureau of Statistics, Office of the Prime Minister (1976b). *1975 Population Census of Japan: Preliminary Count of Population*. Japan Bureau of Statistics, Office of the Prime Minister, Tokyo.

Japan Economic Planning Agency (1975). *Reference Data for an Observation of Regional Structure* (in Japanese). Japan Economic Planning Agency, Tokyo.

Japan Economic Research Center (1975). *The Future of World Economy and Japan*. Japan Economic Research Center, Tokyo.

Japan National Land Agency (1976). *National Land Statistics Outline, 1976* (in Japanese). Japan National Land Agency, Tokyo.

Japan National Land Agency (1974). *The Outline of the National Land Agency*. Japan National Land Agency, Tokyo.

Kornhauser, D. (1976). *Urban Japan: Its Foundations and Growth*. Longman Group Ltd., London and New York.

Kosaka, M. (1972). *100 Million Japanese: The Postwar Experience*. Kodansha, Tokyo.

Lockwood, W. W., ed. (1965). *The State and Economic Enterprise: Essays in the Political Economy of Growth*. Princeton University Press, Princeton, New Jersey.

McNelly, T. (1972). *Contemporary Government of Japan*. Houghton Mifflin, Boston.

Mills, E. S. and K. Ohta (1976). Urbanization and urban problems, in H. Patrick and H. Rosovsky, eds., *Asia's New Giant: How the Japanese Economy Works*. The Brookings Institution, Washington, D.C. Pp. 673–751.

Nakane, C. (1970). *Japanese Society*. University of California Press, Berkeley, California.

Okita, S. (1975). *Japan in the World Economy*. Japan Foundation, Tokyo.

Organization for Economic Cooperation and Development (1975). *OECD Economic Surveys: Japan*. OECD, Paris.

Organization for Economic Cooperation and Development (1976). *Main Economic Indicators: Historical Statistics, 1960–1975*. OECD, Paris.

Organization for Economic Cooperation and Development (1977). *OECD Economic Surveys: Japan*. OECD, Paris.

Patrick, H. and H. Rosovsky, eds. (1976a). *Asia's New Giant: How the Japanese Economy Works*. The Brookings Institution, Washington, D.C.

Patrick, H. and H. Rosovsky (1976b). Japan's economic performance: An overview, in H. Patrick and H. Rosovsky, eds., *Asia's New Giant: How the Japanese Economy Works*. The Brookings Institution, Washington, D.C. Pp. 1–62.

Reischauer, E. O. (1974). *Japan: The Story of a Nation*. Knopf, New York.

Reischauer, E. O. (1977). *The Japanese*. Harvard University Press, Cambridge, Massachusetts.

Stockwin, J. A. A. (1975). *Divided Politics in a Growth Economy*. Norton, New York.

Takahashi, M. (1968). *Modern Japanese Economy*. Kokusai Bunka Shinkokai, Tokyo.

Thayer, N. B. (1971). *How the Conservatives Rule Japan*. Princeton University Press, Princeton, New Jersey.

Tsuru, S. (1958). *Essays on Japanese Economy*. Kinokuniya Bookstore Co. Ltd., Tokyo.

Vogel, E., ed. (1975). *Modern Japanese Organization and Decision Making*. University of California Press, Berkeley, California.

Vogel, E. (1978). Guided enterprise in Japan. *Harvard Business Review 56*, 161–170.

Ward, R. E. (1967). *Japan's Political System*. Prentice-Hall, Englewood Cliffs, New Jersey.

2

The Japanese Urban System
during a Period of Rapid
Economic Development

1 Introduction

This chapter[1] outlines the evolution of the Japanese urban system during a period of significant economic growth. As noted in Chapter 1, between 1950 and 1970, the era under study here, the Japanese economy recovered from extensive war damage, consolidated, and transformed itself into one of the most important industrial powers in the world. Between 1953 and 1971, for instance, real GNP increased by nearly 9% per year.[2] This remarkable economic growth was accompanied by rapid urbanization—the flow of population from rural to urban regions—that was spectacular by most standards. Between 1955 and 1960, 39 of Japan's 46 prefectures lost population, and in 1961 net migration to the three major metropolitan areas from other regions totaled nearly 600,000. By 1970, the population of the Tokyo, Osaka, and Nagoya regions (as measured by prefectural data) had reached 45.6 million people (43.9% of Japan's population), 10 million more than in 1960. Population density in Tokyo prefecture increased by over 70% between 1950 and 1970, while many rural regions were becoming relatively depopulated. Thus, there was high-density urban concentration existing simultaneously with rural depopulation. The central government called for deconcentration policies for the urbanized regions and economic develop-

---

[1] This chapter is an extended version of Glickman (1976).

[2] For analyses of the growth process see Chapter 1 of this volume, Patrick and Rosovsky (1976), and Denison and Chung (1976).

ment policies for the poorer underdeveloped areas (as we shall see in Chapter 6) to remedy this situation of polarity.

But the nature and dimensions of Japanese urban growth has not been analyzed rigorously. Therefore, in what follows, I present an investigation into the evolution of the Japanese urban system during the period from 1950 to 1970. Although there have been several studies of Japanese cities,[3] this work attempts to be comprehensive in its coverage. Whereas most other English language studies have either centered on Tokyo and a few other large cities or have looked at many individual cities, this chapter will view a large number of *metropolitan regions* in their spatial, demographic, and industrial dimensions.

I introduce here a new concept to the study of Japanese urban development: a measure of urban regions by reference to their *functional economic areas*. That is, I observe the commuting patterns and urban character of unified economic regions—central cities and their suburbs—and analyze urban growth using the resulting regional configurations. We call this unit the Regional Economic Cluster (REC). Section 2 of this chapter details the precise definition of the REC and the data-collection process. The analysis of these data are the concern of Sections 3 and 4, in which several interrelated questions are discussed:

1.   What have been the changes within the Japanese system of cities?

2.   Has the system become more or less centralized during the 1950s and 1960s?

3.   What have been the shifts within metropolitan regions with respect to population and employment?

4.   To what extent has there been metropolitan decentralization, that is, suburbanization, during those years of high economic growth?

In Section 5, I observe the development of the Japanese urban system in comparison to other developed and less developed nations such as Great Britain, the United States, the Federal Republic of Germany, and India. I offer some concluding remarks in Section 6.

2   Analytic Units: Regional Economic Clusters and Standard Consolidated Areas

2.1   Definition of Regional Economic Clusters

As noted in Section 1, it was necessary to find a meaningful measure of urbanization. In designing research, it was useful to have a definition that

---

[3] Among the many studies of Japanese urbanism, one should include Isida (1969), Kornhauser (1976), Mills and Ohta (1976), Orishima (1973), and Yamaguchi (1969).

would be consistent with efficient methods of data collection as well. In this research a significant data-related problem was encountered: The Japanese government collects data primarily for individual cities (*shi*), towns (*machi*), villages (*mura*), and prefectures (*ken, to,* and *fu*), not on a functional urban region basis.[4] If, however, one views urbanization only in terms of individual cities or prefectures, one may miss suburbanization effects and ignore the interaction among cities. Rather, a more meaningful aggregation technique involves a system in which a central city and its surrounding hinterland are combined into regions. Thus, it is necessary to have a classification scheme similar to that of the United States' Standard Metropolitan Statistical Area[5] (SMSA) or the British Standard Metropolitan Labour Area (SMLA) or Metropolitan Economic Labour Area (MELA).[6] Since we want to compare Japanese urban growth with that of other nations such as the United States and the United Kingdom (Section 5), such comparative research is facilitated by this analysis being undertaken on a basis similar to the analyses of those countries. In order to carry out this research, we specified a set of Regional Economic Clusters (RECs) and Standard Consolidated Areas (SCAs), which included a central city and the cities, towns, and villages in the central city's commuting fields. The RECs are defined in Sections 2.1.1 and 2.1.2, and the SCAs are defined in Section 2.1.3.

2.1.1 Choice of Central Cities of Regional Economic Clusters

First, it was necessary to choose a set of central cities. There were three criteria for choosing a potential central city:

[4] There was a total of 3,276 cities, towns, and villages in Japan in 1970. Some regional data are available for 1970, but only for the seven largest metropolitan areas. Another way that the government has collected urban data is through the Densely Inhabited Districts (DID), which are contiguous enumeration districts with 4,000 inhabitants or more per square kilometer and more than 5000 in total population.

[5] The Standard Metropolitan Statistical Area (SMSA) is defined as a set of counties having a core of a city (or twin-cities) with a population of 50,000 or more and surrounding countries having "metropolitan character" and "metropolitan integration." Metropolitan character requires that at least 75% of the labor force is nonagricultural and has a population density of 58 persons per square kilometer. If 15% of resident workers commute to the central county (or counties) or if 25% of those working in a county live in the central county (or counties), then the metropolitan integration criterion is fulfilled. This definition has been criticized and extended by Berry (1973a, b) and applied to Kanagawa-*ken* by Nagashima (1974).

[6] Standard Metropolitan Labour Areas (SMLAs) have been defined for Great Britain. They involve criteria for metropolitan character with a labor center or core and metropolitan ring areas related to the core. The labor center is defined with respect to employment density (2.02 jobs per hectare), total employment (20,000 jobs), and contiguous spatial arrangment of sub-areas. The Metropolitan Economic Labour Area (MELA) consists of the SMLA and an outer metropolitan ring less strongly related to the core. Whereas "metropolitan integration" for the SMLA includes areas sending 15% of resident employed to the core, the MELA includes areas sending commuters to the core provided they do not send more to another core.

1a.   The 1970 population must be greater than 100,000 persons.

1b.   The ratio of daytime to nighttime population must be greater than 1.

1c.   Seventy-five percent of the economic households are employed in nonagricultural or "mixed" nonagricultural–agricultural pursuits.

Criterion 1a allowed me to eliminate small cities and reduce to approximately 150 the potential number of central cities; in terms of research design this also made the data collection process more manageable. Criterion 1b was added to exclude cities that had net out-commuting during the day. These cities were primarily those near large urban centers that sent large numbers of workers to the centers during the work day. We included Criterion 1c so that the central cities had a substantially urban character; one measure of urbanization is the way in which residents of a particular city are employed, and I included only cities in which workers were primarily employed in nonagricultural pursuits.

If Criteria 1a–c were met, the city was classified as a potential central city. Since there was the problem of central cities being located very close to each other, I had to take account of the possibility of "twin-cities" and/or relationship between central and satellite cities. Thus, I added Criteria 1d and 1e:

1d.   The minimum distance between potential central city A and potential central city B must be greater than some arbitrary distance ℓ. If the distance between the cities is greater than ℓ, then both A and B are central cities. I used $\ell = 20$ km as the cutoff point.

1e.   If the distance between the cities is less than ℓ, then the central city is determined by the criteria that the number of commuters from city A to city B is greater than or less than the number of commuters from city B to city A. If the number of commuters going from A to B is greater, then A is the central city and B is the satellite city.

2.1.2   The Choice of Municipalities for the Rings in the Regional Economic Clusters

The next problem concerned selecting the towns (*machi*), satellite cities (*eiseitoshi*), and villages (*mura*) that are in the commuting fields of the central cities determined in Section 2.1.1. I set four criteria for the classification of cities, towns, and villages within regions so that functional urban regions resulted:

2a.   The number of commuters from the satellite cities, towns or villages to city A must be greater than 500. This eliminated many small cities, towns, and villages from the commuting ring.

2b.   The ratio of commuters in each city/town/village to city A to total employment in each city/town/village must be greater than 5%.

Since it is possible for Conditions 2a and b to hold for more than one central city, then:

> 2c. The town or village would be classified as part of region A if more commuters went to A than to B.

Finally, to guarantee urban character for the rings:

> 2d. Seventy-five percent of the economic households must be employed in nonagricultural or mixed nonagricultural–agricultural pursuits.

This process yielded a definition of the Japanese version of the SMSA.[7] The definitions are not exactly the same because of data constraints, but the spirit of the RECs and SMSAs are consistent. Both are functional urban regions.

2.1.3 Definition of Standard Consolidated Areas

Since I also wanted to isolate significant agglomerations of population, I defined a set of regions that I call Standard Consolidated Areas (SCAs). These consisted of three or more contiguous RECs. Such regions also exist for the United States (with the same name, although not exactly the same definition, for agglomerations of SMSAs) for major metropolitan centers such as New York and Chicago.

A listing of the component municipalities of the RECs is given in Appendix 1 and the RECs that make up the SCAs are listed in the body of Table 2.3.

2.2 Data Collection

The process of hand collecting (data were not available in machine-readable form) and coding the data yielded 80 RECs as defined in Sections 2.1.1 and 2.1.2. In all, there are 903 cities, towns, and villages in the RECs: 4 RECs on the northernmost island of Hokkaido, 57 on the island of Honshu, 6 on Shikoku, and 13 on Kyushu. Okinawa was ignored since it did not revert to Japan until after 1970. The spatial configuration of the RECs are given in Figure 2.1.

Data were collected for a large number of economic, social, and political variables for each of the component municipalities of the RECs. The result-

---

[7] Note that, in some cases, jurisdictions that failed to meet urban criteria 2a–2d were completely surrounded by those towns that did. In such situations, when I found a "hole" in the REC, I included the nonqualifying jurisdiction in the REC. There were also cases in which a significant group of towns that met criteria 2a–2d for a given REC were "separated" from the REC by one or more jurisdictions that did not qualify. In these cases, I included the separated and the nonqualifying towns in the REC. These adjustments to the preceding rules were necessary in a few occasions and were followed for the sake of logic and geographical neatness. See also Footnote 8 (page 36) for a further adjustment of the definition. Finally, Kawashima (1977), using the same basic data set and similar classification procedures, defined 84 regions called "J-SMSAa."

ing data collection has been coalesced into our Regional Data Bank, listed in Appendix 2. This data bank is available to interested researchers and is capable of being easily updated and expanded. For example, I originally collected data for 1950–1970, but later added 1975 population figures for 1975 in order to complete Chapter 3.

There are 8 SCAs, comprising 35 RECs. The RECs of the SCAs have the heavily scored boundaries in Figure 2.1. Note the nearly continuous urbanized area stretching from the Kanto plain (RECs 19–24 and 37) to the Kinki region (RECs 44–50) in Figure 2.1. There are some breaks in this built-up area between Hamamatsu (36) and Toyohashi (39) and larger rural areas between the Nagoya area and the set of RECs that surround Osaka. Other concentrations of urban centers exist near Sendai (RECs 6, 9, 10, and 12), Okayama (RECs 54, 55, and 57), Kitakyushu (RECs 68, 69, and 71), Matsuyama (RECs 64–66), and Kanazawa (RECs 27–29).

One further note should be added relating to Figure 2.1. Much has been made of the term *megalopolis* (see Gottmann, 1961) and its application to Japanese cities. The term megalopolis has been applied to the Tokaido region, which stretches from north of Tokyo to west of Kobe. Unfortunately, there is little agreement among Japanese urbanists as to a precise definition of the Tokaido megalopolis. Gottmann's definition is itself not completely precise, and this, too, has led to certain definition problems; see for instance, Japan Center for Area Development Research (JCADR) (1973). From Figure 2.1 it appears that the Tokaido region consists of the Tokyo, Nagoya, and Osaka SCAs, and a few RECs such as Shizuoka, Hamamatsu, and Toyohashi. The rest of what is known as the Tokaido megalopolis is primarily rural according to our analysis as it is depicted in Figure 2.1. One could, therefore, view this megalopolis as a set of interrelated large urban regions (Tokyo, Osaka, etc.), combined with some intervening nonurban areas.

2.3   The Nature of the Regional Economic Clusters and Standard Consolidated Areas

One of the advantages of the REC definition is that RECs form natural economic regions. That is, they relate cities within the same commuting field. Also, the RECs can vary in size and can cross prefectural boundaries. Other regions for Japan have been defined by the Economic Planning Agency (EPA); see Chapter 1, Section 3.1 for some definitions. In the cases of the EPA definitions, prefectural boundaries are strictly adhered to and no calculation of commuting areas is made, with the exception of some definitions of major metropolitan areas for 1970. As an example, the Tokyo metropolitan area is defined by the EPA in two ways. First, there is Coastal Kanto, which consists of the Tokyo, Kanagawa, Chiba, and Saitama prefectures. There is a still more encompassing definition of Tokyo that also

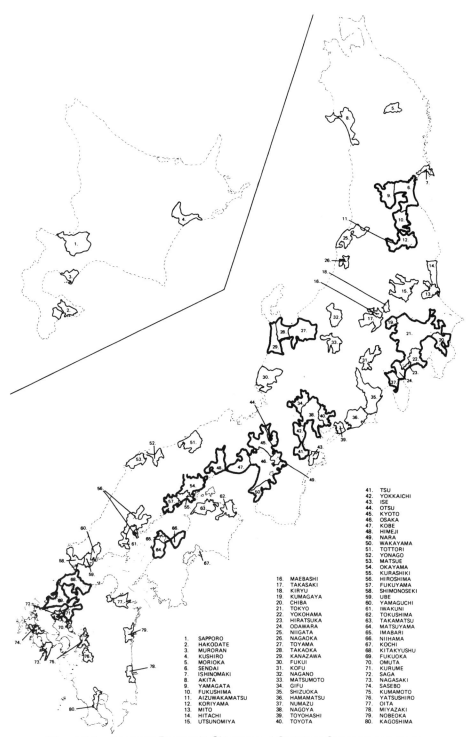

41.	TSU
42.	YOKKAICHI
43.	ISE
44.	OTSU
45.	KYOTO
46.	OSAKA
47.	KOBE
48.	HIMEJI
49.	NARA
50.	WAKAYAMA
51.	TOTTORI
52.	YONAGO
53.	MATSUE
54.	OKAYAMA
55.	KURASHIKI
56.	HIROSHIMA
57.	FUKUYAMA
58.	SHIMONOSEKI
59.	UBE
60.	YAMAGUCHI
61.	IWAKUNI
62.	TOKUSHIMA
63.	TAKAMATSU
64.	MATSUYAMA
65.	IMABARI
66.	NIIHAMA
67.	KOCHI
68.	KITAKYUSHU
69.	FUKUOKA
70.	OMUTA
71.	KURUME
72.	SAGA
73.	NAGASAKI
74.	SASEBO
75.	KUMAMOTO
76.	YATSUSHIRO
77.	OITA
78.	MIYAZAKI
79.	NOBEOKA
80.	KAGOSHIMA

16.	MAEBASHI
17.	TAKASAKI
18.	KIRYU
19.	KUMAGAYA
20.	CHIBA
21.	TOKYO
22.	YOKOHAMA
23.	HIRATSUKA
24.	ODAWARA
25.	NIIGATA
26.	NAGAOKA
27.	TOYAMA
28.	TAKAOKA
29.	KANAZAWA
30.	FUKUI
31.	KOFU
32.	NAGANO
33.	MATSUMOTO
34.	GIFU
35.	SHIZUOKA
36.	HAMAMATSU
37.	NUMAZU
38.	NAGOYA
39.	TOYOHASHI
40.	TOYOTA

1.	SAPPORO
2.	HAKODATE
3.	MURORAN
4.	KUSHIRO
5.	MORIOKA
6.	SENDAI
7.	ISHINOMAKI
8.	AKITA
9.	YAMAGATA
10.	FUKUSHIMA
11.	AIZUWAKAMATSU
12.	KORIYAMA
13.	MITO
14.	HITACHI
15.	UTSUNOMIYA

Figure 2.1. Regional Economic Clusters and Standard Consolidated Areas.

TABLE 2.1

Population of RECs and SCAs Compared to EPA Prefectural Definitions, 1950–1970 (in thousands)

	1950	1960	1970	Ratio of 1970 population to 1950 population
Tokyo REC	8,857	13,099	17,712	2.000
Coastal Kanto[a]	13,051	17,864	24,113	1.848
Tokyo SCA	11,727	16,675	22,940	1.956
Inland and Coastal Kanto[b]	21,114	25,767	32,214	1.526
Osaka REC	4,784	6,781	9,495	1.985
Coastal Kinki[c]	8,149	10,413	13,331	1.636
Osaka SCA	8,762	11,405	15,032	1.716
Inland and Coastal Kinki[d]	11,617	14,030	17,401	1.498
Nagoya REC	2,462	3,268	4,123	1.675
Chukyo region[e]	6,396	7,330	8,688	1.358

[a] Tokyo, Chiba, Kanagawa, and Saitama prefectures.
[b] Those prefectures in Footnote a plus Ibaraki, Tochigi, and Gumma prefectures.
[c] Osaka, Kyoto, and Hyogo prefectures.
[d] Those prefectures in Footnote c plus Nara, Wakayama, and Shiga prefectures.
[e] Aichi, Gifu, and Mie prefectures.

includes the inland portions of the region: Ibaraki, Tochigi, and Gumma prefectures. However, there are many portions of these regions that make them unsuitable for inclusion as part of the urbanized portion of the Tokyo urban region. Many of them are significantly rural, do not send many commuters to Tokyo during the work day, or both. They should not, under reasonable economic criteria, be included in the Tokyo region. The same argument holds for other satellite cities of the central cities of other RECs. Although my classification system requires more effort to collect data and to process it, I feel that it is a preferable urbanization measure to the simpler prefecture-based versions.

Another advantage of the REC data system lies with its coverage of cities beyond the confines of the major metropolitan centers. For purposes of both normative and positive analyses, it is important to catalogue activity in regions such as Sendai or Hiroshima that are not covered by current central government data systems, at least in the sense of this study.

The regions vary greatly in size. For instance, the Yamaguchi REC has only two cities (Yamaguchi and its suburb Ogori) in Yamaguchi prefecture and a total 1970 population of 117,000 persons.[8] On the other hand, the Tokyo REC covers 106 municipalities in portions of six prefectures (Tokyo,

---

[8] I amended my analysis to exclude regions that had no suburban ring. Monocentric regions were inconsistent with some of the analysis in this chapter and Chapter 3. This was a decision that eliminated Aomori, for instance, from my original list of RECs.

Ibaragi, Tochigi, Saitama, Chiba, and Kanagawa) and had a 1970 population over 17 million; the Tokyo SCA (with more cities in the same prefectures) had nearly 23 million people in 1970.

Table 2.1 gives some comparative data for our RECs and SCAs and for those regions defined by the EPA for the three major metropolitan areas. In all cases the EPA definitions include more population. For instance, the four-prefecture definition of Coastal Kanto contains 24.1 million people compared to the Tokyo REC figure of 17.7 million in 1970. The more encompassing EPA definition of Kanto (which includes the inland portions) exceeds the Tokyo SCA population as well. Similar ratios exist for my and the EPA definitions of the other metropolitan areas. Reflecting the greater emphasis on urban regions given by the RECs, the RECs and SCAs are growing faster than the EPA regions. The Tokyo REC population doubled between 1950 and 1970 (see Column 4 of Table 2.1), while Coastal Kanto increased by 85%. In all other cases, the REC/SCA regions' growth exceeded that of the EPA regions.

3 The Growth of the Japanese Urban System, 1950–1970

3.1 Some Basic Data for Regional Economic Clusters and Standard Consolidated Areas

Table 2.2 shows some basic data for the RECs and compares these data with that for Japan as a whole. The total population of the 80 RECs is 70.4 million persons in 1970, 67.9% of the 103.7 million persons in all of Japan.

TABLE 2.2

Regional Economic Clusters Major Economic Variables, 1970 (in thousands)

	(1) Total REC	(2) Mean	(3) Total, Japan	(4) REC/ Japan (1)/(3) (%)
Population	70,435.7	77.232	103,720.1	67.9
Total employment	34,961.6	38.674	52,041.7	67.2
Primary employment	3,410.3	3.772	10,006.1	34.1
Secondary employment	13,349.3	14.767	17,651.4	75.6
Manufacturing employment	10,594.7	11.720	13,442.4	78.8
Wholesale and retail employment	7,748.4	8.571	10,013.8	77.4
Services employment	5,456.5	6.036	7,658.8	71.2
Government employment	1,214.4	1.343	1,740.1	69.8
White-collar workers	10,095.6	11.178	12,806.3	78.8

Similarly, total employment in the RECs is 34.9 million workers as compared to 52.0 million for Japan. Consequently, the RECs have 67.2% of all workers in the country. Within the detailed employment categories, manufacturing and wholesale/retail involve 78.8 and 77.4%, respectively, of the total workers in those categories. Also, nearly 79% of all white-collar employees reside within the RECs. Column 2 of Table 2.2 shows the average number of residents and employees within the RECs. There are 77,232 persons residing within the average municipality within the RECs[9] and a mean of 38,674 employees (of which 11,720 are in manufacturing).

These data clearly indicate the comprehensive coverage of the RECs and SCAs. The REC definition does not exhaust all Japanese national territory, as does Berry's (1973a) Daily Urban Systems for the United States, but it gives coverage of the primary *urban* activity in Japan. Most of the 2,373 cities, towns, and villages not included in the RECs are rural (their average population is 14,685 persons) in character and, therefore, not of primary interest to this study.[10]

Table 2.3 shows the RECs that constitute the SCAs and the 1970 population of each. Note the heavy concentration in the Tokyo (22,940,400 people), Osaka (15,032,200 people), and Nagoya (6,082,700 people) SCAs. The Matsuyama, Kanazawa, and Okayama SCAs are the smallest. In total, the SCA population is 53,147,200, 75.4% of the total REC population and 51.2% of the total population of Japan.

For a presentation of data for individual RECs, see Appendix 3. There I indicate total population and employment as well as the percentage of distribution for each employment category.

3.2 Regional Growth and Industrial Structure

Table 2.4 indicates population and total employment levels, growth rates, and industrial structure for all of the RECs between 1950 and 1970. It is seen that population grew at similar rates for both decades: 24.5% between 1950 and 1960 and 24.0% between 1960 and 1970. Total employment grew at a rate of 33.1% between 1960 and 1970, much higher than for Japan as a whole. For individual industrial groupings, there was a large fall in the share of primary employment (47.2%) and small gains in the shares of government (1.8%) and secondary (6.2%) industry. Major proportional growth occurred in the shares of wholesale and retail employment (16.9%), services (13.0%), and other tertiary industry (14.9%). Thus, there was a large relative expansion in the tertiary sector at the expense of primary and secondary employment.

[9] This compares to about 32,000 for the average municipality in all of Japan.

[10] Work is currently underway at the International Institute for Applied Systems Analysis (Laxenburg, Austria) by Professor Tatsuhiko Kawashima and me to extend the REC definitions to exhaust the entire country, consistent with the Berry work.

TABLE 2.3
Population of Japanese Standard Consolidated Areas, 1970 (in thousands)

Sendai SCA		Nagoya SCA		Kanazawa SCA		Osaka SCA	
Sendai	975.6	Nagoya	3795.6	Toyama	493.5	Osaka	9,495.2
Yamagata	391.3	Toyota	445.1	Takaoka	364.1	Kyoto	1,809.4
Fukushima	327.0	Gifu	749.6	Kanazawa	540.3	Kobe	1,741.0
Koriyama	332.7	Tsu	312.1	TOTAL SCA	1,397.9	Himeji	782.6
TOTAL SCA	2,026.6	Yokkaichi	453.3			Wakayama	563.1
		TOTAL SCA	6,082.7			Nara	284.7
						Otsu	356.2
						TOTAL SCA	15,032.2

Tokyo SCA		Okayama SCA		Matsuyama SCA		Kitakyushu SCA	
Tokyo	17,711.5	Okayama	641.8	Matsuyama	428.5	Kitakyushu	1,501.6
Yokohama	3,323.8	Kurashiki	418.5	Imabari	171.2	Fukuoka	1,324.4
Chiba	816.0	Fukuyama	544.9	Niihama	193.2	Kurume	443.4
Kumagaya	269.5	TOTAL SCA	1,605.2	TOTAL SCA	792.9	TOTAL SCA	3,269.4
Hiratsuka	234.4						
Odawara	283.7						
Numazu	421.5						
TOTAL SCA	22,940.4						

TABLE 2.4
Growth Rates of Population and Employment by Industrial Class in Japanese RECs, 1950–1970

	1950	1960	Percentage of change in population 1950–1960	1970	Percentage of change in population and employment 1960–1970
Population (in thousands)	45,491.712	56,651.491	24.531	70,268.576	24.037
Total employment (in thousands)		26,264.958		34,952.627	33.077
Percent primary employment		18.448		9.747	−47.161
Percent secondary employment		35.953		38.188	6.217
Percent wholesale and retail employment		18.967		22.164	16.855
Percent services employment		13.806		15.607	13.044
Percent other tertiary employment		9.415		10.820	14.922
Percent government employment		3.411		3.474	1.825

Table 2.5 gives the percentage of change in population for 5-year intervals between 1950 and 1970 for individual RECs. The table indicates that the cities with the largest growth were primarily those near Tokyo and Osaka. These include Tokyo, Yokohama, Chiba, and Hiratsuka, in addition to Sapporo and Osaka. Those cities losing population absolutely were Tottori, Omuta, Yatsushiro, and Ube, all at the periphery of the urban system. One can see some leveling of the growth rates in the latter part of the period of the study. That is, the cities that grew the fastest for the 1950–1970 era grew less quickly during the period of 1965–1970 than earlier; conversely, cities that previously grew the slowest seemed to grow less slowly (or to have less negative growth) during 1965–1970. As I show in Chapter 3, this trend continued into the 1970s.

One also can see that the period 1960–1965 brought with it a burst of urbanization in the larger cities and some draining down of the population of the smaller and more peripheral cities. In general, 1960–1965 found fast-growing cities registering their highest growth rates among the four periods and the slower growing cities having their slowest growth then.

Among the major metropolitan centers, Tokyo's growth rate declined in each period: from 23.7% (1950–1955) to 13.7% (1965–1970). The outlying suburban areas of Chiba and Hiratsuka increased their growth rates with the passage of time; Chiba, for instance, grew only at a rate of 6.2% from 1950 to 1955, but grew by 31.5% from 1965 to 1970. Osaka's growth rate declined in each period, except for 1960–1965. The outer suburbs of Osaka also grew more rapidly in the later periods; see, for instance, the data for Himeji and Wakayama. The growth rates of Osaka's outer suburbs were not as great as those of Tokyo, however. I discuss this further in Section 3.3.

The slow-growing cities on the periphery of the urban system declined relative to the fast-growing cities between 1950 and 1970. In some cases, growth rates went from positive to negative. For instance, Yatsushiro grew by 6.5% during the first period but declined at a rate of 3.3% in the last. Ube grew by 6.1% in 1950–1955 but declined by 4.0% in 1965–1970; however, the decline of Ube was 9.1% during 1960–1965.

Examining the patterns of 1960–1970 employment growth in Table 2.5, one also finds that many fast-growing regions expanded less rapidly during 1965–1970 than during 1960–1965. Sapporo added 33.4% to its work rolls in the earlier and 23.1% in the later period. Tokyo's 25.4% increase was cut to 13.4%, and Osaka went from 31.2 to 14.4%. On the other hand, fast-growing suburbs, such as Chiba and such independent centers as Sendai and Fukuoka, increased their growth rates in the late 1960s. For slow-growing regions, the employment picture brightened somewhat during the 1965–1970 period. In general, negative growth rates from 1960 to 1965 were replaced by positive growth rates fron 1965 to 1970 and, overall, there were greater positive rates of increase. However, the slower expansion in 1965–1970 of the fast-growing regions was still greater than the more rapid additions to employment of the slower growing, peripheral regions.

TABLE 2.5
Growth Rates of Population and Employment for Individual RECs, 1950–1970

	Population					Employment	
	Percent change 1950–1955	Percent change 1955–1960	Percent change 1960–1965	Percent change 1965–1970	Percent change 1950–1970	Percent change 1960–1965	Percent change 1965–1970
Sapporo	18.589	18.227	24.440	18.977	76.958	33.429	23.098
Hakodate	5.686	.31	3.092	3.700	13.345	13.792	9.552
Muroran	11.812	16.280	12.911	4.814	53.868	18.901	11.637
Kushiro	24.421	25.153	12.256	7.812	88.456	20.745	15.623
Morioka	10.895	9.274	11.676	10.833	49.988	20.102	15.539
Sendai	6.549	5.863	8.120	11.359	35.808	14.670	18.255
Ishinomaki	1.887	2.935	2.813	6.203	14.515	5.047	14.284
Akita	3.839	2.716	1.911	4.111	13.168	6.241	12.963
Yamagata	.223	.402	-.245	2.403	2.791	2.886	9.231
Fukushima	7.969	.051	2.184	4.254	15.078	6.356	11.338
Aizuwakamatsu	4.103	.864	.759	.403	6.225	6.527	10.583
Koriyama	24.547	-15.996	2.252	5.219	12.564	4.494	14.488
Mito	6.173	3.342	5.982	8.771	26.484	6.977	13.813
Hitachi	6.560	10.925	4.176	1.128	24.527	5.587	6.556
Utsunomiya	1.762	.163	4.316	7.826	14.649	9.416	15.354
Maebashi	4.177	.783	6.369	8.043	20.662	13.336	13.314
Takasaki	2.641	2.650	4.328	6.196	16.732	10.071	12.314
Kiryu	2.276	-.086	3.750	4.702	11.006	11.984	9.256
Kumagaya	1.586	-.987	4.073	7.172	12.187	8.111	11.589
Chiba	6.246	8.490	19.453	31.468	81.016	21.282	31.168
Tokyo	23.722	19.537	18.922	13.695	99.965	25.351	13.447
Yokohama	17.146	16.116	28.429	24.613	117.692	39.344	25.439
Hiratsuka	13.322	6.787	22.922	22.462	82.165	34.470	24.821
Odawara	8.603	6.913	12.766	7.725	41.047	21.477	11.335
Niigata	4.917	2.784	4.375	4.448	17.563	10.106	10.302

Nagaoka	7.501	1.484	2.532	2.724	14.906	6.393	9.351
Toyama	4.716	3.668	.502	2.776	12.130	3.970	7.594
Takaoka	1.820	-.561	-1.148	.212	.299	3.434	6.994
Kanazawa	6.752	3.159	5.183	6.374	23.215	10.310	9.333
Fukui	1.148	1.704	1.778	1.181	5.936	4.742	5.785
Kofu	5.297	-1.093	.961	3.852	9.197	5.624	9.150
Nagano	4.736	.569	2.937	4.564	13.375	7.486	9.892
Matsumoto	.328	1.954	2.335	4.899	9.805	6.985	10.366
Gifu	9.986	6.213	10.823	8.973	41.080	15.440	12.538
Shizuoka	11.493	7.959	8.040	8.149	40.642	13.824	14.375
Hamamatsu	15.405	3.710	4.753	6.205	33.156	8.112	13.476
Numazu	8.420	8.511	13.295	12.443	49.873	17.743	19.179
Nagoya	11.534	19.002	15.675	9.068	67.455	18.531	12.238
Toyohashi	6.198	3.447	8.810	-9.497	8.184	13.698	11.686
Toyota	18.609	9.692	17.120	22.143	86.219	23.060	25.869
Tsu	3.767	-0.516	2.837	4.274	10.698	5.449	8.363
Yokkaichi	5.438	5.316	9.597	7.623	30.977	10.906	9.681
Ise	2.475	0.290	2.038	.596	5.493	1.740	7.210
Otsu	3.423	2.658	6.634	10.516	25.121	10.198	14.709
Kyoto	9.172	5.460	8.850	10.007	37.864	17.137	10.241
Osaka	20.423	17.698	21.990	14.781	98.460	31.164	14.432
Kobe	16.704	9.588	10.168	9.614	54.445	-3.461	11.514
Himeji	2.369	3.672	7.372	6.841	21.748	12.265	11.668
Nara	6.280	1.906	14.456	21.331	50.404	18.553	24.106
Wakayama	7.268	3.022	8.863	7.282	29.064	14.598	10.318
Tottori	4.337	-2.374	-2.299	-.504	-.985	-.660	10.887
Yonago	5.182	-0.752	.523	2.052	7.091	4.233	8.862
Matsue	3.997	-0.317	-.921	1.687	4.446	-.181	10.003
Okayama	5.694	2.523	3.748	6.979	20.267	9.882	11.692
Kurashiki	17.701	1.407	5.415	17.755	48.160	8.491	20.053
Hiroshima	11.998	10.490	16.496	14.794	65.486	18.565	18.023
Fukuyama	2.095	1.727	3.190	10.974	18.933	5.419	15.170
Shimonoseki	10.182	2.751	.045	-.970	12.165	3.986	5.379
Ube	6.076	2.190	-9.137	3.984	-5.429	-1.990	6.286

TABLE 2.5 *(Continued)*

	Population					Employment	
	Percent change 1950–1955	Percent change 1955–1960	Percent change 1960–1965	Percent change 1965–1970	Percent change 1950–1970	Percent change 1960–1965	Percent change 1965–1970
Yamaguchi	4.598	2.666	−2.406	2.307	7.221	0.308	7.505
Iwakuni	10.619	5.612	−1.038	4.873	21.249	1.278	9.421
Tokushima	6.417	.249	1.092	2.566	10.615	3.892	10.755
Takamatsu	1.766	−.731	.306	3.655	5.035	5.510	9.937
Matsuyama	7.185	4.997	6.910	8.668	30.746	−24.444	15.249
Imabari	1.724	.734	1.027	3.357	6.998	7.393	10.635
Niihama	3.105	.952	−1.367	−.674	1.952	5.631	10.420
Kochi	5.652	2.886	5.764	6.800	22.784	9.977	12.806
Kitakyushu	13.438	7.419	−.181	−.933	20.500	3.582	5.972
Fukuoka	12.872	8.700	10.326	12.859	52.768	16.836	18.194
Omuta	4.329	−.146	−5.760	−9.160	−10.818	3.403	2.921
Kurume	7.578	−1.257	−2.053	.816	4.887	0.605	6.952
Saga	6.325	−.531	−3.107	−.960	1.490	1.408	7.294
Nagasaki	11.443	7.755	3.383	4.150	29.299	7.213	10.469
Sasebo	13.541	−.823	−7.932	−.453	3.205	−3.316	8.596
Kumamoto	14.869	5.437	6.636	6.875	38.031	11.750	13.751
Yatsushiro	6.546	.901	−4.255	−3.306	−.471	−2.381	6.435
Oita	7.624	2.203	6.800	8.360	27.296	−11.905	13.569
Miyazaki	8.624	4.649	8.418	10.474	36.152	13.689	19.160
Nobeoka	11.159	3.909	0.626	3.360	20.131	3.068	11.214
Kagoshima	13.474	3.649	7.905	7.398	36.302	9.908	13.107

3.3   Metropolitan Spatial Structure

Table 2.6 indicates the relationship between the 80 central cities and the 823 satellite cities, towns, and villages for 1950–1970 on a place of residence basis. Central city population was 55.5% of the total REC population in 1950 and rose to 58.5% in 1960. Therefore, there was an increasing centralization of metropolitan regions in Japan during that decade. Between 1960 and 1970 there was some decentralization: 54.8% of the population in the RECs lived in central cities in 1970. Thus there was some metropolitan decentralization, although not to the extent previously noted by Berry (1973a, b) and Hall (1973a, b) for the United States and the United Kingdom, respectively. The extent of decentralization in these countries was massive as we shall discuss in Section 5. Although no employment data are available for 1950, the percentage of employees living in central cities declined from 58.0% to 54.3% between 1960 and 1970.

Concerning metropolitan decentralization, wholesale and retail employees were the least decentralized in 1970 with 63.2% of the employees in that category living in central cities; comparable figures for primary, manufacturing, services, and government were 29.6, 51.0, 59.4, and 55.1%, respectively. Table 2.6 shows that the growth in the central city employment was slower than in the suburbs across industrial classes: The growth rate was more than twice as much in the suburbs as in the central cities; in manufacturing, central cities' employment grew by 17.3% compared to 79.1% in the suburbs (see Table 2.8).

Distribution of employment in central cities and suburbs for 1960 and 1970 is shown Table 2.7. One immediately sees the relative shift of secondary industry to the suburbs during the 1960s. In 1960, central cities had 37.9% of all of their employees in secondary industry but had only 36.7% in 1970. During that decade, the share of secondary employment in the suburbs rose from 33.3 to 40.0%. Therefore, there was a relative suburbanization of manufacturing employees in that the suburbs were more concentrated in

TABLE 2.6

Central Cities as a Percentage of Total REC on the Basis of Place of Residence, 1950–1970

	1950	1960	1970
Population	55.0	58.5	54.8
Total employment	NA[a]	58.0	54.3
Primary employment	NA	30.1	29.6
Secondary employment	NA	61.1	52.1
Manufacturing employment	NA	61.4	51.0
Wholesale and retail employment	NA	69.7	63.2
Services employment	NA	65.6	59.4
Government employment	NA	60.7	55.1

[a] NA = Not available.

TABLE 2.7
Percentage of Distribution of Employment by Industrial Class for Central Cities and Suburbs, 1960 and 1970

	Central cities			Suburbs		
	1960	1970	Percent change, 1960–1970	1960	1970	Percent change, 1960–1970
Primary employment	9.585	5.319	−44.512	30.714	15.017	−51.106
Secondary employment	37.865	36.652	−3.205	33.305	40.016	20.148
Wholesale and retail employment	22.790	25.771	13.083	13.676	17.872	30.678
Services employment	15.601	17.061	9.361	11.323	13.877	22.561
Other tertiary employment	10.591	11.671	10.193	7.786	9.807	25.949
Government employment	3.567	3.526	−1.155	3.195	3.411	6.749

TABLE 2.8
Growth Rates of RECs and Components, 1950–1960 and 1960–1970

	1950–1960		1960–1970	
	Central cities	Suburbs	Central cities	Suburbs
Population	32.9	15.2	15.0	33.8
Total employment	NA[a]	NA	24.6	44.9
Primary employment	NA	NA	−30.9	−29.2
Secondary employment	NA	NA	20.6	74.1
Manufacturing employment	NA	NA	17.3	79.1
Wholesale and retail employment	NA	NA	40.8	89.3
Services employment	NA	NA	36.2	77.6
Government employment	NA	NA	23.1	54.7

[a] NA = Not available.

secondary employees than were the central cities by 1970. Looking at other employment categories, the central cities were more concentrated in wholesale and retail employment, services employment, "other" tertiary employment, and government employment than the suburbs. On the other hand, the suburbs continued to be more concentrated in primary employees as small-scale farming continued there.

Table 2.8 shows the population and employment growth rates for central cities and suburban areas for 1950–1970. In the 1950s, population grew at a rate of 32.9% in central cities compared to only 15.2% in the suburbs. In the 1960s, the growth rates were reversed: Central cities grew at 15.0% and the suburbs at 33.8%. Table 2.8 also reveals the much more substantial growth of the suburbs in employment categories for the period 1960–1970 than the growth of the central cities.

The data exhibited thus far are on a place of residence basis. Table 2.9 shows employment patterns by place of work, in which it can be seen that the concentration in central cities by place of work is higher than by place of residence. For instance, manufacturing employment by place of work registers an 88.8% ratio of central city to REC, whereas on a place of residence basis (Table 2.6) it is only 51.0%. Similarly, wholesale and retail employment and services have 79.7 and 60.0%, respectively, of employment compared to

TABLE 2.9
Employment by Place of Work, 1970

	Central city as a percentage of REC
Manufacturing employment	88.8
Wholesale and retail employment	79.7
Services employment	60.0

place of residence figures of 63.2 and 59.4%, respectively. Thus, services are more evenly distributed with population, consistent with a priori expectations; wholesale and retail trade are much more highly centralized.

The suburbanization of the major metropolitan regions is shown in Table 2.10, which displays the spatial patterns of growth for Tokyo, Osaka, and Nagoya metropolitan areas. Within the Tokyo SCA, the Tokyo REC's growth rate declined in each 5-year period from 23.7% (1950–1955) to 13.7% (1965–1970). Tokyo's major suburbs—Yokohama, Chiba, and Hiratsuka—showed increasing growth in later years, and, by 1970, were growing faster than Tokyo. Kumagaya, Odawara, and Numazu, further away from central Tokyo, had increasing growth rates, but ones that were absolutely lower than the inner RECs. For Osaka, higher growth rates were recorded in later periods for Nara (which grew 1.9% during 1955–1960 and 21.3% in 1965–1970) and Otsu. Even though the Osaka REC's growth rate fell over time, it was still higher than all but Nara's in the last period of this study.

Tables 2.6–2.10 clearly show the beginning of the suburbanization process that was to continue into the 1970s, as will be discussed in Chapter 3. Population began to shift toward the suburbs in the 1960s, although employment continued to be highly centralized on a place of work basis. Suburbanization, however, was concentrated in the larger metropolitan regions such as

TABLE 2.10
Growth Rates of RECs within Tokyo, Osaka and Nagoya SCAs, 1950–1970

	1950–1955	1955–1960	1960–1965	1965–1970
Tokyo SCA				
Tokyo	23.7	19.5	18.9	13.7
Yokohama	17.1	16.1	28.4	24.6
Chiba	6.2	8.5	19.5	31.5
Kumagaya	1.6	−1.0	4.1	7.2
Hiratsuka	13.3	6.8	22.9	22.5
Odawara	8.6	6.9	12.8	7.7
Numazu	8.4	8.5	13.3	12.4
Osaka SCA				
Osaka	20.4	17.7	22.0	14.8
Kyoto	9.2	5.5	8.9	10.0
Kobe	16.7	9.6	10.2	9.6
Himeji	2.4	3.7	7.4	6.8
Wakayama	7.3	3.0	8.9	7.3
Nara	6.3	1.9	14.5	21.3
Otsu	3.4	2.7	6.6	10.5
Nagoya SCA				
Nagoya	11.5	19.0	15.7	9.1
Toyota	18.6	9.7	17.1	22.1
Gifu	10.0	6.2	10.8	9.0
Tsu	3.8	−0.5	2.8	4.3
Yokkaichi	5.4	5.3	9.6	7.6

Tokyo, Osaka, and Nagoya. The smaller and more peripherally located RECs exhibited centralization as migrants were drawn from nearby small towns to REC central cities. The central cities grew faster than the component suburban cities in those outlying RECs.

3.4 Industrial Distribution and Growth by Size of Region

How has industrial employment structure varied according to region size? How has regional growth varied with the size of each region? I answer these questions in this section through Tables 2.11 and 2.12.

Table 2.11 presents data by size of region on the industrial structure for 1970. What is striking here is the remarkable stability of industrial structure according to city size. For instance, secondary industry had 38.2% of all employees for all cities. But the range of concentration in the different size classes is small with the exception of the 600,000–700,000 and 700,000–800,000 groups. All other industrial sectors, save primary industry (which falls as a percentage of total employment as size of city increases), show the same sort of stability.

Table 2.12 shows rates of growth among the regions by size of region for population and for the various employment categories. Here, there is the phenomenon of considerably faster growth for both population and employment among the larger RECs. For the smallest category, less than 200,000 people in a REC, population grew by only 1.8% between 1960 and 1970. For regions larger than 700,000, there were significantly higher growth rates; the 10 RECs comprising the size class 1 million or greater grew 33.8% between 1960 and 1970. The range of growth rates for cities of 700,000 or larger was between 17.6 and 33.8%, whereas for cities of less than 700,000 the growth rates were between 1.7 and 12.8%. For total employment, the growth rates were between 27 and 41% for cities above 700,000 compared to only 16 to 23% for the smaller regions.

The relationship between region size and region growth is given in a regression equation in Chapter 3 in which the region's population is a good predictor of a region's growth in the 1960s; see also Figure 3.1. We see in Chapter 3 that the relationship between region size and region population growth changes in the 1970s as the large regions began to lose their preeminence; after 1970, medium-sized regions grew quickly relative to other regions.

3.5 Major Regions

I have aggregated the RECs into nine major regions (see Table 2.13), according to the regions defined by the Japan Economic Planning Agency. The nine regions are Hokkaido, Tohoku, Kanto, Tokai, Hokuriku, Kinki,

TABLE 2.11
Industrial Structure of RECs by Population Size Class of Region, 1970

	0–200,000	200,000–300,000	300,000–400,000	400,000–500,000
Percentage of primary employment	20.115	17.186	20.452	19.060
Percentage of secondary employment	33.880	30.224	33.317	33.075
Percentage of wholesale and retail employment	18.492	21.878	18.678	19.231
Percentage of services employment	15.300	16.399	14.859	15.273
Percentage of other tertiary employment	8.667	9.113	9.142	9.563
Percentage of government employment	3.545	5.200	3.553	3.799
TOTAL	100.000	100.000	100.000	100.000

	500,000–600,000	600,000–700,000	700,000–800,000	800,000–900,000
Percentage of primary employment	15.801	20.248	13.122	17.436
Percentage of secondary employment	33.099	28.428	44.618	39.794
Percentage of wholesale and retail employment	21.258	21.009	18.217	17.452
Percentage of services employment	15.860	15.875	12.524	13.139
Percentage of other tertiary employment	9.979	10.683	8.590	8.834
Percentage of government employment	4.003	3.756	2.929	3.344
TOTAL	100.000	100.000	100.000	100.000

	900,000–1,000,000	1,000,000+	All RECs
Percentage of primary employment	14.939	4.280	9.747
Percentage of secondary employment	31.489	41.275	38.188
Percentage of wholesale and retail employment	23.037	23.651	22.164
Percentage of services employment	15.664	15.881	15.607
Percentage of other tertiary employment	10.944	11.694	10.820
Percentage of government employment	3.926	3.219	3.474
TOTAL	100.000	100.000	100.000

TABLE 2.12

Percentage of Change in Population and Employment by Population Size Class of Region, 1960–1970

	0–200,000	200,000–300,000	300,000–400,000	400,000–500,000
Population	1.774	9.132	6.601	11.473
Total employment	13.650	22.925	21.232	16.347
Primary employment	−28.192	−24.669	−27.545	−30.104
Secondary employment	33.812	33.897	50.415	44.353
Wholesale and retail employment	31.631	53.796	45.411	44.051
Services employment	36.809	42.990	50.666	53.949
Other tertiary employment	34.985	27.514	39.858	0.172
Government employment	17.977	66.491	23.965	28.730

	500,000–600,000	600,000–700,000	700,000–800,000	800,000–900,000
Population	12.822	8.021	17.600	30.087
Total employment	23.338	20.090	27.633	37.352
Primary employment	−31.099	−30.145	−30.202	−31.842
Secondary employment	42.381	43.588	46.902	81.422
Wholesale and retail employment	44.253	56.808	47.318	71.831
Services employment	51.508	56.381	50.271	78.393
Other tertiary employment	51.865	29.387	42.538	66.099
Government employment	28.195	40.147	19.524	36.599

	900,000–1,000,000	1,000,000+	All RECs
Population	18.624	33.792	24.037
Total employment	32.784	41.439	33.077
Primary employment	−23.629	−32.583	−29.684
Secondary employment	48.008	39.148	41.350
Wholesale and retail employment	61.775	59.614	55.507
Services employment	58.539	49.888	50.436
Other tertiary employment	58.242	68.158	52.935
Government employment	14.230	38.543	35.506

TABLE 2.13

Levels and Growth Rates of Population and Employment by Industrial Class in Nine Japanese Major Regions, 1950–1970

	1950	1960	Percentage of change 1950–1960	1970	Percentage of change 1960–1970
HOKKAIDO					
Population (in thousands)	1185.933	1563.286	31.819	2079.833	33.042
Total employment (in thousands)		637.691		957.912	50.216
Percentage of primary employment		10.286		4.787	−53.464
Percentage of secondary employment		29.277		28.092	−4.047
Percentage of wholesale and retail employment		22.931		26.992	17.709
Percentage of services employment		16.356		19.708	20.491
Percentage of other tertiary employment		14.375		14.833	3.186
Percentage of government employment		6.775		5.589	−17.505
TOHOKU					
Population (in thousands)	2385.451	2578.888	8.109	2869.240	11.259
Total employment (in thousands)		1144.248		1421.612	24.240
Percentage of primary employment		35.605		21.426	−39.824
Percentage of secondary employment		20.016		25.239	26.096
Percentage of wholesale and retail employment		17.143		21.393	24.790
Percentage of services employment		13.328		16.730	25.522
Percentage of other tertiary employment		8.839		10.450	18.226
Percentage of government employment		5.069		4.763	−6.048
KANTO					
Population (in thousands)	13608.624	18669.214	37.187	25228.235	35.133
Total employment (in thousands)		8668.191		12419.931	43.282
Percentage of primary employment		13.052		6.350	−51.345
Percentage of secondary employment		38.659		40.028	3.542
Percentage of wholesale and retail employment		20.370		22.784	11.849
Percentage of services employment		14.934		16.300	9.149
Percentage of other tertiary employment		9.449		11.157	18.076
Percentage of government employment		3.536		3.380	−4.408

TOKAI

Population (in thousands)	5938.683	7298.250	22.893	8715.443	19.418
Total employment (in thousands)		3605.745		4704.627	30.476
Percentage of primary employment		21.687		11.762	-45.766
Percentage of secondary employment		40.575		43.820	7.997
Percentage of wholesale and retail employment		16.585		19.906	20.026
Percentage of services employment		10.561		12.968	22.796
Percentage of other tertiary employment		7.980		9.056	13.488
Percentage of government employment		2.612		2.487	-4.773

HOKURIKU

Population (in thousands)	3127.476	3316.942	6.058	3518.954	6.090
Total employment (in thousands)		1642.403		1906.412	16.075
Percentage of primary employment		34.663		21.004	-39.405
Percentage of secondary employment		27.293		32.275	18.256
Percentage of wholesale and retail employment		16.081		19.649	22.185
Percentage of services employment		11.225		14.607	30.128
Percentage of other tertiary employment		7.767		9.284	19.536
Percentage of government employment		2.971		3.181	7.048

KINKI

Population (in thousands)	8777.205	11405.593	29.946	15032.177	31.797
Total employment (in thousands)		5268.112		7271.129	38.022
Percentage of primary employment		9.612		4.823	-49.826
Percentage of secondary employment		43.580		43.284	-0.680
Percentage of wholesale and retail employment		20.289		23.165	14.177
Percentage of services employment		15.034		14.657	-2.507
Percentage of other tertiary employment		8.727		11.298	29.463
Percentage of government employment		2.759		2.774	0.536

CHUGOKU

Population (in thousands)	3659.219	4059.417	10.937	4520.815	11.366
Total employment (in thousands)		1939.444		2349.261	21.131
Percentage of primary employment		29.767		16.716	-43.843
Percentage of secondary employment		29.177		34.207	17.239

(Table 2.13 Continues on page 54)

TABLE 2.13 *(Continued)*

	1950	1960	Percentage of change 1950–1960	1970	Percentage of change 1960–1970
Percentage of wholesale and retail employment		16.023		19.710	23.015
Percentage of services employment		12.291		15.330	24..723
Percentage of other tertiary employment		9.081		10.290	13.308
Percentage of government employment		3.662		3.748	2.347
SHIKOKU					
Population (in thousands)	1545.984	1630.284	5.453	1757.684	7.815
Total employment (in thousands)		819.961		898.000	9.517
Percentage of primary employment		30.038		18.928	−36.985
Percentage of secondary employment		23.377		30.264	29.457
Percentage of wholesale and retail employment		14.483		20.305	40.192
Percentage of services employment		11.906		16.668	39.994
Percentage of other tertiary employment		17.374		10.168	−41.478
Percentage of government employment		2.821		3.668	30.011
KYUSHU					
Population (in thousands)	5263.137	6129.617	16.463	6546.195	6.796
Total employment (in thousands)		2539.163		3023.743	19.084
Percentage of primary employment		22.041		13.253	−39.872
Percentage of secondary employment		28.020		28.070	0.180
Percentage of wholesale and retail employment		20.208		23.601	16.791
Percentage of services employment		15.037		17.859	18.766
Percentage of other tertiary employment		10.526		11.502	9.272
Percentage of government employment		4.169		5.715	37.103

Chugoku, Shikoku, and Kyushu.[11] In terms of population, Kanto and Kinki were the largest, and Shikoku and Hokkaido were the smallest. Interestingly, the large regions grew the fastest, although Hokkaido also grew quickly. Kanto and Kinki (the regions surrounding Tokyo and Osaka, respectively) had population increases of 35.1 and 31.8% between 1960 and 1970; Hokkaido grew by 33.0%. The slowest growing regions were at the periphery of the urban system: Hokuriku (6.1% growth) and Kyushu (6.8% growth). Between 1950 and 1960, Hokkaido, Kanto, and Kinki were also the fastest growing regions; the growth rates of Hokkaido and Kinki accelerated in the 1960–1970 period, although Kanto's declined slightly. Overall, there is stability of the growth rates in interdecennial periods, and there is a strong tendency toward the system's centralization. Thus, the large major regions were getting even larger, the smaller regions lagging still further.

It is important to note that both Kanto and Kinki were more heavily concentrated in secondary industry than the other major regions. Tokai was also predominantly manufacturing and "other" secondary employment. The lowest concentration in secondary industry was in Tohoku and Kyushu. Kyushu and Hokkaido had the highest concentration in government employment, whereas Tokai and Kinki had the lowest. The tendency for manufacturing-based major regions to grow quickly is in contradistinction to the experience of the United States and the United Kingdom where in the 1950s and 1960s service-based cities grew the most rapidly. However, non-manufacturing industrial development was also important in the regional growth process in Japan as will be shown in Section 4.3.

Table 2.14 presents another aggregation of the RECs into the Tokaido and non-Tokaido[12] regions. We see that the Tokaido region was growing faster than the non-Tokaido area with respect to employment and population in both decades. This is another way of showing the relative centralization of the urban system. We also see a large difference in the proportion of employment in secondary industry (41.7% in Tokaido as opposed to only 30.0% in non-Tokaido area). On the other hand, there is relatively more primary and government employment in the non-Tokaido region.

---

[11] The regions were defined as follows: (1) Hokkaido: Hokkaido prefecture; (2) Tohoku: Aomori, Iwate, Miyagi, Akita, Yamagata, and Fukushima prefectures; (3) Kanto: Ibaragi, Tochigi, Gumma, Saitama, Chiba, Tokyo, Kanagawa, and Yamanashi prefectures; (4) Tokai: Gifu, Shizuoka, Aichi, and Mie prefectures; (5) Hokuriku: Toyama, Ishikawa, Fukui, Nagano, and Niigata prefectures; (6) Kinki: Shiga, Kyoto, Osaka, Hyogo, Nara, and Wakayama prefectures; (7) Chugoku: Tottori, Shimane, Okayama, Hiroshima, Yamaguchi, and Tokushima prefectures; (8) Shikoku: Kagawa, Ehime, Tokushima, and Kochi prefectures; (9) Kyushu: Fukuoka, Saga, Nagasaki, Kumamoto, Oita, Miyazaki, and Kagoshima prefectures. (See Figures 1.4–1.7 for maps of the prefectures.)

[12] For my purposes here, Tokaido region is the summation of the RECs of the Kanto, Tokai, and Kinki major regions. The non-Tokaido major region consists of the RECs in all other prefectures.

TABLE 2.14

Levels and Growth Rates of Population and Employment by Industrial Class in the Tokaido Region and Non-Tokaido Areas, 1950–1970

	1950	1960	Percentage of change 1950–1960	1970	Percentage of change 1960–1970
TOKAIDO					
Population (in thousands)	28,324.512	37,373.057	31.946	48,975.855	31.046
Total employment (in thousands)		17,542.048		24,395.687	39.070
Percentage of primary employment		13.794		6.939	−49.697
Percentage of secondary employment		40.531		41.730	2.958
Percentage of wholesale and retail employment		19.568		22.343	14.181
Percentage of services employment		14.065		15.168	7.841
Percentage of other tertiary employment		8.930		10.794	20.870
Percentage of government employment		3.112		3.027	−2.747
NON-TOKAIDO					
Population (in thousands)	17,167.200	19,278.434	12.298	21,292.721	10.448
Total employment (in thousands)		8,722.910		10,556.940	21.025
Percentage of primary employment		27.807		16.238	−41.603
Percentage of secondary employment		26.746		30.002	12.177
Percentage of wholesale and retail employment		17.759		21.751	22.479
Percentage of services employment		13.287		16.623	25.112
Percentage of other tertiary employment		10.389		10.879	4.714
Percentage of government employment		4.013		4.506	12.295

4 Additional Analysis of Growth Patterns of Japanese Regional Economic Clusters

4.1 Introduction

In this section I further discuss the growth patterns that occurred within the Japanese urban system in the 1950s and 1960s. In Section 4.2 and Appendix 4 I present some shift-share analyses of the growth of the population and employment. Regression analysis of changes in these variables are given in Section 4.3.

4.2 Shift-Share Analysis

Tables 2.15–2.17 summarize a shift-share analysis of the Japanese RECs. Shift-share indicates the growth of a region that would have occurred if the region had grown at the same rate as all RECs. One can then calculate the "expected" growth of a region assuming that it grew at the all-REC rate as in Column 3 of Tables 2.15–2.17. Therefore, the expected growth is compared to the actual growth that is given in Column 2. Column 4 shows the absolute difference between the actual and expected growth for a given region.

In Table 2.15 we see that Sapporo grew from 626,400 population in 1950 to 878,200 in 1960. The expected level of population for 1960, based on the growth of all Japanese RECs, was only 780,000. As a result, the "shift factor" given in column 4 is 98,170, the difference between the actual and expected (878,200 − 780,000). Hakodate, on the other hand, grew only to 312,500 in 1960 rather than the "expected" 367,000; the result is a −54,550 shift factor for that city, since it did not grow as fast as the national rate. The shift index given in Column 5 is the percentage change in a REC's share of all the REC population or for total REC employment. Thus, if the REC had 2.0% of the total in 1960 and had a 2.2% share of the total 1970, then the shift index would be 1.10 (2.2/2.0) since in 1970 it had 10% greater share. In Table 2.15 Sapporo's shift index is 1.13, indicating that its "share" increased by 13% during the period under analysis. This technique allows us to easily highlight which RECS grew at the expense of other RECs within the Japanese urban system. It shows for population (and employment) the redistribution within the urban system that took place during the time period under study.

The 1950s saw relative growth in three of the four Hokkaido RECs (Sapporo, Muroran, and Kushiro), according to Table 2.15. This occurred in part because of the relative depopulation of rural Hokkaido and the migration to these centers that accompanied it. Other net gainers of population were Tokyo, Yokohama, Nagoya, Toyota, Osaka, Kobe, and Hiroshima. All other regions were relative losers of population. Therefore, we have a pattern of growth emerging in which growth occurred in and around the three largest regions—Tokyo, Osaka, and Nagoya—and in Hokkaido.

TABLE 2.15
Shift-Share Analysis of Population, 1950–1960[a]

		Actual 1950 (1)	Actual 1960 (2)	Expected 1960 (3)	Shift factor (2)–(3) (4)	Shift index (5)
1.	Sapporo	626.4	878.2	780.0	98.17	1.13
2.	Hakodate	294.7	312.5	367.0	−54.55	.85
3.	Muroran	154.8	201.2	192.7	8.49	1.04
4.	Kushiro	110.1	171.4	137.1	34.32	1.25
5.	Morioka	141.8	171.8	176.6	−4.75	.97
6.	Sendai	704.6	794.7	877.4	−82.69	.91
7.	Ishinomaki	126.4	132.6	157.5	−24.85	.84
8.	Akita	338.6	361.1	421.7	−60.52	.86
9.	Yamagata	380.7	363.1	474.1	−91.01	.81
10.	Fukushima	284.2	307.0	353.9	−46.91	.87
11.	Aizuwakamatsu	113.6	119.3	141.4	−22.18	.84
12.	Koriyama	295.6	309.2	368.1	−58.84	.84
13.	Mito	326.9	358.7	407.1	−48.42	.88
14.	Hitachi	269.1	318.1	335.2	−17.03	.95
15.	Utsunomiya	508.9	518.7	633.8	−115.03	.82
16.	Maebashi	253.2	285.8	315.3	−49.47	.84
17.	Takasaki	335.3	353.3	417.5	−64.27	.85
18.	Kiryu	146.2	149.4	182.1	−32.67	.82
19.	Kumagaya	258.1	259.6	321.4	−61.81	.81
20.	Chiba	450.8	519.6	561.4	−41.77	.93
21.	Tokyo	8857.3	13099.3	11030.1	2069.21	1.19
22.	Yokohama	1526.8	2076.8	1901.4	175.48	1.09
23.	Hiratsuka	128.7	155.7	160.3	−4.53	.97
24.	Odawara	201.2	263.6	250.5	−16.94	.93
25.	Niigata	588.3	634.4	732.6	−98.20	.87
26.	Nagaoka	195.0	212.8	242.9	−30.11	.88
27.	Toyama	440.1	477.8	548.1	−70.31	.87
28.	Takaoka	363.0	367.5	452.1	−84.52	.81
29.	Kanazawa	438.5	482.9	546.0	−63.17	.88
30.	Fukui	471.6	485.1	587.3	−102.14	.83
31.	Kofu	346.1	360.4	431.0	−70.55	.84
32.	Nagano	363.1	382.4	452.1	−69.71	.85
33.	Matsumoto	267.9	274.0	333.6	−59.59	.82
34.	Gifu	531.3	620.7	661.7	−40.98	.94
35.	Shizuoka	659.5	793.8	821.3	−27.46	.97
36.	Hamamatsu	621.4	743.7	773.8	−30.10	.96
37.	Numazu	281.2	330.9	350.2	−19.36	.94
38.	Nagoya	2461.9	3267.6	3065.9	201.76	1.07
39.	Toyohashi	346.8	381.0	431.9	−50.89	.88
40.	Toyota	239.1	311.1	297.8	13.33	1.04
41.	Tsu	281.9	291.0	351.1	−60.05	.83
42.	Yokkaichi	346.1	384.3	431.0	−46.69	.89
43.	Ise	169.3	174.0	210.8	−36.84	.83
44.	Otsu	264.7	302.2	354.5	−52.26	.85
45.	Kyoto	1312.5	1511.1	1634.4	−123.35	.92
46.	Osaka	4784.4	6781.2	5958.1	823.10	1.14

TABLE 2.15 *(Continued)*

		Actual 1950 (1)	Actual 1960 (2)	Expected 1960 (3)	Shift factor (2)–(3) (4)	Shift index (5)
47.	Kobe	1127.3	1441.7	1403.8	37.91	1.03
48.	Himeji	642.8	682.2	800.5	−118.30	.85
49.	Nara	189.3	205.0	235.7	−30.72	.87
50.	Wakayama	436.3	482.1	543.3	−61.17	.89
51.	Tottori	201.0	204.8	250.3	−45.57	.82
52.	Yonago	173.9	181.6	216.6	−35.03	.84
53.	Matsue	218.2	226.2	271.7	−45.52	.83
54.	Okayama	533.6	578.2	664.5	−86.29	.87
55.	Kurashiki	282.4	337.1	351.7	−14.61	.96
56.	Hiroshima	619.9	767.1	771.9	−4.87	.99
57.	Fukuyama	458.2	475.9	570.6	−94.72	.83
58.	Shimonoseki	293.1	331.9	365.1	−33.18	.91
59.	Ube	223.4	242.2	278.3	−36.05	.87
60.	Yamaguchi	109.2	117.3	136.0	−18.72	.86
61.	Iwakuni	143.9	168.1	179.1	−11.08	.94
62.	Tokushima	402.3	429.2	501.0	−71.81	.86
63.	Takamatsu	574.0	579.9	714.9	−134.96	.81
64.	Matsuyama	327.8	368.9	408.2	−39.30	.90
65.	Imabari	160.0	164.0	199.3	−35.30	.82
66.	Niihama	189.5	197.3	236.0	−38.75	.84
67.	Kochi	294.6	320.2	366.9	−46.64	.87
68.	Kitakyushu	1246.1	1518.5	1551.8	−33.35	.98
69.	Fukuoka	866.9	1063.7	1079.6	−15.95	.99
70.	Omuta	295.2	307.5	367.6	−60.08	.84
71.	Kurume	422.8	449.1	526.5	−77.39	.85
72.	Saga	252.4	266.9	314.3	−47.38	.85
73.	Nagasaki	421.8	506.6	525.3	−18.76	.96
74.	Sasebo	263.8	297.1	328.6	−31.46	.90
75.	Kumamoto	374.0	453.0	465.7	−12.78	.97
76.	Yatsushiro	141.5	152.1	176.2	−24.09	.86
77.	Oita	351.1	386.1	437.2	−51.03	.88
78.	Miyazaki	163.5	185.9	203.6	−17.75	.91
79.	Nobeoka	119.7	138.3	149.1	−10.81	.93
80.	Kagoshima	344.3	405.0	428.8	−23.82	.94
Regional totals						
1.	Hokkaido	1185.9	1563.3	1476.9	86.43	1.06
2.	Tohoku	2385.5	2578.9	2970.6	−391.75	.87
3.	Kanto	13608.6	18669.2	16947.0	1722.19	1.10
4.	Tokai	5938.7	7298.2	7395.5	−97.28	.99
5.	Hokuriku	3127.5	3316.9	3894.7	−577.75	.85
6.	Kinki	8777.2	11405.6	10930.4	475.21	1.04
7.	Chugoku	3659.2	4059.4	4556.9	−497.46	.89
8.	Shikoku	1546.0	1630.3	1925.2	−294.95	.85
9.	Kyushu	5263.1	6129.6	6554.3	−424.64	.94

[a] Population and employment values are given in thousands.

TABLE 2.16
Shift-Share Analysis of Population, 1960–1970[a]

		Actual 1960 (1)	Actual 1970 (2)	Expected 1970 (3)	Shift factor (2)–(3) (4)	Shift index (5)
1.	Sapporo	878.2	1108.4	1089.3	210.93	1.19
2.	Hakodate	312.5	334.1	387.6	−53.53	.86
3.	Muroran	201.2	238.1	249.6	−11.45	.95
4.	Kushiro	171.4	207.4	212.6	−5.16	.98
5.	Morioka	171.8	212.7	213.1	−.45	1.00
6.	Sendai	794.7	956.9	985.8	−28.89	.97
7.	Ishinomaki	132.6	144.8	164.5	−19.69	.88
8.	Akita	361.1	383.2	447.9	−64.78	.86
9.	Yamagata	383.1	391.3	475.2	−83.84	.82
10.	Fukushima	307.0	327.0	380.8	−53.74	.86
11.	Aizuwakamatsu	119.3	120.6	147.9	−27.28	.82
12.	Koriyama	309.2	332.7	383.6	−50.86	.87
13.	Mito	358.7	413.5	444.9	−31.42	.93
14.	Hitachi	318.1	335.2	394.6	−59.45	.85
15.	Utsunomiya	518.7	583.5	643.4	−59.95	.91
16.	Maebashi	265.8	305.5	329.7	−24.22	.93
17.	Takasaki	353.3	391.4	438.2	−46.79	.89
18.	Kiryu	149.4	162.3	185.3	−23.02	.88
19.	Kumagaya	259.6	289.5	322.0	−32.45	.90
20.	Chiba	519.6	816.0	644.5	171.50	1.27
21.	Tokyo	13099.3	17711.5	16248.0	1463.50	1.09
22.	Yokohama	2076.8	3323.8	2576.0	747.71	1.29
23.	Hiratsuka	155.7	234.4	193.2	41.26	1.21
24.	Odawara	233.6	283.7	289.7	−5.98	.98
25.	Niigata	634.4	691.6	786.9	−95.27	.88
26.	Nagaoka	212.8	224.1	263.9	−39.82	.85
27.	Toyama	477.8	493.5	592.6	−99.12	.83
28.	Takaoka	367.5	364.1	455.9	−91.79	.80
29.	Kanazawa	482.9	540.3	598.9	−58.67	.90
30.	Fukui	485.1	499.6	601.7	−102.15	.83
31.	Kofu	360.4	377.9	447.1	−69.16	.85
32.	Nagano	382.4	411.6	474.3	−62.72	.87
33.	Matsumoto	274.0	294.2	339.9	−45.73	.87
34.	Gifu	620.7	749.6	769.9	−20.29	.97
35.	Shizuoka	793.8	927.6	984.7	−57.10	.94
36.	Hamamatsu	743.7	827.4	922.5	−95.07	.90
37.	Numazu	330.9	421.5	410.4	11.10	1.03
38.	Nagoya	3267.6	4122.6	4053.1	69.54	1.02
39.	Toyohashi	381.0	435.5	472.6	−37.06	.92
40.	Toyota	311.1	445.1	385.9	59.20	1.15
41.	Tsu	291.0	312.1	361.0	−48.90	.86
42.	Yokkaichi	384.3	453.3	476.7	−23.39	.95
43.	Ise	174.0	178.6	215.8	−37.22	.83
44.	Otsu	302.2	356.2	374.9	−18.71	.95
45.	Kyoto	1511.1	1809.4	1874.3	−64.88	.97
46.	Osaka	6781.2	9495.2	8411.2	1083.98	1.13

TABLE 2.16 *(Continued)*

	Actual 1960 (1)	Actual 1970 (2)	Expected 1970 (3)	Shift factor (2)–(3) (4)	Shift index (5)
47. Kobe	1441.7	1741.0	1788.2	−47.24	.97
48. Himeji	682.2	782.6	846.2	−63.58	.92
49. Nara	205.0	284.7	254.3	30.41	1.12
50. Wakayama	482.1	563.1	598.0	−34.94	.94
51. Tottori	204.8	199.0	254.0	−54.93	.78
52. Yonago	181.6	186.3	225.2	−38.95	.83
53. Matsue	226.2	227.9	280.5	−52.67	.81
54. Okayama	578.2	641.8	717.2	−75.45	.89
55. Kurashiki	337.1	418.5	418.1	.32	1.00
56. Hiroshima	767.1	1025.8	951.4	74.36	1.08
57. Fukuyama	475.9	544.9	590.3	−45.31	.92
58. Shimonoseki	331.9	328.8	411.6	−82.84	.80
59. Ube	242.2	211.3	300.4	−89.12	.70
60. Yamaguchi	117.3	117.1	145.5	−28.37	.80
61. Iwakuni	168.1	174.4	208.5	−34.04	.84
62. Tokushima	429.2	445.0	532.3	−87.34	.84
63. Takamatsu	579.9	602.9	719.3	−116.35	.84
64. Matsuyama	368.9	428.5	457.5	−28.99	.94
65. Imabari	164.0	171.2	203.4	−32.17	.84
66. Niihama	197.3	193.2	244.7	−51.47	.79
67. Kochi	320.2	361.7	397.2	−35.48	.91
68. Kitakyushu	1518.5	1501.6	1883.4	−381.87	.80
69. Fukuoka	1063.7	1324.4	1319.3	5.07	1.00
70. Omuta	307.5	263.2	381.4	−118.17	.69
71. Kurume	449.1	443.4	557.0	−113.60	.80
72. Saga	266.9	256.2	331.1	−74.94	.77
73. Nagasaki	506.6	545.4	628.3	−82.89	.87
74. Sasebo	297.1	272.3	368.5	−96.22	.74
75. Kumamoto	453.0	516.2	561.8	−45.61	.92
76. Yatsushiro	152.1	140.8	188.7	−47.84	.75
77. Oita	386.1	446.9	479.0	−32.08	.93
78. Miyazaki	185.9	222.6	230.5	−7.92	.97
79. Nobeoka	138.3	143.8	171.5	−27.70	.84
80. Kagoshima	405.0	469.3	502.3	−33.00	.93
Regional totals					
1. Hokkaido	1563.3	2079.8	1939.0	140.78	1.07
2. Tohoku	2578.9	2869.2	3198.8	−329.53	.90
3. Kanto	18669.2	25228.2	23156.7	2071.52	1.09
4. Tokai	7298.2	8715.4	9052.5	−337.07	.96
5. Hokuriku	3316.9	3519.0	4114.2	−595.27	.86
6. Kinki	11405.6	15032.2	14147.1	885.05	1.06
7. Chugoku	4059.4	4520.8	5035.2	−514.36	.90
8. Shikoku	1630.3	1757.7	2022.2	−264.47	.87
9. Kyushu	6129.6	6546.2	7603.0	−1056.79	.86

[a] Population and employment values are in thousands.

For the 1960s (Table 2.16), the analysis of population shows the important growth centers were Sapporo, Chiba, Tokyo, Yokohama, Hiratsuka, Osaka, and Wakayama. Again, all but Sapporo are in the Tokyo or Osaka conurbations. This again indicates considerable centralization within the urban system. Those that lost the biggest shares were in the periphery of the system: Odawara, Tottori, Ube, Omuta, Saga, Sasebo, and Yatsushiro.

Table 2.17 gives the shift-share analysis for 1950–1970, and the centralization of the urban system over the two decades is shown again. In Figure 2.2 we show the fast-growing regions in terms of population between 1960 and 1970 as the RECs with shift indices greater than 1 are highlighted. Appendix 4 gives shift-share tables for employment by type of employment for 1960–1970.

The shift-share analysis yields some interesting conclusions as shown in Tables 2.18 and 2.19, which are extracted from Tables 2.15–2.17. Here we have the 10 fastest growing regions for 1950–1970 and the 9 slowest growing for the same period. The fastest growing regions in Japan were Sapporo, Kushiro, Chiba, Tokyo, Yokohama, Osaka, and Hiroshima as shown in Table 2.18. The fastest growing major regions were Hokkaido, Kanto, and Kinki. Most of the fast-growing cities increased their shares more in the period 1960–1970 than they did during the period 1950–1960. This is true for Sapporo, Chiba, Yokohama, Hiratsuka, Osaka, Nara, and Hiroshima. Many of these are suburban cities of the major urban centers, especially Tokyo. For instance, Chiba and Hiratsuka grew less rapidly during the period 1950–1960 than did the REC average but grew quite rapidly as the Tokyo metropolitan region expanded and decentralized greatly during the 1960s. Sapporo appears to be a large independent growth center that increased its population greatly over both periods. Other cities, such as Tokyo and Kobe, grew more slowly in the latter period than in the earlier period. It is seen that Tokyo's preeminence was fading and so is that of the older industrial city of Kobe.

Turning to Table 2.19, we can see that most of the slow-growing cities are away from the major conurbations of Japan. Yamagata is in the Tohoku region, and Takaoka and Tottori are on the Japan Sea; Omuta, Saga, and Yatsushiro are in Kyushu, and Niihama is on the island of Shikoku. A perusal of Table 2.19 indicates that most of the slow-growing regions grew relatively more slowly during the 1960s than during the 1950s: Odawara, Takaoka, Toyohashi, Tottori, Ube, Niihama, Omuta, Saga, and Yatsushiro all followed such a pattern.[13]

Table 2.20 summarizes additional shift-share analysis for employment by industrial class for several of the fast- and slow-growing metropolitan areas. It is important to see what some of the growth characteristics are of

---

[13] This is not, however, true when one sees the major regions noted in Table 2.19. They seem to have grown slightly more quickly (or less slowly) during the 1960–1970 decade.

TABLE 2.17
Shift-Share Analysis of Population, 1950–1970[a]

		Actual 1950 (1)	Actual 1970 (2)	Expected 1970 (3)	Shift factor (2)–(3) (4)	Shift index (5)
1.	Sapporo	626.4	1108.4	967.5	332.69	1.11
2.	Hakodate	294.7	334.1	455.3	−121.20	.73
3.	Muroran	154.8	238.1	239.1	−.92	1.00
4.	Kushiro	110.1	207.4	170.0	37.41	1.22
5.	Morioka	141.8	212.7	219.0	−6.35	.97
6.	Sendai	704.6	956.9	1088.3	−131.45	.86
7.	Ishinomaki	126.4	144.8	195.3	−50.52	.74
8.	Akita	338.6	383.2	523.0	−139.84	.73
9.	Yamagata	380.7	391.3	588.1	−196.73	.67
10.	Fukushima	284.2	327.0	439.0	−111.93	.75
11.	Aizuwakamatsu	113.6	120.6	175.4	−54.79	.69
12.	Koriyama	295.6	332.7	456.5	−123.84	.73
13.	Mito	326.9	413.5	505.0	−91.48	.82
14.	Hitachi	269.1	335.2	415.7	−80.57	.81
15.	Utsunomiya	508.9	583.5	786.1	−202.63	.74
16.	Maebashi	253.2	305.5	391.1	−85.58	.78
17.	Takasaki	335.3	391.4	517.9	−126.51	.76
18.	Kiryu	146.2	162.3	225.8	−63.54	.72
19.	Kumagaya	258.1	289.5	398.7	−109.11	.73
20.	Chiba	450.8	816.0	696.3	119.69	1.17
21.	Tokyo	8857.3	17711.5	13681.4	4030.08	1.29
22.	Yokohama	1526.8	3323.8	2358.4	965.36	1.41
23.	Hiratsuka	128.7	234.4	198.8	35.65	1.18
24.	Odawara	201.2	283.7	310.7	−26.99	.91
25.	Niigata	588.3	691.6	908.7	−217.08	.76
26.	Nagaoka	195.0	224.1	301.3	−77.16	.74
27.	Toyama	440.1	493.5	679.9	−186.33	.73
28.	Takaoka	363.0	364.1	560.7	−196.62	.65
29.	Kanazawa	438.5	540.3	677.3	−137.02	.80
30.	Fukui	471.6	499.6	728.4	−228.85	.69
31.	Kofu	346.1	377.9	534.6	−156.67	.71
32.	Nagano	363.1	411.6	560.8	−149.18	.73
33.	Matsumoto	267.9	294.2	413.8	−119.65	.71
34.	Gifu	531.3	749.6	820.7	−71.12	.91
35.	Shizuoka	659.5	927.6	1018.7	−91.17	.91
36.	Hamamatsu	621.4	827.4	959.8	−132.41	.86
37.	Numazu	281.2	421.5	434.4	−12.91	.97
38.	Nagoya	2461.9	4122.6	3802.8	319.80	1.08
39.	Toyohashi	346.8	435.5	535.7	−100.16	.81
40.	Toyota	239.1	445.1	369.4	75.70	1.21
41.	Tsu	281.9	312.1	435.5	−123.39	.72
42.	Yokkaichi	346.1	453.3	534.6	−81.30	.85
43.	Ise	169.3	178.6	261.5	−82.91	.68
44.	Otsu	284.7	356.2	439.7	−83.53	.81
45.	Kyoto	1312.5	1809.4	2027.3	−217.88	.89
46.	Osaka	4784.4	9495.2	7390.3	2104.93	1.28

TABLE 2.17 *(Continued)*

		Actual 1950 (1)	Actual 1970 (2)	Expected 1970 (3)	Shift factor (2)–(3) (4)	Shift index (5)
47.	Kobe	1127.3	1741.0	1741.2	−.23	1.00
48.	Himeji	642.8	782.6	993.0	−210.32	.79
49.	Nara	189.3	284.7	292.4	−7.69	.97
50.	Wakayama	436.3	563.1	673.9	−110.81	.84
51.	Tottori	201.0	199.0	310.5	−111.46	.64
52.	Yonago	173.9	186.3	268.7	−82.40	.69
53.	Matsue	218.2	227.9	337.0	−109.13	.68
54.	Okayama	533.6	641.8	824.3	−182.49	.78
55.	Kurashiki	282.4	418.5	436.3	−17.81	.96
56.	Hiroshima	619.9	1025.8	957.5	68.31	1.07
57.	Fukuyama	458.2	544.9	707.7	−162.80	.77
58.	Shimonoseki	293.1	328.8	452.8	−124.00	.73
59.	Ube	223.4	211.3	345.1	−133.83	.61
60.	Yamaguchi	109.2	117.1	168.7	−51.60	.69
61.	Iwakuni	143.9	174.4	222.2	−47.78	.78
62.	Tokushima	402.3	445.0	621.4	−176.40	.72
63.	Takamatsu	574.0	602.9	886.7	−283.75	.68
64.	Matsuyama	327.8	428.5	506.3	−77.74	.85
65.	Imabari	160.0	171.2	247.2	−75.96	.69
66.	Niihama	189.5	193.2	292.8	−99.53	.66
67.	Kochi	294.6	361.7	455.1	−93.34	.79
68.	Kitakyushu	1246.1	1501.6	1924.8	−423.25	.78
69.	Fukuoka	866.9	1324.4	1339.1	−14.71	.99
70.	Omuta	295.2	263.2	455.9	−192.70	.58
71.	Kurume	422.8	443.4	653.0	−209.59	.68
72.	Saga	252.4	256.2	389.9	−133.71	.66
73.	Nagasaki	421.8	545.4	651.6	−106.16	.84
74.	Sasebo	263.8	272.3	407.5	−135.24	.67
75.	Kumamoto	374.0	516.2	577.7	−61.46	.89
76.	Yatsushiro	141.5	140.8	218.5	−77.72	.64
77.	Oita	351.1	446.9	542.3	−95.38	.82
78.	Miyazaki	163.5	222.6	252.5	−29.94	.88
79.	Nobeoka	119.7	143.8	184.9	−41.11	.78
80.	Kagoshima	344.3	469.3	531.9	−62.54	.88
Regional totals						
1.	Hokkaido	1185.9	2079.8	1831.8	247.98	1.14
2.	Tohoku	2385.5	2869.2	3684.7	−815.44	.78
3.	Kanto	13608.6	25228.2	21020.5	4207.65	1.20
4.	Tokai	5938.7	8715.4	9173.2	−457.74	.95
5.	Hokuriku	3127.5	3519.0	4830.9	−1311.90	.73
6.	Kinki	8777.2	15032.2	13357.7	1474.48	1.11
7.	Chugoku	3659.2	4520.8	5652.2	−1131.39	.80
8.	Shikoku	1546.0	1757.7	2388.0	−630.32	.74
9.	Kyushu	5263.1	6546.2	8129.7	−1583.50	.81

64 [a] Population and employment values are given in thousands.

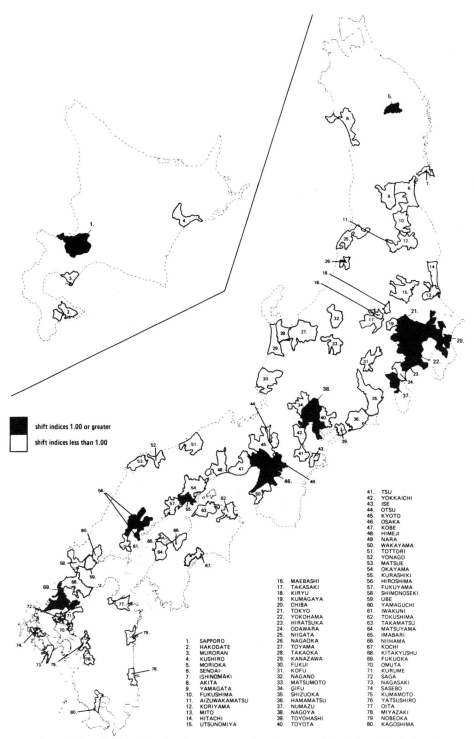

Figure 2.2. Shift indices for Japanese Regional Economic Clusters, 1960–1970.

shift indices 1.00 or greater

shift indices less than 1.00

1.	SAPPORO
2.	HAKODATE
3.	MURORAN
4.	KUSHIRO
5.	MORIOKA
6.	SENDAI
7.	ISHINOMAKI
8.	AKITA
9.	YAMAGATA
10.	FUKUSHIMA
11.	AIZUWAKAMATSU
12.	KORIYAMA
13.	MITO
14.	HITACHI
15.	UTSUNOMIYA

16.	MAEBASHI
17.	TAKASAKI
18.	KIRYU
19.	KUMAGAYA
20.	CHIBA
21.	TOKYO
22.	YOKOHAMA
23.	HIRATSUKA
24.	ODAWARA
25.	NIIGATA
26.	NAGAOKA
27.	TOYAMA
28.	TAKAOKA
29.	KANAZAWA
30.	FUKUI
31.	KOFU
32.	NAGANO
33.	MATSUMOTO
34.	GIFU
35.	SHIZUOKA
36.	HAMAMATSU
37.	NUMAZU
38.	NAGOYA
39.	TOYOHASHI
40.	TOYOTA

41.	TSU
42.	YOKKAICHI
43.	ISE
44.	OTSU
45.	KYOTO
46.	OSAKA
47.	KOBE
48.	HIMEJI
49.	NARA
50.	WAKAYAMA
51.	TOTTORI
52.	YONAGO
53.	MATSUE
54.	OKAYAMA
55.	KURASHIKI
56.	HIROSHIMA
57.	FUKUYAMA
58.	SHIMONOSEKI
59.	UBE
60.	YAMAGUCHI
61.	IWAKUNI
62.	TOKUSHIMA
63.	TAKAMATSU
64.	MATSUYAMA
65.	IMABARI
66.	NIIHAMA
67.	KOCHI
68.	KITAKYUSHU
69.	FUKUOKA
70.	OMUTA
71.	KURUME
72.	SAGA
73.	NAGASAKI
74.	SASEBO
75.	KUMAMOTO
76.	YATSUSHIRO
77.	OITA
78.	MIYAZAKI
79.	NOBEOKA
80.	KAGOSHIMA

65

TABLE 2.18

Shift-Share Analysis: Fastest Growing RECs and Major Regions, 1950–1970

City	Population shift index		
	1950–1960	1960–1970	1950–1970
Sapporo	1.13	1.19	1.11
Kushiro	1.25	.98	1.22
Chiba	.93	1.27	1.17
Tokyo	1.19	1.09	1.29
Yokohama	1.09	1.29	1.41
Hiratsuka	.97	1.21	1.18
Osaka	1.14	1.16	1.29
Kobe	1.03	.97	1.00
Nara	.87	1.12	.97
Hiroshima	.99	1.08	1.07
Hokkaido	1.06	1.07	1.14
Kanto	1.10	1.09	1.20
Kinki	1.04	1.06	1.11

these regions and to see if generalizations can be drawn from these trends. It is clear from Table 2.20 that the fast-growing regions were growing most quickly in the areas of secondary and service employment. For instance, Chiba had a shift index of 1.77, Yokohama had 1.33, and Hiratsuka had 1.41 for secondary employment. Fast-growing regions also show relative increases in services and wholesale and retail trade. The slow-growing regions, on the other hand, had mostly low coefficients for secondary employment. For instance, Omuta and Ube had shift indices of .64 and .65, respectively. It is

TABLE 2.19

Shift-Share Analysis: Slowest Growing RECs and Major Regions, 1950–1970

City	Population shift index		
	1950–1960	1960–1970	1950–1970
Yamagata	.84	.82	.67
Takaoka	.81	.80	.65
Toyohashi	.88	.92	.81
Tottori	.82	.78	.64
Ube	.87	.70	.61
Niihama	.84	.79	.66
Omuta	.84	.69	.58
Saga	.85	.77	.66
Yatsuhiro	.86	.75	.64
Tohoku	.87	.90	.78
Hokuriku	.85	.86	.73
Shikoku	.85	.87	.74

TABLE 2.20

Industrial Structure of Fast-Growing and Slow-Growing RECs: Shift Indices, 1960–1970

	Sapporo	Kushiro	Chiba	Tokyo	Yokohama	Hiratsuka	Osaka	Kobe	Nara	Hiroshima
Population	1.21	.99	1.28	1.10	1.30	1.23	1.16	.82	1.13	1.06
Total employment	1.23	1.05	1.20	1.07	1.31	1.26	1.13	.81	1.11	1.05
Primary employment	.93	1.35	.94	.96	.90	1.10	.92	.94	1.11	.84
Secondary employment	1.20	.81	1.77	.99	1.33	1.41	1.03	.70	1.22	1.07
Wholesale and retail employment	1.21	1.07	1.40	1.00	1.17	1.14	1.07	.88	1.15	1.14
Services employment	1.27	1.25	1.43	1.02	1.15	1.19	1.08	.95	1.19	1.09
Government employment	.87	1.04	1.30	1.01	1.07	1.15	1.07	1.07	1.01	1.01

	Yamagata	Takaoka	Toyohashi	Tottori	Ube	Niihama	Omuta	Saga	Yatsushiro
Population	.83	.81	.92	.79	.71	.80	.70	.78	.75
Total employment	.84	.83	1.00	.83	.78	.88	.80	.82	.75
Primary employment	1.00	.95	1.10	.96	1.13	1.07	1.16	1.16	1.10
Secondary employment	1.12	1.03	1.08	1.27	.65	.86	.64	.77	.86
Wholesale and retail employment	.91	.82	.94	.85	.79	.88	.78	.64	.76
Services employment	.97	.93	1.01	.94	.87	.92	.90	.25	.83
Government employment	.80	.99	.82	.83	.86	.90	2.03	4.07	.89

clear that the slow-growing regions had high concentrations in primary industry; see for instance the relatively high shift indices for Saga, and Omuta.

The data in this section bring the conclusions drawn in Section 3 into
even clearer focus. The centralization of the Japanese urban system—and a
centralization reinforced by manufacturing and service expansion—proceeded through the 1950s and 1960s. The growth of employment as a
determinant of population change is emphasized in Section 4.3.

4.3   Regression Analysis of Population and
Employment Growth between 1960 and 1970

In order to understand further the growth of population and employment of the Japanese urban system during the 1960s, I estimated some
regression equations to predict these variables. The independent variables
(taken from our Regional Data Bank in Appendix 2) in these regressions are
the economic characteristics of the RECs. Although there are other (non-
economic) determinants of growth, I present these regressions as a first
step toward a fuller understanding of the growth process.

In Eq. (1) the percentage of change in REC population between 1960
and 1970 (PCN) is regressed on several characteristics of the REC's labor
force and other variables that were hypothesized to influence employment
and population growth.

$$PCN = 16.64 + .38\,PCWSG - .96\,PYNG60 + .89\,PWC70$$
$$(1.19)\quad(7.82)\qquad\quad(2.33)\qquad\qquad(3.83)$$

$$- 106.45\;LGEHPC70 - .45\,PEP70 - 3.88\,PUNE70 \quad (1)$$
$$(-2.14)\qquad\qquad\quad(-3.12)\qquad\quad(-2.39)$$
$$R^2 = .80$$

where the numbers in parentheses under each of the regression coefficients
are the t-statistics; all are significant at a 95% confidence level. In Eq. (1)

$PCWSG$	= percent change in wholesale, services, and government employment, 1960–1970.
$PYNG60$	= percentage of the RECs' population 0–14 years of age in 1960.
$PWC70$	= percentage of the RECs' employment in white-collar jobs in 1970.
$LGEHPC70$	= local government expenditure per capita on housing measures in 1970.
$PEP70$	= percentage of the RECs' employees in primary sector in 1970.
$PUNE70$	= percentage of the RECs' labor force unemployed in 1970.

Equation (1) indicates that population growth was positively related to percent change in tertiary employment (*PCWSG*), and also to percentage of employment in white-collar jobs during the decade (*PWC70*). Not surprisingly, the growth in REC population was negatively related to percentage of population very young in 1960 (*PYNG60*), percentage of 1970 employment in primary sector (*PEP70*), and the percentage of unemployed labor force (*PUNE70*). Population growth did not occur in RECs where there were great amounts of local public housing built; this can be seen with the negative sign attached to *LGEHPC70* and can be explained by the fact that local public housing was built in largely poor and declining regions.

To assess the relative quantitative importance of the relationships between each of the variables in Eq. (1) and the dependent variable, Eq. (1) was evaluated at the mean of each of the independent variables to yield Eq. (2).

$$PCN = 16.64 + \frac{PCWSG \quad PYNG60 \quad PWC70 \quad LGEHPC70 \quad PEP70 \quad PUNE70}{18.08 \quad - \quad 28.63 \quad + \quad 22.09 \quad - \quad 2.47 \quad - \quad 7.54 \quad - \quad 5.59} \quad (2)$$

Equation (2) indicates that percentage of young (*PYNG60*) was the largest negative contributor to population growth and percentage of white-collar (*PWC70*) was the largest positive contributor.

Next we estimated, in Eq. (3), a regression to predict the percent change in total employment (*PCE*) between 1960 and 1970. Here, the independent variables are as follows:

PCWSG = percent change in wholesale, services, and government employment, 1960–1970.
PEP70 = percentage of employment in primary industry in 1970.
PUNE70 = percentage of the labor force unemployed in 1970.
PWSG60 = percentage of employment in wholesale, services, and government in 1960.
NMVAN = percentage of population who have moved in between 1965 and 1970.
PRAPVD70 = percentage of RECs roads that were paved in 1970.

$$PCE = 15.46 + .45 \, PCWSG - .38 \, PEP70 - 7.94 \, PUNE70$$
$$\quad\quad\quad\quad (6.93) \quad\quad\quad (1.72) \quad\quad\quad (4.75)$$

$$.54 \, PWSG60 + .63 \, NMVDN + .11 \, PRAPVD70 \quad (3)$$
$$(3.16) \quad\quad\quad (1.62) \quad\quad\quad (1.39)$$

$$R^2 = .76$$

Equation (3) shows that employment growth was positively related to percentage of employment in tertiary jobs (*PWSG60*) in 1960 as well as to the percentage of change in the employment in this category over the decade

(*PCWSG*). Employment growth was also positively related to percentage of the population recently moved (*NMVDN*) and the percentage of the REC's roads that were paved (*PRAPVD*). Employment growth is seen to be negatively related to percentage of labor force unemployed in 1970 (*PUNE70*).

The relative quantitative importance of each of the independent variables to the dependent variable is highlighted in Eq. (4), which presents Eq. (3) evaluated at the means of each of the independent variables.

$$PCE = 15.46 + \frac{PCWSG}{21.4} \frac{PEP70}{-6.38} \frac{PUNE70}{-11.43} \frac{PWSG60}{-18.26}$$

$$- \frac{NMVDN}{14.80} \frac{PRAPVD}{+2.20} \tag{4}$$

From Eq. (4) it is seen that the most important contributor to employment growth was percentage of change in wholesale, services, and government employment.

5 Japanese Urbanization in a Worldwide Context, 1950–1970

5.1 Introduction

In this section, I present some views of Japanese urban development in comparison to the experiences of other industrialized countries and some less developed Asian countries. I wish to show to what extent the rapid urbanization in Japan was replicated in other countries, to what extent suburbanization took place elsewhere in the world, and to look at other matters pertaining to our analysis in Section 3. Whenever possible, I make use of functional urban regions as my unit of comparative analysis, but in many countries such definitions are not available. In these cases, I used the individual countries' definition of what constituted urban areas. Some data are derived from the work of Davis (1969), whose study attempts comprehensively to catalogue world urbanization.

Here I concentrate on the postwar period, with particular emphasis on the 1960s; however, in some instances, I extend my analysis back to 1920. It should be noted that international comparisons of urbanization are difficult to make even for contemporaneous examples, owing to differing definitions and data collection methods. Attempts to compare phenomenon over time are even more difficult. This brief analysis should be considered in that light.[14] Clearly, further analysis must be done.[15]

---

[14] Davis (1969, Chap. 2) contains a discussion of some of these problems.

[15] A project at the International Institute for Applied Systems Analysis on comparative

TABLE 2.21
Percentage of Population in Urban Regions, Japan, India, Sweden, United States, and U.S.S.R., 1920–1970

							Ratio of Years		
							$\frac{1940}{1920}$	$\frac{1970}{1950}$	$\frac{1970}{1920}$
	1920	1930	1940	1950	1960	1970			
Japan	18.1	24.1	37.9	37.5	63.5	72.2	1.93	1.93	3.99
India	11.2	12.0	13.9	17.3	17.9	19.9	1.24	1.15	1.78
Sweden	45.2	48.5	56.2	66.2	72.7	81.4	1.24	1.23	1.80
United States	51.2	56.1	56.5	59.0	69.8	73.4	1.10	1.24	1.43
U.S.S.R.	17.9	19.6	32.5	38.9	48.8	56.3	1.81	1.44	3.14

Sources: For Japan, Japan Bureau of Statistics, Office of the Prime Minister (1971); for India, Tanifuji (1977); for Sweden, Falk (1976); for the United States, U.S. Department of Commerce, Bureau of the Census (1975); for U.S.S.R., Mickiewicz (1973).

5.2 Comparative Urban Development in the Twentieth Century[16]

5.2.1 Population in Urban Regions

This section will trace the growth of urbanization in several developed countries (Japan, Sweden, the United States, and the Soviet Union) and one less developed country (India) for the period 1920–1970 in Table 2.21 and Figure 2.3 as measured by the percentage of national population in urban regions. An interesting aspect of Table 2.21 is a comparison between the experiences of Japan and the United States. In 1920, Japan was about one-third as urbanized as the United States, but Japan's dynamic urban growth made it almost as urbanized as the United States by 1970. Japan's population in urban regions increased 3.99 times between 1920 and 1970, compared to an increase of 1.43 times for the United States. Also, note that Japan's urbanization was rapid prior to World War II, nearly doubling between 1920 and 1940 (see Column 7 of Table 2.21), and the rate of increase between 1920 and 1940 is exactly what it was between 1950 and 1970. Therefore, Japanese modern urban development can be viewed as substantial both before and after the war. It is not merely a postwar phenomenon, as was shown in Chapter 1. Table 2.21 also allows a comparison between Japan and another Asian country—India. The data indicate that Indian urbanization is quite low in relation to Japan (19.9% urbanized in 1970 versus 72.2%

urban development has as its principal aim the development of a consistent cross-country data base for functional urban regions. We employ some of the data collected in that project in this section.

[16] Sources of data for this section include Berry (1973a,b), London School of Economics and Political Science (1974–1975), Great Britain Department of the Environment (1976), Sherrill (1976, 1977), Hay and Hall (1977a–d), Falk (1976), Ödmann and Dahlberg (1970), and Drewett, Goddard, and Spence (1975).

PERCENT OF
NATIONAL POPULATION
IN URBAN REGIONS

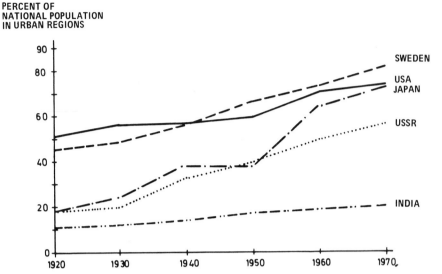

Figure 2.3. Percentage of population in urban regions, Japan, India, Sweden, United States, and U.S.S.R., 1920–1970.

for Japan), and that the rate of urbanization has been proceeding more slowly (see columns 7–9 of Table 2.21).

Table 2.22 shows data derived from the Davis study for Japan and nine other countries for 1950–1970.[17] Again, the table displays the percentage of the total population that was urbanized and the average annual growth rates of population for the 1950s and 1960s. Japan shows consistently higher growth than all countries in Table 2.22, with the exception of the Peoples Republic of China, for which accurate data probably were not really available to Davis. In nearly all cases, the population growth rates slowed between the decades. Japan's growth relative to the other countries is particularly great in the 1950s.

5.2.2 The Population of the Large Cities in Relation to National Population

There has been much discussion in the urbanism literature about the importance of large cities and their primacy within the city system. In order to better understand these relationships in a cross-cultural setting, I present Tables 2.23 and 2.24. Table 2.23 shows the "Four City Index" (FCI) of first city primacy as defined by Davis (1969, pp. 242–246). The FCI is a measure of dominance of the largest city in a country, for example, Tokyo, with respect to the size of the next three largest, for example, Osaka, Nagoya,

[17] The data for Tables 2.21 and 2.22 are not strictly comparable since Davis used somewhat different sources and estimated his data for 1970. However, Davis argues that, to a significant degree, his data are internally consistent.

TABLE 2.22
Comparative Statistics on Worldwide Urbanization, 1950–1970

	Percentage of population in urban regions			Average annual growth rates (%)	
	1950	1970	Ratio of 1970 to 1950	1950–1960	1960–1970
Japan	37.4	83.2	2.22	6.6	3.7
France	54.1	67.9	1.26	2.2	2.2
Federal Republic of Germany	72.5	82.2	1.13	1.6	1.7
United Kingdom	77.5	79.1	1.02	.5	.7
Sweden	55.4	66.1	1.19	1.6	1.6
India	17.1	18.8	1.10	2.4	2.9
U.S.S.R.	42.5	62.3	1.47	3.5	3.5
Austria	49.0	51.0	1.04	.4	.8
United States	64.0	75.2	1.18	2.7	2.1
People's Republic of China	11.0	16.5	2.14	6.4	6.0

Source: Davis (Tables C and D).

and Yokohama, and is calculated as the ratio of the population of the first largest city to the sum of the next three largest.[18] An examination of Table 2.23 indicates that Tokyo's dominance of the city system is not as great as in some other countries. France, with the importance of Paris (see also Chapter 6, Section 4) has the highest FCI of the countries listed there. Tokyo's role vis-à-vis the three next largest cities is most like that of London's. India and the United States have the least dominant largest cities, Calcutta and New York, respectively.

Table 2.24, which is based on data for functional urban regions, indicates the relative importance of the largest, 3 largest, and 10 largest regions in each country compared to the entire national population. We see that Tokyo's dominance over the Japanese urban system is somewhat greater than New York's relative to the United States (17.1% versus 9.0%) in 1970 if one uses the Daily Urban System definition of regions for the United States, and the share of the 3 and 10 larger regions is also greater. Note, in addition, that Japan's largest cities are increasing their relative share of population whereas in the United States the share is declining temporally.[19] This is consistent with the analysis in Section 3. In comparison to the smaller countries such as Denmark, Sweden, and Austria, however, Japan's larger

[18] Davis justifies this calculation because it always contains the same number of cities in each country and ought to have the same relationship to the urban hierarchy in each. The index is independent of the total number of cities in a country and has enough cities to allow one to get some information about the largest city's position relative to others. Although the number of cities is arbitrary, Davis (p. 243) says that the 4-city index is highly correlated with 10- and 2-city indices. Despite its imperfections, it is a useful tool for our comparative purposes here.

[19] Sweden's large regions also had an increasing share of total population while the FRG had mixed results. India's largest cities have had slight gains in their share.

TABLE 2.23

Four-City Index of First-City Primacy for Japan and Other Countries, 1950–1970

	1950	1960	1970
Japan	1.54	1.62	1.53
United States	1.04	.88	.77
France	3.65	3.57	3.10
Federal Republic of Germany	.85	.96	1.03
United Kingdom	1.48	1.51	1.53
Sweden	NA[a]	NA	1.14
India	.76	.72	.68
U.S.S.R.	1.20	1.10	.98
Austria	2.87	2.80	2.70

Source: Davis (1969, Table G).

[a] NA = Not available.

cities are clearly less dominant within the city system. Therefore, Japan's large cities are in the middle of the countries surveyed with respect to this dimension of urban development.

5.2.3 Spatial Structure of Urban Regions

Tables 2.25 and 2.26 give some indications of the spatial structure of metropolitan regions in several countries during the postwar period. Table 2.25 shows the percentage of functional urban regions' population residing in central cities. These central–suburban breakdowns[20] reveal that Japan's regions are somewhat more centralized that the SMSAs of the United States, but less than the SMLAs of Great Britain, both of which are readily comparable with regard to regional definitions. Concerning the rate of decentralization, we show percentage of change of the central city proportion in Columns 4 and 5 of Table 2.25. Thus, the proportion of 1970 population in Japanese REC central cities is 93.7% of that in 1960, and the proportion in 1970 is 99.6% of the 1950 figure. These measure the relative decentralization of Japanese regions.[21] Columns 4 and 5 show that Japan has decentralized much less rapidly than the United States and Great Britain during the postwar period; these countries had 1970 central city proportions less than 90% of the 1950 counterparts. We also see that the relative rates of suburbanization were not greatly different among these three countries during the 1960s. The more rapid suburbanization in the United States and Great Britain occurred in the 1950s.

Table 2.26 gives yet another view of the suburbanization process, show-

[20] For the FRG, Denmark, Austria, and the United Kingdom (using the MELA definition), the areal definitions involve more hinterland than is commonly thought of as "suburban." For these countries, the functional urban regions collectively exhaust or nearly exhaust the entire national territory.

[21] See also Chapter 5 of this volume for cross-cultural comparisons of decentralization.

TABLE 2.24

Largest Functional Urban Regions as a Percentage of Total National Population, 1950–1971 (in percentages)

Nation	Name of urban region	Year	Largest region	Three largest regions	Ten largest regions
Japan	Regional Economic	1950	10.6	19.4	28.2
	Cluster	1960	14.0	24.8	34.7
		1970	17.1	30.2	41.8
United States	Daily Urban System	1960	9.1	17.7	35.2
		1970	9.0	18.1	35.4
	Standard Metropolitan	1960	6.1	12.4	23.9
	Statistical Area	1970	5.7	12.6	23.7
Great Britain	Metropolitan Economic Labour Area	1971	16.4	25.5	40.0
Sweden	A-Region	1950	16.8	34.8	47.7
		1960	18.2	37.1	50.5
		1970	19.1	38.8	52.4
Denmark	Urban Region	1970	38.6	56.3	82.6
Austria	Functional Urban Region	1971	34.4	54.8	90.0
Federal Republic of Germany	Functional Urban Region				
		1961	5.1	12.9	34.6
		1970	4.9	13.4	33.9
India	Urban Agglomerations	1961	1.3	2.9	4.6
		1971	1.3	3.0	5.2

ing the decennial growth rates for central cities and their hinterlands for the 1960s. For Japan and the United States, the hinterland growth rates were approximately twice those of the cores, although the ratio was somewhat greater for the United States; for West Germany, the rate of hinterland growth was more than three times that of German central cities. Great Britain showed an absolute decline of the central cores cities, the only country to experience absolute decline among the four.[22]

5.2.4 Regional Growth and Region Size

How does region size relate to regional growth? Table 2.27 attempts to answer this question. We have already seen (in Section 3) that in the 1960s large Japanese regions grew much faster than smaller ones. Another pattern is seen in the data for West Germany. The growth rates there are much more similar across region size categories (the standard deviation of growth rates from the mean is smaller than that for Japan both absolutely and in relation to the mean), and the highest growth is attained for the middle-sized regions between 500,000 and 700,000 population. A similar situation exists for India,

[22] I further discuss comparative spatial structure in Chapter 5.

TABLE 2.25
Metropolitan Spatial Structure of Functional Urban Regions, 1950–1971

Country	Percentage of functional urban regions in central cities, 1950–1970			Rate of metropolitan decentralization (percentage of base year)	
	1950 or 1951	1960 or 1961	1970 or 1971	Ratio of 1960–1961 to 1970–1971	Ratio of 1950–1951 to 1970–1971
Japan	55.0	58.5	54.8	93.7	99.6
Denmark	NA*a*	NA	44.0	NA	NA
Austria	NA	NA	39.8	NA	NA
Great Britain—SMLA	66.6	64.2	59.8	93.1	89.8
Great Britain—MELA	55.4	53.7	49.5	92.2	89.4
Federal Republic of Germany	NA	34.6	32.9	95.1	NA
United States—SMSA	55.3	51.4	45.8	89.1	82.8

a NA = Not available.

TABLE 2.26

Percentage of Change in Population in Core and Hinterland Subregions for Japan, Federal Republic of Germany, and United Kingdom, 1960–1970

	Core	Hinterland
Japan	15.0	33.8
Federal Republic of Germany[a]	3.2	11.3
United Kingdom[b]	−2.8	17.2
United States[c]	10.0	23.5

[a] 1961 to 1970.
[b] 1961 to 1971.
[c] For SMSAs.

although the overall growth rates are much higher in most instances: The highest growth rate category is for these cities between 700,000 and 800,000 persons. The U.S. case is different from others in that it is the smallest regions that are growing the fastest.

6 Conclusions

This chapter has traced the development of the Japanese urban system from 1950 to 1970. This period was one of high economic growth, and the transformation of the Japanese economy that occurred in those years was accompanied by great changes in the spatial structure of society. These alterations in living patterns—as shown by rapid urbanization (which were continuations of prewar trends)—have been charted in the first four sections of this chapter. After discussing the usefulness of functional urban regions as units of urban analysis, we introduced the REC, a functional urban region definition for Japan. Then, in Sections 3 and 4, we analyzed population and employment data for the RECs.

Several conclusions emerge from this analysis. First, the Japanese population is highly concentrated in a relatively small land area and number of city-regions. Two-thirds of the 1970 population lived in the 80 RECs and a full one-half in eight SCAs. Second, the system of cities appeared to centralize between 1950 and 1970 as there was relatively faster growth in a few large population centers, especially those near Tokyo and Osaka. Third, not only were the "big getting bigger," but many of the important growth centers were manufacturing-based. Fourth, there was centralization in the 1950s within metropolitan areas followed by some decentralization—that is, the suburbs grew more quickly than the central cities—in the 1960s. Finally, employment by place of work was more heavily centralized within metropolitan areas than employment by place of residence.

These results show that Japanese urban development followed a some-what different pattern than that of other industrialized countries. I have

TABLE 2.27

Population Growth by Region Size for Japan, Federal Republic of Germany, India, and United States, 1960–1970

Population size (in thousands)	Japan	Federal Republic of Germany	India[a]	United States[b]
100–200	1.8	6.1	32.8	22.6
200–300	9.1	6.0	40.8	-3.0
300–400	6.6	8.6	44.6	
400–500	11.5	8.0	48.3	
500–600	12.8	10.5	34.9	
600–700	8.0	14.1	33.3	
700–800	17.6	—	54.2	16.7
800–900	30.1	4.1	24.1	
900–1,000	18.6	8.6	34.8	
1,000+	33.8	8.5	39.8	7.3
Average growth in these size classes	24.0	8.5	39.5	10.7
Standard Deviation	10.3	2.8	8.7	NA[c]
Ratio of growth rate of smallest city size class to all city growth rate	.075	.718	.830	2.112
Ratio of growth rate of largest city size class to all city growth rate	1.408	1.000	1.008	.682

[a] 1961–1971.

[b] Categories are 100,000–250,000, 250,000–500,000, 500,000–1,000,000 and 1,000,000+.

[c] NA = Not available.

indicated briefly some comparative statistics in Section 5. First, Japanese urban development was much more rapid than that of other industrialized countries. Second, the large cities of Japan relative to other cities in city system was not as great as some other large countries. However, the dominance of Tokyo was increasing over time; New York's and London's importance, on the other hand, were decreasing. Third, Japan's regions were more spatially centralized than those of other countries and that metropolitan decentralization was less than in the United States and Great Britain, especially in the 1950s.

The major phenomenon of the 1950s and 1960s—that of large Japanese regions growing at the expense of smaller ones—came in the face of central government policy aimed at dispersing population in an effort to relieve negative externalities in the core. These policies are the topic of Chapter 6, where it is shown that they were relatively ineffective. Such programs as those instituting New Industrial Cities in backward regions to provide growth poles seemed not to be very effective.

However, we shall see (in Chapter 3) that population dispersal increased in the 1970s. Then, although the "big getting bigger" phenomenon continued, it was on a much less significant scale and was principally due to higher urban natural growth rates; net out-migration from the large centers was also apparent, especially beginning in the late 1960s. The 1970s pattern, I argue in Chapters 3 and 6, occurred independent of public policy and more closely resembled situations in the United States and Western Europe than the phenomenon reviewed in this chapter. I argue here that Japan went through a stage of urban development in the 1950s and 1960s that other developed nations passed through earlier in this century. Japan had rapid urbanization, growth of large cities, and little metropolitan decentralization in these decades in the same way that the United States passed through such a stage during the first half of the twentieth century.

Appendix 1 Components of Japanese Regional Economic Clusters

Listed below are the cities, towns and villages which constitute the eighty Regional Economic Clusters. The RECs are given according to prefecture (<u>ken</u>) and attached prefectural code (Hokkaido = 01, Iwate = 03,..., Kagoshima = 46). Central cities are recorded in capital letters followed by the component cities, towns, and villages. Each municipality has a city code (from the <u>1970 Population Census</u>). For instance, Sapporo-<u>shi</u> is 01201 (city 201 in the 01st prefecture). Cities which are in prefectures other than their REC's central city have a parenthesis after their city code, representing the prefecture in which that city is located.

01 - HOKKAIDO

    201 - SAPPORO-SHI

        203 Otaru-shi
        217 Ebetsu-shi
        307 Eniwa-cho

    202 - HAKODATE-SHI

        335 Kamiiso-cho
        337 Nanae-cho
        338 Kameda -cho

    205 - MURORAN-SHI

        230 Noboribetsu-shi
        576 Date-cho

    206 - KUSHIRO-SHI

        668 Shiranuka-cho

03 - IWATE-KEN

    201 - MORIOKA-SHI

        323 Tonan-mura

04 - MIYAGI-KEN

    201 - SENDAI-SHI

        203 Shiogama-shi
        206 Shiraishi-shi
        207 Natori-shi
        208 Kakuda-shi
        321 Ogawara-machi
        322 Murata-machi
        323 Shibata-machi
        361 Watari-cho
        362 Yamamoto-cho
        381 Iwanuma-machi
        382 Akiu-machi
        401 Matsushima-cho
        402 Tagajo-machi
        403 Izumi-machi

```
201 - SENDAI-SHI (continued)       202 - AIZUWAKAMATSU-SHI          10 - GUMMA-KEN               13 - TOKYO-TO
      405 Miyagi-machi                   424 Kawahigashi-mura
      406 Rifu-cho                       442 Hongo-machi             201 - MAEBASHI-SHI          100 - TOKYO KU
      503 Kogota-cho                                                      208 Shibukawa-shi
                                   203 - KORIYAMA-SHI                    301 Kitatachibana-mura        201 Hachioji-shi
202 - ISHINOMAKI                         207 Sukagawa-shi                304 Ogo-machi                 202 Tachikawa-shi
      562 Yamoto-cho                     323 Motomiya-machi             345 Yoshioka-mura             203 Musashino-shi
      581 Onagawa-cho                    521 Miharu-machi                                              204 Mitaku-shi
                                                                    202 - TAKASAKI-SHI                206 Fuchu-shi
05 - AKITA-KEN                     08 - IBARAGI-KEN                      209 Fujioka-shi               207 Akishima-shi
                                                                        211 Annaka-shi                208 Choiu-shi
201 - AKITA-SHI                    201 - MITO-SHI                        321 Haruna-machi              209 Machida-shi
      205 Honjo-shi                      209 Nakaminato-shi              323 Misato-machi              210 Koganei-shi
      206 Oga-shi                        213 Katsuta-shi                 324 Gumma-machi               211 Kodaira-shi
      361 Gojome-machi                   216 Kasama-shi                  361 Shin-machi                212 Hino-shi
      362 Showa-machi                    305 Uchihara-machi             363 Yoshii-machi               213 Higashimurayama-shi
      363 Hachirogata-machi              309 Oorai-machi                 401 Matsuida-machi            214 Kokubunji-shi
      364 Iitagawa-machi                 321 Tomobe-machi                464 Tamamura-machi            215 Kunitachi-shi
      365 Tenno-machi                    342 Naka-machi                                                216 Tanashi-shi
      366 Ikawa-mura                     344 Omiya-machi             203 - KIRYU-SHI                   217 Hoya-shi
      405 Iwaki-machi                                                    484 Kasakake-mura             218 Fussa-shi
                                   202 - HITACHI-SHI                     501 Omama-machi               219 Komae-shi
06 - YAMAGATA-SHI                        212 Hitachiota-shi                                            220 Higashiyamato-shi
                                         214 Takahagi-shi           11 - SAITAMA-KEN                  221 Kiyose-shi
201 - YAMAGATA-SHI                       215 Kitaibaraki-shi                                           222 Higashikurume-shi
      206 Sagae-shi                      341 Tokai-mura             202 - KUMAGAYA-SHI                302 Hamura-machi
      207 Kaminoyama-shi                 381 Juo-machi                   218 Fukaya-shi                304 Akita-machi
      210 Tendo-shi                                                     346 Kawajima-mura             321 Tama-machi
      211 Higashine-shi             09 - TOCHIGI-KEN                     347 Yoshimi-mura              322 Inagi-machi
      301 Yamanobe-machi                                                401 Osato-mura                342 Murayama-machi
      302 Nakoyama-machi            201 - UTSUNOMIYA-SHI                 402 Konan-mura                203 (08) Tsuchiura-shi
                                         205 Kanuma-shi                  403 Menuma-machi              204 (08) Koga-shi
07 - FUKUSHIMA-KEN                       207 Imaichi-shi                 406 Kawamoto-mura             208 (08) Ryugasaki-shi
                                         211 Yaita-shi                   407 Hanazono-mura             217 (08) Toride-shi
201 - FUKUSHIMA-SHI                      304 Kawachi-machi                                             444 (08) Ushiku-machi
      210 Nihonmatsu-shi                 361 Mibu-machi              12 - CHIBA-KEN                    563 (08) Fujishiro-machi
      301 Kori-machi                     362 Ishibashi-machi                                           364 (09) Nogi-machi
      302 Date-machi                     385 Ujiie-machi             201 - CHIBA-SHI                   366 (09) Fujioka-machi
      303 Kunimi-machi                   386 Takanezawa-machi             210 Mobara-shi               201 (11) Kawagoe-shi
      305 Hobara-machi                   401 Minaminasu-mura             213 Togane-shi                203 (11) Kawaguchi-shi
      309 Iino-machi                     402 Karasuyama-machi            219 Ichihara-shi              204 (11) Urawa-shi
                                                                        321 Yotsukaido-machi          205 (11) Omiya-shi
                                                                        402 Omaishirasato-machi       208 (11) Tokorozawa-shi
                                                                        403 Kujukuri-machi            209 (11) Hanno-shi
                                                                        425 Honno-machi               210 (11) Kasu-shi
                                                                        444 Ohara-machi               212 (11) Higashimatsu-
                                                                                                               yama-shi
                                                                                                      213 (11) Iwatsuki-shi
                                                                                                      214 (11) Kasukabe-shi
                                                                                                      215 (11) Sayama-shi
                                                                                                      216 (11) Hanyu-shi
                                                                                                      217 (11) Konosu-shi
                                                                                                      218 (11) Ageo-shi
```

TOYOTA-SHI (continued)
541 Asuke-cho

24 MIE-KEN
201 TSU-SHI
204 Matsusaka-shi
213 Hisai-shi
402 Karasu-cho
403 Ichishi-cho
404 Hakusan-cho
405 Ureshino-cho
497 Mikumo-mura

202 YOKKAICHI-SHI
207 Suzuka-shi
210 Kameyama-shi
323 Daian-cho
341 Komono-cho
342 Kusu-cho
344 Kawagoe-cho
381 Kawage-cho

203 ISE-SHI
211 Toba-shi
461 Tamaki-cho
462 Futami-cho
463 Obata-cho

468 Misono-mura
470 Watarai-cho

25 SHIGA-KEN
201 OTSU-SHI
204 Omihachiman-shi
206 Kusatsu-shi
207 Moriyama-shi
301 Shiga-cho
343 Yasu-cho
321 Ritto-cho
342 Chuzu-cho

26 KYOTO-FU
100 KYOTO
204 Uji-shi
206 Kameoka-shi
301 Muko-machi
302 Nagaoka-cho
303 Oyamazaki-cho
321 Joyo-cho
322 Kumiyama-cho
341 Yawata-cho
342 Tanabe-cho

343 Ide-cho

366 Seika-cho
401 Sonobe-cho
402 Yagi-cho
404 Hiyoshi-cho

27 OSAKA-FU
100 OSAKA-SHI
201 Sakai-shi
202 Kishiwada-shi
203 Toyonaka-shi
204 Ikeda-shi
205 Suita-shi

206 Izumiotsu-shi
207 Takatsuki-shi
208 Kaizuka-shi
209 Moriguchi-shi
210 Hirakata-shi
211 Ibaraki-shi
212 Yao-shi
213 Izumisano-shi
214 Tondabayashi-shi
215 Neyagawa-shi
216 Kawachinagano-shi
217 Matsubara-shi
218 Daito-shi
219 Izumi-shi
220 Mino-shi
221 Kashiwara-shi
223 Kadoma-shi
224 Settsu-shi
225 Takaishi-shi
226 Fujiidera-shi
227 Higashiosaka-shi
228 Sennan-shi
229 Shijonawate-shi
301 Shimamoto-cho
341 Tadaoka-cho
361 Kumatori-cho
364 Nankai-cho
365 Higashitottori-cho
366 Misaki-cho
381 Taishi-cho

100 - OSAKA-SHI (continued)
382 Kanan-cho
384 Sayama-cho
385 Mihara-cho
401 Katano-cho
202 (28) Amagasaki-shi
204 (28) Nishinomiya-shi
206 (28) Ashiya-shi
207 (28) Itami-shi
214 (28) Takarazuka-shi
217 (28) Kawanishi-shi
202 (29) Yamatotakada-shi
203 (29) Yamatokoriyamā-shi
205 (29) Kashiwara-shi
206 (29) Sakurai-shi
208 (29) Gose-shi
341 (29) Ikoma-shi
342 (29) Heguri-mura
343 (29) Sango-cho
344 (29) Ikagura-cho
363 (29) Tawaramoto-cho
383 (29) Haibara-cho
401 (29) Takatori-cho
421 (29) Shinjo-cho
422 (29) Taima-cho
423 (29) Kashiba-cho
425 (29) Oji-cho
426 (29) Koryo-cho
427 (29) Kawai-mura
442 (29) Oyodo-cho
203 (30) Hashimoto-shi
222 (30) Habikino-shi
362 (30) Tajiri-cho

28 - HYOGO-KEN

100 - KOBE-SHI
203 Akashi-shi
210 Kakogawa-shi
215 Miki-shi
219 Sanda-shi
381 Inami-cho
382 Harima-cho
682 Awaji-cho

201 - HIMEJI-SHI
208 Aioi-shi
211 Tatsuno-shi
212 Ako-shi

216 Takasago-shi
441 Yumesaki-cho
442 Ichikawa-cho
443 Fukusaki-cho
444 Kodera-cho
445 Okochi-cho
461 Shingu-cho
462 Ibogawa-cho
463 Mitsu-cho
464 Taishi-cho
481 Kamigori-cho
521 Yamasaki-cho
523 Ichinomiya-cho

29 - NARA-KEN

201 - NARA-SHI
204 Tenri-shi
362 (26) Kizu-cho
363 (26) Kamo-cho
424 (26) Kanmaki-mura

30 - WAKAYAMA-KEN

201 - WAKAYAMA-SHI
202 Kainan-shi
204 Arida-shi
301 Shimotsu-chi
321 Uchita-cho
322 Kokawa-cho
323 Naga-cho
325 Kishigawa-cho
326 Iwade-cho
341 Katsuragi-cho

31 - TOTTORI-KEN

201 - TOTTORI-SHI
301 Kokufu-cho
302 Iwami-cho
303 Fukube-son
321 Koge-cho
322 Funaoka-cho
323 Kawahara-cho
324 Hatto-cho
326 Mochigase-cho

201 - TOTTORI-SHI (continued)
341 Ketaka-cho
343 Aoya-cho

202 - YONAGO-SHI
204 Sakaiminato-shi
381 Saihaku-cho
382 Aimi-cho
383 Kishimoto-cho
384 Hiezu-son
385 Yodoe-cho
386 Daisen-cho
387 Nawa-cho

32 - SHIMANE-KEN

201 - MATSUE-SHI
208 Hirata-shi
301 Kashima-cho
304 Higashiizumo-cho
305 Yakumo-muro
306 Tamayu-cho
307 Shinji-machi
361 Daito-cho
401 Hikawa-cho

33 - OKAYAMA-KEN

201 - OKAYAMA-SHI
208 Soja-shi
301 Mitsu-cho
302 Ichinomiya-cho
303 Takebe-cho
304 Tsudaka-cho
321 Seto-cho
322 Sanyo-cho
323 Akasaka-cho
324 Kumayama-cho
341 Bizen-cho
346 Wake-cho
361 Ushimado-cho
362 Oku-cho
363 Osafune-cho
381 Joto-cho
401 Nadasaki-cho
402 Kojo-son
421 Kibi-cho

423 Hayashima-cho
424 Senoo-cho
425 Sho-mura
426 Fukuda-mura
501 Takamatsu-cho
502 Ashimori-cho

202 - KURASHIKI-SHI
427 Yamate-son
428 Kiyone-son
441 Funao-cho
442 Konko-cho
443 Kamagata-cho
444 Yorishima-cho
461 Yakage-cho
503 Mabi-cho

34 - HIROSHIMA-KEN

201 - HIROSHIMA-SHI
301 Aki-cho
302 Fuchu-cho
303 Funakoshi-chi
304 Kaita-cho
305 Senogawa-cho
306 Kumanoata-mura
307 Kumaano-cho
308 Yano-cho
309 Saka-cho
310 Etajima-cho
311 Ondo-cho
312 Kurahashi-cho
313 Shimokamagari-cho
321 Itsukaichi-cho
322 Hatsukaichi-cho
323 Ono-cho
328 Nomi-cho
329 Okimi-cho
330 Ogaki-cho
341 Gion-cho
342 Yasufuruichi-cho
343 Sato-cho
344 Numata-cho
345 Asa-cho
346 Kabe-cho
347 Koyo-cho
386 Mukaihara-cho
387 Shiraki-chi
401 Saijo-cho

201.- HIROSHIMA-SHI (continued)
402 Kurose-cho
403 Hachihonmatsu-cho
409 Takayalcho

207 - FUKUYAMA-SHI
205 Onomichi-shi
482 Numakuma-cho
501 Kannabe-cho
502 Kamo-cho
523 Ekiya-cho
524 Shinichi-cho
205 (33) Kasaoka-shi
207 (33) Ibara-shi

35 - YAMAGUCHI-KEN
201 - SHIMONOSEKI-SHI
422 Sanyo-cho
441 Kikugawa-cho
443 Toyoura-cho
444 Hohoku-cho

202 - UBE-SHI
209 Onoda-shi
403 Ajisu-cho
421 Kusunoki-cho

203 - YAMAGUCHI-SHI
402 Ogori-cho

208 - IWAKUNI-SHI
322 Yuu-cho
323 Kuga-cho
325 Shuto-cho
211 (34) Otake-shi

36 - TOKUSHIMA-KEN
201 - TOKUSHIMA-SHI
202 Naruto-shi
203 Komatsushima-shi

341 Ishii-cho
401 Matsushigo-cho
402 Kitajima-cho
403 Aizumi-cho
404 Itano-cho
405 Kamiita-cho
441 Kamojima-cho
442 Kawashima-cho
443 Yamakawa-cho

37 - KAGAWA-Ken
201 - TAKAMATSU-SHI
202 Marugame-shi
203 Sakaide-shi
303 Ouchi-cho
304 Tsuda-cho
306 Shido-cho
307 Sangawa-cho
308 Nagao-cho
341 Miki-cho
342 Mure-cho
343 Aji-cho
362 Kagawa-cho
381 Ayakami-cho
382 Ryonan-cho
383 Kokubunji-cho
384 Ayauta-cho
385 Hanzan-cho
386 Utazu-cho
404 Tadotsu-cho

38 - EHIME-KEN
201 - MATSUYAMA-SHI
210 Iyo-shi
211 Hojo-shi
361 Shigenobu-sho
401 Masaki-cho
402 Tobe-cho

202 - IMABARI-SHI
322 Nyugawa-cho
324 Miyoshi-cho
343 Namikata-cho
344 Onishi-cho
345 Kikuma-cho

205 - NIHAMA-SHI
206 Saijo-shi
302 Doi-cho

39 - KOCHI-KEN
201 - KOCHI-SHI
204 Nankoku-shi
323 Tosayamada-cho
324 Noichi-cho
342 Otsu-mura
343 Kera-mura
381 Ino-cho
402 Sakawa-cho
410 Hidaka-mura

40 - FUKUOKA-KEN
100 - KITAKYUSHU-SHI
204 Nagata-shi
206 Tagawa-shi
213 Yukuhashi-shi
214 Buzen-shi
215 Nakama-shi
361 Munakata-machi
381 Ashiya-machi
382 Mizunaki-machi
383 Okagaki-machi
384 Ouga-machi
402 Kurate-machi
601 Kawara-machi
605 Kawasaki-machi
621 Kanda-machi
622 Saigawa-machi
624 Toyotsu-machi
641 Shida-machi
643 Tsuiki-machi

201 - FUKUOKA-SHI
209 Amagi-shi
301 Chikushino-machi
302 Dazaifu-machi
304 Ono-machi
305 Nakagawa-machi
321 Sawara-machi
341 Umi-machi

342 Sasaguri-machi
343 Shime-machi
344 Sue-machi
345 Shingu-machi
346 Shika-machi
347 Koga-machi
348 Hisayama-machi
349 Kasuya-machi
362 Fukuma-machi
363 Tsuyazaki-machi
443 Miwa-machi
461 Maebaru-machi
462 Nijo-machi
502 Ogori-machi
203 (41) Tosu-shi
341 (41) Kiyama-cho

202 - OMUTA-SHI
581 Takata-machi
204 (43) Arao-shi
368 (43) Nagasu-machi

203 - KURUME-SHI
210 Yame-shi
211 Chikugo-shi
481 Yoshii-machi
482 Tanushimaru-machi
483 Ukiha-machi
501 Kitano-machi
521 Jojima-machi
522 Oki-machi
523 Mizuma-machi
544 Hirokawa-machi
561 Setaka-machi
343 (41) Kitashigeyasu-cho
433 (41) Mine-cho

41 - SAGA-KEN
201 - SAGA-SHI
204 Taku-shi
301 Morodomi-cho
304 Kubota-cho
305 Yamato-cho
321 Kanzaki-machi
322 Chiyoda-cho

201 - SAGA-SHI (continued)
   361 Ogi-machi
   362 Mikatsuki-cho

45 - MIYAZAKI-KEN
201 - MIYAZAKI-SHI
   303 Sadowara-cho

203 - NOBEOKA-SHI
   421 Kadogawa-cho

46 - KAGOSHIMA-KEN
201 - KAGOSHIMA-SHI
   363 Ijuin-cho
   441 Kajiki-cho

42 - NAGASAKI-KEN
201 - NAGASAKI-SHI
   204 Isahaya-shi
   301 Koyagi-cho
   304 Nomozaki-cho
   305 Sanwa-cho
   306 Tarami-cho
   307 Nagayo-cho
   308 Togitsu-cho

202 - SASEBO-SHI
   322 Kawatana-cho
   391 Saza-cho

43 - KUMAMOTO-KEN
201 - KUMAMOTO-SHI
   211 Uto-shi
   303 Akita-mura
   342 Tomiai-mura
   343 Matsubase-machi
   407 Nishigoshi-machi

202 - YATSUSHIRO-SHI
   461 Sakamoto-mura
   462 Sencho-mura
   463 Kagami-machi

44 - OITA-KEN
201 - OITA-SHI
   202 Beppu-shi
   206 Usuki-shi
   381 Saganoseki-machi

Appendix 2 Variables in the Regional Data Bank

Variables Available for 1970

Variable Number	Variable Name
1	Population, all ages[1]
2	Population, Percent by age 0∿14 years old
3	Population, Percent by age 15∿64 years old
4	Number of Quasi-household members
5	Percent of persons who have completed Junior college or University
6	Total labor force[2]
7	Total employment[2]
8	Percent distribution by industry, Primary industries, Total[2]
9	Percent distribution by industry, Primary industries, Agriculture[2]
10	Percent distribution by industry, Secondary industries, Total[2]
11	Percent distribution by industry, Secondary industries, Manufacturing[2]
12	Population 15 years old and over by level of education, Total
13	Percent distribution by industry, Wholesale and Retail Trade[2]
14	Percent distribution by industry, Services[2]
15	Percent distribution by industry, Government[2]
16	Employed persons 15 years and over by occupation, percent by occupation, Professional and Technical Workers and Managers and Officials and Clerical and related workers[2]
17	Percent by tenure of house, Owned house
18	Number of Quasi-households
19	Rooms per household (ordinary household)
20	Tatami per household (ordinary household)
21	Percent by economic type of ordinary households, Agricultural workers' households

22	Percent by economic type of ordinary house-holds, Agricultural and non-agricultural workers, mixed households
23	Non-agricultural workers' households, Total
24	Employed persons 15 years old and over by employment status, %, Family workers Population by time of last move, locality of previous residence
25	Lived in same residence since birth
26	Lived in same residence from 1959 or before
27	Lived in same residence from 1960 to 1964
28	Lived in same residence from January,1965 ∿September, 1969, Total
29	Lived in same residence from January,1965 ∿September, 1969, Same shi, ku, machi and mura
30	Lived in same residence from January,1965 ∿September, 1969, Different ku of the same shi
31	Lived in same residence from January,1965 ∿September, 1969, Other prefecture
32	Deaths, Total
33	Deaths, Male
34	Ischemic heart disease, Total
35	Ischemic heart disease, Male
36	Wholesale Industry, number of stores,
37	Wholesale Industry, number of employees
38	Wholesale Industry, total annual sales
39	Retail trade, number of stores
40	Retail trade, number of employees
41	Retail trade, Total annual sales
42	Number of manufacturing employees (by place of work)
43	Number of Wholesale and Retail trade employ-ees (by place of work)
44	Number of Service employees (by place of work)

Variables Available for 1960

Variable numbers	Variable Names
1	Population by sex, Males per 100 females
2	Ordinary households, Total
3	Ordinary households, Persons per household
4	Industry of employed persons 15 years old and over, Agriculture
5	Industry of employed persons 15 years old and over, Manufacturing
6	Industry of employed persons 15 years old and over, Wholesale and Retail trade
7	Industry of employed persons 15 years old and over, Services
8	Industry of employed persons 15 years old and over, Government
9	Population, All ages
10	Population, Percent by age, $0 \sim 14$ years old
11	Population, Percent by age, $15 \sim 64$ years old
12	Labor force, Total
13	Number of Unemployed
14	Percent by industry, Primary industry
15	Percent by industry, Secondary industry
16	Employed persons 15 years old and over by occupation, Professional and Technical workers and Managers and Officials and Clerical and related workers
17	Industry by employed persons 15 years old and over, by place of work, Total
18	Industry by employed persons 15 years old and over, by place of work, Living in other shi, machi, mura

Variables Available for 1971

Variable Number	Variable Name
1	Area of roads
2	Number of libraries (Shi-cho-son libraries)
3	Number of libraries (non Shi-cho-son libraries
4	Area of cultivated field
5	Number of sea ports (exceptionally important)
6	Number of sea ports (important)
7	Number of sea ports (local)
8	Percent of paved roads
9	Area of parks (within city planning areas)
10	Area of parks (within local government boundary)
11	Number of public apartments for 100 households
12	Diffusion rate of water supply facilities
13	Diffusion rate of drainage facilities
14	Excrements collection ratio
15	Garbage collection ratio
16	Local government expenditures (LGE) on LG assembly
17	Local government expenditures on general affairs
18	Local government expenditures on general welfare
19	Local government expenditures on welfare for the aged
20	Local government expenditures on welfare for children
21	Local government expenditures on sanitation
22	Local government expenditures on cleaning and sweeping
23	Local government expenditures on labor
24	Local government expenditures on the activities relating to agriculture, forestry and fishing industries
25	Local government expenditures on the activities relating to commerce and industry
26	Local government expenditures on civil engineering works (general)
27	Local government expenditures on the construction of roads and bridge

28	Local government expenditures on city planning activities
29	Local government expenditures on housing
30	Local government expenditures on fire service
31	Local government expenditures on education
32	Local government expenditures local bonds
33	Total local government expenditures
34	Area of forest and woods
35	Number of books stocked in shi-cho-son libraries[3]
36	Number of books stocked in non shi-cho-son libraries[3]
37	Registered population
38	Population in city planning areas
39	Annual collection of excrements
40	Annual collection of garbage

Footnotes to Appendix 2

The data are available for the date noted in the text of Appendix 2 and for the following additional years.

1. 1950, 1955 1965, 1975

2. 1960, 1965

3. 1972 not 1971

Appendix 3 Population and Employment Distribution for Individual RECs, 1960–1970

	1960	1970	% CHANGE 1960-1970
SAPPORO	----	----	---------
POPULATION (1000'S)	876.177	1106.388	26.215
TOTAL EMPLOYMENT (1000'S)	370.424	608.418	64.249
% PRIMARY EMPLOYMENT	9.069	3.626	-60.013
% SECONDARY EMPLOYMENT	26.097	26.905	3.016
% WHOLESALE & RETAIL EMPLOYMENT	24.889	28.616	14.978
% SERVICES EMPLOYMENT	17.355	20.237	16.619
% OTHER TERTIARY EMPLOYMENT	13.606	14.308	3.623
% GOVERNMENT EMPLOYMENT	8.785	6.328	-27.962
HAKODATE			
POPULATION (1000'S)	312.494	334.076	6.906
TOTAL EMPLOYMENT (1000'S)	121.837	151.864	24.662
% PRIMARY EMPLOYMENT	15.613	8.520	-45.431
% SECONDARY EMPLOYMENT	28.151	26.455	-6.025
% WHOLESALE & RETAIL EMPLOYMENT	21.579	25.153	16.565
% SERVICES EMPLOYMENT	15.449	19.631	27.064
% OTHER TERTIARY EMPLOYMENT	14.912	15.220	2.068
% GOVERNMENT EMPLOYMENT	4.296	5.021	16.879
MURORAN			
POPULATION (1000'S)	201.221	238.137	18.346
TOTAL EMPLOYMENT (1000'S)	78.916	104.751	32.737
% PRIMARY EMPLOYMENT	8.771	4.869	-44.486
% SECONDARY EMPLOYMENT	39.655	35.510	-10.453
% WHOLESALE & RETAIL EMPLOYMENT	17.127	21.507	25.576
% SERVICES EMPLOYMENT	15.669	18.420	17.561
% OTHER TERTIARY EMPLOYMENT	15.330	16.268	6.117
% GOVERNMENT EMPLOYMENT	3.448	3.425	-0.670
KUSHIRO			
POPULATION (1000'S)	171.394	207.430	21.025
TOTAL EMPLOYMENT (1000'S)	66.514	92.859	39.608
% PRIMARY EMPLOYMENT	9.108	6.191	-32.021
% SECONDARY EMPLOYMENT	36.726	30.308	-17.481
% WHOLESALE & RETAIL EMPLOYMENT	21.389	25.540	19.403
% SERVICES EMPLOYMENT	13.283	17.821	34.164
% OTHER TERTIARY EMPLOYMENT	15.422	16.026	3.915
% GOVERNMENT EMPLOYMENT	4.076	4.115	1.104
MORIOKA			
POPULATION (1000'S)	171.838	212.690	23.774
TOTAL EMPLOYMENT (1000'S)	73.999	102.684	38.764
% PRIMARY EMPLOYMENT	22.150	11.890	-46.322
% SECONDARY EMPLOYMENT	17.294	18.746	8.396
% WHOLESALE & RETAIL EMPLOYMENT	22.210	26.382	18.786
% SERVICES EMPLOYMENT	19.192	23.419	22.022
% OTHER TERTIARY EMPLOYMENT	13.443	13.873	3.195
% GOVERNMENT EMPLOYMENT	5.711	5.691	-0.348
SENDAI			
POPULATION (1000'S)	794.739	956.876	20.401
TOTAL EMPLOYMENT (1000'S)	337.504	457.663	35.602
% PRIMARY EMPLOYMENT	27.905	15.367	-44.930
% SECONDARY EMPLOYMENT	20.131	24.608	22.243
% WHOLESALE & RETAIL EMPLOYMENT	19.777	24.553	24.148
% SERVICES EMPLOYMENT	14.776	17.809	20.527
% OTHER TERTIARY EMPLOYMENT	10.771	12.171	12.998
% GOVERNMENT EMPLOYMENT	6.641	5.492	-17.300

Population and Employment Distribution for Individual RECs, 1960–1970

ISHIMAKI	1960	1970	% CHANGE 1960-1970
POPULATION (1000'S)	132.616	144.803	9.190
TOTAL EMPLOYMENT (1000'S)	56.829	68.224	20.051
% PRIMARY EMPLOYMENT	34.144	26.168	-23.362
% SECONDARY EMPLOYMENT	25.088	27.798	10.803
% WHOLESALE & RETAIL EMPLOYMENT	18.784	19.816	5.492
% SERVICES EMPLOYMENT	10.878	12.891	18.503
% OTHER TERTIARY EMPLOYMENT	6.563	8.835	34.612
% GOVERNMENT EMPLOYMENT	4.542	4.492	-1.092

AKITA	1960	1970	% CHANGE
POPULATION (1000'S)	361.143	383.175	6.101
TOTAL EMPLOYMENT (1000'S)	154.556	185.488	20.013
% PRIMARY EMPLOYMENT	37.617	22.882	-39.171
% SECONDARY EMPLOYMENT	19.347	22.450	16.041
% WHOLESALE & RETAIL EMPLOYMENT	15.220	20.810	36.730
% SERVICES EMPLOYMENT	12.672	16.950	33.751
% OTHER TERTIARY EMPLOYMENT	10.067	12.000	19.210
% GOVERNMENT EMPLOYMENT	5.078	4.908	-3.339

YAMAGATA	1960	1970	% CHANGE
POPULATION (1000'S)	383.092	391.335	2.152
TOTAL EMPLOYMENT (1000'S)	185.754	208.756	12.383
% PRIMARY EMPLOYMENT	44.435	27.937	-37.129
% SECONDARY EMPLOYMENT	16.743	26.510	41.440
% WHOLESALE & RETAIL EMPLOYMENT	14.532	18.352	26.289
% SERVICES EMPLOYMENT	11.473	14.866	29.569
% OTHER TERTIARY EMPLOYMENT	5.860	7.582	29.388
% GOVERNMENT EMPLOYMENT	4.958	4.754	-4.112

FUKUSHIMA	1960	1970	% CHANGE
POPULATION (1000'S)	306.985	327.032	6.530
TOTAL EMPLOYMENT (1000'S)	143.103	169.456	18.415
% PRIMARY EMPLOYMENT	40.577	25.332	-37.571
% SECONDARY EMPLOYMENT	20.467	27.653	35.111
% WHOLESALE & RETAIL EMPLOYMENT	14.642	17.712	20.970
% SERVICES EMPLOYMENT	12.763	16.022	25.537
% OTHER TERTIARY EMPLOYMENT	7.175	8.450	17.772
% GOVERNMENT EMPLOYMENT	4.377	4.831	10.374

AIZUWAKAMATSU	1960	1970	% CHANGE
POPULATION (1000'S)	119.252	120.641	1.165
TOTAL EMPLOYMENT (1000'S)	52.199	61.491	17.801
% PRIMARY EMPLOYMENT	29.759	18.618	-37.437
% SECONDARY EMPLOYMENT	24.358	30.515	25.277
% WHOLESALE & RETAIL EMPLOYMENT	20.234	21.796	7.718
% SERVICES EMPLOYMENT	14.926	17.140	14.834
% OTHER TERTIARY EMPLOYMENT	8.263	9.352	13.178
% GOVERNMENT EMPLOYMENT	2.460	2.579	4.845

KORIYAMA	1960	1970	% CHANGE
POPULATION (1000'S)	309.223	332.688	7.588
TOTAL EMPLOYMENT (1000'S)	140.304	167.850	19.633
% PRIMARY EMPLOYMENT	45.012	29.229	-35.064
% SECONDARY EMPLOYMENT	19.465	27.021	38.813
% WHOLESALE & RETAIL EMPLOYMENT	14.446	18.359	27.088
% SERVICES EMPLOYMENT	10.905	13.894	27.415
% OTHER TERTIARY EMPLOYMENT	7.191	8.599	19.572
% GOVERNMENT EMPLOYMENT	2.980	2.898	-2.755

APPENDIX 3—(Continued)

Population and Employment Distribution for Individual RECs, 1960–1970

	1960	1970	% CHANGE 1960-1970
MITO			
POPULATION (1000'S)	358.708	413.508	15.277
TOTAL EMPLOYMENT (1000'S)	168.505	205.161	21.754
% PRIMARY EMPLOYMENT	41.329	23.766	-42.496
% SECONDARY EMPLOYMENT	19.584	27.836	42.134
% WHOLESALE & RETAIL EMPLOYMENT	15.494	19.225	24.078
% SERVICES EMPLOYMENT	11.845	15.738	32.861
% OTHER TERTIARY EMPLOYMENT	6.887	9.051	31.425
% GOVERNMENT EMPLOYMENT	4.860	4.384	-9.791
HITACHI			
POPULATION (1000'S)	318.134	335.157	5.351
TOTAL EMPLOYMENT (1000'S)	146.354	164.662	12.509
% PRIMARY EMPLOYMENT	24.202	14.420	-40.416
% SECONDARY EMPLOYMENT	47.934	49.680	.3.642
% WHOLESALE & RETAIL EMPLOYMENT	11.144	14.082	26.358
% SERVICES EMPLOYMENT	10.281	12.904	25.522
% OTHER TERTIARY EMPLOYMENT	4.745	6.795	43.215
% GOVERNMENT EMPLOYMENT	1.695	2.119	25.035
UTSUNOMIYA			
POPULATION (1000'S)	518.732	583.470	12.480
TOTAL EMPLOYMENT (1000'S)	237.866	300.227	26.216
% PRIMARY EMPLOYMENT	40.309	23.975	-40.523
% SECONDARY EMPLOYMENT	21.575	31.719	47.016
% WHOLESALE & RETAIL EMPLOYMENT	16.892	19.389	14.784
% SERVICES EMPLOYMENT	11.034	13.623	23.462
% OTHER TERTIARY EMPLOYMENT	6.021	7.328	21.709
% GOVERNMENT EMPLOYMENT	4.169	3.967	-4.849
MAEBASHI			
POPULATION (1000'S)	265.816	305.489	14.925
TOTAL EMPLOYMENT (1000'S)	122.638	157.499	28.426
% PRIMARY EMPLOYMENT	33.592	19.466	-42.053
% SECONDARY EMPLOYMENT	25.286	31.307	23.812
% WHOLESALE & RETAIL EMPLOYMENT	17.063	20.638	20.948
% SERVICES EMPLOYMENT	13.436	16.368	21.821
% OTHER TERTIARY EMPLOYMENT	6.644	8.368	25.963
% GOVERNMENT EMPLOYMENT	3.979	3.854	-3.158
TAKASAKI			
POPULATION (1000'S)	353.262	391.387	10.792
TOTAL EMPLOYMENT (1000'S)	165.718	204.868	23.624
% PRIMARY EMPLOYMENT	41.116	24.525	-40.353
% SECONDARY EMPLOYMENT	24.406	33.446	37.042
% WHOLESALE & RETAIL EMPLOYMENT	14.202	18.309	28.918
% SERVICES EMPLOYMENT	9.726	12.209	25.538
% OTHER TERTIARY EMPLOYMENT	7.991	8.941	11.888
% GOVERNMENT EMPLOYMENT	2.560	2.571	0.421
KIRYU			
POPULATION (1000'S)	149.404	162.296	8.629
TOTAL EMPLOYMENT (1000'S)	73.080	89.413	22.349
% PRIMARY EMPLOYMENT	13.300	6.992	-47.432
% SECONDARY EMPLOYMENT	53.081	56.104	5.696
% WHOLESALE & RETAIL EMPLOYMENT	16.961	18.085	6.626
% SERVICES EMPLOYMENT	10.739	11.824	10.107
% OTHER TERTIARY EMPLOYMENT	4.425	5.530	24.980
% GOVERNMENT EMPLOYMENT	1.494	1.465	-1.980

Population and Employment Distribution for Individual RECs, 1960–1970

	1960	1970	% CHANGE 1960-1970
KUMAGAYA			
POPULATION (1000'S)	259.595	289.544	11.537
TOTAL EMPLOYMENT (1000'S)	127.917	154.319	20.640
% PRIMARY EMPLOYMENT	48.682	29.494	-39.415
% SECONDARY EMPLOYMENT	21.178	31.863	50.451
% WHOLESALE & RETAIL EMPLOYMENT	12.625	16.153	27.943
% SERVICES EMPLOYMENT	8.834	10.899	23.380
% OTHER TERTIARY EMPLOYMENT	5.577	7.963	42.770
% GOVERNMENT EMPLOYMENT	3.104	3.628	16.898
CHIBA			
POPULATION (1000'S)	519.621	816.025	57.042
TOTAL EMPLOYMENT (1000'S)	247.660	393.921	59.057
% PRIMARY EMPLOYMENT	40.283	16.728	-58.474
% SECONDARY EMPLOYMENT	22.348	35.144	57.254
% WHOLESALE & RETAIL EMPLOYMENT	13.392	18.370	37.171
% SERVICES EMPLOYMENT	10.710	14.439	34.819
% OTHER TERTIARY EMPLOYMENT	9.263	10.875	17.393
% GOVERNMENT EMPLOYMENT	4.003	4.444	11.031
POPULATION (1000'S)	13099.351	17711.518	35.209
TOTAL EMPLOYMENT (1000'S)	6136.391	8726.403	42.207
% PRIMARY EMPLOYMENT	8.113	3.860	-52.415
% SECONDARY EMPLOYMENT	41.322	40.493	-2.007
% WHOLESALE & RETAIL EMPLOYMENT	21.915	24.056	9.770
% SERVICES EMPLOYMENT	15.600	16.808	7.747
% OTHER TERTIARY EMPLOYMENT	9.646	11.519	19.414
% GOVERNMENT EMPLOYMENT	3.404	3.263	-4.133
YOKOHAMA			
POPULATION (1000'S)	2076.841	3323.751	60.039
TOTAL EMPLOYMENT (1000'S)	899.511	1572.277	74.792
% PRIMARY EMPLOYMENT	6.608	2.391	-63.815
% SECONDARY EMPLOYMENT	40.442	43.556	7.702
% WHOLESALE & RETAIL EMPLOYMENT	19.440	20.192	3.866
% SERVICES EMPLOYMENT	16.371	16.143	-1.389
% OTHER TERTIARY EMPLOYMENT	12.395	13.798	11.317
% GOVERNMENT EMPLOYMENT	4.744	3.919	-17.384
HIRATSUKA			
POPULATION (1000'S)	155.728	234.421	50.532
TOTAL EMPLOYMENT (1000'S)	66.519	111.650	67.847
% PRIMARY EMPLOYMENT	17.775	8.181	-53.975
% SECONDARY EMPLOYMENT	38.517	45.698	18.643
% WHOLESALE & RETAIL EMPLOYMENT	17.412	18.370	5.503
% SERVICES EMPLOYMENT	13.930	14.828	6.448
% OTHER TERTIARY EMPLOYMENT	9.278	10.056	8.387
% GOVERNMENT EMPLOYMENT	3.088	2.867	-7.161
ODAWARA			
POPULATION (1000'S)	233.572	283.736	21.477
TOTAL EMPLOYMENT (1000'S)	106.721	144.337	35.247
% PRIMARY EMPLOYMENT	17.285	10.831	-37.339
% SECONDARY EMPLOYMENT	35.341	36.935	4.512
% WHOLESALE & RETAIL EMPLOYMENT	15.455	33.918	119.459
% SERVICES EMPLOYMENT	19.286	20.051	3.966
% OTHER TERTIARY EMPLOYMENT	10.270	4.206	
% GOVERNMENT EMPLOYMENT	2.363	2.471	4.580

Population and Employment Distribution for Individual RECs, 1960–1970

	1960	1970	% CHANGE 1960-1970
NIIGATA	----	----	---------
POPULATION (1000'S)	634.379	691.590	9.018
TOTAL EMPLOYMENT (1000'S)	293.395	356.329	21.449
% PRIMARY EMPLOYMENT	32.639	19.486	-40.299
% SECONDARY EMPLOYMENT	23.483	25.340	7.907
% WHOLESALE & RETAIL EMPLOYMENT	18.146	22.605	24.576
% SERVICES EMPLOYMENT	12.378	16.526	33.508
% OTHER TERTIARY EMPLOYMENT	9.645	11.903	23.404
% GOVERNMENT EMPLOYMENT	3.709	4.141	11.652
NAGAOKA			
POPULATION (1000'S)	212.790	224.121	5.325
TOTAL EMPLOYMENT (1000'S)	105.305	122.514	16.342
% PRIMARY EMPLOYMENT	36.487	22.310	-38.855
% SECONDARY EMPLOYMENT	27.079	32.791	21.091
% WHOLESALE & RETAIL EMPLOYMENT	16.946	20.902	23.344
% SERVICES EMPLOYMENT	10.748	13.859	28.946
% OTHER TERTIARY EMPLOYMENT	6.837	8.191	19.812
% GOVERNMENT EMPLOYMENT	1.903	• 1.947	2.331
TOYAMA			
POPULATION (1000'S)	477.794	493.522	3.292
TOTAL EMPLOYMENT (1000'S)	240.429	268.957	11.865
% PRIMARY EMPLOYMENT	33.237	21.825	-34.336
% SECONDARY EMPLOYMENT	30.453	33.079	8.621
% WHOLESALE & RETAIL EMPLOYMENT	16.207	19.384	19.601
% SERVICES EMPLOYMENT	10.417	14.025	34.632
% OTHER TERTIARY EMPLOYMENT	7.045	8.820	25.195
% GOVERNMENT EMPLOYMENT	2.641	2.868	8.612
TAKAOKA			
POPULATION (1000'S)	367.534	364.085	-0.938
TOTAL EMPLOYMENT (1000'S)	183.655	203.247	10.668
% PRIMARY EMPLOYMENT	39.355	23.871	-39.343
% SECONDARY EMPLOYMENT	27.869	36.598	31.322
% WHOLESALE & RETAIL EMPLOYMENT	14.571	16.865	15.741
% SERVICES EMPLOYMENT	10.019	12.612	25.878
% OTHER TERTIARY EMPLOYMENT	6.129	7.560	23.332
% GOVERNMENT EMPLOYMENT	2.056	2.494	21.289
KANAZAWA			
POPULATION (1000'S)	482.871	540.268	11.887
TOTAL EMPLOYMENT (1000'S)	235.953	284.572	20.605
% PRIMARY EMPLOYMENT	26.750	14.139	-47.144
% SECONDARY EMPLOYMENT	31.053	34.422	10.851
% WHOLESALE & RETAIL EMPLOYMENT	17.127	21.614	26.199
% SERVICES EMPLOYMENT	12.739	16.233	27.420
% OTHER TERTIARY EMPLOYMENT	9.055	10.265	13.360
% GOVERNMENT EMPLOYMENT	3.276	3.327	1.567
FUKUI			
POPULATION (1000'S)	485.114	499.568	2.980
TOTAL EMPLOYMENT (1000'S)	253.626	281.020	10.801
% PRIMARY EMPLOYMENT	35.162	21.101	-39.989
% SECONDARY EMPLOYMENT	31.408	37.481	19.337
% WHOLESALE & RETAIL EMPLOYMENT	14.430	17.431	20.804
% SERVICES EMPLOYMENT	10.066	13.558	34.768
% OTHER TERTIARY EMPLOYMENT	6.390	7.569	18.442
% GOVERNMENT EMPLOYMENT	2.549	2.859	12.147

Population and Employment Distribution for Individual RECs, 1960–1970

	1960	1970	% CHANGE 1960-1970
KOFU	----	----	---------
POPULATION (1000'S)	360.450	377.933	4.850
TOTAL EMPLOYMENT (1000'S)	169.309	195.194	15.289
% PRIMARY EMPLOYMENT	36.502	23.792	-34.820
% SECONDARY EMPLOYMENT	24.257	30.234	24.638
% WHOLESALE & RETAIL EMPLOYMENT	17.274	20.132	16.545
% SERVICES EMPLOYMENT	12.153	14.782	21.632
% OTHER TERTIARY EMPLOYMENT	6.477	7.757	19.757
% GOVERNMENT EMPLOYMENT	3.337	3.304	-0.982
NAGANO			
POPULATION (1000'S)	382.416	411.616	7.636
TOTAL EMPLOYMENT (1000'S)	186.750	222.949	16.119
% PRIMARY EMPLOYMENT	38.420	24.005	-37.518
% SECONDARY EMPLOYMENT	21.625	29.570	36.741
% WHOLESALE & RETAIL EMPLOYMENT	15.463	18.155	17.409
% SERVICES EMPLOYMENT	11.435	14.287	24.935
% OTHER TERTIARY EMPLOYMENT	9.057	10.190	12.508
% GOVERNMENT EMPLOYMENT	4.000	3.793	-5.174
MATSUMOTO			
POPULATION (1000'S)	274.044	294.184	7.349
TOTAL EMPLOYMENT (1000'S)	141.266	166.824	18.075
% PRIMARY EMPLOYMENT	41.132	26.007	-36.772
% SECONDARY EMPLOYMENT	23.141	31.332	35.396
% WHOLESALE & RETAIL EMPLOYMENT	14.942	18.613	24.565
% SERVICES EMPLOYMENT	11.412	13.852	21.375
% OTHER TERTIARY EMPLOYMENT	6.506	7.345	12.854
% GOVERNMENT EMPLOYMENT	2.865	2.853	-0.439
GIFU			
POPULATION (1000'S)	620.691	749.594	20.768
TOTAL EMPLOYMENT (1000'S)	310.384	403.231	29.914
% PRIMARY EMPLOYMENT	24.610	13.169	-46.491
% SECONDARY EMPLOYMENT	37.686	44.341	17.652
% WHOLESALE & RETAIL EMPLOYMENT	17.026	19.133	12.367
% SERVICES EMPLOYMENT	11.013	12.929	17.395
% OTHER TERTIARY EMPLOYMENT	6.121	7.380	20.579
% GOVERNMENT EMPLOYMENT	3.540	3.048	-13.913
SHIZUOKA			
POPULATION (1000'S)	793.846	927.563	16.844
TOTAL EMPLOYMENT (1000'S)	366.115	476.629	30.186
% PRIMARY EMPLOYMENT	24.195	14.529	-39.952
% SECONDARY EMPLOYMENT	35.735	38.096	6.607
% WHOLESALE & RETAIL EMPLOYMENT	18.108	21.581	19.182
% SERVICES EMPLOYMENT	11.593	13.605	17.357
% OTHER TERTIARY EMPLOYMENT	7.720	9.767	26.504
% GOVERNMENT EMPLOYMENT	2.649	2.423	-8.552
HAMAMATSU			
POPULATION (1000'S)	743.710	827.403	11.253
TOTAL EMPLOYMENT (1000'S)	366.424	449.537	22.682
% PRIMARY EMPLOYMENT	31.660	18.057	-42.966
% SECONDARY EMPLOYMENT	35.386	43.870	23.975
% WHOLESALE & RETAIL EMPLOYMENT	14.327	16.647	16.193
% SERVICES EMPLOYMENT	9.715	11.999	23.517
% OTHER TERTIARY EMPLOYMENT	5.982	7.046	17.794
% GOVERNMENT EMPLOYMENT	2.930	2.380	-18.762

Population and Employment Distribution for Individual RECs, 1960–1970

	1960	1970	% CHANGE 1960-1970
	----	----	---------
NUMAZU			
POPULATION (1000'S)	330.878	421.513	27.392
TOTAL EMPLOYMENT (1000'S)	149.364	209.623	40.325
% PRIMARY EMPLOYMENT	23.086	11.174	-51.600
% SECONDARY EMPLOYMENT	33.418	39.736	18.906
% WHOLESALE & RETAIL EMPLOYMENT	17.082	20.073	17.506
% SERVICES EMPLOYMENT	12.434	14.389	15.722
% OTHER TERTIARY EMPLOYMENT	9.468	10.297	8.761
% GOVERNMENT EMPLOYMENT	4.512	4.331	-4.000
NAGOYA			
POPULATION (1000'S)	3267.621	4122.595	26.165
TOTAL EMPLOYMENT (1000'S)	1646.750	2190.774	33.036
% PRIMARY EMPLOYMENT	13.139	6.829	-48.029
% SECONDARY EMPLOYMENT	47.746	46.338	-2.950
% WHOLESALE & RETAIL EMPLOYMENT	17.764	21.870	23.118
% SERVICES EMPLOYMENT	10.182	12.893	26.619
% OTHER TERTIARY EMPLOYMENT	9.013	9.927	10.144
% GOVERNMENT EMPLOYMENT	2.156	2.144	-0.558
TOYOHASHI			
POPULATION (1000'S)	380.991	375.187	-1.523
TOTAL EMPLOYMENT (1000'S)	191.063	242.621	26.985
% PRIMARY EMPLOYMENT	31.967	19.436	-39.199
% SECONDARY EMPLOYMENT	32.141	38.737	20.522
% WHOLESALE & RETAIL EMPLOYMENT	15.757	18.146	15.163
% SERVICES EMPLOYMENT	11.054	13.238	19.753
% OTHER TERTIARY EMPLOYMENT	6.052	7.786	28.664
% GOVERNMENT EMPLOYMENT	3.029	2.657	-12.308
TOYOTA			
POPULATION (1000'S)	311.142	445.103	43.055
TOTAL EMPLOYMENT (1000'S)	158.259	245.133	54.894
% PRIMARY EMPLOYMENT	29.417	12.386	-57.895
% SECONDARY EMPLOYMENT	36.425	54.013	40.567
% WHOLESALE & RETAIL EMPLOYMENT	12.476	14.087	12.892
% SERVICES EMPLOYMENT	9.625	11.076	15.067
% OTHER TERTIARY EMPLOYMENT	8.059	6.481	-19.581
% GOVERNMENT EMPLOYMENT	1.995	1.957	-1.896
TSU			
POPULATION (1000'S)	291.021	312.070	7.233
TOTAL EMPLOYMENT (1000'S)	139.990	159.964	14.268
% PRIMARY EMPLOYMENT	35.905	22.686	-36.817
% SECONDARY EMPLOYMENT	24.253	29.514	21.691
% WHOLESALE & RETAIL EMPLOYMENT	15.823	18.330	15.849
% SERVICES EMPLOYMENT	12.582	15.663	24.493
% OTHER TERTIARY EMPLOYMENT	7.285	8.855	21.553
% GOVERNMENT EMPLOYMENT	4.152	4.951	19.243
YOKKAICHI			
POPULATION (1000'S)	384.347	453.344	17.952
TOTAL EMPLOYMENT (1000'S)	195.477	237.783	21.642
% PRIMARY EMPLOYMENT	32.572	18.468	-43.302
% SECONDARY EMPLOYMENT	36.527	43.565	19.268
% WHOLESALE & RETAIL EMPLOYMENT	12.255	15.160	23.709
% SERVICES EMPLOYMENT	9.068	11.487	26.677
% OTHER TERTIARY EMPLOYMENT	7.772	9.399	20.935
% GOVERNMENT EMPLOYMENT	1.806	1.921	6.370

Population and Employment Distribution for Individual RECs, 1960–1970

	1960	1970	% CHANGE 1960-1970
	----	----	---------
ISE			
POPULATION (1000'S)	174.001	178.606	2.647
TOTAL EMPLOYMENT (1000'S)	81.899	89.332	9.076
% PRIMARY EMPLOYMENT	34.899	21.368	-38.771
% SECONDARY EMPLOYMENT	26.630	31.736	19.175
% WHOLESALE & RETAIL EMPLOYMENT	15.081	18.480	22.539
% SERVICES EMPLOYMENT	12.992	16.738	28.834
% OTHER TERTIARY EMPLOYMENT	7.663	8.655	12.648
% GOVERNMENT EMPLOYMENT	2.716	3.023	11.320
OTSU			
POPULATION (1000'S)	302.222	356.159	17.847
TOTAL EMPLOYMENT (1000'S)	148.656	188.167	26.407
% PRIMARY EMPLOYMENT	31.751	18.542	-41.602
% SECONDARY EMPLOYMENT	31.086	37.159	19.531
% WHOLESALE & RETAIL EMPLOYMENT	13.173	16.117	22.349
% SERVICES EMPLOYMENT	11.314	14.887	31.582
% OTHER TERTIARY EMPLOYMENT	8.592	9.263	7.812
% GOVERNMENT EMPLOYMENT	4.083	4.032	-1.251
KYOTO			
POPULATION (1000'S)	1511.077	1809.412	19.743
TOTAL EMPLOYMENT (1000'S)	685.412	885.094	29.133
% PRIMARY EMPLOYMENT	8.140	4.460	-45.206
% SECONDARY EMPLOYMENT	39.585	39.608	0.058
% WHOLESALE & RETAIL EMPLOYMENT	22.435	24.818	10.622
% SERVICES EMPLOYMENT	32.173	18.339	-43.000
% OTHER TERTIARY EMPLOYMENT	5.644	9.683	
% GOVERNMENT EMPLOYMENT	3.311	3.092	-6.624
OSAKA			
POPULATION (1000'S)	6781.229	9495.198	40.022
TOTAL EMPLOYMENT (1000'S)	3044.325	4569.322	50.093
% PRIMARY EMPLOYMENT	6.482	2.791	-56.935
% SECONDARY EMPLOYMENT	47.012	45.699	-2.794
% WHOLESALE & RETAIL EMPLOYMENT	21.616	23.989	10.976
% SERVICES EMPLOYMENT	12.903	13.915	7.849
% OTHER TERTIARY EMPLOYMENT	9.460	11.156	17.920
% GOVERNMENT EMPLOYMENT	2.527	2.450	-3.033
KOBE			
POPULATION (1000'S)	1441.703	1740.999	20.760
TOTAL EMPLOYMENT (1000'S)	764.895	823.438	7.654
% PRIMARY EMPLOYMENT	7.073	4.344	-38.585
% SECONDARY EMPLOYMENT	42.316	39.061	-7.693
% WHOLESALE & RETAIL EMPLOYMENT	18.075	22.683	26.598
% SERVICES EMPLOYMENT	11.566	15.297	32.262
% OTHER TERTIARY EMPLOYMENT	18.403	14.969	-18.659
% GOVERNMENT EMPLOYMENT	2.567	3.446	34.269
HIMEJI			
POPULATION (1000'S)	682.238	782.646	14.717
TOTAL EMPLOYMENT (1000'S)	312.019	391.158	25.364
% PRIMARY EMPLOYMENT	23.384	13.074	-44.087
% SECONDARY EMPLOYMENT	39.837	44.903	12.718
% WHOLESALE & RETAIL EMPLOYMENT	14.544	17.272	18.755
% SERVICES EMPLOYMENT	10.263	12.106	17.961
% OTHER TERTIARY EMPLOYMENT	9.255	9.837	6.294
% GOVERNMENT EMPLOYMENT	2.718	2.808	3.283

Population and Employment Distribution for Individual RECs, 1960–1970

	1960	1970	% CHANGE 1960-1970
NAPA	----	----	---------
POPULATION (1000'S)	205.020	284.712	38.870
TOTAL EMPLOYMENT (1000'S)	90.552	133.230	47.131
% PRIMARY EMPLOYMENT	26.833	14.260	-46.856
% SECONDARY EMPLOYMENT	23.524	27.523	16.998
% WHOLESALE & RETAIL EMPLOYMENT	17.414	21.116	21.258
% SERVICES EMPLOYMENT	17.065	20.843	22.009
% OTHER TERTIARY EMPLOYMENT	10.039	11.531	14.869
% GOVERNMENT EMPLOYMENT	5.106	4.726	-7.444
WAKAYAMA			
POPULATION (1000'S)	482.104	563.051	16.790
TOTAL EMPLOYMENT (1000'S)	222.051	280.720	26.421
% PRIMARY EMPLOYMENT	24.598	15.259	-37.965
% SECONDARY EMPLOYMENT	35.021	37.281	6.454
% WHOLESALE & RETAIL EMPLOYMENT	17.105	19.283	12.737
% SERVICES EMPLOYMENT	11.652	13.701	17.587
% OTHER TERTIARY EMPLOYMENT	8.517	11.232	31.877
% GOVERNMENT EMPLOYMENT	3.107	3.243	4.368
TOTTORI			
POPULATION (1000'S)	204.752	199.035	-2.792
TOTAL EMPLOYMENT (1000'S)	96.652	106.467	10.155
% PRIMARY EMPLOYMENT	46.432	28.509	-38.601
% SECONDARY EMPLOYMENT	16.361	26.567	62.380
% WHOLESALE & RETAIL EMPLOYMENT	13.254	15.823	19.389
% SERVICES EMPLOYMENT	12.956	16.710	28.980
% OTHER TERTIARY EMPLOYMENT	6.831	8.152	19.347
% GOVERNMENT EMPLOYMENT	4.166	4.238	1.707
YONAGO			
POPULATION (1000'S)	181.576	186.272	2.586
TOTAL EMPLOYMENT (1000'S)	89.403	101.445	13.469
% PRIMARY EMPLOYMENT	40.610	25.287	-37.733
% SECONDARY EMPLOYMENT	16.567	23.788	28.123
% WHOLESALE & RETAIL EMPLOYMENT	14.766	18.806	27.341
% SERVICES EMPLOYMENT	12.435	16.760	34.785
% OTHER TERTIARY EMPLOYMENT	9.693	10.386	7.150
% GOVERNMENT EMPLOYMENT	3.928	4.974	26.619
MATSUE			
POPULATION (1000'S)	226.178	227.877	0.751
TOTAL EMPLOYMENT (1000'S)	111.494	122.424	9.803
% PRIMARY EMPLOYMENT	44.935	29.999	-33.239
% SECONDARY EMPLOYMENT	16.800	21.758	29.512
% WHOLESALE & RETAIL EMPLOYMENT	14.626	19.064	30.341
% SERVICES EMPLOYMENT	13.050	17.339	32.865
% OTHER TERTIARY EMPLOYMENT	6.366	7.692	20.816
% GOVERNMENT EMPLOYMENT	4.224	4.149	-1.753
OKAYAMA			
POPULATION (1000'S)	578.238	641.775	10.988
TOTAL EMPLOYMENT (1000'S)	278.889	342.278	22.729
% PRIMARY EMPLOYMENT	34.014	19.992	-41.224
% SECONDARY EMPLOYMENT	25.396	30.222	18.993
% WHOLESALE & RETAIL EMPLOYMENT	16.707	20.855	24.833
% SERVICES EMPLOYMENT	12.400	15.855	27.863
% OTHER TERTIARY EMPLOYMENT	8.130	9.662	18.841
% GOVERNMENT EMPLOYMENT	3.352	3.414	1.861

Population and Employment Distribution for Individual RECs, 1960–1970

	1960	1970	% CHANGE 1960–1970
KURASHIKI	----	----	---------
POPULATION (1000'S)	337.115	418.465	24.131
TOTAL EMPLOYMENT (1000'S)	174.078	226.730	30.246
% PRIMARY EMPLOYMENT	31.215	15.480	-50.408
% SECONDARY EMPLOYMENT	40.543	49.145	21.217
% WHOLESALE & RETAIL EMPLOYMENT	11.971	14.128	18.022
% SERVICES EMPLOYMENT	8.986	11.337	26.166
% OTHER TERTIARY EMPLOYMENT	5.394	8.034	48.946
% GOVERNMENT EMPLOYMENT	1.892	1.876	-0.833
HIROSHIMA			
POPULATION (1000'S)	767.071	1025.807	33.730
TOTAL EMPLOYMENT (1000'S)	374.063	523.443	39.934
% PRIMARY EMPLOYMENT	18.364	7.798	-57.538
% SECONDARY EMPLOYMENT	32.885	35.477	7.882
% WHOLESALE & RETAIL EMPLOYMENT	16.448	23.426	26.983
% SERVICES EMPLOYMENT	13.566	16.359	20.588
% OTHER TERTIARY EMPLOYMENT	11.763	12.063	2.550
% GOVERNMENT EMPLOYMENT	4.974	4.877	-1.941
FUKUYAMA			
POPULATION (1000'S)	475.869	544.938	14.514
TOTAL EMPLOYMENT (1000'S)	239.162	290.370	21.411
% PRIMARY EMPLOYMENT	31.123	15.294	-50.861
% SECONDARY EMPLOYMENT	35.395	43.279	22.282
% WHOLESALE & RETAIL EMPLOYMENT	14.757	17.937	21.553
% SERVICES EMPLOYMENT	10.032	12.587	25.464
% OTHER TERTIARY EMPLOYMENT	6.707	8.930	33.139
% GOVERNMENT EMPLOYMENT	1.966	1.974	-0.736
SHIMONOSEKI			
POPULATION (1000'S)	331.874	328.801	-0.926
TOTAL EMPLOYMENT (1000'S)	143.161	156.874	9.579
% PRIMARY EMPLOYMENT	24.230	16.781	-30.799
% SECONDARY EMPLOYMENT	25.359	27.987	10.363
% WHOLESALE & RETAIL EMPLOYMENT	19.199	20.907	8.898
% SERVICES EMPLOYMENT	13.706	15.105	10.259
% OTHER TERTIARY EMPLOYMENT	13.886	15.946	14.885
% GOVERNMENT EMPLOYMENT	3.613	3.274	-9.387
UBE			
POPULATION (1000'S)	242.216	211.317	-12.757
TOTAL EMPLOYMENT (1000'S)	101.387	105.615	4.170
% PRIMARY EMPLOYMENT	18.113	13.850	-23.538
% SECONDARY EMPLOYMENT	41.087	36.146	-12.026
% WHOLESALE & RETAIL EMPLOYMENT	17.275	20.434	18.286
% SERVICES EMPLOYMENT	12.813	16.072	25.429
% OTHER TERTIARY EMPLOYMENT	8.301	10.809	30.206
% GOVERNMENT EMPLOYMENT	2.410	2.690	11.626
YAMAGUCHI			
POPULATION (1000'S)	117.285	117.104	-0.154
TOTAL EMPLOYMENT (1000'S)	56.758	61.206	7.837
% PRIMARY EMPLOYMENT	34.071	23.170	-31.995
% SECONDARY EMPLOYMENT	11.690	14.935	27.757
% WHOLESALE & RETAIL EMPLOYMENT	17.330	20.733	19.637
% SERVICES EMPLOYMENT	16.354	20.508	25.403
% OTHER TERTIARY EMPLOYMENT	9.625	10.877	13.015
% GOVERNMENT EMPLOYMENT	10.931	9.777	-10.555

Population and Employment Distribution for Individual RECs, 1960–1970

	1960	1970	% CHANGE 1960–1970
IWAKUNI			
POPULATION (1000'S)	168.067	174.427	3.784
TOTAL EMPLOYMENT (1000'S)	78.356	86.833	10.819
% PRIMARY EMPLOYMENT	24.069	13.142	-45.398
% SECONDARY EMPLOYMENT	35.467	40.495	14.176
% WHOLESALE & RETAIL EMPLOYMENT	15.319	17.766	15.979
% SERVICES EMPLOYMENT	14.106	15.256	8.150
% OTHER TERTIARY EMPLOYMENT	7.726	10.102	30.709
% GOVERNMENT EMPLOYMENT	3.311	3.239	-2.164
TOKUSHIMA			
POPULATION (1000'S)	429.176	444.997	3.686
TOTAL EMPLOYMENT (1000'S)	196.041	225.576	15.066
% PRIMARY EMPLOYMENT	31.840	19.806	-37.795
% SECONDARY EMPLOYMENT	27.174	31.885	17.336
% WHOLESALE & RETAIL EMPLOYMENT	15.230	19.133	25.628
% SERVICES EMPLOYMENT	11.366	15.733	38.417
% OTHER TERTIARY EMPLOYMENT	11.147	9.260	-16.927
% GOVERNMENT EMPLOYMENT	3.243	4.183	28.985
TAKAMATSU			
POPULATION (1000'S)	579.910	602.948	3.973
TOTAL EMPLOYMENT (1000'S)	277.099	321.419	15.994
% PRIMARY EMPLOYMENT	37.908	21.366	-43.636
% SECONDARY EMPLOYMENT	22.454	29.942	33.351
% WHOLESALE & RETAIL EMPLOYMENT	13.292	19.403	45.982
% SERVICES EMPLOYMENT	11.783	15.176	28.796
% OTHER TERTIARY EMPLOYMENT	11.999	10.419	-13.167
% GOVERNMENT EMPLOYMENT	2.565	3.693	43.979
MATSUYAMA			
POPULATION (1000'S)	368.872	428.545	16.177
TOTAL EMPLOYMENT (1000'S)	235.399	204.981	-12.922
% PRIMARY EMPLOYMENT	23.417	19.032	-18.725
% SECONDARY EMPLOYMENT	15.905	25.968	63.268
% WHOLESALE & RETAIL EMPLOYMENT	12.163	21.508	76.835
% SERVICES EMPLOYMENT	9.423	18.109	92.186
% OTHER TERTIARY EMPLOYMENT	36.144	11.043	-69.446
% GOVERNMENT EMPLOYMENT	2.946	4.339	47.177
IMABARI			
POPULATION (1000'S)	163.971	171.216	4.418
TOTAL EMPLOYMENT (1000'S)	75.018	89.132	18.814
% PRIMARY EMPLOYMENT	29.257	18.108	-38.109
% SECONDARY EMPLOYMENT	34.947	41.641	19.157
% WHOLESALE & RETAIL EMPLOYMENT	15.722	17.420	10.801
% SERVICES EMPLOYMENT	11.431	12.786	11.855
% OTHER TERTIARY EMPLOYMENT	6.695	8.030	19.939
% GOVERNMENT EMPLOYMENT	1.949	2.016	3.439
NIIHAMA			
POPULATION (1000'S)	197.286	193.238	-2.052
TOTAL EMPLOYMENT (1000'S)	79.526	92.757	16.637
% PRIMARY EMPLOYMENT	24.442	15.821	-35.273
% SECONDARY EMPLOYMENT	39.556	41.390	4.637
% WHOLESALE & RETAIL EMPLOYMENT	14.052	16.564	17.880
% SERVICES EMPLOYMENT	11.991	14.261	18.932
% OTHER TERTIARY EMPLOYMENT	7.890	9.798	24.179
% GOVERNMENT EMPLOYMENT	2.069	2.165	4.688

Population and Employment Distribution for Individual RECs, 1960–1970

	1960	1970	% CHANGE 1960-1970
KOCHI			
POPULATION (1000'S)	320.245	361.737	12.956
TOTAL EMPLOYMENT (1000'S)	152.919	189.711	24.060
% PRIMARY EMPLOYMENT	29.259	16.589	-43.303
% SECONDARY EMPLOYMENT	22.464	24.664	9.791
% WHOLESALE & RETAIL EMPLOYMENT	19.835	23.716	19.581
% SERVICES EMPLOYMENT	16.142	20.640	27.664
% OTHER TERTIARY EMPLOYMENT	8.394	9.982	18.924
% GOVERNMENT EMPLOYMENT	3.908	4.409	12.822
KITAKYUSHU			
POPULATION (1000'S)	1518.451	1501.563	-1.112
TOTAL EMPLOYMENT (1000'S)	609.503	668.908	9.746
% PRIMARY EMPLOYMENT	12.026	7.937	-34.019
% SECONDARY EMPLOYMENT	40.076	36.262	-9.516
% WHOLESALE & RETAIL EMPLOYMENT	18.923	21.576	14.017
% SERVICES EMPLOYMENT	13.947	16.547	18.640
% OTHER TERTIARY EMPLOYMENT	12.030	13.572	12.811
% GOVERNMENT EMPLOYMENT	2.995	4.107	37.132
FUKUOKA			
POPULATION (1000'S)	1063.653	1324.394	24.514
TOTAL EMPLOYMENT (1000'S)	451.869	624.000	38.093
% PRIMARY EMPLOYMENT	19.679	10.286	-47.732
% SECONDARY EMPLOYMENT	24.380	25.835	5.965
% WHOLESALE & RETAIL EMPLOYMENT	22.440	27.422	22.205
% SERVICES EMPLOYMENT	15.782	19.053	20.724
% OTHER TERTIARY EMPLOYMENT	14.026	12.658	-9.753
% GOVERNMENT EMPLOYMENT	3.693	4.746	28.526
OMUTA			
POPULATION (1000'S)	307.501	263.243	-14.393
TOTAL EMPLOYMENT (1000'S)	108.231	115.183	6.423
% PRIMARY EMPLOYMENT	19.810	15.156	-23.493
% SECONDARY EMPLOYMENT	40.943	34.828	-14.937
% WHOLESALE & RETAIL EMPLOYMENT	17.149	19.460	13.479
% SERVICES EMPLOYMENT	12.402	15.805	27.438
% OTHER TERTIARY EMPLOYMENT	7.326	8.606	17.560
% GOVERNMENT EMPLOYMENT	2.375	6.146	158.712
KURUME			
POPULATION (1000'S)	449.080	443.424	-1.259
TOTAL EMPLOYMENT (1000'S)	207.301	223.054	7.599
% PRIMARY EMPLOYMENT	35.409	26.428	-25.363
% SECONDARY EMPLOYMENT	21.295	27.136	27.432
% WHOLESALE & RETAIL EMPLOYMENT	16.442	19.591	19.154
% SERVICES EMPLOYMENT	12.483	14.891	19.290
% OTHER TERTIARY EMPLOYMENT	10.193	7.564	-25.793
% GOVERNMENT EMPLOYMENT	4.176	4.389	5.048
SAGA			
POPULATION (1000'S)	266.944	256.165	-4.038
TOTAL EMPLOYMENT (1000'S)	113.040	122.993	8.805
% PRIMARY EMPLOYMENT	32.716	24.529	-25.029
% SECONDARY EMPLOYMENT	23.633	23.731	0.415
% WHOLESALE & RETAIL EMPLOYMENT	18.815	17.162	-8.785
% SERVICES EMPLOYMENT	13.911	4.815	-65.386
% OTHER TERTIARY EMPLOYMENT	6.722	8.472	26.045
% GOVERNMENT EMPLOYMENT	4.202	21.291	406.683

Population and Employment Distribution for Individual RECs, 1960–1970

NAGASAKI	1960	1970	% CHANGE 1960–1970
POPULATION (1000'S)	506.565	545.435	7.673
TOTAL EMPLOYMENT (1000'S)	199.010	235.702	18.437
% PRIMARY EMPLOYMENT	23.311	12.735	-45.370
% SECONDARY EMPLOYMENT	27.906	28.223	1.135
% WHOLESALE & RETAIL EMPLOYMENT	20.420	24.260	18.803
% SERVICES EMPLOYMENT	15.209	19.029	25.119
% OTHER TERTIARY EMPLOYMENT	9.158	11.304	23.428
% GOVERNMENT EMPLOYMENT	3.996	4.450	11.358
SASEBO			
POPULATION (1000'S)	297.099	272.294	-8.349
TOTAL EMPLOYMENT (1000'S)	119.438	125.404	4.995
% PRIMARY EMPLOYMENT	16.230	11.129	-38.953
% SECONDARY EMPLOYMENT	24.726	26.775	8.288
% WHOLESALE & RETAIL EMPLOYMENT	21.976	24.809	12.890
% SERVICES EMPLOYMENT	17.553	19.229	9.549
% OTHER TERTIARY EMPLOYMENT	9.465	10.613	12.126
% GOVERNMENT EMPLOYMENT	8.050	7.445	-7.518
KUMAMOTO			
POPULATION (1000'S)	452.960	516.223	13.967
TOTAL EMPLOYMENT (1000'S)	188.361	239.439	27.117
% PRIMARY EMPLOYMENT	21.022	11.796	-43.886
% SECONDARY EMPLOYMENT	19.445	20.810	7.015
% WHOLESALE & RETAIL EMPLOYMENT	24.343	26.564	9.126
% SERVICES EMPLOYMENT	18.212	21.607	18.641
% OTHER TERTIARY EMPLOYMENT	9.717	11.459	17.932
% GOVERNMENT EMPLOYMENT	7.262	7.764	6.924
YATSUSHIRO			
POPULATION (1000'S)	152.094	140.809	-7.420
TOTAL EMPLOYMENT (1000'S)	63.585	66.065	3.900
% PRIMARY EMPLOYMENT	40.856	30.321	-25.750
% SECONDARY EMPLOYMENT	20.510	24.113	17.566
% WHOLESALE & RETAIL EMPLOYMENT	17.575	20.094	14.332
% SERVICES EMPLOYMENT	12.254	14.654	19.582
% OTHER TERTIARY EMPLOYMENT	6.326	7.918	25.163
% GOVERNMENT EMPLOYMENT	2.497	2.900	16.102
OITA			
POPULATION (1000'S)	386.147	446.885	15.729
TOTAL EMPLOYMENT (1000'S)	167.593	213.011	27.100
% PRIMARY EMPLOYMENT	26.151	13.408	-48.730
% SECONDARY EMPLOYMENT	22.675	24.528	8.171
% WHOLESALE & RETAIL EMPLOYMENT	19.492	22.906	17.513
% SERVICES EMPLOYMENT	17.587	21.565	22.619
% OTHER TERTIARY EMPLOYMENT	8.956	11.969	33.612
% GOVERNMENT EMPLOYMENT	5.137	5.625	9.501
MIYAZAKI			
POPULATION (1000'S)	185.852	222.602	19.774
TOTAL EMPLOYMENT (1000'S)	80.505	109.042	35.447
% PRIMARY EMPLOYMENT	33.478	17.574	-47.505
% SECONDARY EMPLOYMENT	14.320	17.748	23.933
% WHOLESALE & RETAIL EMPLOYMENT	22.163	26.717	20.549
% SERVICES EMPLOYMENT	16.395	22.215	35.494
% OTHER TERTIARY EMPLOYMENT	8.283	10.443	26.076
% GOVERNMENT EMPLOYMENT	5.361	5.304	-1.067

Population and Employment Distribution for Individual RECs, 1960–1970

	1960	1970	% CHANGE 1960-1970
NOBECKA	----	----	---------
POPULATION (1000'S)	138.291	143.832	4.007
TOTAL EMPLOYMENT (1000'S)	60.731	69.613	14.625
% PRIMARY EMPLOYMENT	24.864	14.998	-39.681
% SECONDARY EMPLOYMENT	36.700	40.641	5.015
% WHOLESALE & RETAIL EMPLOYMENT	16.427	19.802	20.550
% SERVICES EMPLOYMENT	12.322	15.066	22.272
% OTHER TERTIARY EMPLOYMENT	5.560	6.514	17.164
% GOVERNMENT EMPLOYMENT	2.127	2.979	40.021
KAGOSHIMA			
POPULATION (1000'S)	404.980	469.326	15.889
TOTAL EMPLOYMENT (1000'S)	169.996	211.329	24.314
% PRIMARY EMPLOYMENT	27.046	12.524	-53.696
% SECONDARY EMPLOYMENT	20.053	23.383	16.608
% WHOLESALE & RETAIL EMPLOYMENT	22.391	25.596	14.317
% SERVICES EMPLOYMENT	15.877	19.910	25.399
% OTHER TERTIARY EMPLOYMENT	9.996	12.668	26.715
% GOVERNMENT EMPLOYMENT	4.633	5.917	27.720

Appendix 4 Shift Share Analysis of Employment

TABLE 1
Total Employment

		1. ACTUAL 1960	2. ACTUAL 1970	3. EXPECTED 1970	4. SHIFT FACTOR (2-3)	5. SHIFT INDEX
1.	SAPPORO	370.4	608.4	492.9	115.47	1.23
2.	HAKODATE	121.8	151.9	162.1	-10.25	0.94
3.	MURORAN	78.9	104.8	105.0	-0.27	1.00
4.	KUSHIRO	66.5	92.9	88.5	4.34	1.05
5.	MORIOKA	74.0	102.7	98.5	4.21	1.04
6.	SENDAI	337.5	457.7	449.1	8.52	1.02
7.	ISHINOMACHI	56.8	68.2	75.6	-7.40	0.90
8.	AKITA	154.6	185.5	205.7	-20.19	0.90
9.	YAMAGATA	185.8	208.8	247.2	-38.44	0.84
10.	FUKUSHIMA	143.1	169.5	190.4	-20.98	0.89
11.	AIZUWAKAMATSU	52.2	61.5	69.5	-7.97	0.89
12.	KORIYAMA	140.3	167.8	186.7	-18.86	0.90
13.	MITO	168.5	205.2	224.2	-19.08	0.91
14.	HITACHI	146.4	164.7	194.8	-30.10	0.85
15.	UTSUNOMIYA	237.9	300.2	316.5	-16.32	0.95
16.	MAEBASHI	122.6	157.5	163.2	-5.70	0.97
17.	TAKASAKI	165.7	204.9	220.5	-15.66	0.93
18.	KIRYU	73.1	89.4	97.3	-7.84	0.92
19.	KUMAGAYA	127.9	154.3	170.2	-15.91	0.91
20.	CHIBA	247.7	393.9	329.6	64.34	1.20
21.	TOKYO	6136.4	8726.4	8166.1	560.27	1.07
22.	YOKOHAMA	899.5	1572.3	1197.0	375.23	1.31
23.	HIRATSUKA	66.5	111.6	88.5	23.13	1.26
24.	ODAWARA	106.7	144.3	142.0	2.32	1.02
25.	NIIGATA	293.4	356.3	390.4	-34.12	0.91
26.	NAGAOKA	105.3	122.5	140.1	-17.62	0.87
27.	TOYAMA	240.4	269.0	320.0	-51.00	0.84
28.	TAKAOKA	183.7	203.2	244.4	-41.16	0.83
29.	KANAZAWA	236.0	284.6	314.0	-29.43	0.91
30.	FUKUI	253.6	281.0	337.5	-56.50	0.83
31.	KOFU	169.3	195.2	225.3	-30.12	0.87
32.	NAGANO	188.7	222.9	251.2	-28.23	0.89
33.	MATSUMOTO	141.3	166.8	188.0	-21.20	0.89
34.	GIFU	310.4	403.2	413.1	-9.82	0.98
35.	SHIZUOKA	366.1	476.6	487.2	-10.59	0.98
36.	HAMAMATSU	366.4	449.5	487.6	-38.09	0.92
37.	NUMAZU	149.4	209.6	198.8	10.83	1.05
38.	NAGOYA	1646.7	2190.8	2191.4	-0.67	1.00
39.	TOYOHASHI	191.1	242.6	254.3	-11.64	0.95
40.	TOYOTA	158.3	245.1	210.6	34.53	1.16
41.	TSU	140.0	160.0	186.3	-26.33	0.86
42.	YOKKAICHI	195.5	237.8	260.1	-22.35	0.91
43.	ISE	81.9	89.3	109.0	-19.66	0.82
44.	OTSU	148.9	188.2	198.1	-9.93	0.95
45.	KYOTO	685.4	865.1	912.1	-27.03	0.97

POPULATION AND EMPLOYMENT VALUES IN THOUSANDS

TABLE 1—(Continued)
Total Employment

		1. ACTUAL 1960	2. ACTUAL 1970	3. EXPECTED 1970	4. SHIFT FACTOR (2-3)	5. SHIFT INDEX
46.	OSAKA	3044.3	4569.3	4051.3	518.02	1.13
47.	KOBE	764.9	823.4	1017.9	-194.46	0.81
48.	HIMEJI	312.0	391.2	415.2	-24.07	0.94
49.	NARA	90.6	133.2	120.5	12.73	1.11
50.	WAKAYAMA	222.1	280.7	295.5	-14.78	0.95
51.	TOTTORI	96.7	106.5	128.6	-22.15	0.83
52.	YONAGO	89.4	101.4	119.0	-17.53	0.85
53.	MATSUE	111.5	122.4	148.4	-25.95	0.83
54.	OKAYAMA	278.9	342.3	371.1	-28.86	0.92
55.	KURASHIKI	174.1	226.7	231.7	-4.93	0.98
56.	HIROSHIMA	374.1	523.4	497.8	25.65	1.05
57.	FUKUYAMA	239.2	290.4	318.3	-27.90	0.91
58.	SHIMONOSEKI	143.2	156.9	190.5	-33.64	0.82
59.	UBE	101.4	105.6	134.9	-29.31	0.78
60.	YAMAGUCHI	56.8	61.2	75.5	-14.33	0.81
61.	IWAKUNI	78.4	86.8	104.3	-17.44	0.83
62.	TOKUSHIMASHI	196.0	225.6	260.9	-35.31	0.86
63.	TAKAMATSU	277.1	321.4	368.8	-47.34	0.87
64.	MATSUYAMA	235.4	205.0	313.3	-108.28	0.65
65.	IMABARI	75.0	89.1	99.8	-10.70	0.89
66.	NIIHAMA	73.5	92.8	105.8	-13.07	0.88
67.	KOCHI	152.9	189.7	203.5	-13.79	0.93
68.	KITAKYUSHU	609.5	668.9	811.1	-142.20	0.82
69.	FUKUOKA	451.9	624.0	601.3	22.67	1.04
70.	OMUTA	108.2	115.2	144.0	-28.85	0.80
71.	KURUME	207.3	223.1	275.9	-52.82	0.81
72.	SAGA	113.0	123.0	150.4	-27.44	0.82
73.	NAGASAKI	199.0	235.7	264.8	-29.13	0.89
74.	SASEBO	119.4	125.4	158.9	-33.54	0.79
75.	KUMAMOTO	188.4	239.4	250.7	-11.23	0.96
76.	YATSUSHIRO	63.6	66.1	84.6	-18.55	0.78
77.	OITA	167.6	213.0	223.0	-10.02	0.96
78.	MIYAZAKI	80.5	109.0	107.1	1.91	1.02
79.	NOBEOKA	60.7	69.6	80.8	-11.21	0.86
80.	KAGOSHIMA	170.0	211.3	226.2	-14.90	0.93

REGIONAL TOTALS

1.	HOKKAIDO	637.7	957.9	848.6	109.29	1.13
2.	TOHOKU	1144.2	1421.6	1522.7	-101.12	0.93
3.	KANTO	8668.2	12419.9	11535.4	884.55	1.08
4.	TOKAI	3605.7	4704.6	4798.4	-93.79	0.98
5.	HOKURIKU	1642.4	1906.4	2185.7	-279.25	0.87
6.	KINKI	5268.1	7271.1	7010.7	260.47	1.04
7.	CHUGOKU	1939.4	2349.3	2581.0	-231.70	0.91
8.	SHIKOKU	820.0	898.0	1091.2	-193.18	0.82
9.	KYUSHU	2539.2	3023.7	3379.0	-355.30	0.89

POPULATION AND EMPLOYMENT VALUES IN THOUSANDS

TABLE 2

Primary Employment

		1. ACTUAL 1960	2. ACTUAL 1970	3. EXPECTED 1970	4. SHIFT FACTOR (2-3)	5. SHIFT INDEX
1.	SAPPORO	33.6	22.1	23.6	-1.56	0.93
2.	HAKODATE	19.0	12.9	13.4	-0.44	0.97
3.	MURORAN	6.9	5.1	4.9	0.23	1.05
4.	KUSHIRO	6.1	5.7	4.3	1.49	1.35
5.	MORIOKA	16.4	12.2	11.5	0.68	1.06
6.	SENDAI	94.2	70.3	66.2	4.11	1.06
7.	ISHINOMACHI	19.4	17.9	13.6	4.21	1.31
8.	AKITA	58.1	42.4	40.9	1.56	1.04
9.	YANAGATA	82.5	58.3	58.0	0.28	1.00
10.	FUKUSHIMA	53.1	42.9	40.8	2.10	1.05
11.	AIZUWAKAMATSU	15.5	11.4	10.9	0.53	1.05
12.	KORIYAMA	63.2	49.1	44.4	4.65	1.10
13.	MITO	69.6	48.8	49.0	-0.21	1.00
14.	HITACHI	35.4	23.7	24.9	-1.16	0.95
15.	UTSUNOMIYA	95.9	72.0	67.4	4.56	1.07
16.	MAEBASHI	41.2	30.7	29.0	1.69	1.06
17.	TAKASAKI	68.1	50.2	47.9	2.33	1.05
18.	KIRYU	9.7	6.3	6.8	-0.58	0.91
19.	KUMAGAYA	62.3	45.5	43.8	1.73	1.04
20.	CHIBA	99.8	65.9	70.2	-4.26	0.94
21.	TOKYO	497.8	336.9	350.0	-13.17	0.96
22.	YOKOHAMA	59.4	37.6	41.8	-4.20	0.90
23.	HIRATSUKA	11.8	9.1	8.3	0.82	1.10
24.	ODAWARA	18.4	15.6	13.0	2.66	1.21
25.	NIIGATA	95.8	69.4	67.3	2.10	1.03
26.	NAGAOKA	38.4	27.3	27.0	0.32	1.01
27.	TOYAMA	79.9	58.7	56.2	2.51	1.04
28.	TAKAOKA	72.3	48.5	50.8	-2.30	0.95
29.	KANAZAWA	63.1	40.2	44.4	-4.15	0.91
30.	FUKUI	89.2	59.3	62.7	-3.41	0.95
31.	KOFU	61.8	46.4	43.5	2.98	1.07
32.	NAGANO	72.5	53.5	51.0	2.53	1.05
33.	MATSUMOTO	58.1	43.4	40.9	2.52	1.06
34.	GIFU	76.4	53.1	53.7	-0.61	0.99
35.	SHIZUOKA	88.6	69.2	62.3	6.96	1.11
36.	HAMAMATSU	116.0	81.2	81.6	-0.40	1.00
37.	NUMAZU	34.5	23.4	24.2	-0.83	0.97
38.	NAGOYA	216.4	149.6	152.1	-2.54	0.98
39.	TOYOHASHI	61.1	47.2	42.9	4.21	1.10
40.	TOYOTA	46.6	30.4	32.7	-2.37	0.93
41.	TSU	50.3	36.3	35.3	0.95	1.03
42.	YOKKAICHI	63.7	43.9	44.8	-0.86	0.98
43.	ISE	28.6	19.1	20.1	-1.01	0.95
44.	OTSU	47.3	34.9	33.2	1.66	1.05
45.	KYOTO	55.8	39.5	39.2	0.25	1.01

POPULATION AND EMPLOYMENT VALUES IN THOUSANDS

TABLE 2—(Continued)

Primary Employment

		1. ACTUAL 1960	2. ACTUAL 1970	3. EXPECTED 1970	4. SHIFT FACTOR (2-3)	5. SHIFT INDEX
46.	OSAKA	197.3	127.5	138.8	-11.20	0.92
47.	KOBE	54.1	35.8	38.0	-2.27	0.94
48.	HIMEJI	73.0	51.1	51.3	-0.16	1.00
49.	NARA	24.3	19.0	17.1	1.91	1.11
50.	WAKAYAMA	54.6	42.8	38.4	4.43	1.12
51.	TOTTORI	44.9	30.4	31.6	-1.20	0.96
52.	YONAGO	36.3	25.7	25.5	0.12	1.00
53.	MATSUE	50.1	36.7	35.2	1.50	1.04
54.	OKAYAMA	94.9	68.4	66.7	1.73	1.03
55.	KURASHIKI	54.3	35.1	38.2	-3.11	0.92
56.	HIROSHIMA	68.7	40.8	48.3	-7.49	0.85
57.	FUKUYAMA	74.4	44.4	52.3	-7.93	0.85
58.	SHIMONOSEKI	34.7	26.3	24.4	1.91	1.08
59.	UBE	18.4	14.6	12.9	1.71	1.13
60.	YAMAGUCHI	19.3	14.2	13.6	0.58	1.04
61.	IWAKUNI	18.9	11.4	13.3	-1.85	0.86
62.	TOKUSHIMASHI	62.4	44.7	43.9	0.79	1.02
63.	TAKAMATSU	105.0	68.7	73.9	-5.19	0.93
64.	MATSUYAMA	55.1	39.0	38.8	0.25	1.01
65.	IMABARI	21.9	16.1	15.4	0.71	1.05
66.	NIIHAMA	19.4	14.7	13.7	1.01	1.07
67.	KOCHI	44.7	31.5	31.5	0.01	1.00
68.	KITAKYUSHU	73.3	53.1	51.6	1.54	1.03
69.	FUKUOKA	88.9	64.2	62.5	1.66	1.03
70.	OMUTA	21.4	17.5	15.1	2.38	1.16
71.	KURUME	73.4	58.9	51.6	7.34	1.14
72.	SAGA	37.0	30.2	26.0	4.16	1.16
73.	NAGASAKI	46.4	30.0	32.6	-2.60	0.92
74.	SASEBO	21.8	14.0	15.3	-1.35	0.91
75.	KUMAMOTO	39.6	28.2	27.8	0.40	1.01
76.	YATSUSHIRO	26.0	20.0	18.3	1.77	1.10
77.	OITA	43.6	28.6	30.8	-2.26	0.93
78.	MIYAZAKI	27.0	19.2	19.0	0.21	1.01
79.	NOBEOKA	15.1	10.4	10.6	-0.18	0.98
80.	KAGOSHIMA	46.0	26.5	32.3	-5.86	0.82

REGIONAL TOTALS

1.	HOKKAIDO	65.6	45.9	46.1	-0.27	0.99
2.	TOHOKU	407.4	304.6	286.5	18.12	1.06
3.	KANTO	1131.4	788.7	795.5	-6.81	0.99
4.	TOKAI	782.0	553.4	549.9	3.50	1.01
5.	HOKURIKU	569.3	400.4	400.3	0.11	1.00
6.	KINKI	506.4	350.7	356.1	-5.39	0.98
7.	CHUGOKU	577.3	392.7	405.9	-13.23	0.97
8.	SHIKOKU	246.3	170.0	173.2	-3.21	0.98
9.	KYUSHU	559.6	400.7	393.5	7.20	1.02

TABLE 3

Secondary Employment

		1. ACTUAL 1960	2. ACTUAL 1970	3. EXPECTED 1970	4. SHIFT FACTOR (2-3)	5. SHIFT INDEX
1.	SAPPORO	96.7	163.6	136.6	26.93	1.20
2.	HAKODATE	34.3	40.2	48.5	-8.30	0.83
3.	MURORAN	31.3	37.2	44.2	-7.04	0.84
4.	KUSHIRO	24.4	28.1	34.5	-6.39	0.82
5.	MORIOKA	12.8	19.2	18.1	1.16	1.06
6.	SENDAI	67.9	112.6	96.0	16.59	1.17
7.	ISHINOMACHI	14.3	19.0	20.2	-1.19	0.94
8.	AKITA	29.9	41.6	42.3	-0.62	0.99
9.	YAMAGATA	34.8	55.3	49.2	6.13	1.12
10.	FUKUSHIMA	29.3	46.9	41.4	5.46	1.13
11.	AIZUWAKAMATSU	12.7	18.8	18.0	0.79	1.04
12.	KORIYAMA	27.3	45.4	38.6	6.75	1.17
13.	MITO	33.0	57.1	46.6	10.46	1.22
14.	HITACHI	70.2	81.8	99.2	-17.36	0.82
15.	UTSUNOMIYA	51.3	95.2	72.5	22.69	1.31
16.	MAEBASHI	31.0	49.3	43.8	5.48	1.12
17.	TAKASAKI	40.4	68.5	57.2	11.35	1.20
18.	KIRYU	38.8	50.2	54.8	-4.67	0.91
19.	KUMAGAYA	27.1	49.2	38.3	10.88	1.28
20.	CHIBA	55.3	138.4	78.2	60.20	1.77
21.	TOKYO	2535.7	3533.6	3584.2	-50.65	0.99
22.	YOKOHAMA	363.8	684.8	514.2	170.63	1.33
23.	HIRATSUKA	25.6	51.0	36.2	14.81	1.41
24.	ODAWARA	37.7	53.3	53.3	-0.00	1.00
25.	NIIGATA	68.9	90.3	97.4	-7.10	0.93
26.	NAGAOKA	28.5	40.2	40.3	-0.13	1.00
27.	TOYAMA	73.2	89.0	103.5	-14.53	0.86
28.	TAKAOKA	51.2	74.4	72.3	2.04	1.03
29.	KANAZAWA	73.3	98.0	103.6	-5.61	0.95
30.	FUKUI	79.7	105.3	112.6	-7.27	0.94
31.	KOFU	41.1	59.0	58.1	0.96	1.02
32.	NAGANO	40.8	65.9	57.7	8.23	1.14
33.	MATSUMOTO	32.7	52.3	46.2	6.05	1.13
34.	GIFU	117.0	178.8	165.3	13.45	1.08
35.	SHIZUOKA	130.8	181.6	184.9	-3.35	0.98
36.	HAMAMATSU	129.7	197.2	183.3	13.93	1.08
37.	NUMAZU	49.9	83.3	70.6	12.73	1.18
38.	NAGOYA	786.3	1015.2	1111.4	-96.23	0.91
39.	TOYOHASHI	61.4	94.0	86.8	7.18	1.08
40.	TOYOTA	60.8	132.4	86.0	46.45	1.54
41.	TSU	34.0	47.2	48.0	-0.78	0.98
42.	YOKKAICHI	71.4	103.6	100.9	2.66	1.03
43.	ISE	21.8	28.4	30.8	-2.48	0.92
44.	OTSU	46.3	69.9	65.4	4.51	1.07
45.	KYOTO	271.3	350.6	383.5	-32.94	0.91

TABLE 3—(Continued)
Secondary Employment

		1. ACTUAL 1960	2. ACTUAL 1970	3. EXPECTED 1970	4. SHIFT FACTOR (2-3)	5. SHIFT INDEX
46.	OSAKA	1431.2	2088.1	2023.0	65.10	1.03
47.	KOBE	323.7	321.6	457.5	-135.88	0.70
48.	HIMEJI	124.3	175.6	175.7	-0.05	1.00
49.	NARA	21.3	56.7	30.1	6.56	1.22
50.	WAKAYAMA	77.8	104.7	109.9	-5.26	0.95
51.	TOTTORI	15.8	28.3	22.4	5.93	1.27
52.	YONAGO	16.6	24.1	23.5	0.67	1.03
53.	MATSUE	19.7	26.6	26.5	0.16	1.01
54.	OKAYAMA	70.8	103.4	100.1	3.32	1.03
55.	KURASHIKI	70.6	111.4	99.8	11.67	1.12
56.	HIROSHIMA	123.0	185.7	173.9	11.83	1.07
57.	FUKUYAMA	84.6	125.7	119.6	6.02	1.05
58.	SHIMONOSEKI	36.3	43.9	51.3	-7.41	0.86
59.	UBE	41.7	38.2	58.9	-20.71	0.65
60.	YAMAGUCHI	6.6	9.1	9.4	-0.24	0.97
61.	IWAKUNI	27.8	35.2	39.3	-4.12	0.90
62.	TOKUSHIMASHI	53.3	71.9	75.3	-3.38	0.96
63.	TAKAMATSU	62.2	96.2	87.9	8.29	1.09
64.	MATSUYAMA	37.4	53.2	52.9	0.31	1.01
65.	IMABARI	26.2	37.1	37.1	0.06	1.00
66.	NIIHAMA	31.5	38.4	44.5	-6.07	0.86
67.	KOCHI	34.4	46.8	48.6	-1.77	0.96
68.	KITAKYUSHU	244.3	242.6	345.3	-102.71	0.70
69.	FUKUOKA	110.2	161.2	155.7	5.49	1.04
70.	OMUTA	44.3	40.1	62.6	-22.52	0.64
71.	KURUME	44.1	60.5	62.4	-1.87	0.97
72.	SAGA	26.7	29.2	37.8	-8.57	0.77
73.	NAGASAKI	55.5	66.5	78.5	-11.98	0.85
74.	SASEBO	29.5	33.6	41.7	-8.17	0.80
75.	KUMAMOTO	36.6	49.8	51.8	-1.95	0.96
76.	YATSUSHIRO	13.0	15.9	18.4	-2.50	0.86
77.	OITA	38.0	52.2	53.7	-1.47	0.97
78.	MIYAZAKI	11.5	19.4	16.3	3.06	1.19
79.	NOBEOKA	23.5	28.3	33.2	-4.93	0.85
80.	KAGOSHIMA	34.1	49.4	48.2	1.23	1.03

REGIONAL TOTALS

1.	HOKKAIDO	186.7	269.1	263.9	5.20	1.02
2.	TOHOKU	229.0	358.8	323.7	35.07	1.11
3.	KANTO	3351.0	4971.5	4736.7	234.78	1.05
4.	TOKAI	1463.0	2061.6	2068.0	-6.44	1.00
5.	HOKURIKU	448.3	615.3	633.6	-18.31	0.97
6.	KINKI	2295.8	3147.2	3245.2	-97.96	0.97
7.	CHUGOKU	565.9	803.6	799.9	3.75	1.00
8.	SHIKOKU	191.7	271.8	270.9	0.82	1.00
9.	KYUSHU	711.5	848.8	1005.7	-156.89	0.84

TABLE 4

Wholesale and Retail Employment

		1. ACTUAL 1960	2. ACTUAL 1970	3. EXPECTED 1970	4. SHIFT FACTOR (2-3)	5. SHIFT INDEX
1.	SAPPORO	92.2	174.1	143.4	30.74	1.21
2.	HAKODATE	26.3	38.2	40.9	-2.68	0.93
3.	MUROKAN	13.5	22.5	21.0	1.51	1.07
4.	KUSHIRO	14.2	23.7	22.1	1.59	1.07
5.	MORIOKA	16.4	27.1	25.6	1.53	1.06
6.	SENDAI	66.7	112.4	103.8	8.57	1.08
7.	ISHINOMACHI	10.7	13.5	16.6	-3.08	0.81
8.	AKITA	23.5	38.6	36.6	2.02	1.06
9.	YAMAGATA	27.0	38.3	42.0	-3.67	0.91
10.	FUKUSHIMA	21.0	30.0	32.6	-2.57	0.92
11.	AIZUWAKAMATSU	10.6	13.4	16.4	-3.02	0.82
12.	KORIYAMA	20.3	30.8	31.5	-0.70	0.98
13.	MITO	26.1	39.4	40.6	-1.16	0.97
14.	HITACHI	16.3	23.2	25.4	-2.18	0.91
15.	UTSUNOMIYA	40.2	58.2	62.5	-4.27	0.93
16.	MAEBASHI	20.9	32.5	32.5	-0.04	1.00
17.	TAKASAKI	23.5	37.5	36.6	0.91	1.02
18.	KIRYU	12.4	16.2	19.3	-3.10	0.84
19.	KUMAGAYA	16.1	24.9	25.1	-0.19	0.99
20.	CHIBA	33.2	72.4	51.6	20.79	1.40
21.	TOKYO	1344.8	2099.2	2091.2	7.99	1.00
22.	YOKOHAMA	174.9	317.5	271.9	45.54	1.17
23.	HIRATSUKA	11.6	20.5	18.0	2.50	1.14
24.	ODAWARA	16.5	49.0	25.6	23.31	1.91
25.	NIIGATA	53.2	60.5	82.8	-2.24	0.97
26.	NAGAOKA	17.8	25.6	27.8	-2.14	0.92
27.	TOYAMA	39.0	52.1	60.6	-8.46	0.86
28.	TAKAOKA	26.8	34.3	41.6	-7.34	0.82
29.	KANAZAWA	40.4	61.5	62.8	-1.33	0.98
30.	FUKUI	36.6	49.0	56.9	-7.93	0.86
31.	KOFU	29.2	39.3	45.5	-6.18	0.86
32.	NAGANO	29.2	40.5	45.4	-4.91	0.89
33.	MATSUMOTO	21.1	31.1	32.8	-1.78	0.95
34.	GIFU	52.9	77.2	82.2	-5.03	0.94
35.	SHIZUOKA	66.3	102.9	103.1	-0.23	1.00
36.	HAMAMATSU	52.5	74.8	81.6	-6.80	0.92
37.	NUMAZU	25.5	42.1	39.7	2.39	1.06
38.	NAGOYA	292.5	479.1	454.9	24.23	1.05
39.	TOYOHASHI	30.1	44.0	46.8	-2.79	0.94
40.	TOYOTA	19.7	34.5	30.7	3.82	1.12
41.	TSU	22.1	29.3	34.4	-5.12	0.85
42.	YOKKAICHI	24.0	36.0	37.3	-1.20	0.97
43.	ISE	12.4	16.5	19.2	-2.70	0.86
44.	OTSU	19.6	30.3	30.5	-0.17	0.99
45.	KYOTO	153.8	219.7	239.1	-19.46	0.92

TABLE 4—(Continued)

Wholesale and Retail Employment

		1. ACTUAL 1960	2. ACTUAL 1970	3. EXPECTED 1970	4. SHIFT FACTOR (2-3)	5. SHIFT INDEX
46.	OSAKA	658.1	1096.1	1023.3	72.79	1.07
47.	KOBE	138.3	188.4	215.0	-26.57	0.88
48.	HIMEJI	45.4	67.6	70.6	-3.01	0.96
49.	NARA	15.8	28.1	24.5	3.61	1.15
50.	WAKAYAMA	38.0	54.1	59.1	-4.93	0.92
51.	TOTTORI	12.8	16.8	19.9	-3.07	0.85
52.	YONAGO	13.2	19.1	20.5	-1.45	0.93
53.	MATSUE	16.3	23.3	25.4	-2.02	0.92
54.	OKAYAMA	46.6	71.4	72.5	-1.07	0.99
55.	KURASHIKI	20.8	32.0	32.4	-0.37	0.99
56.	HIROSHIMA	69.0	122.6	107.3	15.31	1.14
57.	FUKUYAMA	35.3	52.1	54.9	-2.80	0.95
58.	SHIMONOSEKI	27.5	32.8	42.7	-9.94	0.77
59.	UBE	17.5	21.6	27.2	-5.66	0.79
60.	YAMAGUCHI	9.8	12.7	15.3	-2.61	0.83
61.	IWAKUNI	12.0	15.4	18.7	-3.24	0.83
62.	TOKUSHIMASHI	29.9	43.2	46.4	-3.27	0.93
63.	TAKAMATSU	36.8	62.4	57.3	5.09	1.09
64.	MATSUYAMA	28.6	44.1	44.5	-0.44	0.99
65.	IMABARI	11.8	15.5	18.3	-2.81	0.85
66.	NIIHAMA	11.2	15.4	17.4	-2.01	0.88
67.	KOCHI	30.3	45.0	47.2	-2.17	0.95
68.	KITAKYUSHU	115.3	144.3	179.4	-35.04	0.80
69.	FUKUOKA	101.4	171.1	157.7	13.43	1.09
70.	OMUTA	18.6	22.4	28.9	-6.45	0.78
71.	KURUME	34.1	43.7	53.0	-9.30	0.82
72.	SAGA	21.3	21.1	33.1	-11.97	0.64
73.	NAGASAKI	40.6	57.2	63.2	-6.01	0.90
74.	SASEBO	26.2	31.1	40.8	-9.71	0.76
75.	KUMAMOTO	45.9	63.6	71.3	-7.70	0.89
76.	YATSUSHIRO	11.2	13.3	17.4	-4.10	0.76
77.	OITA	32.7	48.8	50.8	-2.01	0.96
78.	MIYAZAKI	17.8	29.1	27.7	1.39	1.05
79.	NOBEOKA	10.0	13.8	15.5	-1.73	0.89
80.	KAGOSHIMA	38.1	54.1	59.2	-5.10	0.91

REGIONAL TOTALS

		1. ACTUAL 1960	2. ACTUAL 1970	3. EXPECTED 1970	4. SHIFT FACTOR (2-3)	5. SHIFT INDEX
1.	HOKKAIDO	146.2	258.6	227.4	31.16	1.14
2.	TOHOKU	196.2	304.1	305.0	-0.92	1.00
3.	KANTO	1765.8	2829.8	2745.9	83.92	1.03
4.	TOKAI	598.0	936.5	929.9	6.57	1.01
5.	HOKURIKU	264.1	374.6	410.7	-36.13	0.91
6.	KINKI	1068.8	1684.4	1662.1	22.26	1.01
7.	CHUGOKU	310.7	463.0	483.2	-20.19	0.96
8.	SHIKOKU	118.8	182.3	184.7	-2.34	0.99
9.	KYUSHU	513.1	713.6	797.9	-84.29	0.89

TABLE 5

Service Employment

		1. ACTUAL 1960	2. ACTUAL 1970	3. EXPECTED 1970	4. SHIFT FACTOR (2-3)	5. SHIFT INDEX
1.	SAPPORO	64.3	123.1	96.7	26.43	1.27
2.	HAKODATE	18.8	29.8	28.3	1.50	1.05
3.	MURORAN	12.4	19.3	18.6	0.69	1.04
4.	KUSHIRO	8.8	16.5	13.3	3.26	1.25
5.	MORIOKA	14.2	24.0	21.4	2.68	1.13
6.	SENDAI	49.9	81.5	75.0	6.48	1.09
7.	ISHINOMACHI	6.2	8.8	9.3	-0.51	0.95
8.	AKITA	19.6	31.4	29.5	1.98	1.07
9.	YAMAGATA	21.3	31.0	32.1	-1.03	0.97
10.	FUKUSHIMA	18.3	27.2	27.5	-0.32	0.99
11.	AIZUWAKAMATSU	7.8	10.5	11.7	-1.18	0.90
12.	KORIYAMA	15.3	23.3	23.0	0.31	1.01
13.	MITO	20.0	32.3	30.0	2.26	1.08
14.	HITACHI	15.0	21.2	22.6	-1.39	0.94
15.	UTSUNOMIYA	26.2	40.9	39.5	1.42	1.04
16.	MAEBASHI	16.5	25.8	24.8	0.99	1.04
17.	TAKASAKI	16.1	25.0	24.2	0.77	1.03
18.	KIRYU	7.8	10.6	11.8	-1.23	0.90
19.	KUMAGAYA	11.3	16.8	17.0	-0.18	0.99
20.	CHIBA	26.5	56.9	39.9	16.98	1.43
21.	TOKYO	957.3	1466.8	1440.1	26.70	1.02
22.	YOKOHAMA	147.3	253.8	221.5	32.29	1.15
23.	HIRATSUKA	9.3	16.6	13.9	2.62	1.19
24.	ODAWARA	20.6	28.9	31.0	-2.02	0.93
25.	NIIGATA	36.3	58.9	54.6	4.25	1.08
26.	NAGAOKA	11.3	17.0	17.0	-0.05	1.00
27.	TOYAMA	25.0	37.7	37.7	0.04	1.00
28.	TAKAOKA	18.4	25.6	27.7	-2.05	0.93
29.	KANAZAWA	30.1	46.2	45.2	0.97	1.02
30.	FUKUI	25.5	38.1	38.4	-0.28	0.99
31.	KOFU	20.6	28.9	31.0	-2.10	0.93
32.	NAGANO	21.6	31.9	32.5	-0.62	0.98
33.	MATSUMOTO	16.1	23.1	24.3	-1.15	0.95
34.	GIFU	34.2	52.1	51.4	0.71	1.01
35.	SHIZUOKA	42.4	64.8	63.8	1.00	1.02
36.	HAMAMATSU	35.6	53.9	53.6	0.39	1.01
37.	NUMAZU	18.6	30.2	27.9	2.22	1.08
38.	NAGOYA	167.7	282.4	252.2	30.21	1.12
39.	TOYOHASHI	21.1	32.1	31.8	0.35	1.01
40.	TOYOTA	15.2	27.2	22.9	4.23	1.18
41.	TSU	17.6	25.1	26.5	-1.44	0.95
42.	YOKKAICHI	17.7	27.3	26.7	0.65	1.02
43.	ISE	10.6	15.0	16.0	-1.05	0.93
44.	OTSU	16.8	28.0	25.3	2.68	1.11
45.	KYOTO	220.5	162.3	331.7	-169.42	0.49

TABLE 5—(Continued)
Service Employment

		1. ACTUAL 1960	2. ACTUAL 1970	3. EXPECTED 1970	4. SHIFT FACTOR (2-3)	5. SHIFT INDEX
46.	OSAKA	392.8	635.8	590.9	44.93	1.08
47.	KOBE	85.5	126.0	133.1	-7.12	0.95
48.	HIMEJI	32.0	47.4	48.2	-0.82	0.98
49.	NARA	15.5	27.8	23.3	4.50	1.19
50.	WAKAYAMA	25.9	38.5	38.9	-0.46	0.99
51.	TOTTORI	12.5	17.8	18.8	-1.05	0.94
52.	YONAGO	11.1	17.0	16.7	0.28	1.02
53.	MATSUE	14.5	21.2	21.9	-0.66	0.97
54.	OKAYAMA	34.6	54.3	52.0	2.24	1.04
55.	KURASHIKI	15.6	25.7	23.5	2.17	1.09
56.	HIROSHIMA	50.7	85.6	76.3	9.29	1.12
57.	FUKUYAMA	24.0	36.5	36.1	0.45	1.01
58.	SHIMONOSEKI	19.6	23.7	29.5	-5.81	0.80
59.	UBE	13.0	17.0	19.5	-2.57	0.87
60.	YAMAGUCHI	9.3	12.6	14.0	-1.41	0.90
61.	IWAKUNI	11.1	13.2	16.6	-3.38	0.80
62.	TOKUSHIMASHI	22.3	35.5	33.5	1.97	1.06
63.	TAKAMATSU	32.7	48.8	49.1	-0.34	0.99
64.	MATSUYAMA	22.2	37.1	33.4	3.75	1.11
65.	IMABARI	8.6	11.4	12.9	-1.50	0.88
66.	NIIHAMA	9.5	13.2	14.3	-1.12	0.92
67.	KOCHI	24.7	39.2	37.1	2.02	1.05
68.	KITAKYUSHU	85.0	110.7	127.9	-17.20	0.87
69.	FUKUOKA	71.3	118.9	107.3	11.51	1.11
70.	OMUTA	13.4	16.2	20.2	-1.99	0.90
71.	KURUME	25.9	33.2	38.9	-5.71	0.85
72.	SAGA	15.7	5.9	23.7	-17.73	0.25
73.	NAGASAKI	30.3	44.9	45.5	-0.68	0.99
74.	SASEBO	21.0	24.1	31.5	-7.42	0.76
75.	KUMAMOTO	34.3	51.7	51.6	0.13	1.00
76.	YATSUSHIRO	7.8	9.7	11.7	-2.04	0.83
77.	OITA	29.5	45.9	44.3	1.60	1.04
78.	MIYAZAKI	13.2	24.2	19.9	4.37	1.22
79.	NOBEOKA	7.5	10.5	11.3	-0.77	0.93
80.	KAGOSHIMA	27.0	42.1	40.6	1.47	1.04

REGIONAL TOTALS

1.	HOKKAIDO	104.3	188.8	156.9	31.88	1.20
2.	TOHOKU	152.5	237.8	229.4	8.41	1.04
3.	KANTO	1294.5	2024.4	1947.3	77.10	1.04
4.	TOKAI	380.8	610.1	572.9	37.26	1.07
5.	HOKURIKU	184.4	278.5	277.4	1.13	1.00
6.	KINKI	792.0	1065.7	1191.4	-125.71	0.89
7.	CHUGOKU	238.4	360.1	358.6	1.53	1.00
8.	SHIKOKU	97.6	149.7	146.9	2.81	1.02
9.	KYUSHU	381.8	540.0	574.4	-34.38	0.94

TABLE 6

Government Employment

		1. ACTUAL 1960	2. ACTUAL 1970	3. EXPECTED 1970	4. SHIFT FACTOR (2-3)	5. SHIFT INDEX
1.	SAPPORO	32.5	38.5	44.1	-5.59	0.87
2.	HAKODATE	5.2	7.6	7.1	0.53	1.08
3.	MUROHAN	2.7	3.6	3.7	-0.10	0.97
4.	KUSHIRO	2.7	3.8	3.7	0.15	1.04
5.	MORIOKA	4.2	5.8	5.7	0.12	1.02
6.	SENDAI	22.4	25.1	30.4	-5.24	0.83
7.	ISHINOMACHI	2.6	3.1	3.5	-0.43	0.88
8.	AKITA	7.8	9.1	10.6	-1.53	0.86
9.	YAMAGATA	9.2	9.9	12.5	-2.55	0.80
10.	FUKUSHIMA	6.3	8.2	8.5	-0.30	0.96
11.	AIZUWAKAMATSU	1.3	1.6	1.7	-0.15	0.91
12.	KORIYAMA	4.2	4.9	5.7	-0.80	0.86
13.	MITO	8.2	9.0	11.1	-2.10	0.81
14.	HITACHI	2.5	3.5	3.4	0.13	1.04
15.	UTSUNOMIYA	9.9	11.9	13.4	-1.53	0.89
16.	MAEBASHI	4.9	6.1	6.6	-0.54	0.92
17.	TAKASAKI	4.2	5.3	5.7	-0.48	0.92
18.	KIRYU	1.1	1.3	1.5	-0.17	0.89
19.	KUMAGAYA	4.0	5.6	5.4	0.22	1.04
20.	CHIBA	9.9	17.5	13.4	4.07	1.30
21.	TOKYO	208.9	284.8	283.1	1.72	1.01
22.	YOKOHAMA	42.7	61.6	57.8	3.80	1.07
23.	HIRATSUKA	2.1	3.2	2.8	0.42	1.15
24.	ODAWARA	2.5	3.6	3.4	0.15	1.04
25.	NIIGATA	10.9	14.8	14.7	0.01	1.00
26.	NAGAOKA	2.0	2.4	2.7	-0.33	0.88
27.	TOYAMA	6.3	7.7	8.6	-0.89	0.90
28.	TAKAOKA	3.8	5.1	5.1	-0.05	0.99
29.	KANAZAWA	7.7	9.5	10.5	-1.01	0.90
30.	FUKUI	6.5	8.0	8.8	-0.73	0.92
31.	KOFU	5.6	6.4	7.7	-1.21	0.84
32.	NAGANO	7.5	8.5	10.2	-1.77	0.83
33.	MATSUMOTO	4.0	4.8	5.5	-0.73	0.87
34.	GIFU	11.0	12.3	14.9	-2.60	0.83
35.	SHIZUOKA	9.7	11.5	13.1	-1.60	0.88
36.	HAMAMATSU	10.7	10.7	14.5	-3.85	0.74
37.	NUMAZU	6.7	9.1	9.1	-0.05	0.99
38.	NAGOYA	35.5	47.0	48.1	-1.14	0.98
39.	TOYOHASHI	5.8	6.4	7.8	-1.40	0.82
40.	TOYOTA	3.2	4.8	4.3	0.52	1.12
41.	TSU	5.8	7.9	7.9	0.04	1.01
42.	YOKKAICHI	3.5	4.6	4.8	-0.22	0.95
43.	ISE	2.2	2.7	3.0	-0.31	0.90
44.	OTSU	6.1	7.6	8.2	-0.65	0.92
45.	KYOTO	22.7	27.4	30.8	-3.39	0.89

TABLE 6—(Continued)

Government Employment

		1. ACTUAL 1960	2. ACTUAL 1970	3. EXPECTED 1970	4. SHIFT FACTOR (2-3)	5. SHIFT INDEX
46.	OSAKA	76.9	112.0	104.2	7.72	1.07
47.	KOBE	19.6	28.4	26.6	1.77	1.07
48.	HIMEJI	8.5	11.0	11.5	-0.51	0.96
49.	NARA	4.6	6.3	6.3	0.03	1.00
50.	WAKAYAMA	6.9	9.1	9.3	-0.25	0.97
51.	TOTTORI	4.0	4.5	5.5	-0.95	0.83
52.	YONAGO	3.5	5.0	4.8	0.29	1.06
53.	MATSUE	4.7	5.1	6.4	-1.30	0.80
54.	OKAYAMA	9.3	11.7	12.7	-0.98	0.92
55.	KURASHIKI	3.3	4.3	4.5	-0.21	0.95
56.	HIROSHIMA	18.6	25.5	25.2	0.32	1.01
57.	FUKUYAMA	4.8	5.7	6.4	-0.71	0.89
58.	SHIMONOSEKI	5.2	5.1	7.0	-1.87	0.73
59.	UBE	2.4	2.8	3.3	-0.47	0.86
60.	YAMAGUCHI	6.2	6.0	8.4	-2.42	0.71
61.	IWAKUNI	2.6	2.8	3.5	-0.70	0.80
62.	TOKUSHIMASHI	6.4	9.4	8.6	0.82	1.10
63.	TAKAMATSU	7.1	11.9	9.6	2.24	1.23
64.	MATSUYAMA	6.9	8.9	9.4	-0.51	0.95
65.	IMABARI	1.5	1.8	2.0	-0.18	0.91
66.	NIIHAMA	1.6	2.0	2.2	-0.22	0.90
67.	KOCHI	6.0	8.4	8.1	0.27	1.03
68.	KITAKYUSHU	18.3	27.5	24.7	2.74	1.11
69.	FUKUOKA	16.7	29.6	22.6	7.01	1.31
70.	OMUTA	2.6	7.1	3.5	3.59	2.03
71.	KURUME	8.7	9.8	11.7	-1.95	0.83
72.	SAGA	4.7	26.2	6.4	19.75	4.07
73.	NAGASAKI	8.0	10.5	10.8	-0.29	0.97
74.	SASEBO	9.6	9.3	13.0	-3.69	0.72
75.	KUMAMOTO	13.7	18.6	18.5	0.06	1.00
76.	YATSUSHIRO	1.6	1.9	2.2	-0.24	0.89
77.	OITA	8.6	12.0	11.7	0.32	1.03
78.	MIYAZAKI	4.3	5.8	5.8	-0.06	0.99
79.	NOBEOKA	1.3	2.1	1.8	0.32	1.18
80.	KAGOSHIMA	7.9	12.5	10.7	1.83	1.17

REGIONAL TOTALS

1.	HOKKAIDO	43.2	53.5	58.5	-5.00	0.91
2.	TOHOKU	58.0	67.7	78.6	-10.89	0.86
3.	KANTO	306.5	419.8	415.3	4.48	1.01
4.	TOKAI	94.2	117.0	127.6	-10.60	0.92
5.	HOKURIKU	48.8	60.6	66.1	-5.49	0.92
6.	KINKI	145.3	201.7	196.9	4.73	1.02
7.	CHUGOKU	71.0	88.0	96.2	-8.19	0.91
8.	SHIKOKU	23.1	32.9	31.3	1.59	1.05
9.	KYUSHU	105.9	172.8	143.4	29.39	1.20

References

Berry, B. J. L. (1973a). *Growth Centers in the American Urban System, Vol. 1.* Ballinger Publishing Co., Cambridge, Mass.

Berry, B. J. L. (1973b). The changing scale and nature of American urbanization, in Japan Center for Area Development Research, *Seminar on the International Comparative Study of Megalopolises* (JCADR, Tokyo), Pp. 44–99.

Davis, K. (1969) *World Urbanization 1950–1970: Vol. 1.* University of California Institute of International Studies, Berkeley, California.

Denison, E. F. and W. K. Chung (1976). Economic growth and its sources, in H. Patrick and H. Rosovsky, eds., *Asia's New Giant: How the Japanese Economy Works.* The Brookings Institution, Washington, D.C. Pp. 63–151.

Drewett, R., J. Goddard and N. Spence (1975). What's happening to British cities? *Town and Country Planning, 43,* 1–8.

Falk, T. (1976). *Urban Sweden: Changes in the Distribution of Population—the 1960s in Focus.* The Economic Research Institute of the Stockholm School of Economics, Stockholm.

Glickman, N. J. (1976). On the Japanese urban system. *Journal of Regional Science, 16,* 317–336.

Gottmann, J. (1961). *Megalopolis.* Twentieth Century Fund, New York.

Great Britain Department of the Environment (1976). *British Cities: Urban Population and Employment Trends 1951–71,* Research Report No. 10. Great Britain Department of the Environment, London.

Hall, P., R. Thomas, H. Gracey and R. Drewett (1973a). *The Containment of Urban England.* George Allen and Unwin, London.

Hall, P. (1973b). Urban trends in North-Western Europe 1950–1970: A megalopolis in formation, in Japan Center for Area Development Research, *Seminar on the International Comparative Study of Megalopolises.* (JCADR, Tokyo), Pp. 99–142.

Hay, D. and P. Hall (1977a). *Urban Regionalization of Great Britain, 1971,* University of Reading Department of Geography, European Urban Systems Working Paper I, Part 1. Department of Geography, Reading, England.

Hay, D. and P. Hall (1977b). *Urban Regionalization of Sweden, 1970,* University of Reading Department of Geography, European Urban Systems Working Paper II, Part 1. Department of Geography, Reading, England.

Hay, D. and P. Hall (1977c). *Urban Regionalization of Denmark, 1970,* University of Reading Department of Geography, European Urban Systems Working Paper III, Part 1. Department of Geography, Reading, England.

Hay, D. and P. Hall (1977d). *Urban Regionalization of Norway, 1970,* University of Reading Department of Geography, European Urban Systems Working Paper IV, Part 1, Department of Geography, Reading, England.

Isida, R. (1969). *Geography of Japan.* Kokusai Bunka Shinkokai, Tokyo.

Japan Bureau of Statistics, Office of the Prime Minister (1971). *1970 Population Census of Japan, Vol. 1.* Japan Bureau of Statistics, Office of the Prime Minister, Tokyo.

Japan Center for Area Development Research (1973). *Seminar on the International Comparative Study of Megalopolises* (JCADR, Tokyo).

Kawashima, T. (1977). *Changes in the Spatial Population Structure of Japan,* IIASA Research Memorandum 77-25. Luxenburg, Austria.

Kornhauser, D. (1976). *Urban Japan: Its Foundations and Growth.* Longman, London and New York.

London School of Economics and Political Science (1974–1975) *Urban Change in Britain: 1961–1971,* Department of Geography, Working Reports Nos. 1, 8 and 15. London School of Economics and Political Science, London.

Mickiewicz, E. (1973). *Handbook of Soviet Social Science Data.* Free Press, New York.

Mills, E. S. and K. Ohta (1976). Urbanization and urban problems, in H. Patrick and H. Rosovsky, eds., *Asia's New Giant: How the Japanese Economy Works*. The Brookings Institution, Washington, D.C. Pp. 673–751.

Nagashima, C. (1974). Standard definitions of metropolitan areas and patterns of decentralization with reference to Kanagawa-ken. *Area Development in Japan, 8,* 9–23.

Ödmann, E. and G. B. Dahlberg (1970). *Urbanization in Sweden: Means and Methods of Planning*. National Institute of Building and Urban Planning Research, Stockholm.

Orishima, I. (1973). Land use and land price. *Real Estate Appraisal*.

Patrick, H. and H. Rosovsky (1976). Japan's economic reformance: An overview, in Patrick, H. and H. Rosovsky, eds., *Asia's New Giant: How the Japanese Economy Works*. The Brookings Institution, Washington, D.C. Pp. 1–61.

Sherrill, K. (1976). *Functional Urban Regions in Austria*, IIASA Research Memorandum 76-17. Luxenburg, Austria.

Sherrill, K. (1977). *Functional Urban Regions and Central Place Regions in the Federal Republic of Germany and Switzerland*, IIASA Research Memorandum 77-17. Luxenburg, Austria.

Tanifuji, M. (1977). *Reference Data on Indian Urban Development*. Mimeo.

U.S. Department of Commerce, Bureau of the Census (1975). *Historical Statistics of the United States: Colonial Times to 1970*. U.S. Government Printing Office, Washington, D.C.

Yamaguchi, T. (1969). Japanese cities: Their functions and characteristics. *Papers and Proceedings of the Third Far East Conference of the Regional Science Association, 3,* 141–156.

Growth and Change in the Japanese Urban System: The Experience of the 1970s

1 Introduction

In Chapter 2 (and Glickman, 1976), I outlined the development of the Japanese urban system in the period 1950–1970. There, I defined the Regional Economic Cluster (REC),[1] analogous to the U.S. Standard Metropolitan Statistical Area, as a unit of analysis. There was rapid urbanization and a high spatial concentration of population and economic activity in Japan: Two-thirds of the 1970 population was in 903 cities, towns, and villages that constitute the 80 RECs. Moreover, a full one-half of the population was located in only 33 of the RECs that made up eight Standard Consolidated Areas (SCA).[2] Over time, we found that the system of cities was centralizing: The large, centrally located metropolitan regions were growing at the

---

[1] A REC is defined as a central city with a surrounding commuting field. Central cities with a population of 100,000 or more in 1970, net in-commuting during the work day, and a substantially urban character were selected. The satellite cities, towns, and villages were related to the central city via commuting patterns: 500 workers, or a least 5% of total employment, must commute daily. Also, the suburban cities had to have urban character as well. For further details see Chapter 2, Section 2. For another use of this data set see Kawashima (1977). Please note that, owing to some boundary changes, there are some minor differences in the data in the following tables and those in Chapter 2.

[2] The SCAs are defined as three or more contiguous RECs.

expense of the smaller, more peripheral ones. This rapid urbanization and highly centralized urban system was accentuated by rapid economic growth and the spatial concentration of public investment in the Tokaido megalopolis; see Patrick and Rosovsky (1976) and Chapter 6. Thus, there was heavy growth near Tokyo, Osaka, and Nagoya (particularly their suburban areas such as Chiba, Hiratsuka, and Yokohama) as well as some independent growth in the area surrounding Sapporo and near Sendai.

Furthermore, when compared to other developed capitalist countries, there was relatively little metropolitan decentralization between 1950 and 1970. For instance, the percentage of the REC population living in central cities declined only from 55.0 to 54.8 over that 20-year period; it actually increased (denoting relative metropolitan centralization) during the 1950s. These patterns are different from those in North America and Western Europe, where population concentration was much less and there was considerable systemic and metropolitan decentralization. Finally, Japan's important growth regions were manufacturing-oriented, rather than service-based as in the United States and elsewhere.

Mera (1976) and Vining and Kontuly (1976), among others, have examined migration data and have found evidence of low in-migration to the major metropolitan centers during the 1970s. There has also been considerable discussion in Japan of what has been called the "U-turn phenomenon." It has been seen that many people have migrated from rural areas to large metropolitan centers and then have return-migrated to areas near their home cities ("U-turn").[3] Most of the U-turners are young (20–29 years old), according to Kuroda (1977). Economic, social and "quality of life" reasons are commonly given as explanations of these trends.

Does this mean that there has been a changing pattern of urbanization within Japan in the 1970s? Has there been significant development in smaller regions at the expense of the larger ones? Has Japan moved into a stage of urban growth in which decentralization of both the urban system and individual regions is paramount?

In Chapter 2 it was argued that some of these questions might be answered with the publication of the 1975 population census. The preliminary count of that census (Japan Bureau of Statistics, Office of the Prime Minister, 1975b) has been released, and this chapter presents some highlights of that enumeration as well as an examination of the intercensal migration data. Following a presentation of the census data in Section 2, an examination of the migration data is offered in Section 3. Japan's interregional migration is compared to that of other countries in Section 4. Section 5 presents some concluding remarks.

---

[3] For additional discussion of Japanese migration, see Chapter 4 and Glickman and McHone (1977).

2 Growth and Change in the Japanese Urban System, 1970–1975

2.1 Aggregative Growth for Regional Economic Clusters and Standard Consolidated Areas

Using the REC and SCA concepts of Japanese city-regions, I collected data for the 903 cities, towns, and villages that make up the RECs for 1975. The data for this enumeration are summarized in Table 3.1, where aggregates and comparisons between 1970 and 1975 are made. According to the census figures, overall population growth for Japan was 6.926%, from 104.7 million to 111.9 million persons from 1970 to 1975. However, this growth was highly concentrated in the 80 RECs and 8 SCAs. Of the 7.2-million-person increase in population in Japan, 6.2 million (86.1%) was accounted for by the RECs and 4.6 million (63.9%) by the SCAs. In the more than 2,000 cities, towns, and villages in Japan that were not part of the RECs, population increased by only 1 million persons, or only 13.9% of all population growth. Thus, REC and SCA growth rates were 8.705 and 8.716%, respectively, for 1970–1975, both considerably faster than the national rate of increase. Non-REC areas grew by only 3.264% over the period. As a result of these differential growth rates, the REC share in total population increased from 67.30 to 68.42%. Also, if one examines the three major metropolitan areas—Tokyo, Osaka, and Nagoya—their combined growth

TABLE 3.1

Growth of Regional Economic Clusters, Standard Consolidated Regions, and All Japan, 1970–1975[a]

Area	Population (millions)		Percent change 1970–1975
	1975	1970	
All Japan	111.9	104.7	6.926
All Regional Economic Clusters	76.6	70.4	8.705
All Standard Consolidated Areas	57.9	53.3	8.716
Tokyo, Nagoya, and Osaka SCAs	48.0	44.2	8.659
All Non-REC Japan	35.3	34.2	3.264
RECs as percentage of all Japan	68.42	67.30	—
SCAs as percentage of all Japan	51.73	50.89	—
SCAs as percentage of RECs	75.61	75.63	—
Tokyo, Nagoya, and Osaka SCAs as percentage of all RECs	62.89	62.73	—

[a] Percentages are calculated on the basis of unrounded data and may not agree with data in Table 3.1 if calculations made with Table 3.1's rounded data are employed.

was 8.659%, a very high rate for such large and congested areas.[4] Finally, there is some indication of greater growth in the non-SCA RECs than those in the SCAs. The former grew by 9.357% and the ratio of SCA to REC population fell slightly over the period.

This means that the Japanese urban system continued to centralize during the early 1970s, as there was increased concentration in a relatively small number of metropolitan regions—despite the U-turn movement. Thus, to a certain extent, the experience of the 1950s and 1960s continued. I shall discuss this in more detail in what follows.

2.2 The Growth of Individual RECs

Table 3.2 presents data for the 80 individual RECs, which shows the 1975 population, the percent change in population between 1970 and 1975 for each REC and its component central city, the average annual growth rates for the 1960s and the 1970s, and the 1970–1975 "shift index."[5] The total REC population in 1975 was 76.6 million, compared to 70.4 million in 1970; this growth, as noted previously, was 8.705%, which must be compared to the central city growth of 6.794%. Thus, for the RECs taken as a whole, there was relative metropolitan decentralization since suburban growth (11.010%) exceeded that of central cities. Central city population was 54.7% of the REC population in 1970, but fell to 53.7% in 1975. This is a continuation of the slight amount of decentralization that occurred in the 1960s.[6]

Table 3.2 also shows that there was a decline in the REC growth rates from 2.177% per year in the 1960s to 1.683% per year in the 1970s. But even though the REC growth rate fell, it was still much higher than the 1970–1975 growth rate for all of Japan, the latter being 1.352% per year.[7]

The most rapid growth of the RECs occurred in the regions near the major metropolitan centers. For instance, if we look at the shift indices (which compare the growth of each region with that of all RECs as shown in Column 5 of Table 3.2) we see that indices of greater than 1.05, that is, relatively fast growth, are recorded for the Tokyo suburbs of Chiba, Yokohama, and Hiratsuka, the Nagoya suburb of Toyota, and Otsu and Nara near Kyoto. As was the case in the 1960s, there were several indepen-

---

[4] These three SCAs had a total population of 48 million people, nearly 63% of all those in Japanese RECs and 43% of all in Japan.

[5] The shift index indicates the relative growth of a region with respect to all RECs. An index value of 1.0 shows the same growth as all RECs, a value below 1.0 indicates slower growth; see Chapter 2, Section 4.2.

[6] I shall return to a discussion of decentralization in the discussion of Table 3.4 (Section 2.4). As will be seen, the composition of spatial development holds some interesting conclusions.

[7] The declining growth rate was largely a reflection of the relative decline of the largest cities. A comparison of the unweighted interdecade growth rates by population shows an increase over time (1.150%/year for 1960–1970 to 1.620%/year for 1970–1975). It also reflects a declining national growth rate of the population in general.

TABLE 3.2
Population of RECs, REC and Central City Growth Rates, and Shift Index, 1960–1975

City	REC population (thousands) 1975 (1)	Percent change REC population 1970–1975 (2)	Percent change central city population 1970–1975 (3)	Average annual growth rates of REC population (4)		Shift index 1970–1975 (5)
				1960–1970	1970–1975	
Sapporo	1,542.5	39.166	22.807	4.002	6.833	1.28
Hakodate	353.3	5.798	5.165	.670	1.130	.97
Muroran	242.9	2.016	-2.097	1.699	.400	.94
Kushiro	221.6	6.847	7.712	1.927	1.333	.98
Morioka	237.7	11.754	10.306	2.156	2.247	1.03
Sendai	1,113.4	14.136	12.915	1.874	2.680	1.07
Ishinomaki	154.2	6.492	7.875	.883	1.266	.98
Akita	408.4	6.604	10.725	.594	1.287	.98
Yamagata	410.1	4.778	7.692	.213	.938	.96
Fukushima	347.2	6.177	8.352	.635	1.206	.98
Aizuwakamatsu	124.4	3.151	4.419	.116	.622	.95
Koriyama	356.6	7.184	9.475	.734	1.397	.99
Mito	459.0	10.923	13.924	1.432	2.095	1.02
Hitachi	348.3	3.939	4.762	.523	.776	.96
Utsunomiya	650.5	11.482	14.343	1.183	2.198	1.03
Maebashi	326.5	6.874	7.106	1.401	1.338	.98
Takasaki	424.8	8.533	9.425	1.030	1.651	1.00
Kiryu	169.1	4.190	.083	.831	.824	.96
Kumagaya	296.0	9.833	8.858	1.098	1.894	1.01
Chiba	1,051.9	28.909	36.416	4.617	5.211	1.19
Tokyo	18,503.9	4.474	-2.241	3.062	.879	.96
Yokohama	3,931.0	18.268	17.124	4.815	3.413	1.09
Hiratsuka	279.1	19.019	19.486	4.175	3.544	1.09
Odawara	302.5	6.627	6.051	1.965	1.292	.98

(Table 3.2 Continues on page 126)

TABLE 3.2 (Continued)
Population of RECs, REC and Central City Growth Rates, and Shift Index, 1960–1975

City	REC population (thousands) 1975 (1)	Percent change REC population 1970–1975 (2)	Percent change central city population 1970–1975 (3)	Average annual growth rates of REC (4)		Shift index 1970–1975 (5)
				1960–1970	1970–1975	
Niigata	740.8	7.114	10.237	.867	1.384	.99
Nagaoka	233.0	3.971	5.792	.520	.782	.96
Toyama	522.4	5.856	7.724	.324	1.146	.97
Takaoka	376.2	-3.323	6.199	-.094	.656	.95
Kanazawa	565.1	4.571	-.058	1.130	.898	.96
Fukui	532.7	-6.625	7.578	.294	1.291	.98
Kofu	401.8	6.324	6.130	.475	1.234	.98
Nagano	443.8	7.823	7.428	.739	1.518	.99
Matsumoto	315.6	7.274	6.057	.712	1.414	.99
Gifu	821.5	9.592	5.963	1.905	1.849	1.01
Shizuoka	993.4	7.094	7.349	1.569	1.380	.99
Hamamatsu	891.9	7.796	8.491	1.072	1.513	.99
Numazu	468.5	11.151	5.450	2.451	2.137	1.02
Nagoya	4,641.6	12.589	2.141	2.351	2.400	1.04
Toyohashi	489.9	10.080	9.745	-.153	1.877	1.01
Toyota	525.9	18.153	26.166	3.645	3.392	1.09
Tsu	339.0	8.619	6.897	.701	1.667	1.00
Yokkaichi	500.2	10.322	7.766	1.665	1.984	1.01
Ise	183.7	2.856	1.351	.262	.564	.95
Otsu	424.4	19.180	11.467	1.656	3.572	1.10
Kyoto	1,984.8	9.694	2.952	1.818	1.868	1.01
Osaka	10,252.2	7.972	-6.761	3.424	1.546	.99
Kobe	1,908.2	9.645	5.555	1.904	1.859	1.01
Himeji	838.7	7.141	6.783	1.382	1.389	.99
Nara	341.3	19.881	23.620	3.338	3.693	1.10

Wakayama	589.1	4.617	6.704	1.564	.907	.96
Kurashiki	480.2	14.743	10.741	2.185	2.789	1.06
Tottori	205.0	3.015	8.039	-.283	.596	.95
Yonago	197.8	6.173	8.433	.256	1.205	.98
Matsue	236.7	3.861	7.692	.075	.761	.96
Okayama	719.9	12.169	11.468	1.048	2.323	1.03
Hiroshima	1,196.1	16.613	57.306	2.949	3.122	1.07
Fukuyama	605.0	11.030	29.283	1.364	2.115	1.02
Shimonoseki	336.8	2.433	3.173	-.093	.482	.94
Ube	221.9	5.017	5.952	-1.355	.984	.97
Yamaguchi	123.3	5.295	4.950	-.015	1.037	.97
Iwakuni	181.5	4.071	4.713	.372	.801	.96
Tokushima	472.7	6.225	7.069	.363	1.215	.98
Takamatsu	647.7	7.431	8.965	.390	1.444	.99
Matsuyama	482.5	12.602	13.812	1.511	2.402	1.04
Imabari	182.1	6.367	7.201	.433	1.242	.98
Niihama	200.7	3.882	4.524	-.207	.765	.96
Kochi	399.2	10.368	13.260	1.226	1.993	1.02
Kitakyushu	1,554.3	3.510	1.516	-.112	.692	.95
Fukuoka	1,540.5	16.317	14.971	2.217	3.069	1.07
Omuta	258.4	-1.861	-5.197	-1.542	-.375	.90
Kurume	453.3	2.233	5.304	-.127	.443	.94
Saga	263.1	2.693	6.132	-.411	.533	.94
Nagasaki	592.0	8.544	5.507	.742	1.653	1.00
Sasebo	275.6	1.212	1.129	-.868	.241	.93
Kumamoto	568.6	10.151	8.636	1.316	1.952	1.01
Yatsushiro	140.1	-.497	1.766	-.768	-.010	.92
Oita	514.2	15.059	22.870	1.472	2.845	1.06
Miyazaki	257.0	15.454	15.475	1.821	2.916	1.06
Nobeoka	151.2	5.146	4.832	.394	1.009	.97
Kagoshima	527.6	12.423	13.266	1.486	2.370	1.03
All RECs	76567.1	8.705	6.794	2.177	1.683	1.00

dent urban growth centers such a Sapporo, Sendai, Miyazaki, and Hiroshima. Note that there was rapid growth only for relatively few regions. Shift indices of greater than 1.05 are recorded only for the RECs noted previously and for Kurashiki and Fukuoka. All but Sapporo, Sendai, and the three RECs in Kyushu (Fukuoka, Oita, and Miyazaki) are in or near the Tokaido belt.

If one looks at the RECs that had shift indices between 1.00 and 1.05, about half are in the spheres of Tokyo, Nagoya, and Osaka. However, there is considerable growth among five RECs in Tohoku (in northern Honshu) such as Sendai, Morioka, and Utsunomiya. This is probably a result of the spillover of population and industry from the Tokyo region. There is also some substantial growth among certain RECs in Shikoku (Matsuyama and Kochi) and in Kyushu (Nagasaki, Kumamoto, and Kagoshima). Thus, there is evidence of some growth of regions away from the metropolitan core. This is a somewhat different pattern when compared to previous decades. However, most of the regions that grew relatively slowly (those with shift indices of less than 1.00) were situated away from the major metropolitan areas: the other RECs in Tohoku, those bordering on the Japan Sea, and those in Kyushu.[8]

A detailed examination of Column 4 of Table 3.2 also reveals that 63 of the 80 RECs had higher growth rates during the 1970s than they did in the 1960s. Of the 17 RECs with declining growth rates, several were large metropolitan centers (for instance, Tokyo, Osaka, and Kobe[9]), independent centers such as Sapporo and Shizuoka, and suburban regions such as Yokohama, Hiratsuka, and Toyota. But, overall, the group with declining growth rates is dominated by large central RECs.

There was some considerable convergence toward the mean growth rate for the group of urban regions. Fifty-nine cities with growth rates below the average for 1960–1970 had faster growth during 1970–1975; seven additional cities with faster-than-average growth in the earlier period had declining rates in the 1970s. (These were principally some suburban regions around major centers.) There were only 15 regions that showed polarizing effects: 7 fast-growing regions in the 1960s grew even faster in the 1970s, and 8 with slow growth in the 1960s grew even more slowly in the 1970s. The "fast-getting-faster" group (Chiba, Nagoya, Nara, Kurashiki, Hiroshima, Fukuoka, and Sapporo) was a mixture of large centers and suburbs. The 8 regions that diverged from the mean in a negative way were generally at the periphery of the Japanese urban system.[10]

---

[8] Table 3.2 shows relatively little growth for such regions as Muroran, Aizuwakamatsu, Takaoka, Ise, Tottori, Shimonoseki, Kitakyushu, Kurume, and Sasebo. In addition, the RECs of Omuta and Yatsushiro, both in Kyushu, were the only RECs that lost population absolutely.

[9] Tokyo and Osaka grew at rates above the mean for all RECs in the 1960s but below the mean in the 1970s.

[10] These were Muroran, Kushiro, Maebashi, Kiryu, Odawara, Kanazawa, Shizuoka, and Wakayama.

2.3   Regional Growth and Regional Size

The changing relationship between regional growth and region size is presented in Table 3.3 and Figure 3.1. In Table 3.3 the RECs are aggregated into size classes (generally in groups of 100,000) for 1960–1970 and 1970–1975. In the former period, when the average annual growth rate for all RECs was 2.177%, the growth rate for regions with population below 200,000 persons was .176 per annum, only about 6% of the growth rate for the fastest growing category (1,000,000 or more). During the 1960s, the growth rate increased directly with region size. This can be seen from a simple regression relating region population size (*SIZE*) and average annual growth (*AAG*) using grouped data that is given in Eq. (1).

$$AAG = .9189 + \underset{(3.1021)}{.4657\ SIZE} \qquad R^2 = .5462 \qquad (1)$$

where both the *t*-test (given in parentheses) for the *SIZE* variable and the *F*-test for the correlation coefficient are significant at a 95% confidence level.

The 1970s showed a somewhat different pattern between region size and region growth, however. The smaller regions had relatively higher growth rates vis-à-vis the larger ones. For instance, those with populations below 200,000 grew by .862% per year, nearly five times their 1960s' figures and 49% of the growth rate of the largest size class. The fastest growing group in the 1970s was that in the 600,000–700,000 range. Moreover, the relationship between region size and growth is clearly weaker. This mixed pattern with respect to region size is shown in the Eq. (2), where the *SIZE* variable and the correlation coefficient are statistically insignificant at a 95% confidence interval.

$$AAG = 1.4663 + \underset{(.9299)}{.7857\ SIZE} \qquad R^2 = .1008 \qquad (2)$$

Table 3.3 and Figure 3.1 indicate that growth increased with region size up to about 600,000–700,000 population. But for larger regions, the relationship was erratic, falling for the size classes up to 1,000,000 and then rising for the largest class.

I shall return to the consideration of the relationship between region size and regional growth in Chapter 8.

2.4   Metropolitan Decentralization

Some interesting trends are also evident with respect to metropolitan decentralization when viewed from a perspective of region size as shown in Table 3.4. Note that for regions with population of less than 800,000 persons, the central cities were growing faster than the suburbs during the 1970s. Therefore, there was relative centralization of those regions during that period. It is for the larger regions, with the exception of the size class of

TABLE 3.3
Average Annual Growth Rate of Population by Size of Region, 1960–1975

Size of region (in thousands)	Growth rate	
	1960–1970	1970–1975
0–200	.177	.862
201–300	.878	1.118
301–400	.641	1.403
401–500	1.092	1.783
501–600	1.214	1.804
601–700	.775	1.911
701–800	1.634	1.840
801–900	2.665	1.579
901–1 million	1.723	1.380
1 million or more	2.954	1.753
All RECs	2.177	1.683

900,000–1,000,000, that relative decentralization took place. Thus, the slight amount of decentralization noted with respect to my discussion of Table 3.2 must be qualified to indicate that the smaller regions centralized while the larger regions decentralized. It must be remembered that 63 of the 80 RECs in Japan encountered relative centralization during the 1970s as the central cities grew faster than their suburbs.

It is also important to observe closely the development of the SCAs during the 1970s, as shown in Table 3.5. There are eight such agglomerations with a 1975 total population of 57.9 million. If we look at the individual SCAs, we see that Tokyo with 24.8 million people and Osaka (16.3 million people) are the largest, but these two SCAs are growing at the SCA average or below. The overall growth of the SCAs was 8.716% for 1970–1975, but there was a wide variation of SCA growth rates. The fastest growing SCAs, Nagoya (12.256% growth) and Okayama (12.453% growth) were in or near the Tokaido region but were not the two major centers of that belt, Tokyo and Osaka. The slowest-growing SCAs were Kanazawa (4.707%), which is on the Japan Sea, followed by the older regions of Tokyo, Kitakyushu, and Osaka.

The spatial pattern of urban development can be seen from Table 3.5. If we examine the group of SCAs, we see that there was little growth within the central RECs and fast growth in the outlying RECs. For instance, within the Tokyo SCA, the Tokyo REC grew by 4.5%, but Chiba (28.9% growth), Hiratsuka (19.1%), and Yokohama (18.3%) grew much faster. For Osaka, there was a similar pattern since the Osaka REC had a population increase of less than 8%, whereas Otsu and Nara grew by over 19%. Within both large SCAs one can see an interesting pattern of growth. The central RECs

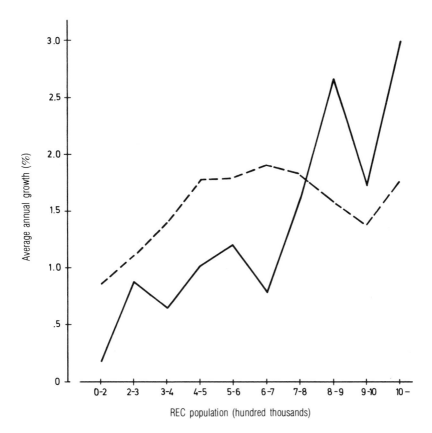

Figure 3.1. Average annual growth rates of RECs by region size, 1960–1970 (——) and 1970–1975 (– – –).

(Tokyo and Osaka) and the outer RECs (Odawara, Numazu, Kumagaya, Wakayama, and Himeji) grew more slowly than the ''middle'' layer of the RECs (e.g., Chiba, Yokohama, Hiratska, and Nara).[11]

Table 3.6 shows some of the ''layers'' of spatial development within the SCAs. There, the central REC is broken out by its own central city, the rest of the REC, and the remaining portions of the SCA. For Tokyo and Osaka (as well as Kanazawa) there was an absolute population loss within the central cities of the RECs. Osaka, for instance, lost nearly 7% of its population between 1970 and 1975. In Tokyo, we find the rest of the REC (the noncentral city portion) growing quickly (11.2%), but the remainder of the

---

[11] This is also true of Nagoya where far away Tsu is the slowest growing REC, and nearby Toyota is the fastest growing.

TABLE 3.4
Regional Population Growth and Decentralization by Size of Region, 1970–1975

Population in region (in thousands)	Percent change in population, 1970–1975		Central city share of regional population	
	Region	Central city	1975	1970
0–200	4.383	4.643	.719	.718
201–300	6.083	6.611	.718	.704
301–400	7.219	8.393	.662	.660
401–500	9.237	9.389	.563	.562
501–600	9.349	9.577	.640	.639
601–700	9.929	17.154	.511	.480
701–800	9.547	10.919	.641	.633
801–900	8.149	7.127	.515	.520
901–1,000	7.094	7.349	.450	.449
1,000 or more	9.086	4.616	.497	.518
All RECs	8.685	6.794	.539	.548

TABLE 3.5
Population and Population Growth of Standard Consolidated Areas, 1970–1975 (in thousands)

SCA and component RECs	1975 Population	1970 Population	Percent change 1970–1975
Sendai SCA			
Sendai REC	1113.4	975.5	14.136
Yamagata REC	410.1	391.4	4.778
Fukushima REC	347.2	327.0	6.177
Koriyama REC	356.6	332.7	7.184
Total SCA	2227.3	2026.6	9.903
Tokyo SCA			
Tokyo REC	18503.9	17711.5	4.474
Yokohama REC	3931.0	3323.8	18.268
Chiba REC	1051.9	816.0	28.909
Kumagaya REC	296.0	269.5	9.833
Hiratsuka REC	279.1	234.4	19.070
Odawara REC	302.5	283.7	6.627
Numazu REC	468.5	421.5	11.151
Total SCA	24832.9	23060.4	7.686
Kanazawa SCA			
Kanazawa REC	561.1	540.3	4.590
Takaoka REC	376.2	364.1	3.323
Toyama REC	522.4	493.5	5.856
Total SCA	1463.7	1397.9	4.707

TABLE 3.5 (Continued)

SCA and component RECs	1975 Population	1970 Population	Percent change 1970–1975
Nagoya SCA			
Nagoya REC	4641.6	4122.6	12.589
Toyota REC	425.9	445.1	18.153
Gifu REC	821.5	749.6	9.592
Tsu REC	339.0	312.1	8.619
Yokkaichi REC	500.2	453.3	10.346
Total SCA	6828.2	6082.7	12.256
Osaka SCA			
Osaka REC	10252.2	9495.2	7.972
Kyoto REC	1984.8	1809.4	9.694
Kobe REC	1908.7	1740.8	9.645
Himeji REC	838.7	782.8	7.141
Wakayama REC	589.1	563.1	4.617
Otsu REC	424.4	356.1	19.180
Nara REC	341.3	284.7	19.881
Total SCA	16339.2	15032.1	8.695
Okayama SCA			
Okayama REC	719.9	641.8	12.169
Kurashiki REC	480.2	418.5	14.743
Fukuyama REC	605.0	544.9	11.030
Total SCA	1805.1	1605.2	12.453
Matsuyama SCA			
Matsuyama REC	482.5	428.5	12.602
Imabari REC	182.1	171.2	6.367
Niihama REC	200.7	193.2	3.882
Total SCA	865.3	792.9	9.131
Kitakyushu SCA			
Kitakyushu REC	1554.3	1501.6	3.510
Fukuoka REC	1540.5	1324.4	16.317
Kurume REC	453.3	443.4	2.233
Total SCA	3548.1	3269.4	8.524
All SCAs	57909.9	53267.2	8.716

SCA grew even more quickly (18.3%). Thus, there is considerable sprawl from the Tokyo-*ku* area. The fast-growing RECs within the SCA were Chiba, Yokohama, and Hiratsuka. For Osaka, the outward flow was mainly to the rest of the Osaka REC—similarly for Nagoya, Kanazawa, and Okayama. For Matsuyama and, to a lesser extent, Sendai, the central cities of the central RECs grew relatively fast. Therefore, if one observes the major metropolitan areas, one sees far more sprawl from Tokyo than from Osaka and Nagoya. In the outlying SCAs there is much less metropolitan decentralization.

TABLE 3.6

Population Growth Rates among Components of Standard Consolidated Areas, 1970–1975

SCA	Percent change of population, 1970–1975
Sendai SCA	
Sendai-*shi*	12.915
Rest of Sendai REC	15.683
Rest of SCA	5.975
Total SCA	8.724
Tokyo SCA	
Tokyo *ku* area	−2.241
Rest of Tokyo REC	11.166
Rest of SCA	18.323
Total SCA	7.686
Kanazawa SCA	
Kanazawa-*shi*	−.058
Rest of Kanazawa REC	14.972
Rest of SCA	4.781
Total SCA	4.707
Nagoya SCA	
Nagoya-*shi*	2.141
Rest of Nagoya REC	22.785
Rest of SCA	11.556
Total SCA	12.256
Osaka SCA	
Osaka-*shi*	−6.761
Rest of Osaka REC	14.713
Rest of SCA	9.935
Total SCA	8.696
Okayama SCA	
Okayama-*shi*	11.488
Rest of Okayama REC	13.900
Rest of SCA	12.642
Total SCA	12.453
Matsuyama SCA	
Matsuyama-*shi*	13.812
Rest of Matsuyama REC	8.902
Rest of SCA	5.049
Total SCA	9.131
Kitakyushu SCA	
Kitakyushu-*shi*	1.516
Rest of Kitakyushu REC	8.034
Rest of SCA	12.784
Total SCA	8.524

2.5 Conclusions from the Census Data

What conclusions can be drawn from the 1975 Census? First, it can be seen that there was a continuation of relatively rapid population growth of the RECs at the expense of nonmetropolitan areas; a full 86% of all population 1970–1975 growth occurred in the RECs. Second, the highest growth rates among the RECs occurred in the regions adjacent to the largest metropolitan centers. The central regions of the SCAs grew less quickly than the suburban regions, and, in fact, the central cities of Tokyo and Osaka lost population absolutely. Third, there were signs that some less central regions were attaining higher population growth rates. However, the more peripheral regions were the slowest growing of all. Fourth, the fastest growing regions were middle-sized rather than large-sized as in the 1960s. Fifth, although there was metropolitan decentralization for the weighted average of all RECs (i.e., all REC suburbs grew faster than all REC central cities), 63 of 80 RECs—most of the smaller ones, obviously—centralized during the 1970s.

Therefore, the urban development experience of the 1960s is repeated in the 1970s, but with much less clear direction. There is an evening of growth rates between large and small regions, and there are signs of more vibrant independent growth outside of the metropolitan core. Yet nonmetropolitan Japan continued to decline relative to the metropolitan areas, and there was still very low growth at the spatial periphery of the metropolitan group.

3 Migration Trends in Postwar Japan

How can we relate these findings to those based on data for migration among regions? Although there are some problems of strict comparability between our RECs and the prefectural data on migration, it is important to examine the latter to see intercensal movements.

If one aggregates prefectures into the nine major regions as defined by the Economic Planning Agency[12] one obtains an interesting picture of inter-regional migration (Table 3.7). For the metropolitan regions—Kanto, Kinki, and Tokai (the regions surrounding Tokyo, Osaka, and Nagoya, respectively)—there was substantial net in-migration until the 1970s. After peaking at 575,700 in 1962, net in-migration fell rapidly to only 32,200 in 1975. By 1975, Kanto was the only region of the three to maintain positive in-migration. The nonmetropolitan regions (Hokkaido, Tohoku, Hokuriku, Shikoku, Kyushu, and Chugoku) had, of course, a mirror image of the metropolitan migration picture, since there is insignificant foreign migration. Thus, from a trough in 1962, net out-migration decreased significantly,

---

[12] For these definitions, see Chapter 2, Footnote 11.

TABLE 3.7
Annual Net Migration to Japanese Regions, 1954–1975 (in thousands)

	Kanto, Kinki, and Tokai regions[a] (1)	Other regions[b] (2)	Core prefectures[c] (3)	Suburban prefectures[d] (4)	Exurban prefectures[e] (5)	Peripheral prefectures[f] (6)	Prefectures other than core, suburbs, exurbs, and periphery[g] (7)
1954	265.3	−265.3	418.8	−35.1	−118.4	−59.2	−206.1
1955	242.2	−242.2	383.0	−27.3	−113.5	−53.0	−189.2
1956	279.5	−326.8	429.9	−24.4	−126.0	−50.8	−228.7
1957	371.2	−371.2	523.9	−10.7	−142.0	−65.1	−306.1
1958	294.7	−294.7	430.0	−3.6	−131.7	−50.3	−244.4
1959	370.4	−370.4	482.8	16.7	−129.1	−82.7	−287.7
1960	491.9	−491.9	552.3	43.8	−104.1	−121.0	−371.0
1961	572.6	−556.5	594.0	62.4	−83.8	−139.7	−432.9
1962	575.7	−575.7	539.1	112.4	−76.2	−128.1	−447.2
1963	557.1	−557.1	477.0	151.9	−71.8	−138.7	−418.6
1964	521.4	−521.4	421.2	166.0	−65.8	−108.2	−413.2
1965	426.1	−426.1	337.9	158.7	−70.5	−78.6	−347.5

1966	348.9	−348.9	251.0	174.2	−76.3	−61.0	−287.9
1967	374.7	−273.8	229.5	195.4	−50.2	−62.2	−312.5
1968	399.6	−399.6	231.3	208.5	−40.2	−60.2	−339.4
1969	430.5	−430.5	212.5	233.1	−15.1	−60.6	−369.9
1970	427.5	−427.5	147.3	265.0	15.2	−49.2	−378.3
1971	318.7	−318.7	77.4	231.7	9.6	−28.7	−290.0
1972	229.1	−229.1	−11.0	259.5	−19.4	−13.0	−216.1
1973	168.5	−167.5	−105.4	244.3	28.6	−5.8	−161.7
1974	78.2	−78.2	−152.8	202.7	28.3	6.0	− 84.2
1975	32.2	−32.2	−151.6	172.2	11.6	19.6	− 51.8

[a] Tokyo, Kanagawa, Chiba, Saitama, Tochigi, Ibaraki, Gumma, Yamanashi, Nagano, Shiga, Kyoto, Nara, Wakayama, Osaka, Hyogo, Shizuoka, Aichi, Gifu, and Mie prefectures.

[b] Prefectures not included in Column (1); see footnote a.

[c] Tokyo, Osaka, Kyoto, Hyogo, Aichi, and Kanagawa prefectures.

[d] Gifu, Nara, Saitama, and Chiba prefectures.

[e] Gumma, Ibaraki, Tochigi, Shizuoka, Mie, Shiga, Wakayama, Yamanashi, and Nagano prefectures.

[f] Miyagi, Fukushima, Okayama, Hiroshima, Yamaguchi, and Fukuoka prefectures.

[g] Prefectures not included in Columns (3) through (6); see footnotes c–f of this table.

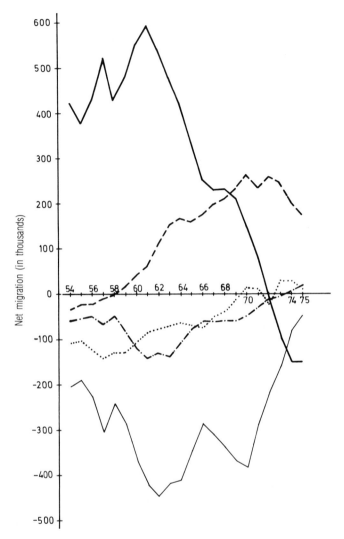

Figure 3.2. Net migration for Japanese regions, 1954–1975. *Key:* (——): Core prefectures; (– – –): Suburban prefectures; (- - -): Exurban prefectures; (– · –): Peripheral prefectures; (——): Other prefectures.

especially in the period after 1970. Still, as late as 1975, all of the nonmetropolitan regions except Kyushu continued to show net out-migration.[13]

Table 3.7 also divides portions of Japan into several categories: "core," "suburban," "exurban," and "periphery" prefectures. The definitions of

[13] See Japan Bureau of Statistics, Office of the Prime Minister (1973, 1975a). Kuroda (1969, 1977) also discusses these issues.

these categories are given in Kornhauser (1976) and summarized in Table 3.7. It is seen that the core prefectures reached their collective peak of in-migration in 1961 (594,000) and declined rapidly thereafter, with net out-migration beginning in 1972. As the core prefectures began to decline in attractiveness for new migrants, the suburban prefectures began to take their place as destinations for interprefectural migrants. Net in-migration to suburban prefectures, negative until 1958, grew significantly until it reached its peak in 1970 (265,000); then decline set in from 1971 to 1975 although net in-migration by 1975 was still strongly positive (172,200). Table 3.7 and Figure 3.2 also show that as suburban net in-migration began to subside in the early 1970s, the exurbs began to grow substantially, first becoming net recipients of migrants in 1970. The peripheral urban regions, which had negative net migration throughout the earlier part of the period, show positive in-migration beginning in 1974. Finally, the remaining prefectures—the most rural in Japan—showed sharply declining amounts of out-migration beginning after 1970, falling from 378,300 (1970) to 51,800 (1975).

Thus, Table 3.7 shows the continuing spread of population movements from the core of the metropolitan centers outward in successive stages to the more peripheral prefectures of Japan.[14] However, Table 3.7 indicates that the metropolitan regions continue to attract migrants from nonmetropolitan areas, albeit fewer in later years than previously. This is a partial explanation for the patterns found in the census data described in Section 2.

Another reason for the higher population growth rates in the metropolitan areas can be found by reference to the relative age structure of the population in metropolitan and nonmetropolitan areas. The in-migrants to the metropolitan areas tend to be concentrated in the prime childbearing ages. As a result, the structure of the metropolitan areas' population is more heavily dominated by those age classes. For instance, although 33.9% of the entire 1974 Japanese population was in the age group 20–39, urbanized areas had much higher percentages: Tokyo had 40.9% of its population in that category, and other urbanized prefectures also had similarly high levels.[15] On the other hand, the more rural prefectures had much lower percentages in the prime childbearing age group: Saga and Iwate had only 27.0 and 29.0%

---

[14] This can also be seen with respect to the Tokyo region. The *ku*-area of Tokyo (Tokyo city) experienced its peak amount of in-migration in 1957; it then had, with the exception of 1964–1965, continuously decreasing amounts of in-migration. By 1967, net in-migration had become negative, peaking at a net out-migration of 172.8 thousand in 1973. (There was less out-migration in 1974 and 1975 than there was in 1973.) The inner ring around Tokyo (Saitama, Chiba, and Kanagawa prefectures) had increasing in-migration until a peak in 1970 (374.7 thousand net in-migrants); thereafter, net in-migration decreased to 194.4 thousand by 1975. The outer ring (Tochigi, Ibaraki, Gumma, Yamanashi, and Nagano prefectures) of Tokyo had net out-migration until 1970, when net in-migration became positive (except for 1972). Thus, here too, the flow of population from the core to the suburbs to the periphery was clear.

[15] For instance, Osaka (38.3%), Chiba (36.5%), and Kanagawa (39.2%).

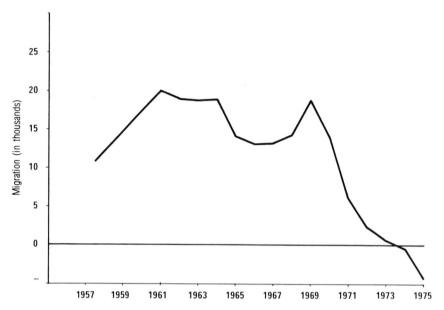

Figure 3.3. Annual net migration in the Swedish Stockholm, western and southern metropolitan regions, 1957–1975.

of their respective populations in the 20–39 age group. This, of course, has led to higher birth rates in the metropolitan regions than in nonmetropolitan regions.[16]

4   Japanese Migration Patterns as Compared to Those of Other Countries

How does the Japanese migration experience compare to other countries? Several authors have written on the subject of population dispersal policies and patterns,[17] and we shall present some interesting data provided by Vining and Kontuly (1976, 1977). They show that Japan's experience was not at all unique. During the late 1960s net migration to the major metropolitan areas of Sweden fell from +18,977 (1969) to −4,379 (1975). Italy's combined Northwest Region and Lazio Province showed sharp declines in net in-migration beginning in 1970. Similarly, Oslo had net out-migration after 1973. These data are presented in Figures 3.3, 3.4, and 3.5, and the

---

[16] Johnson and Vining (1976) show that for the Kanto, Tokai, and Kinki regions the natural increase in population from 1973 to 1974 was 1.42%. However, for the rural regions such as Tohoku (.87%), Shikoku (.77%), and Kyushu (.82%), it was much lower.

[17] For instance, Sundquist (1975).

Figure 3.4. Annual net migration, into the Italian regions in the northwest and Lazio Province, 1957–1974.

reader will likely note the striking similarity to the situation with respect to Japan's core prefectures, shown in Figure 3.2.[18]

Thus, the experience in Japan is not unique. The relative decline of the major metropolitan centers, as noted in Section 3, is repeated in several other industrialized countries at approximately the same time. Section 5 comments on the future of the Japanese urban system.

5 Concluding Remarks

The results from the migration and other demographic data are consistent with the analysis presented in Section 2 of Chapter 2 concerning the relative increase in population in the major metropolitan centers. In-migration, though lower than previously, is positive through 1975 (the last year for which complete data are presently available), and birth rates in these regions are also considerably higher than in the more rural areas. Thus, the metropolitan regions continue to increase their population at the

---

[18] Vining and Kontuly (1976) also note a similar situation for the United States but do not present comparable data. The problems of highly urbanized regions in the Northeast United States, particularly New York City, have been widely discussed; see, for instance, Alcaly and Mermelstein (1977) and Sternlieb and Hughes (1975).

Figure 3.5. Annual net migration into the Ostlandet region of Norway, 1951–1974.

expense of the rural areas. Whether this will continue, in the face of the changing pattern of internal migration, remains to be seen. Should net out-migration accelerate in the highly urbanized areas, then out-migration may be high relative to the natural increase rates there, and such areas will decline not only relatively to the more rural areas, but perhaps even on an absolute basis.

The patterns of the 1970s are a bit closer to those of the United States, the United Kingdom, and other Western developed nations in previous decades: The rate of increase of population of the larger metropolitan centers is declining, and large cities such as Tokyo and Osaka are now experiencing absolute declines. Concomitantly, there is considerable growth of moderately sized cities near the major centers and, to a lesser extent, in more rural areas. If these trends continue—some, for instance, might argue that a portion of the mid-1970s out-migration from the core cities was partly due to cyclical economic causes—then Japan will increasingly appear like Western developed countries in the shape of its urban system. We shall discuss this further in Chapter 8.

References

Alcaly, R. E. and D. Mermelstein (1977). *The Fiscal Crisis of American Cities: Essays on the Political Economy of Urban America with Special Reference to New York.* Random House, New York.

Glickman, N. J. (1976). On the Japanese urban system. *Journal of Regional Science, 16,* 317–336.

Glickman, N. J., and W. W. McHone (1977). Intercity migration and employment growth in the Japanese urban system. *Regional Studies, 11,* 165–181.

Japan Bureau of Statistics, Office of the Prime Minister (1975a). *Population Estimates As of October 1, 1974* (Population Estimate Series, No. 47). Japan Bureau of Statistics, Office of the Prime Minister, Tokyo.

Japan Bureau of Statistics, Office of the Prime Minister (1975b). *Population Census of Japan: Preliminary Count of Population.* Japan Bureau of Statistics, Office of the Prime Minister, Tokyo.

Japan Bureau of Statistics, Office of the Prime Minister (1973). *Internal Migration in Japan 1954–1971.* Japan Bureau of Statistics, Office of the Prime Minister, Tokyo.

Johnson, P. D., and D. R. Vining, Jr. (1976). A note on the equilibrium Hoover Index associated with regional migration and natural growth patterns in Japan, 1955–1974. *Journal of Regional Science, 16,* 337–344.

Kawashima, T. (1977). *Changes in the Spatial Population Structure of Japan,* RM-77-25. International Institute for Applied Systems Analysis, Laxenburg, Austria.

Kornhauser, D. (1976). *Urban Japan: Its Foundations and Growth.* Longman Group Ltd., London.

Kuroda, T. (1969). *A New Dimension of Internal Migration in Japan.* Institute of Population Problems, Japan Ministry of Health and Welfare, Tokyo.

Kuroda, T. (1977). *Migration, Distribution of Population and Development in Japan.* Mimeo.

Mera, K. (1976). The changing pattern of population distribution in Japan and its implication for developing countries, in United Nations Centre for Regional Development, *Growth Pole Strategy and Regional Planning in Asia.* UNCRD, Nagoya, Japan.

Patrick H., and H. Rosovsky (1976). Japan's economic performance: An overview, in H. Patrick and H. Rosovsky, eds., *Asia's New Giant: How the Japanese Economy Works.* The Brookings Institution, Washington, D.C. Pp. 1–62.

Sternlieb G., and J. W. Hughes, eds. (1975). *Post-Industrial America: Metropolitan Decline and Inter-Regional Job Shifts.* Center for Urban Policy Research, New Brunswick, New Jersey.

Sundquist, J. L. (1975). *Dispersing Population: What America Can Learn from Europe.* The Brookings Institution, Washington, D.C.

Vining, D. R., Jr. and T. Kontuly (1976). *Population Dispersal from Metropolitan Regions—A Review of Three Current Hypotheses.* Mimeo.

Vining, D. R., Jr. and T. Kontuly (1977). Increasing returns to city size in the face of an impending decline in the sizes of large cities: Which is the bogus fact? *Environment and Planning A, 9,* 59–62.

4

Migration and Urban Economic Development

1 Introduction

This chapter[1] continues the discussion of the development of the Japanese urban system begun in the last two chapters. Here, I concentrate on the period of the late 1960s and on the relationship among intercity migration, intracity labor force shifts among sectors, and employment growth. Thus, the discussion here is more time- and subject-specific than the efforts of previous chapters. Underlying the discussion in this chapter is the rapid economic growth that was underway in the 1960s, previously outlined in Chapters 1 and 2. Growth resulted in considerable centralization of the urban system and more specialized interdependent production units. To the extent that urban growth was linked to the growth of economic activity and, furthermore, that economic development was associated with shifts in demand for goods and services and technological innovations in the production of these goods and services, a spatial and sectoral redistribution of Japan's labor force was required. This statement is based upon two postulates. First, the distribution of a country's population at any point in time corresponds roughly to the distribution of prevailing economic opportunities. Second, demand shifts and technical innovations are usually industry-specific and have varying impacts on the employment growth in different urban centers depending upon an individual center's level of industrial development and its particular industrial specialization.

In most cases the rapidity and magnitude of changes imposed by de-

[1] This chapter is based on Glickman and McHone (1977).

145

mand shifts and technological innovations are such that the natural processes of accession and retirement can only play a minor role in the adjustment of the nation's labor force to the changing distribution of economic opportunities. Therefore, other mechanisms such as net labor force migration, intracity employment shifts among sectors of the economy, and changes in the labor force participation rates of the city's working-age population must perform the major part of the adjustment task.

In this chapter, the importance of each of these adjustment mechanisms to the employment growth process is investigated for the major industrial sectors of the Japanese urban economy. More specifically, we formulate a simple model in Section 2, which provides the basic framework for estimating the responsiveness of each sector's employment growth to (a) net labor force migration, (b) intracity sectoral shifts in employment, and (c) changes in the labor force participation rates of the city's working-age population. Following the development of this model, the variables used to represent each of the three labor force adjustment mechanisms are defined and then utilized to construct an empirically estimatable model of sectoral employment growth; this is done in Section 3. The empirical results of the analysis are presented in Section 4, which begins with an overview of Japanese sectoral employment growth and labor force migration patterns for the 1965–1970 time period. The discussion then turns to an empirical analysis of the variables used to represent intracity sectoral employment shifts and net migration of the labor force. Section 4 concludes with the empirical estimation of employment growth equations for seven separate industrial sectors of the Japanese urban economy. A set of conclusions is given in Section 5.

The units of observation in the empirical analysis of this chapter are 72 Japanese cities with 1970 populations of 100,000 or more. These cities are a subset of the sample analyzed in Chapters 2 and 3, and they are listed in Appendix 1 of this chapter. Therefore, I continue my use of the REC data base begun in earlier chapters.

2 A Model of Sectoral Employment Growth

Much of the previous work that has been undertaken in this area has adopted the view that differential rates of migration are induced by differential growth of employment opportunities and has thus postulated relationships of the general form

$$M_{c,\,dt} = f(E_{c,\,dt},\,\ldots)$$

where $M_{c,\,dt}$ represents migration into city c over the time interval dt and $E_{c,\,dt}$ represents employment growth in city c over the dt interval; see, for instance, Blanco (1963) and Lowry (1966). An alternative approach that has been used by Borts and Stein (1964) and investigated in some detail by Muth

(1968, 1971) suggests that differential rates of employment growth are induced by differential rates of migration.

One basis for the later approach is as follows. Focusing on sector i of the city's economy, assume that i's demand curve for labor can be represented by the line $D_1 D_1$ in Figure 4.1. Also, assume that the sector's short-run labor supply reaction is characterized by a relationship between wages and employment such as the one depicted by the line $S_1 S_1$ in Figure 4.1. The inelasticity implied by the steep slope of this curve is assumed to arise because the sector's ability to expand employment in the short-run is limited to temporary measures such as overtime or outside contracting. If Figure 4.1 is taken as an accurate depiction of the short-run labor market of sector i, then shifts in demand for the sector's output and the ensuing wage increases that these shifts impart will result in a relatively small increase in the sector's employment in the short-run. However, if the wage increases to a sufficiently high level so that the differential between i's wage rate and those of other sectors in the city's economy exceeds the cost of mobility between these sectors, then employees will tend to change sectors and the short-run labor supply schedule will shift to the right. In a similar fashion, if the differential between i's wage and the wages of sectors in other regions in the country exceed the costs (both spatial and sectoral) of mobility between these sectors, then in-migration into the sector also will occur from outside the city and the schedule $S_1 S_1$ will shift even further to the right. One other source of shift in the sector's labor supply curve is the one that occurs as a result of the increased wage which attracts people into the labor force who

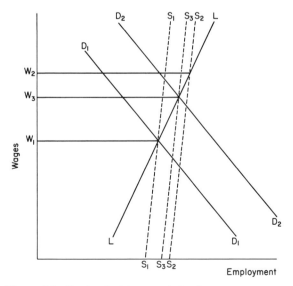

Figure 4.1 Sector i's labor market adjustment process.

had previously withheld their services, that is, increases in the labor force participation rate. This would occur to the extent that the new wage exceeds the opportunity costs of these people in their nonlabor force activities plus their mobility costs of entering the labor force and the sector.

The influx of workers from each of the aforementioned sources will tend to shift the short-run labor supply schedule of sector i to the right. The point of intersection of this shifted short-run supply curve (S_2S_2 in Figure 4.1) with a horizontal line drawn from the increased short-run wage level, W_2, yields one point on the long-run labor supply curve. Other points on this curve can be found by further varying the wage level and observing shifts of the short-run supply curve. Taken together, these intersections trace out a long-run labor supply curve such as LL in Figure 4.1.

Turning to the question of actual employment growth, assume that the workers in sector i are paid the value of their marginal product. If the sector experiences an exogenous increase in the demand for its product that, in turn, causes a shift of its labor demand schedule from D_1D_1 to D_2D_2, then the wage rate offered by the firms in the sector will increase in the short-run from W_1 to W_2. This increased wage will induce ($S_2 - S_1$) additional workers to offer their services. However, if the labor demand is less than perfectly elastic as depicted in Figure 4.1, the sector's employment growth will be ($S_3 - S_1$) rather than ($S_2 - S_1$), and the new equilibrium wage will become W_3. Thus, the migration and intracity sector shifts that determine the elasticity of the long-run labor supply schedule are perceived to be dependent upon wage differentials, while the actual growth of employment is dependent upon labor demand shifts and the elasticities of the labor supply and labor demand schedules. On the basis of this postulated flow of causality, it is possible to develop the following simple model of sectoral employment growth.

At any point in time, the existing employment of an economic sector can be described by decomposing it on the basis of the origins of its component parts. Before proceeding to do this, the discussion will be considerably facilitated if a set of symbolic terms are defined and utilized. For city c let

$E^c_{i,\,t_1}$ = total employment in sector i at time t_1;

$E^c_{i,\,t_0}$ = total employment in sector i at time t_0;

$SE^c_{ij,\,dt}$ = ($E^c_{ji,\,dt} - E^c_{ij,\,dt}$) = the sum of the net shift of employment between sector i and all other sectors, j ($j = 1,...,n; j \neq i$) during the time interval t_0 to t_1; this time interval is designated by dt;

$M^c_{i,\,dt}$ = the net change in sector i's employment as a result of net migration of the city's labor force over dt;

$CLF^c_{i,\,dt}$ = the net change in sector i's employment as a result of changes in labor force participation rates of the city's working-age population over dt;

$N^{i,\,dt}_c$ = the net change in sector i's employment as a result of natural increase in the city's labor force over dt.

Utilizing these terms, sector i's employment at the time t_1 in terms of the origins of its component parts is expressed in Eq. (1).

$$E^c_{i, t_1} = E^c_{i, t_0} + SE^c_{ij, dt} + M^c_{i, dt} + CLF^c_{i, dt} + N^c_{i, dt} \qquad (1)$$

This equation indicates that employment in sector i in city c at time t_1 is equal to the sector's employment in the previous time period, t_0, plus net changes to the sector's employment as the result of intracity sectoral shifts ($SE^c_{ij, dt}$), net migration of the labor force ($M^c_{i, dt}$), changes in the labor force participation rate of the city's working-age population ($CLF^c_{i, dt}$), and natural increase of the labor force ($N^c_{i, dt}$). Dividing both sides of Eq. (1) by E^c_{i, t_0}, an expression for the relative growth of sector i's employment in terms of the sources of this growth is obtained:

$$\frac{E^c_{i, t_1}}{E^c_{i, t_0}} = 1 + \frac{SE^c_{ij, dt}}{E^c_{i, t_0}} + \frac{M^c_{i, dt}}{E^c_{i, t_0}} + \frac{CLF^c_{i, dt}}{E^c_{i, t_0}} + \frac{N^c_{i, dt}}{E^c_{i, t_0}} \qquad (2)$$

If data were available to measure each of the five variables in Eq. (2), it would be possible to determine precisely the degree to which sector i's employment growth depends on each of the three postulated labor force adjustment mechanisms as well as the natural increase. Unfortunately, as is frequently the case in empirical research, the desired set of data measures is unavailable. However, it is possible to estimate the degree to which the sector depends on each of the adjustment mechanisms by observing the relationship between intercity variations in the employment growth of the sector and intercity variations in three variables that are citywide surrogates for sector i's $SE_{ij, dt}$, $M_{i, dt}$, and $CLF_{i, dt}$ variables in Eq. (2). These three citywide variables are, respectively, an index of sector i's growth in employment relative to the growth of all other sectors in the city's economy, the 5-year change in the city's total labor force as a result of net migration of the population, and the 5-year change in the city's labor force as a result of increased labor force participation rates of the city's working-age population.

The other component of employment growth in Eq. (2) is that part that is due to the natural increase of the labor force. Unlike the three adjustment mechanisms just discussed, this source of employment growth does not respond to short-run signals of excess demand in the labor market such as rising wage levels or falling unemployment rates. It is, instead, dependent upon the childbearing decisions made 15 to 20 years previously. Because there is little reason to expect intercity variations in a sector's employment growth to be related in any meaningful sense to intercity variations in the rates of natural increase, it is assumed that the rates at which sectors expand their employment from this source are reasonably constant across cities. In terms of the empirical analysis that follows, this means that the employment growth due to natural increase appears as a shift in the intercept term of the estimated regression equations. Before proceeding with the estimation of these regression equations, it is necessary to discuss in detail each of the three citywide variables that serve as surrogates for the employment adjustment mechanisms. This discussion is provided in Section 3.

3 Employment Adjustment Mechanisms

3.1 Intracity Employment Shifts

The intracity sectoral shift variable that is represented by $SE^c_{ij, dt}$ in Eq. (2) was defined earlier as $(E^c_{ij, dt} - E^c_{ji, dt})$; this expression represents the net change in sector i's employment as a result of attracting employees from, and dispersing employees to, other economic sectors within the city. Unfortunately, the information necessary to calculate such an expression precisely is extremely difficult to obtain and to my knowledge is not available for Japan. However, if the net value of the sectoral shift variable is interpreted as representing a gain (positive net value) or loss (negative net value) of sector i's employment position relative to the other sectors in the urban economy, then the spirit of the net shift can be captured through the use of an index that measures the growth of sector i's employment relative to the growth of every other sector in the city's economy.

Before defining the index, it is necessary to note the measure of sectoral employment growth that is used in this and subsequent sections. The employment growth of sector i is defined in Eq. (3).

$$EG^c_{i, dt} = \frac{E^c_{i, t_1}}{E^c_{i, t_0}} \tag{3}$$

$EG^c_{i, dt}$ represents employment growth in sector i in city c over the time interval dt and E^c_{i, t_0} and E^c_{i, t_1} are respectively the levels of employment in the sector at the beginning and end points of this interval. Utilizing this definition, the index of sectoral shift for sector i is given by:

$$SX^c_{i, dt} = k \sum_{\substack{j=1 \\ j \neq i}}^{n} \frac{EG^c_{i, dt}}{EG^c_{j, dt}} \qquad i = 1, \ldots, 7 \tag{4}$$

In Eq. (4), the index of employment shift for sector i in city c, $SX^c_{i, dt}$, is defined as the sum of the ratios of the employment growth of sector i to that of each of the other sectors in the city's economy.[2] The growth figures for

[2] The values that the sectoral shift index can assume range from zero to infinity. A formal statement of the limiting conditions is presented here.

(a) $\lim SX_{i, dt} \to 0$ as $EG_{i, dt} \to 0$

and

(b) $\lim SX_{i, dt} \to \infty$ as $EG_{i, dt} \to \epsilon$ and $Eg_{j, dt} \to 0$ for at least one j where ϵ is a finite positive number.

the seven sectors, and consequently the shift indices are all measures of change over the time interval dt. The k in Eq. (4) is a scaling factor that makes the range of the index independent of the number of sectors included on the right-hand side of the expression. This factor makes it possible to compare the indices of the broad sectors (i.e., primary, secondary, and tertiary) to the indices of the more narrowly defined sectors (i.e., manufacturing, wholesale/retail, transportation/communication, and services). The obvious advantage of an index such as the one defined in Eq. (4) is that it can be calculated directly with readily available aggregate city employment data. A possible disadvantage of the approach is that it implicitly assumes that changes in the sector's relative position come about solely as a result of shifts among sectors. In reality, changes in the sector's relative position could stem from the sector attracting or dispersing a disproportionate share of the migrants or a disproportionate share of the new labor force participants relative to all other sectors in the city's economy. The impact and severity of this problem will be investigated in more detail in Section 4.

Table 4.1 presents averages and ranges of values for each of the sectoral shift indices for the 72 cities included in the sample or the period 1965–1970. A value of $SX^c_{i,\,dt} = 1$ implies that the sector's employment position has remained the same relative to each of the other sectors in the city's economy. A value of $SX^c_{i,\,dt} > 1$ implies a gain, while a value of $SX^c_{i,\,dt} < 1$ implies a loss in the sector's relative employment position. Table 4.1 shows that, on average, the primary sector experienced losses in its relative position while all other sectors experienced gains over the period 1965–1970. The figures also indicate that the manufacturing and transportation/communication sectors had smaller gains than the wholesale/retail and service sectors. These shifts are, of course, consistent with our findings in Chapter 2. The intercity variation in these indices will be discussed in more detail in Section 4.

3.2 Net Migration of the Labor Force

The discussion now turns to consideration of the second of the labor adjustment mechanisms, net migration of the labor force. The method used to calculate city values of this variable is the well-known cohort survival technique of calculating net migration of the population. The description of this process will be greatly facilitated by delineating the following notation. Let,

$P65_{c,s,a}$ = the number of people in city c in 1965 who were in the s, a sex/age cohort of the population, where s is either male or female and a are the 5 year intervals 10–14 years, 15–19 years, 20–24 years, . . . , 65–69 years;

$P70_{c,s,a}$ = the number of people in city c in 1970 who were in the s, a sex/age cohort, where s and a are as defined previously;

TABLE 4.1
Sectoral Shift Indices for 72 Japanese Cities, 1965–1970

Sector	Mean index value $(SX^c_{i,\,dt})$	High value	Low value
Primary	.75	1.32	.51
Secondary	1.12	1.60	.53
Tertiary	1.19	2.24	.61
Manufacturing	1.06	1.57	.73
Wholesale/Retail	1.10	1.25	.84
Transportation/Communication	1.02	1.33	.72
Services	1.14	1.36	.86

$SR_{s,a}$ = the 5-year national survival rate of the Japanese population who were in the s, a sex/age cohort in 1965;

$MLF_{c,s,a}$ = the 5-year net change in the s, a sex/age cohort of city c's labor force due to net migration of the population;

$LFP_{c,s,a}$ = the labor force participation rate of the s, a sex/age cohort in city c in 1970.

Utilizing this notation, net migration of the labor force by age and sex is calculated for each city in the following way.

$$MLF_{c,s,a+5} = \left[P70_{c,s,a+5} - (SR_{s,a}) \cdot (P65_{c,s,a}) \right] \cdot \left[LFP_{c,s,a+5} \right] \qquad (5)$$

Since the ultimate objective is to determine the change in the city's labor force due to net migration, these numbers are calculated only for the 11 5-year age cohorts between 16 and 69 years of age.[3] Having calculated the net labor force migration for each of these age/sex cohorts in the city, the remaining tasks are to sum across the categories and to divide the result by the total labor force of the city as in Eq. (6).

$$MRLF_{c,\,dt} = \frac{\sum_s \sum_a MLF_{c,s,a}}{LF_c} \qquad (6)$$

This division of the city's net labor force migration by the total city labor force yields a variable that is the citywide economy counterpart of sector i's $M^c_{i,\,dt}/E^c_{i,\,t_0}$ variable in Eq. (2).

---

[3] These survival ratios were calculated with the formula

$$SR_{s,\,a} = P70_{n,s,a+5} / P65_{n,s,a}$$

where $P65_{n,s,a}$ is the number of Japanese people in Japan in 1965 who were in the s, a sex/age cohort and $P70_{n,s,a+5}$ is the number of Japanese people in 1970 who were in the s, $a + 5$ sex/age cohort.

3.3 Labor Force Participation Rate Changes

The third adjustment mechanism in Eq. (2) is the change in sector i's employment as a result of increased labor force participation rates of the city's working-age population. The citywide counterpart of this variable is calculated in the following way:

$$CLFP_{c,\,dt} = \left[LFP_{c,\,t_1} - LFP_{c,\,t_0} \right] \tag{7}$$

where $LFP_{c,\,t_0}$ and $LFP_{c,\,t_1}$ are, respectively, the labor force participation rates of city c's working-age population at the beginning and end points of the dt time interval.

3.4 Other Considerations

Before the variables defined by Eqs. (3), (4), (6), and (7) are utilized to formulate an empirically estimable expression that corresponds to Eq. (2), two other points must be considered. Both concern the question of proper specification of the equation to be estimated. It should be evident that, in a statistical sense, the growth of a sector's employment depends on many other variables in addition to the three postulated adjustment mechanisms. Therefore an equation that is estimated with only these three variables on the right-hand side is likely to be underspecified. In a partial analysis such as the one pursued here, the complete alleviation of the underspecification problem could necessitate the inclusion of a large number of additional variables. An alternative approach often employed in partial analysis is to choose one or more additional variables that are related to a large number of the other excluded variables and to proceed with the estimation procedure. This latter approach is adopted here.

The variable chosen to represent the excluded variables is total city population in 1965. This variable was selected after an investigation of a rather extensive city characteristic correlation matrix revealed that city size was significantly related to many variables that might be expected to enhance employment growth. Of these variables, several of the more significant relationships were those between city size and the education level of the population, volume of retail and wholesale sales per capita, value added by manufacturing per employee, bank loans per capita, and age composition of the city's population.

The second point to be considered is the proper form of the equation to be estimated. Although it is clear that the relationship expressed by Eq. (2) is a linear one, it is not at all clear that the relationship between a sector's employment growth and the variables defined by Eqs. (4), (6), and (7) is necessarily linear; it is possible that the relationship is either logarithmic, semilogarithmic, or of some other form. Perhaps the most straightforward way of resolving the question of proper form is to observe the scatter diagrams of the dependent variable and each of the independent variables. When this was done for the sample used in this analysis, the diagrams revealed that a logarithmic specification was the most appropriate form.[4] This form is particularly desirable in the present analysis because it can be shown that the regression coefficients have the convenient interpretation of *employment elasticities* when each of the variables are entered into the empirical estimation in their logarithmic form. That is, the coefficients represent the percentage of change in the dependent variable given a 1% change in the independent variable.

Combining these two considerations with the citywide employment adjustment mechanism variables and the natural increase of labor force assumption made in the previous section, yields Eq. (8), which can be empirically estimated for each of seven employment sectors of the Japanese urban economy:

$$\ln EG^c_{i,\ dt} = B_0 + B_1 (\ln SX^c_{i,\ dt}) + B_2 (\ln MRLF_{c,\ dt})$$
$$+ B_3 (\ln CLFP_{c,\ dt}) + B_4 (\ln CITYSZ) \qquad (8)$$

where *CITYSZ* represents city c's population in 1965, and the other variables are as previously defined. These estimated equations, an overview of Japanese sectoral employment growth and labor force migration patterns, and an empirical analysis of the intracity shift index and net labor force migration variables are presented in the next section.

4 Empirical Results

4.1 Employment Growth and City Size

Before proceeding to analyze the responsiveness of the urban economy's employment growth to the postulated adjustment mechanisms, it is desirable to present an overview of the patterns of this growth for the urban system represented by the 72-city sample selected for this study. One of the first steps in the provision of this overview is an investigation of the relationship between employment growth and city size. This relationship is summarized in Table 4.2. Appendix 2 gives a set of tables that summarize employment growth by industry according to city size.

To construct Table 4.2, the 1965–1970 employment growth variables (as defined in Section 3) were calculated for each of the sample cities. The cities

---

[4] Since it is not possible to take the logarithm of negative numbers, the *MRLF* and *CLFP* variables were transformed to a strictly positive scale by adding 1 to the values of each of the variables. As a result of these transformations, positive values of the original variables are now represented by numbers greater than 1 and negative values of the original variables are now represented by numbers less than 1 but greater than 0.

TABLE 4.2
Total Employment Growth and City Size

City size (in thousands)	Number of cities in size class	Slowest growing quartile	Second slowest growing quartile	Second fastest growing quartile	Fastest growing quartile	Total
100–200	31	29.0	35.5	16.1	19.4	100.0
201–300	18	22.2	11.1	33.3	33.3	100.0
301–400	7	0	57.1	14.3	28.6	100.0
401–500	7	0	14.3	57.1	28.6	100.0
501–999	3	0	0	66.7	33.3	100.0
999+	6	83.3	0	0	16.7	100.0

were then ranked in ascending order by rates of employment growth and divided into quartiles; then the bivariate frequency distribution of cities by employment growth quartile and city size was produced. Because the 72-city sample was highly skewed toward the smaller city size classes (i.e., 100,000–200,000), the raw frequency distributions tended to present a somewhat nebulous picture of employment growth by city size. To clarify the relationship, the raw frequencies in each of the bivariate frequency cells were replaced by the percentage of cities in a particular city size class that fell into a particular employment growth quartile.

Reference to Table 4.2 reveals that a majority of the cities in the smaller size class (i.e., population less than 200,000) had slow 1965–1970 employment growth rates relative to other cities in the sample. For instance, 64.5% of the cities in the 100,000–200,000 city size class were ranked in the two slowest growing quartiles. The table also indicates that an overwhelming number (83.3%) of the cities in the largest size class (i.e., greater than 999,000) were ranked in the slowest growing quartile. Of the 35 cities in the city size range 201,000–999,000, 11 ranked in the fastest growing quartile and another 13 in the second fastest growing quartile. A final point of interest with respect to Table 4.2 is the consistently high growth rate rankings of the cities in the two size classes between 401,000 and 999,000. Of the combined number of cities in these two classes, 90% ranked in the two fastest growing quartiles. These results, of course, are fully consistent with those of Chapters 2 and 3.

In summary, Table 4.2 presents an interesting picture of the city size patterns of employment growth during the 1965–1970 period. The bivariate frequency distribution has revealed that the smallest and largest cities shared the common distinction of relatively slow employment growth, while the moderately large-sized cities enjoyed the highest rankings on the employment growth scale.

4.2 Labor Force Migration and City Size

Having established the patterns of employment growth by city size, it is now desirable to investigate the relationship between net labor force migration, which was postulated as a major source of employment growth, and city size. Table 4.3 presents the city size/net labor force migration bivariate frequency distribution of the 72 cities in the sample. In constructing this table the net labor force migration rate for each city was calculated in the manner described in Section 3. On the basis of this variable, each of the cities were then classified into one of the four mutually exclusive migration categories identified by the column headings in Table 4.3. Here again, as in Table 4.2, the raw frequencies were replaced with percentages of the city size totals classified in each migration category.

The percentages in Table 4.3 indicate that cities in the smallest size

TABLE 4.3
Labor Force Migration and City Size

City size (in thousands)	Number of cities in size class	In-migration and out-migration of labor force				
		In-migration of less than 5% of labor force	In-migration of more than 5% of labor force	Out-migration of less than 5% of labor force	Out-migration of more than 5% of labor force	Total
100–200	31	22.6	16.1	35.5	25.8	100.0
201–300	18	27.8	44.4	16.6	11.1	100.0
301–400	7	42.8	42.8	14.3	0	100.0
401–500	7	57.1	28.5	14.3	0	100.0
501–999	3	33.3	33.3	33.3	0	100.0
999+	6	0	16.7	50.0	33.3	100.0
Total sample	72	27.8	27.8	27.8	16.7	100.0

class (i.e., population less than 200,000) and cities in the largest class (i.e., population greater than 999,000) experienced net out-migration during the 1965–1970 period; 61.3% of the cities in the 100,000–200,000 size class and 83.3% of the cities in the 999,000–plus size class registered net out-migration. The table also reveals that, in general, the cities in the medium-sized range (i.e., 201,000–999,000) had net in-migration during 1965–1970; 77.1% of the cities in this range had net in-migration rates between 0 and 5% while 40% of the cities exhibited rates greater than 5%.

Comparing the results of Tables 4.3 and 4.2, it is seen that the fastest growing city size classes, in terms of total employment, during 1965–1970 were those classes that experienced the highest rates of in-migration during the same period. This result implies a relationship between net migration rates and employment growth. Additional information on this relationship is provided by Table 4.4, which presents the joint frequency distribution of the 72-city sample by employment growth quartile and net migration rate.

The entries in Table 4.4 indicate that 83.3% of the cities in the fastest growing quartile had 1965–1970 net labor force in-migration rates of 5% or more and 55.5% of the cities in the slowest growth quartile had net out-migration rates of 5% or more. These results provide a preliminary indication of a strong positive association between net in-migration and employment growth. The extent of this association for different industrial sectors of the economy will be investigated in a more rigorous fashion later in the analysis; for the moment, the discussion addresses a problem that was alluded to earlier.

4.3 Relationships among Sectors

In Section 3 it was suggested that one possible problem with using the $SX^c_{i,\,dt}$ index as an indicator of intracity sectoral shifts of employment was the assumption that changes in a sector's relative position of employment importance in the economy occur solely as a result of employment shifts between sectors and are not significantly related to intercity variations in the rates of net migration of the labor force and changes in labor force participation rates of the city's working-age population. The difficulty that arises when this assumption is violated is the classic multicollinearity problem of multivariate statistics. The amount of confidence that can be placed in the estimated regression coefficients of two assumed independent variables must be qualified to the extent that the variables are colinear, or not truly independent. A simple check for multicollinearity between independent variables is provided by their pairwise correlation coefficients.

The correlation coefficients for the independent variables used in the estimated employment growth equations are presented in Table 4.5. Note that it is not necessary to examine coefficients between pairs of shift indices because only one index at a time appears in each estimated employment

TABLE 4.4

Labor Force Migration and Employment Growth (Percentage of Total in Each Employment Growth Quartile)

	In-migration of less than 5% of the labor force	In-migration of more than 5% of the labor force	Out-migration of less than 5% of the labor force	Out-migration of more than 5% of the labor force	Total sample
Slowest growing quartile	0	0	44.4	55.5	100.0
Second slowest growing quartile	44.4	0	50.0	5.6	100.0
Second fastest growing quartile	66.7	27.8	5.6	0	100.0
Fastest growing quartile	0	83.3	11.1	5.6	100.0
Total sample	27.8	27.8	27.8	16.7	100.0

TABLE 4.5

Correlation Coefficients for Independent Variables Used in Employment Growth Equations

	In *MRLF*	In *CLFP*
In *CLFP*	−.052	
In SX_{pri}	.115	.254**
In SX_{scd}	.129	−.180
In SX_{trt}	−.211*	−.065
In SX_{mfg}	.139	−.095
In $SX_{w/r}$	−.034	−.113
In $SX_{t/c}$	−.278**	−.053
In SX_{svc}	−.022	−.192

* $P < .1$.
** $P < .05$.

growth equation. The coefficients in Table 4.5 reveal that, in general, the independence assumption is supported by the data. There are three instances in which assumed independent variables are correlated; but since two of these correlations are only significant at the 5% level and the other one is only significant at the 10% level, the analysis, while subject to qualification in these three cases, is not severely affected by violations of the independence assumptions.

A major point of interest with respect to the shift indices is the direction and strength of the relationship that exists between the indices of any two given sectors. Conceptually, and by virtue of the manner by which they are calculated, it should be expected that, in most cases, values of the index for any particular sector will be inversely related to the values of the index for other sectors of the economy; this is so because one sector can only gain in relative position if another sector loses. One method of investigating the interrelationships between the sectoral shift indices is to regress each of them on all of the other indices used in the analysis. The results obtained when this was done for the 72-city sample are presented in Table 4.6. Each column in Table 5.6 represents one estimated logarithmic equation of the general form of Eq. (9).

$$\ln SX^c_{i,\ dt} = B_0 + \sum_{\substack{j=1 \\ j \neq i}}^{n} B_j\ (\ln SX^c_{j,\ dt}) + B_{n+1}\ (\ln MRLF_c)$$

$$+ B_{n+2}\ (\ln CLFP_c)\ 2 \tag{9}$$

In Eq. (9), the SX^e's, *MRLF*, and *CLFP* are as previously defined, and the *B*'s are the regression coefficients to be estimated by the data. In the case of the three broad sectors (i.e., primary, tertiary, and secondary), the number of indices included on the right-hand side of Eq. (9) is two; in the case of the more narrowly defined sectors (i.e., manufacturing, wholesale/retail, trans-

TABLE 4.6
Shift Index Interrelationships—ln $SX_1 = f(\ln SX_j, \ldots, \ln MRLF, \ln CLFP)^a$

	ln SX_{pri} (1)	ln SX_{scd} (2)	ln SX_{trt} (3)	ln SX_{mfg} (4)	ln $SX_{w/r}$ (5)	ln $SX_{t/c}$ (6)	ln SX_{svc} (7)
Constant	−.128*** (5.77)	−.049** (1.84)	.001 (0.2)	−.062*** (2.16)	−.043*** (3.87)	.022 (.72)	.076*** (6.38)
ln SX_{pri}		−.53*** (5.00)	−.57*** (5.66)	−.48*** (5.09)	−.22*** (5.67)	−.24** (2.10)	.06 (1.08)
ln SX_{scd}	−.52*** (5.00)		.07 (.53)				
ln SX_{trt}	−.58*** (5.66)	.07 (.53)					
ln SX_{mfg}					−.07 (1.43)	−.17 (1.33)	.04 (.69)
ln $SX_{w/r}$				−.42 (1.43)		.53* (1.71)	.86*** (7.73)
ln $SX_{t/c}$				−.16 (1.33)	.08* (1.71)		−.12** (2.00)
ln SX_{svc}				.17 (.69)	.57*** (7.73)	−.50** (2.00)	
ln $MRLF$	.13 (1.00)	.31** (2.44)	−.20 (1.53)	.19 (1.82)	.06 (1.50)	−.20*** (1.85)	−.05 (.94)
ln $CLFP$	.61** (2.09)	.01 (.02)	.38 (1.29)	.25 (1.01)	.21** (2.05)	.01 (.04)	.20 (1.69)
R^2	.68	.51	.54	.39	.80	.34	.65

^{a} Numbers in parentheses under coefficients are t-statistics.
* $P < .1$.
** $P < .05$.
*** $P < .01$.

poration/communications, and services), $n = 4$. The shift index for the broad primary sector was included on the right-hand side of the equations of each of the four narrowly defined sectors because it was felt that a representative of primary employment should be included at this level of analysis. However, due to the relative scarcity of primary activity in the Japanese urban economy, it was not possible to find a detailed sector within the broad primary sector that was consistently represented by sufficiently large numbers for all cities in the sample.

Referring to Column 1 of Table 4.6, it is seen that positive increases in the relative employment position of both the secondary and tertiary sectors were significantly related to decreases in the relative employment position of the primary sector of the urban economy. Recalling the mean index values from Table 4.1, it will be remembered that, on average, the primary sector ($SX_{pri} = .75$) suffered a loss in relative position during the 1965–1970 time interval, while the secondary sector ($SX_{scd} = 1.12$) and tertiary sector ($SX_{trt} = 1.19$) gained relatively. Taken in conjunction with the estimated coefficients in the secondary and tertiary shift indices in Column 1 of Table 4.6, the implication that emerges is that the tertiary sector gained more than the secondary sector at the expense of the primary sector.

In terms of the model of Section 2, these coefficients imply a shift of employment from primary activities to these other two sectors. Referring to Columns 2 and 3 of Table 4.6, it is seen that the coefficients relating the secondary and tertiary sector shifts variables are small, positive, and insignificant. The implication of these coefficients is that neither of these sectors tended to gain at the expense of the other.

Turning to the four more narrowly defined sectors (Columns 4 through 7) in Table 4.6, the first point that should be noted is that, unlike the broad sector, the two coefficients that relate a pair of indices are not symmetrical in terms of magnitude. The reason for this is that the broad sector definition totally accounted for all employment in the city, whereas the narrowly defined sectors only partially exhaust total city employment. Therefore, the shift in relative position by one of the narrowly defined sectors could be associated with a shift of relative position by an excluded sector. Taking each sector in turn, it is seen that the shift in the manufacturing sector's relative employment position was inversely related to shifts in the employment positions of the primary, wholesale/retail, and transportation/communications sectors, and positively related to shifts in the service sector's position. Of these relationships the only one that is significant is the relationship with the primary sector. If the coefficient associating these two sectors is considered along with the mean index values from Table 4.1, the implication is that the manufacturing sector received much of the gain in its relative position at the expense of the primary sector.

The coefficients in Column 5 of Table 4.6 indicate that shifts in the wholesale/retail sector's position were in general inversely related to shifts in the relative position of the primary and manufacturing sectors and positively related to shifts in the transportation/communications and service sectors' positions. Building on the previous discussion of mean index values and the interpretation of significant negative coefficients, it follows that the implication of the coefficient associated with the primary sector shift index is that the wholesale/retail sector gained relative employment at the expense of a loss in position by the primary sector. It is interesting to note that the magnitude of gain by wholesale/retail at the expense of the primary sector was less than half the gain enjoyed by the manufacturing sector at the primary sector's expense. The other interesting point in connection with the regression coefficients of Eq. (9) is the strong, relatively large positive association between wholesale/retail shifts and service sector shifts. The data in Table 4.1 indicated that, on average, these sectors were the largest gainers in relative employment importance in the urban economy. The coefficients in Table 4.6, which relate the shift indices of the two sectors, further indicate that these sectors were growing concurrently in the same urban areas.

Of the remaining coefficients in Table 4.6, those that warrant discussion are the ones relating service sector shifts to shifts of other sectors. The service sector is the only sector whose shift index is not significantly negatively related to the primary sector's shift index. It appears that because services are forward linkages of all other included sectors (with the possible exception of transportation/communications, which is in large part a service sector itself), gains in the relative position of the sector are incompatible with losses in the relative positions of the sectors on which it depends either directly or indirectly for its demand.

Summarizing the results of this section, evidence has been presented that tends to support the hypothesis that the intracity sector shift variables, although highly dependent on each other, are reasonably independent of the migration and change in labor force participation rate variables. Having done this, it is now desirable to explore the source and extent of intercity variation in the net migration of the labor force variable.

4.4 Relationships between Labor Force Migration and City Characteristics

The extent of intercity variation in the rates of net migration of the labor force is summarized in Table 4.7. The figures in Table 4.7 indicate that the rate of net migration of the labor force varied across cities from a low value of -30% of the labor force to a high value of $+39\%$ of the labor force. Table 4.7 also shows that, while the average rate is only slightly higher for males than for females, the variance in the male rates is over twice that of the female rates.

The data in Table 4.7, along with those of Table 4.3, indicate that there is

TABLE 4.7
Rates of Net Migration of Labor Force, 1970

	Mean	Variance	Low-value	High-value
Labor force net migration rates for males	.012	.005	−.21	+.22
Labor force net migration rates for females	.014	.002	−.16	+.13
Labor force net migration rates total	.023	.013	−.30	+.39

considerable intercity variation in the migration rates. To understand the causes of these variations, several variables that provide measures of city job market conditions, residential characteristics, city locational and physical characerics, and characteristics of the city's population were selected, and the relationship between these variables and the logarithm of the net migration rate of the labor force was estimated for the 72-city sample using multiple linear regression techniques. The results that were obtained are presented in Table 4.8.

Variables 1–4 in Table 4.8 were selected to measure important aspects of the city's job market and labor force. The first three (1965 unemployment rate, 1965 median wage and salary level, and 1965 citywide labor force participation rate) were chosen to indicate labor demand conditions in the city. The theoretical discussion in Section 2 predicted that wage and salaries and labor force participation rates will rise and unemployment rates will fall to signify excess demand in a labor market and that one response will be an increase in the rate of in-migration to the labor market; these predictions are supported by the statistically significant coefficients of Variables 1–3 in Table 4.8. The fourth variable in Table 4.8, the growth of manufacturing value added per employee, was included in the analysis as a measure of changes in productivity of the city's labor force. To the extent that the increases in the rates of value added by manufacturing per employee are attributable to the increased productivity of labor, there will be both an output and substitution effect, which will increase the demand for labor. This increased labor demand will, in turn, exert upward pressure on the wage rate and consequently will induce an increase in the rate of in-migration to the city. Here again, the empirical results support the theory; the coefficient of the growth in value added variable is positive and significant.

Variables 5 and 6 in Table 4.8 were chosen to reflect residential characteristics of the city. The coefficient associated with the percentage of new housing variable implies that migrants were attracted to cities with large percentages of new housing. The rate of suburbanization variable (Variable 6 in Table 4.8) is a measure of the rate of change of the city's daytime-

TABLE 4.8
Relationships between Net Migration Rates of Labor Force and City Characteristics—in $MRLF = f$(city characteristics)

Independent variable	Regression coefficient	t-statistic
1. Unemployment rate, 1965	−.04600***	3.28
2. Median wage and salary level, 1965	.3900**	2.06
3. Citywide labor force participation rate, 1965	.05600**	1.81
4. 1965–1970 growth in value added by manufacturing/employee	.00023**	2.37
5. Percentage of housing new, 1970	.00179*	1.73
6. Rate of suburbanization 1965–1970	−.02520***	4.15
7. Percentage of population with only primary education in 1970	−.00970*	1.67
8. Percentage of population less than 15 years of age, 1965	−.01840***	3.57
9. Annual rate of in-migration in 1965 as a percentage of population	.00290***	4.58
10. Index of potential interaction with nearest city, 1965	−.00026***	2.88
11. Index of potential interaction with Tokyo, 1965	.01220*	1.88
12. Age of the city	−.00112***	2.96

* $P < .1$.
** $P < .05$.
*** $P < .01$.

population–nighttime-population ratio over the time interval 1965–1970. If the value of the daytime-population–nighttime-population ratio at any particular point in time is greater than unity, then the city is experiencing in-commutation during the day for the purposes of employment.[5] On the other hand, a value of the rate of suburbanization variable greater than unity implies that the city has become more suburbanized in terms of the residential location of its work force over the time interval 1965–1970. Referring to this variable's coefficient in Table 4.8, it is seen that those cities that were experiencing the greatest rates of suburbanization during this period were also experiencing low or negative rates of net migration. This relationship probably reflects the fact that the largest cities in the sample were experiencing very high rates of suburbanization and very low rates of net migration during the 1965–1970 time period.

Variables 7–9 in Table 4.8 were included in the analysis as measures of the characteristics of the city's population. The coefficient associated with the education variable (Variable 7) implies that people with low levels of education have a lower propensity to migrate than people with higher levels of education. The coefficient of Variable 8, the percentage of the city's population less than 15 years of age in 1965, is negative and significant. This indicates that cities with large numbers of young people in 1965 tended to experience very low in-migration or even net out-migration rates over the 1965–1970 interval. This is most likely a reflection of the radical increase in the propensity to migrate that accompanies moving into the 15- to 19-year age cohort from the less mobile 10- to 14-year age cohorts.[6]

The final population variable presented in Table 4.8 is the annual rate of in-migration to the city in 1965. This variable was included as an additional measure of the propensity to migrate of the city's population. Its sign indicates that cities that were experiencing high rates of in-migration in 1965 also experienced positive net migration rates over the 1965–1970 period.

The next three variables listed in Table 4.8 were included in the analysis to reflect locational and physical characteristics of the city. The two indexes of potential interaction, variables 10 and 11, are the standard gravity-type measures used extensively in regional flow analysis; see Isard (1960, Chap. 11). The formula used to calculate these indices is

$$PI_{ij} = (P_i \cdot P_j)/d_{ij} \tag{10}$$

where PI_{ij} is the index of potential interaction between city i and city j and P_i and P_j are, respectively, the 1965 populations of city i and city j, and d_{ij} is the railroad distance between the two cities. These indices were designed to simultaneously capture the effects of city size and accessibility (distance) on the rate of migration to a city. When each of these factors were entered into the regression analysis as separate independent variables, they were both

---

[5] The daytime-population–nighttime-population variable used in this analysis is a measure of employees by place of work divided by employees by place of residence.

[6] See, for instance, Cordey-Hayes and Gleave (1974) and Lowry (1966) on this issue.

found to be insignificantly related to the dependent variable. However, as Table 4.8 reveals, when the two variables were combined to form the indexes of potential interaction, the result is a variable that is significantly related to the rate of net migration of the labor force. The coefficients associated with the two variables imply that the greater the potential for interaction with the nearest city, the lower the rate of net migration to the city and the greater the potential for interaction with Tokyo, the greater the rate of net migration to the city. It was originally anticipated that both of these variables would be positively related to the rate of net migration; however, these anticipations were not fulfilled with respect to the potential index for interaction with the nearest city. The negative relationship between this variable and the rate of net migration probably reflects the fact that city i's proximity to another large city results in competition for the pool of potential migrants to the general area and thus overshadows the effects of high potential interaction that are implied by large values of the index. The last variable in Table 4.8 is the age of the city, where 1868 = 1. The age of the city could affect the rate of migration in one of two ways. On one hand, it might be hypothesized that older cities emit more negative externalities, such as pollution and congestion, as a result of the obsolescence of the city's public and private physical capital stock. For this reason, migration might be expected to be negatively related to the age of the city. On the other hand, the older cities also might be hypothesized to emit certain positive benefits not available in newer cities, such as better developed cultural centers. To the extent that this is the case, net migration will be positively related to the age of the city. The coefficient of the variable in Table 4.8 implies that the negative benefits outweigh the positive externalities in terms of attracting migrants to the cities in this sample.

Summarizing the results of Table 4.8, it appears that migrants were attracted to cities characterized by *higher-than-average* median wage level, labor force participation rates, growth in manufacturing productivity per employee, percentages of the city's housing stock recently built, annual rates of inmigration in 1965, and indices of potential interaction with Tokyo. It also appears that cities with *lower-than-average* unemployment rates, suburbanization rates, percentages of the population poorly educated, percentages of the population moving into the mobile 15- to 19-year age cohort, and those with indices of potential interaction with (or competition from) adjacent cities also gained migrants. Finally, older cities tended to disperse more migrants than they attracted during the 1965–1970 time period.

4.5 Employment Growth and the Adjustment Mechanisms

The discussion presented thus far has been primarily designed to provide a firm foundation for the investigation of the relationships that exist between the three postulated labor force adjustment mechanisms and the growth of employment in each of the seven sectors of the Japanese urban economy. Being reasonably confident of this foundation, the analysis now moves directly to this investigation.

Table 4.9 presents the results that were obtained when Eq. (8) was empirically estimated for the three broad sectors (i.e., primary, secondary, and tertiary) and for the four more narrowly defined sectors (i.e., manufacturing, wholesale/retail, transportation/communications, and services) of the urban economy. Each of the columns in this table contains the estimated equation for one of the sectors. The column headings identify the sector and the row labels identify the constant term, the right-hand side variables, and the measure of the equation's overall significance. The t-statistic for each of the coefficients is presented in parentheses underneath it.The tilde over the *MRLF* variable indicates that the values used for this variable in each of the equations are predicted values obtained from the first-stage equation of the two-stage least squares (TSLS) regression technique. The use of TSLS is necessitated by the simultaneous equation bias that arises because migration is, to some degree, determined by the same variables that determine employment growth and is therefore correlated with the error terms of the employment growth variables. TSLS provides a method of purging the migration variable of this correlation and thus yields unbiased estimates of the regression coefficients. The first-stage equation used to estimate values for the variable is a slight variant of the equation presented in Table 4.8. In addition to the independent variables presented in that table, the *MRLF* variable was also regressed on the SX_i, $_{dt}$'s and ln *CLFP* variables.[7] The inclusion of there additional variables did not noticeably affect the coefficients or significance levels of any of the variables in Table 4.9; however, the inclusion did increase the equation's R^2 from .70 to .74.

As was indicated in the previous section, entering the variables into the analysis in their logarithmic forms provides a basis for interpreting the coefficients in Table 4.9 as employment growth elasticities.[8] Referring to

---

[7] The necessity for including all exogenous variables in the first-stage estimation is discussed in detail by Johnston (1963, pp. 258–260).

[8] To demonstrate this, consider the equation for primary employment growth in Column 1 of Table 4.6.

$$\ln EG_{pri} = .60 + 1.01(\ln MRLF) + .29(\ln CLFP) + .88(\ln SX_{pri}) - .09(\ln CITYSZ)$$

Taking the partial derivation of EG_{pri} with respect to *MRLF* yields

$$1/EG_{pri} \cdot \partial EG_{pri}/\partial MRLF = 1.01 \ 1/MRLF$$

Multiplying both sides by *MRLF* yields:

$$MRLF/EG_{pri} \cdot \partial EG_{pri}/\partial MRLF = 1.01$$

which is the familiar expression for the elasticity of employment growth in the primary sector

TABLE 4.9
Sectoral Employment Growth Elasticities—ln $EG_i = f(\ln SX_i, \ln MRLF, \ln CLFP, \ln CITYSZ)^a$

	ln EG_{pri} (1)	ln EG_{scd} (2)	ln EG_{trt} (3)	ln EG_{mfg} (4)	ln EG_{wlr} (5)	ln EG_{tlc} (6)	ln EG_{svc} (7)
Constant	.60	.50***	.41***	.48***	.39***	.40***	.39***
	(7.68)	(6.53)	(5.79)	(6.44)	(7.01)	(5.37)	(6.22)
ln MRLF	1.01***	1.06***	.79***	.92***	.87***	.81***	.84***
	(8.99)	(9.92)	(7.71)	(9.05)	(10.89)	(7.40)	(9.40)
ln CLFP	.29	.14	.29*	.30*	.24*	.35**	.20
	(1.22)	(.63)	(1.38)	(1.46)	(1.45)	(1.59)	(1.08)
ln SX_{pri}	.88***						
	(15.33)						
ln SX_{scd}		.21***					
		(3.15)					
ln SC_{trt}			.23***				
			(3.80)				
ln SX_{mfg}				.51***			
				(5.51)			
ln SX_{wlr}					.14*		
					(1.41)		
ln SX_{tlc}						.66***	
						(7.01)	
ln SX_{svc}							.20**
							(1.66)
ln CITYSZ	-.09***	-.07***	-.05***	-.07***	-.04***	-.05***	-.04***
	(6.30)	(5.21)	(3.86)	(5.09)	(4.07)	(4.04)	(3.16)
R^2	.87	.70	.54	.74	.67	.59	.59

[a] Numbers in parentheses under coefficients are t-statistics.
  * $p < .2$
  ** $p < .1$
  *** $P < .01$.

the *MRLF* elasticities of employment growth in Table 4.9, it is seen that of the three broad sectors, the secondary sector's employment growth was the most responsive to changes in the net migration rate of the labor force and the tertiary sector's employment growth was the least responsive to this adjustment mechanism. On the other hand, the *CLFP* elasticities of employment growth for these three sectors indicate that both the primary and tertiary sectors' employment growth response with respect to changes in the labor force participation rate of the city's working-age population was more than twice that of the secondary sector. Finally, the elasticities of employment growth with respect to the intracity sectoral shift variables reveal that the primary sector's employment growth was almost four times more responsive than that of either of the other two broad sectors to this labor force adjustment mechanism.

Turning to the coefficients of the four more narrowly defined sectors, it is seen that manufacturing employment growth was the most responsive to changes in the net migration rate of the labor force and transportation/communications employment was the least responsive. It is interesting to note that the range of variation in the *MRLF* elasticities across the four narrowly defined sectors is very small; this is also true with respect to the *CLFP* employment growth elasticities across these four sectors. Finally, referring to the SX_i employment growth elasticities for these sectors, it is seen that a great deal of variation in the range exists. In particular, the responsiveness of employment growth in both the manufacturing and transportation/communications sectors is quite high with respect to intracity sectoral shifts of employment, whereas the responsiveness of employment growth in the wholesale/retail and service sectors is quite small.

Comparing the elasticities of each of the three postulated labor force adjustment mechanisms for each sector individually, it is seen that in all cases employment is more responsive to changes in the net migration rate of the labor force than to changes in either of the other two adjustment mechanisms. In addition, these comparisons reveal that in five of the seven sectors employment growth is more responsive to change in the shift index variable than it is to changes in the labor force participation rate of the city's working-age population.

The implications of these results are that, in general, the costs of geographic mobility are exceeded by both the costs of intersector mobility (i.e., retraining costs) and also by the costs (opportunity costs plus entry costs) that must be incurred to increase citywide labor force participation rates. The policy directions suggested by these results will be briefly discussed in the concluding section of the chapter.

---

with respect to the rate of net migration of the labor force. In a similar fashion it can be shown that each of the other coefficients in Table 4.6 also represent employment growth elasticities.

5 Conclusions

This chapter has explored the sectoral employment growth process of the Japanese urban economy in some detail. The major result emerging from the analysis is that of the three mechanisms available for adjusting the labor force distribution to the distribution of employment opportunities, migration is the most important for all analyzed industrial sectors. A second result that emerges is that intercity variation in the rates of net labor force migration are significantly related to a variety of labor market, residential, and locational characteristics that, to varying degrees, can be influenced through local and national public policy action. From the viewpoint of local policymakers, these rather tenuous results imply that measures designed to attract migrants will result in a greater response in employment growth in all sectors than measures designed to facilitate intracity sectoral shifts or increases in the labor force participation rate of the city's working-age population. At the national level the results imply that policymakers should address themselves to the social costs, in terms of allocative efficiency, of each of the adjustment tools and also should concentrate on measuring the social benefits realized from facilitating the use of each of the adjustment mechanisms.

In conclusion, the analysis pursued in this chapter has provided some answers to the question of sources of sectoral employment growth and sources of intercity variations in net migration rates of the labor force. However, perhaps the most important result that emerges is the realization of the importance of determining the sources of employment growth for industries and sectors of the economy with a much greater precision than is possible with currently available aggregate data sources. Given this realization, one important direction for future research in this area is the development of more precise data sources so that the questions of sources of sectoral employment growth can be determined and appropriate public policy can be formulated.

Appendix 1   Cities Used in Chapter 4's Analysis

The original sample of cities chosen for this analysis were the 80 REC cities of Chapters 2 and 3. A description of the sample selection process is provided there and is not repeated here. Tokyo and 7 other of the original 80 cities were dropped from the analysis to obtain the sample used in this chapter. Tokyo was deleted because of certain unique characteristics of the city such as its size and international character. The 7 other cities were deleted because of data incongruities between 1965 and 1970. The 72 cities that were included are listed here.

1. Sapporo	25. Hakodate	49. Muroran
2. Kushiro	26. Morioka	50. Sendai
3. Ishinomaki	27. Akita	51. Yamagata
4. Mito	28. Hitachi	52. Utsunomiya
5. Maebashi	29. Takasaki	53. Kiryu
6. Kumagaya	30. Chiba	54. Niigata
7. Nagaoka	31. Toyama	55. Takaoka
8. Kanazawa	32. Fukui	56. Kofu
9. Matsumoto	33. Gifu	57. Shizuoka
10. Hamamatsu	34. Numazu	58. Nagoya
11. Toyohashi	35. Tsu	59. Yokkaichi
12. Ise	36. Otsu	60. Himeji
13. Nara	37. Wakayama	61. Matsue
14. Tottori	38. Yonago	62. Okayama
15. Hiroshima	39. Fukuyama	63. Shimonoseki
16. Yamaguchi	40. Iwakuni	64. Tokushima
17. Takamatsu	41. Matsuyama	65. Imabari
18. Niihama	42. Kochi	66. Kitakyushu
19. Fukuoka	43. Omuta	67. Kurume
20. Saga	44. Ube	68. Nagasaki
21. Sasebo	45. Kumamoto	69. Yatsushiro
22. Oita	46. Miyazaki	70. Nobeoka
23. Kagoshima	47. Nagano	71. Toyota
24. Kyoto	48. Osaka	72. Kobe

Appendix 2   Employment Growth by Industry and City Size

TABLE 4.A1
Primary Employment Growth Quartiles Versus City Size in 1970
(*Primary Employment Growth Quartiles*)

City size (in thousands)	Slowest growth quartile	Second slowest growth quartile	Second fastest growth quartile	Fastest growth quartile	Total
100–200	22.6	25.8	25.8	25.8	100.0
201–300	16.7	16.7	33.3	33.3	100.0
301–400	14.3	28.6	28.6	28.6	100.0
401–500	14.3	42.9	14.3	28.6	100.0
501–999	33.3	66.6	0	0	100.0
999+	83.3	0	16.7	0	100.0

TABLE 4.A2
Secondary Employment Growth Quartiles versus City Size in 1970
(*Secondary Employment Growth Quartiles*)

City size (in thousands)	Slowest growth quartile	Second slowest growth quartile	Second fastest growth quartile	Fastest growth quartile	Total
100–200	25.8	22.6	25.8	25.8	100.0
201–300	5.5	27.8	38.9	27.8	100.0
301–400	28.6	28.6	0	42.9	100.0
401–500	14.3	42.9	28.6	14.3	100.0
501–999	33.3	33.3	33.3	0	100.0
999+	83.4	0	0	16.7	100.0

TABLE 4.A3
Tertiary Employment Growth Quartiles versus City Size in 1970
(*Tertiary Employment Growth Quartiles*)

City size (in thousands)	Slowest growth quartile	Second slowest growth quartile	Second fastest growth quartile	Fastest growth quartile	Total
100–200	25.8	35.5	19.4	19.4	100.0
201–300	22.2	11.1	22.2	44.4	100.0
301–400	14.3	28.6	42.9	14.3	100.0
401–500	0	28.6	42.9	28.6	100.0
501–999	0	33.3	66.6	0	100.0
999+	83.3	0	0	16.7	100.0

TABLE 4.A4
Manufacturing Employment Growth Quartiles versus City Size in 1970
(*Manufacturing Employment Growth Quartiles*)

City size (in thousands)	Slowest growth quartile	Second slowest growth quartile	Second fastest growth quartile	Fastest growth quartile	Total
100–200	22.6	25.8	22.6	29.0	100.0
201–300	11.1	16.7	44.4	27.8	100.0
301–400	28.6	28.6	14.3	28.6	100.0
401–500	14.3	42.9	14.3	28.6	100.0
501–999	33.3	66.7	0	0	100.0
999+	83.3	0	16.7	0	100.0

TABLE 4.A5
Wholesale/Retail Employment Growth Quartiles versus City Size in 1970
(Wholesale/Retail Employment Growth Quartiles)

City size (in thousands)	Slowest growth quartile	Second slowest growth quartile	Second fastest growth quartile	Fastest growth quartile	Total
100–200	32.2	32.2	22.6	12.9	100.0
201–300	16.7	11.1	27.8	44.4	100.0
301–400	0	42.9	28.6	28.6	100.0
401–500	0	28.6	28.6	42.9	100.0
501–999	0	33.3	66.7	0	100.0
999+	83.3	0	0	16.7	100.0

TABLE 4.A6
Transportation/Communication Employment Growth Quartiles versus City Size in 1970
(Transportation/Communication Employment Growth Quartiles)

City size (in thousands)	Slowest growth quartile	Second slowest growth quartile	Second fastest growth quartile	Fastest growth quartile	Total
100–200	19.4	22.6	29.0	29.0	100.0
201–300	22.2	27.8	27.8	22.2	100.0
301–400	28.6	42.9	0	28.6	100.0
401–500	0	28.6	42.9	28.6	100.0
501–999	33.3	33.3	33.3	0	100.0
999+	83.3	0	0	16.7	100.0

TABLE 4.A7
Services Employment Growth Quartiles versus City Size in 1970
(Services Employment Growth Quartiles)

City size (in thousands)	Slowest growth quartile	Second slowest growth quartile	Second fastest growth quartile	Fastest growth quartile	Total
100–200	32.2	32.2	22.6	12.9	100.0
201–300	16.7	11.1	27.8	44.4	100.0
301–400	0	42.9	28.6	28.6	100.0
401–500	0	28.6	42.9	28.6	100.0
501–999	0	33.3	33.3	33.3	100.0
999+	83.3	0	0	16.7	100.0

References

Blanco, C. (1963). The determinants of interstate population movements. *Journal of Regional Science, 5,* 77–84.

Borts, G. H. and L. Stein (1964). *Economic Growth in a Free Market.* Columbia University Press, New York.

Cordy-Hayes, M. and D. Gleave (1974). Migration movements and the differential growth of city regions in England and Wales. *Papers of the Regional Science Association, 33,* 99–123.

Glickman, N. J. (1976). On the Japanese urban system. *Journal of Regional Science, 16,* 317–336.

Glickman, N. J. and W. W. McHone (1977). Intercity migration and employment growth in the Japanese urban system. *Regional Studies, 11,* 165–181.

Greenwood, M. F. (1975). Urban economic growth and migration. *Environmental Planning, 5,* 91–112.

Isard, W., *et al.* (1960). *Methods of Regional Analysis.* MIT Press, Cambridge, Massachusetts.

Johnston, J. (1963). *Econometric Method,* 1st ed. McGraw-Hill, New York.

Kamiya, K. (1963). Korekara no jinko bumpu: shukyoku bumpo to chiiki keizi. (The future population distribution: limiting distributions and regional economics.) *Kinu Janaru (Finance Journal) 4,* 40–43. In Japanese.

Kawashima, T. (1966). Some trends and problems on the recent regional development of manufacturing industry in Japan. *Osaka City University Economic Review, 2,* 33–41.

Kuroda, T. (1969). *A New Dimension of Internal Migration in Japan.* Institute of Population Problems. Tokyo English Pamphlet Series No. 69.

Land, K. (1969). Duration of residence and prospective migration. *Demography, 4,* 293–309.

Lowry, I. S. (1966). *Migration and Metropolitan Growth: Two Analytical Models.* Chandler Publishing Company, San Francisco.

Mills, E. S., and K. Ohta. (1976). Urbanization and urban problems, in Patrick, H. and H. Rosovsky, eds., *Asia's New Giant: How the Japanese Economy Works.* The Brookings Institution, Washington, D. C. Pp. 673–751.

Morrison, P. A. (1971). Chronic movers and future redistributions of population. *Demography, 8,* 171–184.

Muth, R. F. (1968). Differential growth among large U.S. cities, in Quirk, J. P. and A. M. Zarley, eds., *Papers in Quantitative Economics.* University of Kansas Press, Lawrence, Kansas.

Muth, R. F. (1971). Migration: chicken or egg? *Southern Economic Journal, 37,* 295–306.

Okada, M. (1971). Jinko chihokanryu gensho no kenti to sono shakaiteki imi no kaishaku. (U-turn movement in Japan.) *Shakaigatu Hyoron (Japanese Scoiological Review), 22,* 86–93. In Japanese.

Okazaki, Y. (1969). An observation on the relationship between population migration and industrialization. *Annual Report of the Institute of Population Problems, 14.* Institute of Population Problems, Tokyo.

Shimizu, R. (1964), Waga kuni ni okeru jinko ido to sangyo no chiiki kozo. (Migration and regional structure of Japanese industries). *Nogyo Keizai Kenkyu (Journal of Farm Economics), 36,* 1–1. In Japanese.

Vining, D. R. Jr. (1975). The spatial distribution of human populations and its characteristic evolution over time: some recent evidence from Japan. *Papers of the Regional Science Association, 35,* 157–180.

Yamaguchi, T. (1969). Japanese cities: their functions and characteristics. *Papers and Proceedings of the Third Far East Conference of the Regional Science Association, 3,* 141–156.

5

The Spatial Structure of
Japanese Cities

1 Introduction

This chapter extends the analysis of Chapters 2 and 3, as some spatial aspects of Japanese cities are considered. Particularly, the focus is on the spatial distribution of land use patterns and land prices, using microeconomic data. Since Japanese cities are so densely populated, no study of Japanese urbanism would be complete without a rigorous examination of these phenomena. The chapter also looks at land use patterns in Japan in relation to those of other countries, continuing the international comparisons begun in earlier chapters.

Density patterns are examined first. Figure 5.1 shows the growth of total population density between 1920 and 1970, which grew rather steadily over the entire period (parallel to the growth of total population) at approximately 1% per year. Urban density (Figure 5.2) fell nearly continuously from 1920 to 1960, largely because of a greatly expanded definition of what areas are considered "urban." However, urban densities rose between 1960 and 1970; the 1970 level was 791. This can be compared with a density of 1,300 for U.S. urbanized areas. Mills and Ohta (1976, pp. 681–682) argue that Japanese living in the more densely populated portions of cities have much higher density living conditions than Americans. Density in Japanese Densely Inhabited Districts (DIDs) was about 8,700 per square kilometer, nearly five times the average density of the central cities of U.S. SMSAs, for example. Mills and Ohta conclude that Japanese urban densities are really about 1.5 times U.S. levels. This seems to be a reasonable estimate.

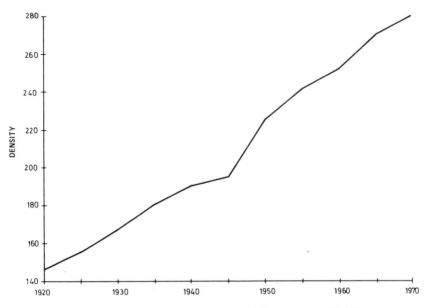

Figure 5.1. Total population density in Japan, 1920–1970.

Next, we observe urban land prices. Parallel to the rapid growth of urban population noted in Chapters 2 and 3, there were astonishing increases in urban land prices. According to the Japan National Land Agency (1976, p. 57), the index of urban land prices increased from a base of 100 in 1955 to 2,691 in 1975, an increase of over 19% per year. When compared to other countries, as is shown in Table 5.1, these land price increases are great. Land price growth has been particularly high in the largest cities such as Tokyo, Osaka, and Kyoto; on this subject, see Japan National Land Agency (1975, p. 27).[1] These high and rising land prices reflect the relative scarcity of a land-poor country and, in recent years, considerable land speculation.

It is toward understanding density and land price patterns that I undertake the analysis in this chapter. There are six additional sections. Section 2 outlines the major analytical tool used in the chapter—the urban density function. Section 3 presents some estimates of density functions for a sample of Japanese cities. Section 4 gives some estimates of the spatial distribution of land prices and, Section 5 presents a model of land use, tying together the work of Sections 3 and 4. Section 6 undertakes a set of cross-cultural comparisons, and concluding remarks are contained in Section 7.

---

[1] For instance, for 1973 when the land price index for rural and urban land was 2,812 (1955 = 100), the index for the six largest cities was 3,444.

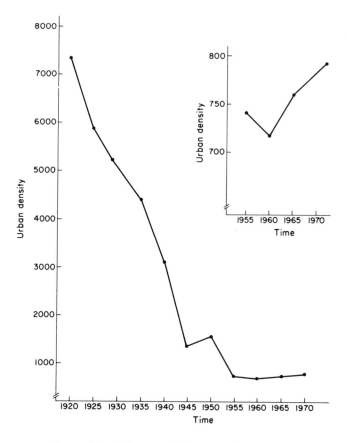

Figure 5.2. Urban population density, 1920–1970.

2 Measures of Urban Spatial Structure

2.1 Introduction

Before any serious analysis of urban form can be undertaken, a good measure must be found of the dimensions of spatial structure. Mills (1972a, 1972b) and others[2] have adopted the negative exponential density function as a good first approximation of how residential density varies as one moves from the center of the city to its periphery. The density function is depicted

---

[2] See, for instance, Clark (1951), Muth (1969), Newling (1969), Kau and Lee (1977), and McDonald and Bowman (1976). McDonald and Bowman provide a good set of references on this subject.

TABLE 5.1
International Comparison of Land Price Changes

Country and years	Average annual growth (percentage)
Japan (1955–1970)	19.3
United States (1956–1966)	4.5–6.0
France (1950–1970)	15.0–21.0
West Germany (1962–1968)	7.5–14.5
United Kingdom (1960–1964)	10.0
Switzerland (1950–1968)	13.0

Source: Japan National Land Agency (1976; p. 60).

in Figure 5.3 and specified in Eq. (1)

$$D_j = D_{01} \exp(-G_1 t_j) \tag{1}$$

where D_j is the density at tract j; t_j is the distance from tract j to the center of the city; D_{01} is the central density; and G_1 is the density gradient. According to Eq. (1), if $t_j = 0$, then D_{01} is the hypothetical central density. Additionally, since G_1 [the slope or gradient of Eq. (1)] is greater than zero, density decreases with each unit distance moved from the core of the city. For example if $G_1 = .4$, then population in that city would fall by 40% per unit t of movement from the center. Furthermore, if the city's population increases by increasing D_{01} (with G_1 constant), then the percentage of population living within any given distance from the center is unchanged. Therefore, it follows that if one compares two density functions, the one with the larger value of G_1 will be less suburbanized. This feature allows us easily to compare the spatial structures of different urban areas independent of legal boundaries.

2.2   The Underlying Theoretical Model[3]

Mills (1972b, Chap. 5) has provided a theoretical model of a monocentric city that predicts that population density decays exponentially with distance from the center. The model assumes that all employment is located in the Central Business District (CBD), that the price elasticity of demand for housing is unity, that all households have the same tastes and income levels, and that commuting costs per mile are constant. Two versions of the model are relevant for predictive purposes: the closed-city and the open-city model. In the former, the city's total population is assumed fixed, independent of exogenous changes; in the latter, households are assumed to migrate frictionlessly among cities in response to utility differentials caused by exogenous changes.

[3] This section draws heavily from Glickman and White (1978).

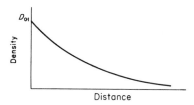

Figure 5.3. The negative exponential density function.

These versions of the basic urban model suggest several hypotheses concerning the way density function parameters shift as exogenous factors change. First, suppose the major effects of the passage of time on the parameters of the model have historically been to raise income levels and to lower transportation costs. If these changes occur uniformly for all large and small cities in a national system of cities, then their effects can be predicted using the closed-city version of the model; the level of household welfare in all cities will increase over time, but no strong interurban migration flows will occur. When, as incomes rise, all cities' density gradients should flatten and their central density levels should fall. Similarly, if travel costs (including both the actual outlay and the value of time spent) fall in all cities, then the same effects should occur.[4] Then, as incomes increase, the density gradients of all cities should fall (i.e., flatten) and their central densities should also decline. Similarly, if travel costs (including both the money outlays and the value of travel time) fall in all cities, then the same effect should occur.

Second, comparing large and small cities contemporaneously, the open-city model is relevant if intercity migration occurs quickly in response to exogenous changes. Suppose the difference between large and small cities is that larger cities benefit from agglomeration economies that push up wages. This draws an increased population to larger cities until, at equilibrium, higher rents eliminate the welfare advantages of living there. Thus, larger cities should have lower density gradients but higher central density levels. This prediction is tested in Sections 3.3 and 6.3 by examining density functions for a group of cities of different sizes.

Also, the effects of changes in large cities' productivity advantage over that of small cities can be traced by their effects on the density function parameters. If large cities' productivity advantage decline over time due to improvements in communications and transportation technology, then we would expect the ratio of large-city to small-city density gradients to decline over time for cities of a given size and vice versa.

---

[4] In addition, the closed city model is relevant for comparisons across countries at a single point in time, since intercountry migration does not occur quickly. Comparing the density gradients of cities of the same size in different countries, we expect that those of higher income countries will have flatter density gradients and lower central density levels. See Section 6 for further consideration of this matter.

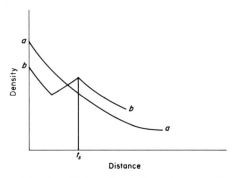

Figure 5.4. Density function with suburban subcenter.

2.3 Extensions of the Simple Model

Like all models, this one is oversimplified, neglecting as it does the effects of several important changes occurring in cities. One obvious trend not considered by the model is that of employment suburbanization: Jobs are moving away from the traditional CBD. Population suburbanization is predicted by the simple model, but job suburbanization is usually assumed away. Under certain conditions, it is possible for job suburbanization to occur without changing the general shape of a city's population density function.[5] However, more commonly, the process of job suburbanization creates suburban subcenters, local concentrations of jobs that have their own declining rent and population density functions in all directions. These tend to flatten an overall estimated density gradient for a city relative to what it would be with only CBD employment. Curve aa of Figure 5.4 shows an exponential density function for a city with all CBD employment, and curve bb shows a density function for a city with a suburban subcenter at distance $t = t_s$ from the center. Incorrect estimation of bb using an exponential form would result in a flatter density gradient than if aa were estimated using an exponential. Thus, cities with greater suburbanization of employment will tend to have flatter density gradients and lower central density levels. If job suburbanization occurs gradually over time, then its effects will tend to reinforce the effects of rising income and falling transportation costs on the estimated density function. But, since job suburbanization tends to cause cities' density functions increasingly to depart from the shape of an exponential, we expect that over time the estimated density functions will fit less well in cities where job suburbanization is occurring.

A second problem of the simple model concerns the assumption that all households have the same income level and the same tastes. If, in fact, several income classes are present in a city, then each will have a separate bid rent function as shown in Figure 5.5. Most urban models predict that the

---

[5] See Solow (1973) and White (1976) for further discussions.

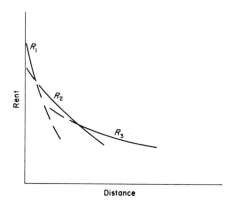

Figure 5.5. Bid rent functions for a city.

poor (R_1) outbid the rich (R_3) for central area housing and the rich outbid the poor in the suburbs, as shown. If so, then the market rent function is the upper envelope in Figure 5.5. Also, the population density function has the same shape as the rent function.[6] If the underlying bid rent functions are exponentials, then the upper envelope cannot be an exponential (even as the number of income classes increases to an infinite number). Rather, the true density function is more convex than an exponential. If an exponential is fit to data for a city with several income classes, the intercept will be biased upward and the gradient will be too steep; also, the extent of the bias will increase as the range of income levels in the city increases and as higher income households form a larger fraction of the city's population. If large cities have relatively more high-income households, then this will reinforce the tendency already noted for larger cities to have flatter density gradients. Furthermore, if large cities have flatter density gradients (due to greater job suburbanization and/or more high-income workers), then intertemporal changes in large cities' productivity advantages over small cities' can be traced by their effect on the density gradient. If large cities' productivity advantage over small cities' declines over time (due, perhaps, to improvements in communications technology), then we expect the ratio of large-city to small-city density gradients to decline over time for cities of a given size.[7]

Third, the simple monocentric model also assumes that each city is spatially independent, that is, that it is surrounded on all sides by agricultural or vacant land and does not abut any other city. In fact, many cities are adjacent to other cities and may indeed be completely surrounded by other cities. This is particularly true of cities in the Tokaido belt in Japan. The existence of abutting cities, like subcenters, tends to flatten the estimated exponential density function and to reduce the explanatory power of the model. The same effect also tends to occur when the rural population density

[6] See Mills (1972b) for derivations of bid rent and density functions.
[7] I shall test this prediction of the model in Section 6.3.

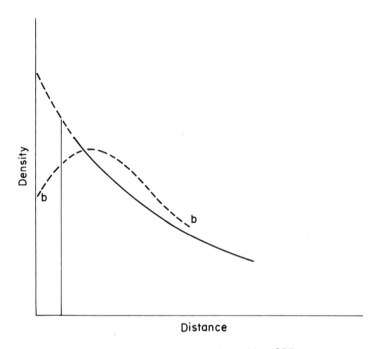

Figure 5.6. Density function with a CBD.

level is relatively high. The model assumes that nonurban land is used entirely for agriculture and that the population of such land is zero. In fact, nonurban population levels in Japan may be quite high as Mills and Ohta (1976) have indicated.

Fourth, the simple model assumes complete spatial separation of residential and nonresidential uses. Thus, D_{01} in Eq. (1) is the hypothetical central density level that would prevail if a city had an infinitesimally small CBD in Figure 5.6. In fact, residential and nonresidential land uses mix in varying proportions all over the city. Near the CBD, population densities fall off as nonresidential uses begin to predominate. Thus, density may decline near the center as shown by *bb* in Figure 5.6. A variety of techniques have been developed to fit density functions other than the exponential that peak and fall off near the center. I experiment with other functional forms in Section 3, although not all such previous attempts have been very successful.[8] I attempt to correct for possible biases by omitting central tracts from my sample. However, to the extent that substantial nonresidential uses occur in included tracts, this tends to bias both the density gradient and the

---

[8] See McDonald and Bowman (1976) for a comparison of several functional forms.

central density level downward. The bias is worse where the CBD is less distinct, that is, where more mixing of residential and nonresidential uses occurs.

2.4   Other Forms of the Urban Density Function

Some authors, such as McDonald and Bowman (1976) and Newling (1969), have considered other forms of the urban density functions including the following.

$$D_j = D_{02} \exp(-G_2 t_j^2) \tag{2}$$

and

$$D_j = D_{03} \exp(G_{31} t_j + G_{32} t_j^2) \tag{3}$$

where the symbols parallel those described in conjunction with Eq. (1). Here, $D_{02}, D_{03}, G_2, G_{31}$, and G_{32} are parameters to be estimated from the data as are D_{01} and G_1. Equation (2) has a standardized normal density function and Eq. (3) a general normal density function. Using Eq. (3) allows for the possibility of a "crater" in the center of the city. That is, density can increase as one moves away from the core, reach a peak, and then decline as t increases further. Such is the case in the various configurations of Figure 5.7. Newling considers the case where G_{32} is less than zero. If so, the density function can have three forms depending on the sign of G_{31}. If G_{31} is greater than zero, then the function is of the form of Figure 5.7a. If G_{31} equals or is less than

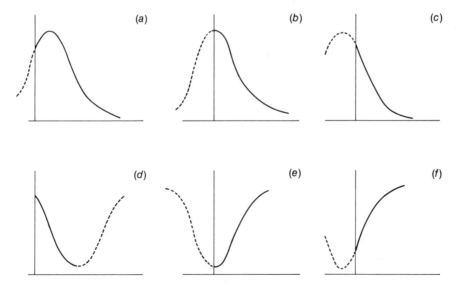

Figure 5.7.   Quadratic forms of urban density functions. (a): $G_{32} < 0$, $G_{31} > 0$; (b): $G_{32} < 0$, $G_{31} = 0$; (c): $G_{32} < 0$, $G_{31} < 0$; (d): $G_{32} > 0$, $G_{31} < 0$; (e): $G_{32} > 0$, $G_{31} = 0$; (f): $G_{32} > 0$, $G_{31} > 0$.

zero, then the function would appear as a decreasing function of distance as in Figures 5.7b and 5.7c. If, on the other hand, G_{32} is greater than zero and G_{31} is less than zero, then we have the odd form given in Figure 5.7d: the inverted quadratic. I shall return to a discussion of this in Section 3.1.3. Finally, if G_{32} is positive and G_{31} is equal to or greater than zero, we have the situation where density is an increasing function of t as depicted in Figures 5.7e and 5.7f.

The viability of using Eqs. (1)–(3) to describe the form of Japanese cities by comparing them with each other with respect to statistical fit, including the case in which G_{32} is greater than zero, a case not considered by Newling, is discussed in Section 3.

3 Estimates of Density Functions for Japanese Cities

3.1 Estimates for Individual Cities

Tables 5.2–5.4 show the results for the forms given in Eqs. (1)–(3).[9] A 25% random sample of census tracts was taken, with a minimum of 15 observations for each city. Employing city maps, I measured the distance from the cities' centers to each of the census tracts in the sample. I thus obtained data for density and distance and used ordinary least squares regressions to estimate the parameters for $D_{01}, \ldots, D_{03}$ and $G_1, \ldots, G_{32}$ summarized in Tables 5.2–5.4. Also given in those tables are the t-test and the coefficient of determination adjusted for degrees of freedom (R^2).

3.1.1 Estimates Using Equation (1)

Let us review the findings for the density function of equations that we have discussed. First, examine Table 5.2 for the negative exponential function. The "prototypical" Japanese city can be constructed by taking a mean of the values for the 84 cities in the sample.

$$D_j = 12{,}992 \exp(-.3184t_j) \qquad R^2 = .531$$

That is, the hypothetical central density was 12,992 persons per square kilometer and the population density decreased at a rate of 31.84% per kilometer movement away from the core. The empirical relationship be-

---

[9] For a use of these estimates, see Section 5 and Glickman and Oguri (1978). Data on population density by census tract are available for each of those cities for 1970 from the *1970 Population Census* (Japan Bureau of Statistics, Office of the Prime Minister, 1972). Each census tract has a population between 5,000 and 20,000 in that year, and census tracts were delineated for cities of 200,000 or more (124 for all of Japan) and for prefectural capitals with populations of less than 200,000.

TABLE 5.2

Estimates of Urban Density Functions Using Equation (1), 1970

		Sample size	D_{01}	G_1	t	R^2
1	Sapporo	30	29,544.125	.35986	(7.244)	.652
2	Hakodate	22	15,017.922	.16760	(2.341)	.215
3	Asahikawa	13	12,874.453	.48730	(14.860)	.952
4	Aomori	30	14,946.168	.39419	(11.576)	.827
5	Hachinohe	21	6,865.270	.37575	(4.325)	.496
6	Morioka	27	11,456.238	.50862	(8.995)	.764
7	Sendai	30	20,212.160	.40786	(5.379)	.508
8	Akita	28	5,935.523	.21835	(2.889)	.243
9	Yamagata	24	12,309.789	.54320	(14.461)	.905
10	Fukushima	23	3,818.223	.29734	(9.508)	.812
11	Kooriyama	26	5,661.418	.29493	(9.569)	.792
12	Utsunomiya	30	13,595.723	.44839	(8.559)	.724
13	Maebashi	30	10,949.180	.34874	(4.512)	.421
14	Kawaguchi	30	19,766.023	.35165	(5.118)	.483
15	Urawa	27	23,400.207	.60153	(10.652)	.819
16	Omiya	30	23,252.539	.59212	(5.943)	.558
17	Chiba	30	11,110.219	.18877	(2.906)	.232
18	Ichikawa	26	22,233.375	.48214	(6.480)	.636
19	Funabashi	30	15,637.852	.19326	(3.065)	.251
20	Hachioji	30	13,437.172	.51980	(10.322)	.792
21	Yokosuka	30	6,360.742	.08435	(.721)	.018
22	Fujisawa	22	8,117.602	.19028	(2.932)	.301
23	Sagamihara	25	3,077.890	.04987	(.689)	.020
24	Niigata	30	11,321.516	.26587	(8.229)	.707
25	Toyama	27	9,455.195	.36119	(7.248)	.678
26	Kanazawa	30	16,460.352	.44144	(9.144)	.749
27	Fukui	17	10,371.941	.50757	(7.765)	.801
28	Kofu	21	22,847.570	.77223	(8.010)	.771
29	Nagano	30	5,680.699	.25356	(5.605)	.529
30	Gifu	30	18,710.312	.47473	(12.120)	.840
31	Shizuoka	29	23,571.168	.49841	(16.778)	.913
32	Hamamatsu	30	10,454.527	.31156	(11.382)	.822
33	Shimizu	32	10,579.777	.39720	(7.916)	.676
34	Toyohashi	24	10,802.469	.40152	(9.103)	.790
35	Okazaki	21	9,979.414	.43393	(7.483)	.747
36	Ichinomiya	16	9,715.422	.33236	(5.231)	.661
37	Tsu	13	7,044.480	.42270	(4.110)	.606
38	Yokkaichi	28	6,098.816	.29716	(7.998)	.711
39	Otsu	15	4,473.828	.21330	(4.786)	.638
40	Kyoto	41	46,166.043	.36490	(10.270)	.730
41	Sakai	30	18,343.680	.28298	(6.665)	.613
42	Toyonaka	25	9,461.629	.01572	(.128)	.001

TABLE 5.2 *(Continued)*

	Sample size	D_{01}	G_1	t	R^2
43 Suita	25	8,883.937	.07927	(1.074)	.048
44 Takatsuki	23	22,986.223	.60542	(5.618)	.600
45 Hirakata	20	15,267.316	.44721	(5.774)	.649
46 Yao	20	4,294.109	.30300	(1.356)	.093
47 Neyagawa	20	17,413.488	.21070	(.669)	.024
48 Higashiosaka	30	20,294.594	.21948	(5.858)	.551
49 Himeji	30	6,512.055	.17389	(3.235)	.272
50 Amagasaki	30	25,143.383	.27939	(3.009)	.245
51 Nishinomiya	30	27,210.004	.44195	(6.627)	.611
52 Nara	22	3,444.520	.11756	(1.169)	.064
53 Wakayama	30	14,144.340	.37521	(9.816)	.775
54 Tottori	15	6,634.246	.46660	(6.450)	.762
55 Matsue	15	8,400.113	.48970	(6.961)	.788
56 Kurashiki	30	2,828.749	.07811	(2.010)	.126
57 Kure	23	9,179.887	.35993	(5.371)	.579
58 Fukuyama	27	5,359.793	.20971	(3.233)	.295
59 Shimonoseki	28	10,632.598	.25327	(9.866)	.789
60 Yamaguchi	12	943.881	.15410	(2.484)	.382
61 Tokushima	21	8,866.629	.44557	(10.995)	.864
62 Takamatsu	29	11,419.641	.38835	(9.127)	.755
63 Matsuyama	30	12,701.559	.40983	(7.221)	.651
64 Kochi	17	15,080.988	.56975	(7.589)	.793
65 Fukuoka	30	14,782.512	.18812	(3.663)	.324
66 Saga	13	8,225.551	.51250	(6.066)	.770
67 Nagasaki	30	19,778.488	.43608	(6.730)	.618
68 Kumamoto	30	12,278.437	.34186	(5.565)	.525
69 Oita	24	6,005.555	.27084	(6.371)	.649
70 Miyazaki	19	5,318.148	.30134	(5.804)	.665
71 Kagoshima	30	14,443.352	.31240	(5.387)	.509
72 Iwaki	28	2,674.987	.14920	(3.796)	.357
73 Mito	14	7,368.723	.37010	(4.351)	.612
74 Matsudo	15	4,230.184	.03870	(.301)	.069
75 Tokyo	89	17,518.273	.01320	(.543)	.003
76 Yokohama	87	17,943.805	.11780	(5.208)	.242
77 Kawasaki	29	18,681.715	.08750	(3.835)	.353
78 Nagoya	46	25,084.367	.17100	(6.214)	.467
79 Osaka	61	16,285.004	−.01430	(−.457)	.004
80 Kobe	40	21,881.562	.16020	(3.747)	.270
81 Okayama	30	9,508.102	.28280	(9.231)	.753
82 Hiroshima	30	17,676.648	.32470	(4.450)	.446
83 Kitakyushu	27	13,218.859	.15540	(3.750)	.360
84 Sasebo	15	9,681.773	.28970	(3.754)	.520
Mean		12,992.164	.31835		.531

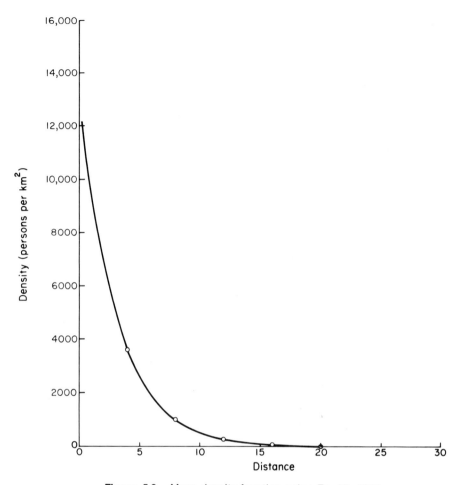

Figure 5.8.   Mean density function using Eq. (1), 1970.

tween density and distance as given by the mean city as estimated by Eq. (1) is shown in Figure 5.8.

Comparing cities within the sample, we find that medium-sized independent cities (those away from major concentrations) have better statistical fits than those in concentrated areas or their suburbs, as one would expect from the discussion in Section 2. Thus, cities such as Asahikawa, Aomori, Fukushima, Urawa, Yamagata, and Tokushima all have R^2s greater than .80; they are largely away from the core of the urban system, being located in Hokkaido, Tohoku, and Shikoku. Large cities such as Tokyo (R^2 = .003), Osaka (R^2 = .004), and Kobe (R^2 = .270) had poor fits. Kyoto and Sapporo are exceptions among the large cities, having high R^2s; Sapporo, however, is an independent center and should have a good fit.

The suburbs of the large cities also have poor fits since their density is affected heavily by the interaction with the central cities of which they are suburbs and the neighboring suburban towns. See, for example, in suburban Osaka the low R^2s for Toyonaka and Suita. These results are expected from previous work on urban density functions and the discussion in Section 2.

Comparing density gradients (G_1) among cities, we know from Section 2.1 that the larger G_1, the faster density falls with distance from the core; the smaller G_1, the slower density declines. Thus, G_1 is a measure of the spatial decentralization within cities. Not surprisingly, we find that Tokyo and Osaka have very small G_1s and that smaller independent centers such as Tokushima, Aomori, and Sendai have much larger G_1s; This indicates less decentralization in the independent cities.

3.1.2   Estimates Using Equation (2)

Table 5.3, gives the estimates obtained using Eq. (2). The statistical fits are inferior to those shown in Table 5.2: The mean R^2 is only .461 for Eq. (2) compared to .531 for Eq. (1). The results here show that there was more decentralization in the larger cities and more compact configurations for the independent and smaller cities. The same estimation problems were found with the large and suburban cities in the sample as in estimating Eq. (1): They performed in an inferior manner with respect to independent cities. The mean city's function for Eq. (2) is depicted in Figure 5.9.

3.1.3   Estimates Using Equation (3)

Tables 5.4a–5.4c show the results for the equations estimated using Eq. (3). There are three possible sets of results for Eq. (3) that are consistent with urban theory as noted in Section 2.[10] Our results for Eq. (3) are somewhat mixed in comparison to our results for Eqs. (1) and (2). In Table 5.4a, we find the case in which $G_{31} > 0$ and $G_{32} < 0$, the "crater" case of Newling and others. Included in the cities that exhibited these tendencies are the large ones such as Hiroshima, Kawasaki, and Fukuoka. The fits are poor and the coefficients for G_{31} are insignificant at a 99% significance test; many of the coefficients for G_{32} are also statistically insignificant. The maximum point of the quadratic is given by the formula $(-G_{31}/2G_{32})$. For the mean city in the sample of seven cities in this category, the maximum point (or peak of density) is 3.074 km from the center; declines in density set in thereafter as we move from the core.[11] In general, the smaller the absolute value of G_{32},

---

[10] The fourth, where $G_{31} \geq 0$ and $G_{32} > 0$, implies a density gradient with a positive slope with distance that is counterintuitive and counterfactual. See Figures 5.7e and 5.7f. The regressions for Tokyo and Osaka fall into this category; I believe these to be spurious empirical results.

[11] The rather large average crater (more than 3 km) occurs because of two extremely large craters for Fukuoka (12.9 km) and Yao (4.9 km). If these outliers are removed, the average crater is a more reasonable value of .7 km.

TABLE 5.3

Estimates of Urban Density Function Using Equation (2), 1970

	D_{02}	G_2	t	R^2
1 Sapporo	10,955.530	.02608	(7.661)	.677
2 Hakodate	12,209.860	.02575	(2.136)	.186
3 Asahikawa	5,497.234	.03675	(14.030)	.947
4 Aomori	6,998.422	.02372	(7.872)	.689
5 Hachinohe	3,088.251	.03268	(3.578)	.402
6 Morioka	4,445.465	.04220	(7.633)	.700
7 Sendai	9,996.301	.04697	(5.589)	.527
8 Akita	3,703.411	.01464	(2.275)	.166
9 Yamagata	5,174.973	.05457	(9.777)	.813
10 Fukushima	1,350.460	.01433	(6.796)	.687
11 Kooriyama	2,396.345	.01154	(4.930)	.503
12 Utsunomiya	5,968.133	.04128	(6.707)	.616
13 Maebashi	6,362.645	.03243	(3.455)	.299
14 Kawaguchi	13,600.330	.05639	(5.804)	.546
15 Urawa	10,956.300	.08342	(7.945)	.716
16 Omiya	11,823.790	.09453	(5.750)	.541
17 Chiba	6,684.121	.01328	(3.075)	.252
18 Ichikawa	13,526.010	.08628	(6.422)	.632
19 Funabashi	10,937.360	.01935	(3.221)	.270
20 Hachioji	5,197.430	.04742	(7.394)	.661
21 Yokosuka	5,534.297	.00935	(.753)	.020
22 Fujisawa	5,615.074	.01700	(2.642)	.259
23 Sagamihara	3,035.100	.00965	(1.241)	.063
24 Niigata	5,283.844	.01452	(5.654)	.533
25 Toyama	5,194.680	.03753	(5.659)	.562
26 Kanazawa	7,188.441	.03830	(8.694)	.730
27 Fukui	4,386.379	.04185	(4.479)	.572
28 Kofu	10,874.650	.14921	(8.519)	.793
29 Nagano	2,766.063	.01549	(4.499)	.420
30 Gifu	7,738.320	.04462	(8.055)	.699
31 Shizuoka	9,402.395	.04299	(10.697)	.809
32 Hamamatsu	4,937.676	.02200	(7.051)	.640
33 Shimizu	4,019.447	.02393	(5.620)	.513
34 Toyohashi	4,898.230	.03341	(6.533)	.660
35 Okazaki	3,832.184	.03736	(6.314)	.677
36 Ichinomiya	6,019.859	.04160	(3.458)	.461
37 Tsu	4,407.219	.06566	(3.620)	.544
38 Yokkaichi	2,968.940	.02065	(5.717)	.557
39 Otsu	2,377.964	.01120	(4.350)	.593
40 Kyoto	19,594.420	.02517	(11.850)	.783
41 Sakai	10,254.680	.02398	(6.326)	.589
42 Toyonaka	9,172.813	.00803	(.358)	.006

TABLE 5.3 *(Continued)*

		D_{02}	G_2	t	R^2
43	Suita	7,769.801	.00713	(.689)	.002
44	Takatsuki	10,843.160	.08982	(6.714)	.682
45	Hirakata	14,447.110	.06409	(7.792)	.771
46	Yao	5,308.152	.08865	(1.262)	.081
47	Neyagawa	14,720.550	.05839	(.552)	.017
48	Higashiosaka	14,370.880	.02525	(5.483)	.518
49	Himeji	4,185.281	.01231	(2.787)	.217
50	Amagasaki	16,742.230	.04194	(2.323)	.162
51	Nishinomiya	13,714.920	.03922	(7.161)	.647
52	Nara	2,716.964	.01052	(1.116)	.059
53	Wakayama	6,715.809	.03277	(7.701)	.679
54	Tottori	3,041.179	.03705	(3.923)	.542
55	Matsue	3,327.577	.03906	(4.023)	.545
56	Kurashiki	2,179.368	.00427	(1.751)	.099
57	Kure	5,118.207	.03786	(4.480)	.489
58	Fukuyama	3,213.418	.01424	(2.196)	.162
59	Shimonoseki	5,262.859	.01244	(6.884)	.646
60	Yamaguchi	521.652	.00614	(1.414)	.166
61	Tokushima	3,839.969	.03898	(7.016)	.721
62	Takamatsu	5,687.297	.03873	(6.974)	.643
63	Matsuyama	6,489.172	.04609	(6.232)	.581
64	Kochi	7,505.191	.08314	(5.817)	.693
65	Fukuoka	9,973.426	.01724	(4.174)	.384
66	Saga	3,554.606	.04968	(3.221)	.485
67	Nagasaki	9,374.789	.04863	(6.121)	.572
68	Kumamoto	6,853.125	.03685	(4.947)	.466
69	Oita	2,917.697	.01633	(4.096)	.433
70	Miyazaki	2,352.467	.01456	(3.419)	.408
71	Kagoshima	6,705.141	.02067	(4.614)	.432
72	Iwaki	1,401.082	.00588	(3.659)	.340
73	Mito	4,052.139	.04016	(4.201)	.595
74	Matsudo	3,688.593	.00063	(.034)	.000
75	Tokyo	18,694.790	.00189	(1.435)	.023
76	Yokohama	12,004.050	.00674	(5.303)	.249
77	Kawasaki	13,867.300	.00423	(4.120)	.386
78	Nagoya	16,514.590	.01360	(6.245)	.470
79	Osaka	17,483.270	−.00016	(−.065)	.000
80	Kobe	12,701.040	.00755	(3.841)	.280
81	Okayama	4,653.430	.01762	(6.113)	.572
82	Hiroshima	12,730.800	.05760	(5.382)	.509
83	Kitakyushu	8,464.191	.00913	(2.912)	.253
84	Sasebo	5,318.785	.02192	(2.994)	.408
Mean		7,397.602	.03281		.461

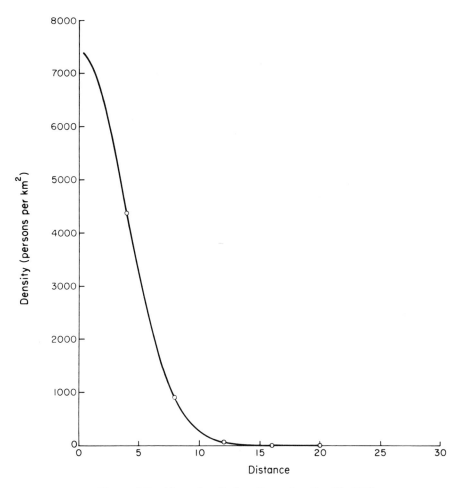

Figure 5.9. Mean density function using Eq. (2), 1970.

the flatter the function will be. Also, the smaller G_{31}, the smaller the size of the crater.

Table 5.4b and Figure 5.7c show the case where G_{31} and G_{32} are both less than zero and thus where the maximum point of the quadratic is in the negative quadrant. Thus, the regressions reflect the right-hand side of the tail of the quadratic function. Here, we have many large- and medium-sized cities such as Nagoya, Kobe, and Sapporo, as well as some suburban cities such as Higashiosaka, Sakai, and Nishinomiya (all near Osaka) and Matsudo, Ichikawa, Funabashi, Chiba, and Yokusuka (which are located close to Tokyo).[12] There are many monocentric independent centers in this group,

[12] The presence of Nagoya in this group (rather than in the group in Table 5.4a) can best be explained by its rebuilding in western grid style after World War II with less distinct "downtown" area (or more decentralized CBD) than other large cities.

TABLE 5.4
Estimates of Urban Density functions Using Equation (3): $G_{31} < 0$, $G_{32} < 0$, 1970

	D_{03}	G_{31}	t_1	G_{32}	t_2	$-G_{31}/2G_{32}$	R^2
A. Group I: G_{31+}, G_{32+}							
1 Takatsuki	10,476.920	.0246	(.084)	-.09305	(-2.270)	.132	.682
2 Kawasaki	13,634.780	.0044	(.055)	-.00442	(-1.192)	.501	.386
3 Hiroshima	11,111.760	.1155	(.484)	-.07606	(-1.920)	.759	.513
4 Kawaguchi	11,011.000	.1728	(.656)	-.08165	(-2.056)	1.058	.553
5 Hirakata	6,083.465	.2299	(1.069)	-.09303	(-3.288)	1.236	.786
6 Yao	3,936.313	.4427	(.492)	-.04518	(-.160)	4.899	.094
7 Fukuoka	7,097.090	.7434	(.743)	-.02874	(-1.793)	12.932	.396
Mean	9,050.191	.2476		-.06030		3.074	.487
B. Group II: G_{31-}, G_{32-}							
1 Morioka	10,836.110	-.4756	(-2.564)	-.00301	(-.187)	-79.063	.764
2 Iwaki	2,398.815	-.1218	(-.829)	-.00115	(-.194)	-53.053	.358
3 Higashiosaka	19,733.640	-.2001	(-1.414)	-.00239	(-.142)	-41.875	.551
4 Sakai	16,013.530	-.2116	(-1.417)	-.00645	(-.500)	-16.395	.617
5 Sasebo	13,121.400	-.4709	(-1.876)	-.01629	(-.760)	-14.454	.542
6 Tsu	8,316.523	-.5932	(-1.322)	-.02878	(-.391)	-10.306	.612
7 Yamaguchi	3,835.288	-.7411	(-6.068)	-.03681	(-5.000)	-10.067	.836
8 Matsue	18,434.870	-1.0280	(-6.066)	-.05392	(-3.344)	-9.533	.891
9 Kanazawa	12,486.330	-.2805	(-1.859)	-.01492	(-1.125)	-9.398	.760
10 Tottori	15,123.410	-1.1090	(-6.094)	-.06306	(-3.681)	-8.793	.888
11 Asahikawa	9,054.344	-.2734	(-2.015)	-.01660	(-1.617)	-8.235	.962
12 Saga	15,946.580	-1.0400	(-6.025)	-.06897	(-3.272)	-7.540	.889
13 Nagoya	19,850.800	-.0736	(-.498)	-.00786	(-.670)	-4.682	.473
14 Kobe	15,044.680	-.0469	(-.308)	-.00540	(-.776)	-4.339	.282
15 Matsudo	9,614.227	-.6885	(-1.378)	-.09758	(-1.343)	-3.528	.137
16 Ichikawa	18,030.490	-.2690	(-.909)	-.03955	(-.744)	-3.401	.645
17 Nishinomiya	17,237.450	-.1297	(-.796)	-.02805	(-1.861)	-2.312	.655

18 Sendai	12,488.200	−.1213	(−.465)	−.03384	(−1.148)	−1.793	.531
19 Kofu	14,223.480	−.2614	(−.775)	−.10130	(−1.575)	−1.290	.799
20 Funabashi	11,553.790	−.0262	(−.127)	−.01694	(−.850)	−.773	.271
21 Sapporo	12,150.070	−.0359	(−.157)	−.02358	(−1.454)	−.761	.677
22 Chiba	6,946.059	−.0131	(−.062)	−.01245	(−.868)	−.525	.253
23 Yokosuka	5,603.180	−.0065	(−.017)	−.00869	(−.214)	−.376	.020
Mean	12,523.590	−.3573		−.02990		−12.717	.583

C. Group III: $G_{31\rightarrow}$, G_{32+}

1 Neyagawa	31,571.160	−1.2220	(−.679)	.34400	(.572)	1.776	.043
2 Kyoto	25,084.360	−.0972	(−1.109)	.01913	(3.274)	2.542	.789
3 Toyonaka	15,803.710	−.4961	(−.942)	.09643	(.999)	2.572	.044
4 Yokohama	13,266.530	−.0276	(−.271)	.00522	(.906)	2.645	.249
5 Sagamihara	9,311.445	−.6586	(−2.369)	.08002	(2.621)	4.115	.253
6 Suita	12,977.850	−.4116	(−1.515)	.04766	(1.269)	4.318	.113
7 Amagasaki	58,495.180	−1.2314	(−2.796)	.14141	(2.094)	4.354	.350
8 Ichinomiya	19,541.570	−.9769	(−5.472)	.10003	(3.736)	4.883	.837
9 Fukuyama	16,500.390	−.8888	(−4.206)	.06447	(3.327)	6.893	.517
10 Maebashi	21,731.100	−.8995	(−3.340)	.06313	(2.124)	7.124	.504
11 Omiya	19,427.790	−.4218	(−1.104)	.02862	(.463)	7.367	.561
12 Toyama	14,589.390	−.6798	(−3.560)	.03756	(1.724)	9.048	.713
13 Akita	10,545.660	−.5524	(−2.128)	.02829	(1.344)	9.762	.294
14 Kure	13,245.190	−.6266	(−2.364)	.03154	(1.039)	9.932	.600
15 Mito	6,235.410	−.2580	(−.776)	.01279	(.350)	10.086	.616
16 Hachinohe	454,584.700	−.7354	(−2.191)	.03593	(1.109)	10.232	.528
17 Kochi	19,375.800	−.8121	(−2.817)	.03924	(.872)	10.349	.804
18 Takamatsu	17,538.780	−.6787	(−4.079)	.03237	(1.800)	10.482	.782
19 Fukui	18,038.060	−.9020	(−5.476)	.04090	(2.546)	11.026	.864
20 Toyohashi	20,110.340	−.7712	(−4.647)	.03471	(2.297)	11.111	.832
21 Fujisawa	10,473.980	−.3408	(−1.206)	.01491	(.548)	11.431	.312
22 Hakodate	15,898.810	−.2222	(−.875)	.00944	(.225)	11.767	.217
23 Oita	11,388.840	−.5904	(−5.226)	.02493	(2.989)	11.841	.753
24 Okayama	18,796.010	−.6154	(−6.599)	.02471	(3.707)	12.449	.836

TABLE 5.4 (Continued)

	D_{03}	G_{31}	t_1	G_{32}	t_2	$-G_{31}/2G_{32}$	R^2
25 Miyazaki	14,567.370	-.7583	(-6.560)	.02976	(4.173)	12.739	.839
26 Kitakyushu	19,319.870	-.3289	(-2.498)	.01278	(1.385)	12.871	.407
27 Gifu	27,142.330	-.7075	(-5.539)	.02510	(1.906)	14.097	.859
28 Kurashiki	3,612.047	-.1697	(-1.118)	.00587	(.625)	14.466	.139
29 Nagano	9,827.602	-.4888	(-3.007)	.01677	(1.504)	14.578	.565
30 Himeji	8,353.613	-.2951	(-1.595)	.01005	(.685)	14.685	.285
31 Shimizu	21,870.850	-.7414	(-4.769)	.02497	(2.322)	14.847	.727
32 Hamamatsu	15,443.750	-.5097	(-6.483)	.01672	(2.656)	15.246	.859
33 Niigata	20,638.630	-.5207	(-5.262)	.01678	(2.695)	15.512	.770
34 Shizuoka	35,498.650	-.7446	(-6.412)	.02323	(2.184)	16.027	.926
35 Tokushima	12,145.080	-.6415	(-4.892)	.01965	(1.565)	16.322	.881
36 Aomori	24,812.410	-.7006	(-5.853)	.02091	(2.650)	16.753	.863
37 Kooriyama	13,338.090	-.6768	(-14.789)	.01986	(8.834)	17.036	.953
38 Yokkaichi	8,392.887	-.4596	(-4.118)	.01349	(1.539)	17.039	.736
39 Utsunomiya	17,794.410	-.6166	(-3.434)	.01754	(.979)	17.577	.733
40 Shimonoseki	18,458.870	-.4959	(-5.463)	.01361	(2.762)	18.213	.839
41 Wakayama	18,172.770	-.5207	(-3.606)	.01407	(1.045)	18.508	.784
42 Hachioji	17,449.040	-.6888	(-4.370)	.01780	(1.131)	19.345	.802
43 Nara	3,721.158	-.1605	(-.343)	.00412	(.094)	19.493	.064
44 Yamagata	15,341.090	-.7014	(-4.764)	.01734	(1.111)	20.230	.910
45 Okazaki	13,249.030	-.5733	(-2.314)	.01298	(.579)	22.092	.751
46 Matsuyama	14,474.730	-.4998	(-2.369)	.01112	(.443)	22.467	.653
47 Nagasaki	22,567.350	-.5193	(-1.824)	.00991	(.300)	26.195	.619
48 Fukushima	5,688.430	-.4291	(-3.983)	.00720	(1.276)	29.803	.826
49 Kumamoto	13,267.450	-.3935	(-1.848)	.00618	(.254)	31.847	.526
50 Kagoshima	17,044.780	-.3888	(-2.110)	.00579	(.437)	33.581	.512
51 Urawa	24,966.750	-.6587	(-3.727)	.00897	(.342)	36.707	.820
52 Otsu	4,171.371	-.1870	(-1.238)	.00151	(.183)	62.04	.639
Mean	25,304.880	-.5710		.03387		14.970	.610

Sendai, Kanazawa, Asahikawa, and Kofu among them. The mean R^2 for this group is .583, which is considerably higher than in Table 5.4a and better than the fits for either Eq. (1) or (2).

In Table 5.4c, we have the case in which $G_{31} < 0$ and $G_{32} > 0$. There are 52 cities in our sample that fell into this category, the most of any group. The mean R^2 is .610, which is the best among all the estimating equations that I attempted. This is the "paradox" case where the quadratic is inverted. That is, the density is seen to *fall* from the core, reach a *minimum* at $(-G_{31}/2G_{32})$, and then *rise* as we move further from the core. An example of this is for the city of Okayama, which has its best fit in Eq. (3):

$$D_j = 18,796 \exp(-.6154t_j + .02471t_j^2) \qquad R^2 = .836$$

The R^2 for Okayama using Eq. (3) is .836, compared to .753 and .572 for Eqs. (1) and (2), respectively. If we evaluate this quadratic at its minimum point, we find that the minimum is 12.449 km from the center. This is well beyond the built up area of the city of Okayama and in fact beyond its city limits. Thus, the paradox is explained. We get only a *truncated* part of the quadratic, that is a part that falls with the distance from the center. The density function for Okayama is given in Figure 5.10. This is generally true of other cities in this group as well: The mean distance for the 52 cities to the minimum point is 14.970 km, with a maximum of 62 km. Figure 5.11 shows the differences among the three forms of Eq. (3).

3.2 A Summary of Results for the Different Functional Forms

Table 5.5 summarizes the results for my analysis of the density functions of various functional forms. The best statistical fits are for the so-called paradox case [Eq. (3) in which $G_{31} < 0$ and $G_{32} > 0$], where the average R^2 is .610. The "crater" case [Eq. (3) where $G_{31} < 0$ and $G_{32} < 0$] had the second highest average fit, followed by Eqs. (1), (2), and (3) (where $G_{31} > 0$ and $G_{32} < 0$). Thus, the quadratic formulation would seem to dominate—at least the paradox and crater cases—the other functional forms.

With regard to predicted central density, the inverted quadratic form $(G_{31} < 0, G_{32} > 0)$ indicates the highest predicted central density, 25,304/km². The crater case, on the other hand, predicts a lower central density (9,050/km²) as one would expect on a priori grounds.

3.3 Density Functions by City Size and Region

Table 5.6 and Figure 5.12 indicate the distribution of the negative exponential density function estimates [Eq. (1)] by city size. Our a priori expectations are that the density gradient (G_1) should fall with city size and

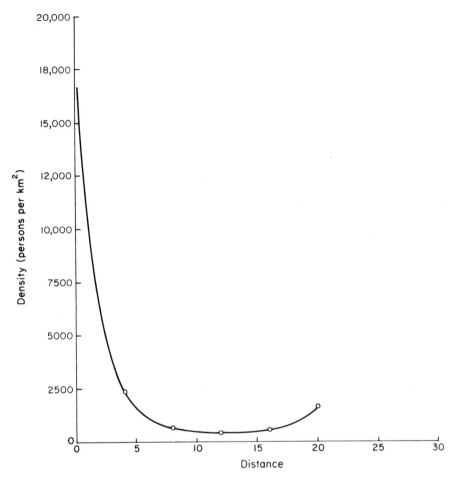

Figure 5.10.   Density function for Okayama using Eq. (3), 1970.

that the central density (D_{01}) should increase. Our statistical results, shown in Table 5.6, indicate that central density does, in fact, increase with city size. For cities with population of less than 200,000, D_0 is 8,600 people per square kilometer; but hypothetical central density increases to 23,500 for cities of more than 1 million. As D_0 increases with city size, G_{01} decreases; the latter phenomenon indicates that larger cities are more decentralized than smaller ones. Thus, there is a 43.4% decrease in residential density per kilometer movement from the city center for the smallest size class of cities, but only a 16.6% decrease in density per kilometer outward movement for the largest cities in our sample. Finally, note that the R^2s are higher for smaller cities than for larger ones; this is so since the smaller cities tend to be independent cities, away from the major metropolitan areas and thus are

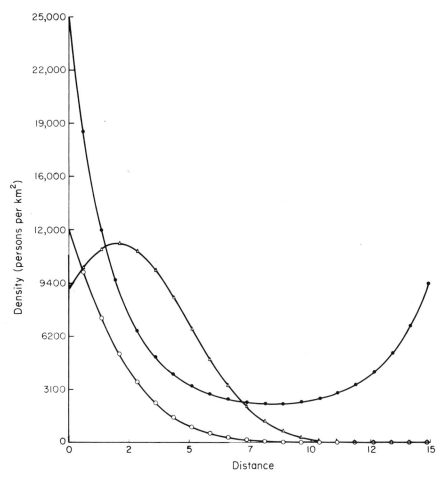

Figure 5.11. Comparison of three functional forms of density function using Eq. (3). $\triangle$: $G_{31} > 0$, $G_{32} < 0$; $\bigcirc$: $G_{31} < 0$, $G_{32} < 0$; $\bullet$: $G_{31} < 0$, $G_{32} > 0$.

more consistent with the theoretical model underlying our statistical estimates than larger cities close to other cities. There is, therefore, less theoretical and statistical "noise" in the estimation of these independent cities.

Another way to look at these density gradient estimations is to observe their distribution according to region. Table 5.7 breaks out the figures according to the following geographical categories: (*a*) Tohoku and Hokkaido, (*b*) the 10 largest cities in the sample, (*c*) suburban Tokyo, and (*d*) suburban Osaka. These results are graphed in Figure 5.13. Thus, Tohoku and Hokkaido, which contain a high proportion of independent and smaller cities, have a relatively steep density gradient (.457) and low central density (12,700 persons per square kilometer); additionally, the goodness-of-fit statistic is high. On the other hand, the 10 largest cities show greater amounts of

TABLE 5.5
Comparison of Estimates of Density Gradients for Japanese Cities, 1970

Functional form	R^2	Predicted central density (per km²)
(1) $D_j = D_{01} \exp(-G_1 t_j)$	.531	12,992
(2) $D_j = D_{02} \exp(-G_1 t_j)$	.461	7,398
(3) $D_j = D_{03} \exp(G_{31} t_j + G_{32} t_j^2)$		
(a) $G_{31} > 0, G_{32} < 0$	.487	9,050
(b) $G_{31} < 0, G_{32} < 0$	.583	12,523
(c) $G_{31} < 0, G_{32} > 0$	.610	25,304

decentralization and higher central density. Also, the R^2s are much lower for these cities. The suburban groups yield intermediate results with respect to all three statistics.

These, then, are the estimates obtained from the data provided in the 1970 Japanese Census. These results are compared to those obtained for other countries in Section 6.

4   Estimates of Land Price Functions for Japanese Cities

4.1   Introduction

Parallel to the analysis of land density in Section 3, this section examines the manner in which the price of land behaves with respect to its spatial position within the city. Few existing studies of the spatial structures of land

TABLE 5.6
Density Gradient Statistics by City Size Class, 1970

City size class	Mean value			Number of cities
	D_0 (in thousands)	G_1	R^2	
Less than 199,999	8.6	.434	.677	9
200,000–299,999	10.3	.336	.552	39
301,000–399,999	12.9	.286	.560	14
401,000–499,999	14.8	.310	.555	8
500,000–599,999	20.3	.323	.453	4
600,000–999,999	16.7	.138	.339	2
1,000,000 or more	23.5	.166	.341	8
All cities	13.0	.318	.531	84

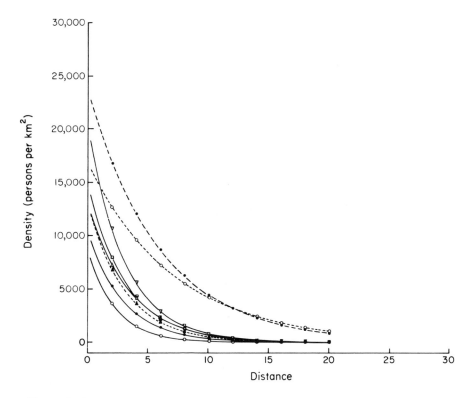

Figure 5.12. Density functions by city size, 1970. ○: less than 200,000; ●: 200,000–299,999; △: 300,000–399,999; □: 400,000–499,999; ▽: 500,000–599,999; ○: 600,000–999,999; ●: 1,000,000 or more; ▲: all cities in sample.

prices exist. Mills (1969), for instance, calculates some regressions involving the relationship between land price and distance from the center of Chicago for various time periods;[13] There are relatively few other rigorous studies of urban land prices, owing mainly to poor data.

This section draws on land price patterns for Japanese cities from a data set collected by the Japan Ministry of Construction (1973). Land appraisers regularly evaluate the value of particular parcels of land (called "standard points") in a large number of cities. I drew a random sample of these points for 71 cities for which density data were available as well. I then measured airline distance to the center of these cities (the same procedure used for the density gradients) and calculated, via ordinary least squares, regression

[13] Mills also summarizes the work of other authors who have done analytic studies of land price such as Brigham (1964), Rickert (1965), and Wendt and Goldner (1966).

TABLE 5.7
Estimates of Density Functions by Region, 1970

Region	D_0	G_1	R^2
Tohoku and Hokkaido			
(12 cities)	12.7	.457	.658
Ten largest cities			
(10 cities)	27.0	.157	.344
Suburban Tokyo			
(11 cities)	14.3	.328	.466
Suburban Osaka			
(11 cities)	16.0	.275	.377
All cities			
(84 cities)	13.0	.318	.531

coefficients for Eqs. (4)–(6):

$$P_j = P_{01} \exp(-H_1 t_j) \tag{4}$$

$$P_j = P_{02} \exp(-H_2 t_j^2) \tag{5}$$

$$P_j = P_{03} \exp(H_{31} t_j + H_{32} t_j^2) \tag{6}$$

where t_j is defined as in Eqs. (1)–(3), P_j is the price of land at point j, and P_{01} ... P_{03} and $H_1, \ldots, H_{32}$ are parameters estimated from the data. The results of this set of regressions are given in Tables 5.8–5.10, a discussion of which follows.

4.2 Estimates of Land Price Functions for Individual Cities

4.2.1 Estimates Using Equation (4)

Table 5.8 and Figure 5.14 show the estimates for Eq. (4), the negative exponential version. It can be seen there that the average predicted central land price is 57,004 *yen* (about $190) per square meter. Furthermore, land prices are seen to decline at a rate of 2.621% per kilometer distance from the center.[14] The average R^2 for this set of regressions was .350. As with the density functions, we can see from Table 5.8 that the cities away from the

---

[14] A comparison of the average value of H_1 in Table 5.8 (.02621) with its counterpart value of G_1 in Table 5.2 (.31835) yields a rather large difference between the two values. One ought to expect, a priori, that the two values be more closely aligned. However, in picking our land price samples, I systematically excluded commercial lots that are centrally located relative to residential lots; for the density gradients, I had more centrally located census tracts (although not the most central). Thus, the regression values of their respective slopes of G_1 and H_1 should also vary systematically with G_1 (estimated from more centrally located data) being greater than H_1.

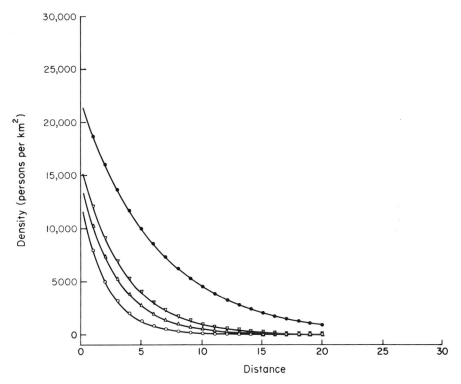

Figure 5.13. Comparison of density functions by region, 1970. ○: Tohoku and Hokkaido; ●: 10 largest cities; △: suburban Tokyo; ▽: suburban Osaka.

core of the urban system have the best statistical fits. See for instance, the results for Takamatsu, Kochi, Akita, Urawa, Niigata, Toyama, and Fukui.

4.2.2 Estimates Using Equation (5)

In Table 5.9, the values of the individual city results are displayed for the estimation of Eq. (5). Here, where the distance term is squared, the prediction is of a lower central land price and an even more gradual distance decay (see Figure 5.14) as we move from the center of the city than appears in Table 5.8. The R^2 also falls to .278.

4.2.3 Estimates Using Equation (6)

Tables 5.10a–5.10c show the regression results for Eq. (6). Most of the cases in Table 5.10 (this table is comparable to Table 5.4) are for the case

TABLE 5.8
Estimates of Land Price Functions Using Equation (4)[a]

	Sample size	P_{01}	H_1	t	R^2
1 Sapporo	135	58.590	.02885	(12.309)	.533
2 Hakodate	21	24.130	.00465	(.486)	.013
3 Asahikawa	38	14.717	.02652	(2.905)	.190
4 Aomori	19	36.905	.02039	(1.582)	.128
5 Hachinohe	26	29.398	.02882	(3.555)	.345
6 Morioka	24	29.366	.02145	(1.535)	.097
7 Sendai	59	65.117	.02458	(6.445)	.421
8 Akita.	89	28.870	.04470	(7.471)	.601
9 Yamagata	13	44.138	.07484	(3.243)	.489
10 Fukushima	29	26.859	.03514	(3.091)	.262
11 Kooriyama	40	39.246	.04455	(3.224)	.215
12 Utsunomiya	60	51.957	.02557	(6.436)	.416
13 Maebashi	25	48.015	.03604	(4.342)	.451
14 Kawaguchi	27	96.437	.02435	(3.472)	.325
15 Urawa	28	113.512	.03642	(6.356)	.608
16 Omiya	31	82.498	.02644	(5.096)	.472
17 Chiba	68	75.430	.02160	(4.891)	.266
18 Ichikawa	26	107.454	.02915	(4.709)	.480
19 Funabashi	42	80.665	.01706	(3.759)	.261
20 Hachioji	53	62.498	.01329	(2.720)	.126
21 Yokosuka	33	53.365	.00386	(1.463)	.063
22 Fujisawa	29	80.315	.01393	(5.038)	.485
23 Sagamihara	33	44.537	.00759	(1.682)	.083
24 Niigata	51	79.002	.03266	(8.955)	.621
25 Toyama	37	45.287	.05468	(9.938)	.738
26 Kanazawa	38	60.462	.04337	(7.456)	.607
27 Fukui	16	65.876	.05541	(7.169)	.786
28 Kofu	16	35.658	.03955	(1.823)	.192
29 Nagano	21	36.644	.04981	(5.193)	.587
30 Gifu	22	77.107	.05479	(4.387)	.490
31 Shizuoka	39	68.499	.03535	(6.837)	.558
32 Hamamatsu	45	38.494	.02132	(5.498)	.413
33 Shimizu	21	49.671	.02044	(2.146)	.196
34 Toyohashi	27	38.121	.01403	(1.650)	.098
35 Okazaki	28	30.460	.01450	(3.644)	.338
36 Ichinomiya	90	33.947	.00676	(.564)	.045
37 Tsu	21	23.796	.01646	(3.567)	.402
38 Yokkaichi	32	24.977	.01519	(2.144)	.133
39 Otsu	26	62.354	.01476	(3.929)	.391

where $H_{31} < 0$ and $H_{32} > 0$.[15] This, it will be recalled, is the "paradox" case. Compared to Eqs. (4) and (5), this gives the highest predicted value of central land price and the highest R^2 (.475).

---

[15] One city, Fukui, had positive values for H_{31} and H_{32}.

TABLE 5.8 (Continued)

	Sample size	P_{01}	H_1	t	R^2
40 Kyoto	92	164.335	.02534	(11.754)	.607
41 Sakai	64	73.356	.01091	(4.352)	.234
42 Toyonaka	28	92.730	.00563	(.847)	.028
43 Suita	31	80.070	.00066	(.139)	.001
44 Takatsuki	24	82.938	.01934	(3.241)	.324
45 Hirakata	32	68.550	.01226	(2.755)	.202
46 Yao	16	84.563	.02949	(2.062)	.234
47 Neyagawa	14	71.013	.01663	(.881)	.062
48 Higashiosaka	33	61.421	.01158	(1.616)	.078
49 Himeji	58	46.310	.01566	(4.606)	.275
50 Amagasaki	26	105.976	.00811	(1.642)	.101
51 Nishinomiya	38	126.304	.01692	(5.049)	.414
52 Nara	33	38.537	.01347	(3.192)	.247
53 Wakayama	42	53.360	.01766	(2.889)	.173
54 Tottori	10	51.275	.05726	(3.178)	.558
55 Matsue	14	27.178	.03363	(3.264)	.470
56 Kurashiki	51	22.387	.00958	(4.172)	.262
57 Kure	17	59.894	.02592	(3.635)	.469
58 Fukuyama	38	43.165	.01738	(4.698)	.380
59 Shimonoseki	35	20.916	.00991	(4.231)	.352
60 Yamaguchi	50	20.587	.04231	(2.076)	.590
61 Tokushima	25	76.372	.05449	(7.779)	.725
62 Takamatsu	29	112.911	.05122	(10.343)	.799
63 Matsuyama	27	66.028	.04307	(3.493)	.328
64 Kochi	28	75.430	.04443	(6.834)	.642
65 Fukuoka	81	55.264	.02511	(7.855)	.439
66 Saga	70	20.938	.04697	(2.140)	.478
67 Nagasaki	36	33.448	.00873	(1.240)	.043
68 Kumamoto	58	23.721	.02403	(5.471)	.348
69 Oita	63	37.267	.02591	(6.911)	.439
70 Miyazaki	28	27.571	.02463	(5.053)	.496
71 Kagoshima	50	59.077	.01414	(2.603)	.124
Mean		57.004	.02621		.350

[a] Land prices in thousands of *yen*.

5 An Econometric Model of the Urban Land Market[16]

5.1 Introduction

This section brings together the analyses of Sections 3 and 4 in an effort to explain the distribution of population and land use in its spatial context. In

[16] This section is based on Glickman and Oguri (1978).

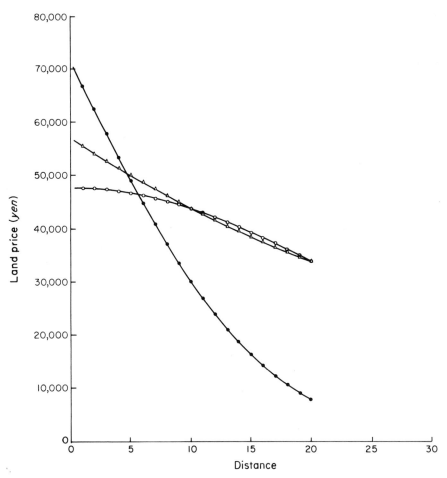

Figure 5.14. Land price functions using Eqs. (4), (5), and (6). △: Eq. (4); ○: Eq. (5); ●: Eq. (6).

several previous efforts, land use models have been constructed that examine the mechanisms of the urban land market. Alonso (1964), Muth (1969), and Mills (1972a) present theoretical models that show the variations in land use within the spatial context of cities. There also has been considerable empirical work on urban density functions that has been discussed and extended in Sections 2 and 3. This section presents an econometric model of urban land use that uses population density and land price gradient functions as the representative measures of internal structure of the city. Thus, it draws upon previous work on density gradients; additionally, it uses concepts from previous theoretical efforts concerning land use. The model causally relates indices of urban spatial structure to other measures of land use in cities.

TABLE 5.9

Estimates of Land Price Functions Using Equation (5), 1970[a]

	P_{02}	H_2	t	R^2
1 Sapporo	41.561	.00052	(10.422)	.451
2 Hakodate	24.272	.00030	(.899)	.041
3 Asahikawa	11.475	.00062	(2.441)	.142
4 Aomori	28.956	.00011	(.402)	.010
5 Hachinohe	23.865	.00077	(3.365)	.321
6 Morioka	24.991	.00054	(.890)	.035
7 Sendai	50.778	.00047	(4.870)	.294
8 Akita	20.581	.00109	(5.700)	.468
9 Yamagata	33.342	.00434	(3.034)	.456
10 Fukushima	22.915	.00139	(2.561)	.196
11 Kooriyama	33.630	.00151	(2.308)	.123
12 Utsunomiya	40.884	.00051	(4.462)	.255
13 Maebashi	37.894	.00112	(3.220)	.311
14 Kawaguchi	81.610	.00073	(3.143)	.283
15 Urawa	88.182	.00093	(4.137)	.397
16 Omiya	69.209	.00082	(4.040)	.360
17 Chiba	58.589	.00038	(3.938)	.190
18 Ichikawa	92.304	.00106	(3.962)	.396
19 Funabashi	71.723	.00050	(3.483)	.233
20 Hachioji	55.208	.00026	(2.098)	.079
21 Yokosuka	51.579	.00008	(1.257)	.047
22 Fujisawa	73.035	.00034	(4.881)	.469
23 Sagamihara	45.597	.00027	(2.344)	.150
24 Niigata	52.917	.00049	(6.590)	.469
25 Toyama	28.920	.00116	(6.841)	.572
26 Kanazawa	43.597	.00117	(6.008)	.501
27 Fukui	45.135	.00152	(5.240)	.662
28 Kofu	29.553	.00180	(1.895)	.204
29 Nagano	28.520	.00194	(4.069)	.466
30 Gifu	57.366	.00210	(4.124)	.460
31 Shizuoka	55.769	.00127	(5.646)	.463
32 Hamamatsu	32.236	.00048	(4.283)	.299
33 Shimizu	42.916	.00062	(1.876)	.157
34 Toyohashi	33.514	.00032	(1.303)	.064
35 Okazaki	26.931	.00030	(2.889)	.243
36 Ichinomiya	33.013	.00031	(.733)	.072
37 Tsu	21.723	.00058	(3.429)	.383
38 Yokkaichi	21.290	.00029	(1.427)	.064
39 Otsu	52.730	.00022	(3.061)	.281
40 Kyoto	124.511	.00049	(9.985)	.528
41 Sakai	66.948	.00025	(3.478)	.164
42 Toyonaka	90.156	.00021	(.567)	.014
43 Suita	78.694	.00007	(.400)	.005
44 Takatsuki	76.066	.00089	(2.998)	.291
45 Hirakata	63.600	.00039	(2.387)	.160
46 Yao	76.971	.00181	(2.501)	.309
47 Neyagawa	67.222	.00107	(1.017)	.080
48 Higashiosaka	65.385	.00045	(1.407)	.060
49 Himeji	38.549	.00024	(3.429)	.173
50 Amagasaki	102.354	.00039	(1.640)	.101

TABLE 5.9 *(Continued)*

	P_{02}	H_2	t	R^2
51 Nishinomiya	113.032	.00043	(6.625)	.549
52 Nara	41.497	.00038	(3.806)	.318
53 Wakayama	44.871	.00036	(2.340)	.120
54 Tottori	37.304	.00173	(2.050)	.345
55 Matsue	22.277	.00097	(2.875)	.408
56 Kurashiki	19.213	.00011	(2.973)	.153
57 Kure	48.403	.00535	(2.440)	.284
58 Fukuyama	35.356	.00027	(3.435)	.247
59 Shimonoseki	18.728	.00015	(4.524)	.383
60 Yamaguchi	17.524	.00198	(1.375)	.387
61 Tokushima	54.877	.00177	(5.677)	.584
62 Takamatsu	77.818	.00143	(7.433)	.672
63 Matsuyama	48.760	.00109	(2.442)	.193
64 Kochi	57.159	.00134	(5.487)	.536
65 Fukuoka	40.189	.00042	(7.543)	.419
66 Saga	17.087	.00210	(1.580)	.333
67 Nagasaki	31.782	.00027	(1.379)	.053
68 Kumamoto	18.451	.00041	(4.004)	.223
69 Oita	27.197	.00033	(4.190)	.223
70 Miyazaki	22.167	.00036	(3.245)	.288
71 Kagoshima	50.311	.00021	(1.954)	.074
Mean	47.645	.00086		.278

[a] Land prices in thousands of *yen*.

    The type of residential activity that takes place within the cities is influenced both by the overall indices of population size and population growth as well as those indices of internal structure. The model set forth here takes account of the types of housing tenure and scale of housing as representative variables of the type of residential activity and explains these variables by the overall and internal indices of the city noted previously.

    The model focuses on two major issues. First, the internal structure of cities can be described by such indices as population density and land price gradients with respect to distance from the city core. Different types of land price and population density gradient functions have been employed by different research workers. I adopt here the negative exponential function of Eqs. (1) and (4) and use the exponent and the constant coefficient as indices of urban spatial structure and land price distribution. Second, economic activity, which takes place in cities, spills over jurisdictional boundaries forming metropolitan areas. Thus, an activity level of a given city is not necessarily explained by other activity levels in the city itself but in part by activity in neighboring cities. This phenomena is typically observed in the context of the central city–suburban relationships that have been well documented in the literature. In order to take account of the

TABLE 5.10

Estimates of Land Price Functions Using Equation (6): $H_{31} < 0$, $H_{32} < 0$[a]

	P_{03}	H_{31}	t_1	H_{32}	t_{21}	$-H_{31}/2H_{32}$	R^2
			A. Group I: H_{31+}, H_{32-}				
1 Kofu	27.189	.0167	(.136)	−.25270	(−.468)	.033	.205
2 Neyagawa	56.196	.0447	(.483)	−.00352	(−.678)	6.352	.099
3 Yao	51.983	.0997	(1.498)	−.00703	(−1.978)	7.096	.411
4 Shimonoseki	18.154	.0026	(.261)	−.00018	(−1.298)	7.097	.385
5 Nishinomiya	104.608	.0106	(1.280)	−.00065	(−3.549)	8.119	.569
6 Nagasaki	29.129	.0126	(.408)	−.00062	(−.711)	10.169	.058
7 Hakodate	13.710	.0935	(2.138)	−.00348	(−2.290)	13.423	.236
8 Ichinomiya	23.699	.0627	(.877)	−.00233	(−.986)	13.468	.178
9 Higashiosaka	53.692	.0410	(1.127)	−.00133	(−.825)	15.436	.098
Mean	42.040	.0427		−.03020		9.021	.249
			B. Group II: H_{31-}, H_{32-}				
1 Tsu	23.779	−.0163	(−.751)	−.00001	(−.006)	−1581.104	.402
2 Hachinohe	27.161	−.0259	(−.931)	−.00008	(−.109)	−154.211	.345
3 Fujisawa	78.631	−.0106	(−.942)	−.00008	(−.302)	−63.501	.487
4 Amagasaki	104.345	−.0044	(−.184)	−.00018	(−.161)	−12.004	.102
Mean	58.479	−.0143		−.0009		−452.705	.334
			C. Group III: H_{31-}, H_{32+}				
1 Toyonaka	104.130	−.0381	(−1.296)	.00188	(1.133)	10.121	.076
2 Yamaguchi	31.630	−.1904	(−4.369)	.00879	(3.480)	10.836	.942
3 Ichikawa	115.837	−.0171	(−3.756)	.00069	(.803)	12.308	.494
4 Morioka	76.333	−.2194	(−3.929)	.00845	(3.618)	12.989	.444
5 Nara	50.557	−.0265	(−1.554)	.00102	(2.407)	13.028	.369
6 Saga	28.593	−.1371	(−1.650)	.00498	(1.122)	13.751	.603
7 Suita	91.168	−.0268	(−1.781)	.00096	(1.823)	13.980	.107

TABLE 5.10 (Continued)

	P_{03}	H_{31}	t_1	H_{32}	t_2	$-H_{31}/2H_{32}$	R^2
8 Sagamihara	62.664	-.0436	(-2.503)	.00137	(3.021)	15.927	.297
9 Kooriyama	49.354	-.1241	(-2.973)	.00377	(2.012)	16.463	.292
10 Tottori	110.317	-.2384	(-6.068)	.00719	(4.748)	16.582	.896
11 Fukushima	33.434	-.0948	(-2.071)	.00280	(1.344)	16.905	.310
12 Maebashi	73.625	-.1161	(-3.915)	.00310	(2.785)	18.712	.594
13 Shizuoka	93.256	-.0970	(-3.985)	.00249	(2.583)	19.510	.627
14 Nagano	47.303	-.1095	(-2.988)	.00270	(1.682)	20.274	.643
15 Toyohashi	64.772	-.0836	(-1.904)	.00206	(.614)	20.296	.187
16 Yokkaichi	45.101	-.0981	(-3.511)	.00236	(3.045)	20.768	.343
17 Matsuyama	119.671	-.1446	(-3.680)	.00348	(2.692)	20.773	.484
18 Omiya	106.549	-.0726	(-3.517)	.00169	(2.300)	21.444	.556
19 Shimizu	62.253	-.0559	(-1.248)	.00122	(.811)	22.844	.224
20 Takatsuki	88.094	-.0341	(-1.136)	.00073	(.502)	23.337	.332
21 Hirakata	74.053	-.0273	(-1.528)	.00056	(.868)	24.326	.222
22 Kochi	106.681	-.1067	(-3.706)	.00210	(2.212)	25.405	.701
23 Utsunomiya	86.998	-.0947	(-7.598)	.00183	(5.736)	25.858	.630
24 Sakai	84.426	-.0322	(-3.396)	.00061	(2.324)	26.235	.297
25 Asahikawa	23.910	-.0860	(-2.103)	.00164	(1.490)	26.271	.238
26 Kawaguchi	117.292	-.0565	(-1.527)	.00106	(.886)	26.728	.347
27 Hamamatsu	53.056	-.0667	(-4.426)	.00124	(3.097)	26.983	.522
28 Kure	82.145	-.0781	(-3.755)	.00144	(2.622)	27.020	.643
29 Urawa	145.760	-.0798	(-5.251)	.00146	(3.023)	27.389	.713
30 Yamagata	49.314	-.1065	(-.849)	.00194	(.257)	27.478	.492
31 Aomori	100.101	-.1513	(-6.319)	.00268	(5.763)	28.247	.717
32 Kanazawa	89.191	-.1024	(-4.124)	.00179	(2.437)	28.525	.664

	Land price[a]						
33 Wakayama	72.083	−.0539	(−2.250)	.00091	(1.563)	29.528	.221
34 Takamatsu	163.645	−.1103	(−5.671)	.00185	(3.116)	29.887	.853
35 Tokushima	95.302	−.0969	(−4.053)	.00160	(1.847)	30.375	.762
36 Sendai	103.756	−.0802	(−5.729)	.00132	(4.094)	30.421	.555
37 Akita	42.328	−.1051	(−4.773)	.00172	(2.832)	30.609	.674
38 Yokosuka	55.702	−.0098	(−.926)	.00015	(.580)	31.742	.074
39 Fukuyama	70.857	−.0729	(−5.410)	.00109	(4.231)	33.354	.590
40 Hachioji	71.616	−.0310	(−2.099)	.00046	(1.269)	33.360	.153
41 Kagoshima	82.948	−.0510	(−2.571)	.00074	(1.927)	34.519	.188
42 Miyazaki	40.727	−.0785	(−6.123)	.00107	(4.393)	36.598	.715
43 Chiba	109.014	−.0595	(−3.590)	.00081	(2.367)	36.650	.324
44 Kagoshima	60.735	−.0453	(−4.051)	.00061	(2.767)	37.387	.363
45 Oita	61.872	−.0827	(−9.187)	.00108	(6.655)	38.251	.677
46 Kumamoto	30.833	−.0549	(−4.287)	.00070	(2.551)	39.447	.417
47 Okazaki	33.468	−.0279	(−2.255)	.00034	(1.144)	40.639	.371
48 Toyama	62.927	−.1008	(−5.879)	.00117	(2.815)	43.224	.788
49 Funabashi	85.505	−.0266	(−1.312)	.00030	(.484)	44.000	.265
50 Matsue	29.836	−.0515	(−1.231)	.00057	(.442)	45.006	.480
51 Kurashiki	28.399	−.0304	(−4.157)	.00032	(2.977)	46.786	.377
52 Sapporo	82.579	−.0612	(−5.983)	.00064	(3.242)	47.453	.568
53 Niigata	112.330	−.0675	(−5.660)	.00063	(3.045)	53.599	.682
54 Otsu	71.537	−.0298	(−2.505)	.00028	(1.331)	53.858	.435
55 Kyoto	177.853	−.0335	(−4.422)	.00018	(1.123)	95.474	.613
56 Gifu	78.791	−.0591	(−1.075)	.00017	(.080)	169.336	.491
57 Fukuoka	55.543	−.2553	(−1.661)	.00001	(.028)	17,656.293	.439
Mean	76.276	−.0813		.00173		340.861[b]	.475

[a] Land prices in thousands of _yen_.

[b] Large figure is due to figure for Fukuoka, which in turn is due to spuriously estimated H_{32}.

impact of interjurisdictional interaction, it is necessary to construct variables that explain the relationship of a city to the metropolitan area in which it is located. In this model I use the REC definitions of metropolitan areas, and I form an accessibility measure of a city in a metropolitan area by combining distance and employment levels of a given city and those in central cities of a metropolitan region.

5.2 The Data Base

5.2.1 Basic Sources of Data

Two basic data sources are employed here. First, I use a subsample of the cities analyzed in Sections 3 and 4. I selected 71 cities that were common to the 1970 Census and Ministry of Construction enumerations for density and land price, respectively. I used estimates of Eqs. (1) and (4) for the 71 cities here; see Table 5.8 for a list of the cities. Second, I used the REC data bank from Chapters 2 and 3. Among the sample cities, 67 are in the RECs; 46 were central cities and 21 were suburban cities. Central city–suburban distinction plays a critical role in defining accessibility measures of the sample cities as is noted in the following sections.

5.2.2 Construction of Other Variables for the Model

The model, outlined in Section 5.3, employs the estimated parameters of the residential density and land price functions (D_{01}, G_1, P_{01}, H_1) from Eqs. (1) and (4) for the 71 cities. In addition, it was necessary to use some other land use variables. This section contains a discussion of the construction of these variables.

Average Land Price. It was desirable to compute the *average land price* for each city using the land price gradient data from Section 4. This computation was carried out in the following way. Four variables were used:

$\tilde{k}$:   the radius of the residential area;
A: the total residential area;
P_{01}: the land price at the central location;
H_1: the land price gradient.

Using the variables, one can calculate the average land price, $\bar{P}$, using Eq. (7);

$$\bar{P} = \int_0^{\tilde{k}} P_{01} \exp(-H_1 k) 2\Pi k / A \tag{7}$$

This computation yielded results showing very large variances in the average land price. Past experience with the Japanese land indicated that many of these estimations were probably inaccurate. There are several possible explanations for this:

1. There was low statistical significance of some of the price gradient (H_1) estimates.
2. It was necessary to approximate the total residential area by subtracting from the total urban area land used for forests, agriculture, and roads; these estimates were sometimes difficult to make.
3. There were many irregularities in city shapes; this, too, would tend to make for error in the estimates.

Thus the results from Eq. (7) were abandoned, and a simple arithmetic average of land price ($\bar{P}$) from the "standard" points in each city was calculated as in Eq. (8).

$$\bar{P} = \frac{\Sigma_j^n P_j}{N} \tag{8}$$

where P_j is the jth standard point and N is the number of standard points.

Accessibility. A variable for *accessibility* was also constructed. The areal differentiations of residential land price and population density are caused principally by the interarea differences of the demand for residential land and for housing. This demand at a given point in space is generated in part by employees who work at certain job sites. It is essential, therefore, to associate land price and density variables of cities with some measure of accessibility to job opportunities, either in the same city or in neighboring cities. My measure of accessibility of city i to job opportunities in city j, A_{ij}, is constructed as follows:

$$A_{ij} = E_j[f(t_{ij})]^{-1} \tag{9}$$

where E_j is employment in city j, t_{ij} is the distance between the two cities, and $f(t_{ij})$ is a friction function between the two cities that is specified either by an exponential or by the power function given in Eq. (10).

$$f(t_{ij}) = \begin{cases} \exp(\gamma t_{ij}) \\ t_{ij}^\sigma \end{cases} \tag{10}$$

where γ and σ are parameters. The two types of functions can be used interchangeably as shown by Harris (1966). The theoretical derivation of the exponential friction function is made through such trip distribution models as gravity models, accessibility–opportunity models and maximum entropy models; see Schneider (1959) and Wilson (1967, 1970).

If A_{ij} is the individual accessibility of city i with respect to city j, then the aggregative accessibility of city i is

$$A_i = \sum_j A_{ij} \tag{11}$$

To compute the accessibility measure for each city, we need to take account of the relationships between the city concerned with all its neighboring cities. We may, however, limit our perspective to central city–suburban city relationships since the central cities in metropolitan areas have the largest amount of job opportunities and, thus, the accessibility to the central city is most likely to dominate the aggregative accessibility of the city concerned.[17]

Here we employ an exponential friction function as shown in Eq. (12).

$$A_{ij} = E_j[\exp(-\gamma t_{ij})] \tag{12}$$

Note that by this specification, the accessibility of a city to itself is identical to the total employment of the city since $E_i[\exp(-\gamma t_{ii})] = E_i$ for $t_{ii} = 0$. Thus, for central cities, the aggegative accessibility measure A_i is identical to the number of employees of the cities themselves E_i. For suburban cities, taking account of the accessibility to the central city and the suburban city itself, the aggregative accessibility measure is

$$A_i = E_i + E_{ci}[\exp(-\gamma t_{ic})] \tag{13}$$

where E_i and E_{ci} are the employment in the city itself and the employment of its central city, respectively, and t_{ic} is the distance between city i and its central city.

It remains to indicate the value of the friction function parameter γ. Oguri (1974) estimated exponential functions of commuting population of the cities of Kanagawa and Tokyo prefectures by specifying

$$C_{ij}/L_i = A_j \exp(-\gamma_j t_{ij}) \tag{14}$$

where C_{ij} is the number of commuters from city i to city j, L_i is the total area of city i, and A_j and E_j are estimated parameters for city j. Oguri found a mean for γ equal to .102 and a relatively small standard deviation of .0431. The estimates of A_j, on the other hand, are highly correlated with the total employment of each city; the simple correlation coefficient is .997. Thus, I calibrated the friction parameter γ with a value of .102, consistent with Oguri's work.

5.3 A Model of Land Use

5.3.1 Outline of the Model

This section outlines a model of land use in Japanese cities that consists of nine endogenous and five exogenous variables. The endogenous variables are calculated in eight stochastic and one identity equations. The model's

---

[17] As I noted in Section 5.2.1, among the 67 cities that are included in the Regional Economic Clusters, 46 cities are central cities and 21 as suburban cities. For cities not included in the RECs, I treat these cities as equivalent to central cities.

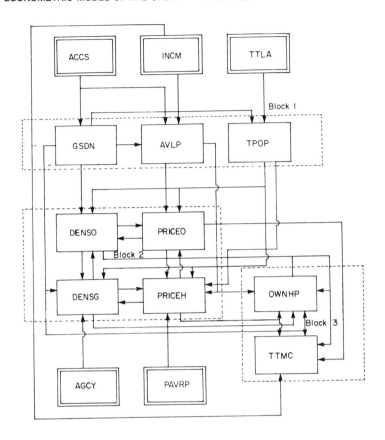

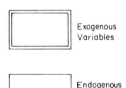

Exogenous
Variables

Endogenous
Variables

Figure 5.15. Causal relationships within the model.

causal relations are depicted in Figure 5.15 and its equations are summarized in Table 5.11.

The model calculates the following *endogenous* variables

1. *AVLP:* average land price (1,000 *yen* per square meter);
2. *TPOP:* total population (in thousands);
3. *DENSO:* estimated value of the constant term of the population

TABLE 5.11
A Model of Urban Land Use

Equation number	Equations and ordinary least squares and two-stage least squares estimates	R^2	SE
Block 1			
(15) GSDN	$= 484.0947 + 6.7849ACCS$ $\qquad\qquad\quad(13.936)$	.738	1185.950
(16) TPOP	$= (TTLA) \cdot (GSDN)$		
(17) AVLP	$= -48.0307 + .0016GSDN + .0381ACCS + .9347INCM$ $\qquad\qquad\quad(1.223)\qquad\quad(3.680)\qquad\quad(4.335)$	.687	12.829
Block 2			
(22) DENSO	$= 6.9867 + 2.9225DENSG + .00010GSDN + .1458PRICEO + .000027TPOP$ $\qquad\qquad(9.031)\qquad\quad(4.377)\qquad\quad(1.430)\qquad\quad(6.024)$	.748	.335
(23) DENSG	$= -1.4806 + .1992DENSO - .00003GSDN + 3.4280PRICEH - .00003TPOP$ $\qquad\qquad(11.811)\qquad(5.249)\qquad\quad(4.933)\qquad\quad(5.356)$ $\quad + .0010AGCY$ $\qquad(1.870)$	.702	.076
(24) PRICEO	$= 2.0356 + 9.6366PRICEH + .0207AVLP + .0718DENSO + .0002TPOP$ $\qquad\qquad(6.407)\qquad\quad(17.437)\qquad(1.658)\qquad\quad(1.532)$	.869	.187
(25) PRICEH	$= -.0719 + .0328PRICEO - .00077AVLP + .0285DENSG$ $\qquad\qquad(5.519)\qquad\quad(5.645)\qquad\quad(2.972)$ $\quad -.00001TPOP - .00012PAVRP$ $\qquad(1.268)\qquad\quad(1.705)$	.500	.011

Block 3

(26) $OWNHP = 88.6917 - .0015GSDN - .0444AVLP - 4.1937DENSO$
$\qquad\qquad\quad (2.961)\qquad (.868)\qquad\quad (2.418)$
$\qquad\qquad + 136.5827PRICEH + 13.1454DENSG$
$\qquad\qquad\quad (2.348)\qquad\qquad (1.681)$

$\qquad\qquad\qquad\qquad\qquad\qquad\qquad\qquad .601\qquad 6.172$

(27) $TTMC = 7.1301 - .00009GSDN - .1869DENSO - .316PRICEO$
$\qquad\qquad\qquad (2.498)\qquad\quad (1.668)\qquad (1.731)$
$\qquad\qquad + 19.8340PRICEH + .0179INCM$
$\qquad\qquad\quad (4.150)\qquad\qquad (1.821)$

$\qquad\qquad\qquad\qquad\qquad\qquad\qquad\qquad .510\qquad .508$

Note:
1. The numbers in the parentheses are t-statistics.
2. Although OLS method was used, it is more desirable to apply simultaneous equations estimating method of Eqs. (22)–(25). The results of Two-Stage Least Squares estimation are:

(22)' $DENSO = 6.8627 + 5.4649DENSG + .0002GSDN - .1191PRICEO + .0002TPOP$
$\qquad\qquad\qquad (1.047)\qquad\quad (1.075)\qquad (.201)\qquad\quad (2.366)$

$\qquad\qquad\qquad\qquad\qquad\qquad\qquad\qquad .474\qquad .484$

(23)' $DENSG = -1.5687 + .2161DENSO - .00003GSDN = 2.1059PRICEH - .00003TPOP$
$\qquad\qquad\qquad (3.861)\qquad\quad (3.853)\qquad\quad (.755)\qquad\quad (3.335)$
$\qquad\qquad + .0006AGCY$
$\qquad\qquad\quad (.665)$

$\qquad\qquad\qquad\qquad\qquad\qquad\qquad\qquad .746\qquad .078$

(24)' $PRICEO = -.2822 + 11.9026PRICEH + .0186AVLP + .3362DENSO - .000001TPOP$
$\qquad\qquad\qquad (2.590)\qquad\qquad (4.373)\qquad (.936)\qquad\quad (.253)$

$\qquad\qquad\qquad\qquad\qquad\qquad\qquad\qquad .795\qquad .241$

Some variables ($PRICEO$ of Eq. (22)' and $TPOP$ of Eq. (24)' have changed their sign with low t values. Equation (25)' is not shown here because of its low $\bar{R}^2$.

density gradient (D_{01}) given in Eq. (1) (log of persons per square kilometer);

4. *DENSG:* the estimated value of the population density gradient (G_1) given in Eq. (1);

5. *GSDN:* the gross residential density (population per square kilometer);

6. *PRICEO:* the estimated value of the constant term in the land price gradient function (P_{01}) given in Eq. (4) (log of 1,000 *yen* per square meter);

7. *PRICEH:* the estimated value of the land price gradient (H_1) given in Eq. (4);

8. *TTMC:* *tatami* per capita (one *tatami* = 1.65 m²);

9. *OWNHP:* proportion of homes that are owner-occupied (percentage).

The *exogenous* variables are:

1. *ACCS:* the accessibility to job opportunities (1.0 employees);
2. *INCM:* average income (1,000 *yen*);
3. *PAVRP:* proportion of paved roads in a city (percentage);
4. *TTLA:* total area (km²);
5. *AGCY:* the age of the city (year 1876 = 1).

The model was constructed under the assumption that the internal spatial structure of a city (i.e., the population and land price distribution), is determined by the overall indices of residential activity of the city, that is, average gross population density and average land price, as well as the mutual influence of the indices of internal structure. The model also assumes that the types of residential activity represented by tenure relationships and size of dwelling units are determined by the indices of overall and internal residential activity. Thus, the model is composed of three blocks as shown in Figure 5.15. Block 1 determines gross population density and average land price. Block 2 contains forecasts of the parameters of the population density and the land price functions. Finally, Block 3, shows tenure relationships and the scale of housing.[18]

---

[18] I recognize other possible logical relationships of the indices of residential activity, in which individual demand for housing, that is, tenure relationship, size, and location of dwelling units, and market structure of residential area, that is, the population and land price distribution both in a metropolitan area and in each city, are simultaneously determined. A model that incorporates such a relationship is, however, only possible after data are collected for each city in each metropolitan area, a task beyond the resources of this project. A metropolitan model also may treat such factors as income level and public facilities, which were assumed to be exogenous in this model, endogenously.

5.3.2 Block 1

As already stated, the first block of the model determines the gross population density ($GSDN$), total population ($TPOP$), and average land price ($AVLP$).

Since it is assumed that each of the sample cities constitutes a portion of a different metropolitan area, it would be desirable to construct a location model for each metropolitan area and to allocate residential activity to subdivided zones (cities) in the area; this would take account of the simultaneous relationship of population density and land price. Limited data availability, however, made this work intractable. Thus the perspective is limited to identifying the cross-sectional statistical relationships among overall residential activity indices of the sample cities.

Hansen's (1959) model of residential population location assumes that the incremental population in a region is allocated to subdivided zones of the region proportionally to the product of the amount of remaining developable land and the levels of accessibility of the subdivided zone. This assumption can be interpreted as saying that the population density per remaining developable land is proportional to the level of accessibility in a subdivided zone. If we are to allocate residential population at a point in time, assuming that all the area is usable for residential activity, we may say (according to the conceptualization of Hansen) that the gross population density is proportional to the level of accessibility. Taking account of the fact that the sample cities are located in different metropolitan areas, I construct a simple model of residential location that relates the gross population density ($GSDN$) with the accessibility measure ($ACCS$) of the city in linear form. The Ordinary Least Squares estimation is:

$$GSDN = \quad 484.0947 + \quad 6.7849\, ACCS \qquad (15)$$
$$(13.936)$$
$$R^2 = .738 \qquad SE = 1185.95$$

where the number in parentheses is the t value, R^2 is the coefficient of multiple determination adjusted for degrees of freedom, and SE is the standard error of the estimate.

Multiplying the gross population density ($GSDN$) by total area ($TTLA$), we obtain the total population ($TPOP$) of the city.

$$TPOP = (GSDN) \cdot (TTLA) \qquad (16)$$

Residential land price may be increased by both actual and potential demand for a parcel. The former is represented by gross population density ($GSDN$) and the latter by accessibility ($ACCS$) to the city's employment. The land price may also be increased by greater ability to pay for land, which may be represented by the income level ($INCM$) of residents. Thus, I estimate the following equation:

$$AVLP = -48.037 + .0016\,GSDN + .0381\,ACCS + .9347\,INCM \quad (17)$$
$$(1.233) \qquad\qquad (3.680) \qquad\qquad (4.335)$$
$$R^2 = .687 \qquad SE = 12.829$$

5.3.3   Block 2

Block 2 determines population density and land price gradients as indices of the internal structure of Japanese cities. These functions are two-parameter functions: for the density function, the central density, and the density gradient itself. The price function is determined by the price at a central location and the price gradient. Thus, there are four variables: central density ($DENSO$), the density gradient ($DENSG$), the central land price ($PRICEO$), and the price gradient ($PRICEH$). These variables are determined simultaneously in the "real world," and the model is constructed to reflect this fact. The relationships among these variables and between them and the variables in Block 2 ($GSDN$, $TPOP$, and $AVLP$) are determined in Block 1 and are considered exogenous to Block 2.

First, let us view Eq. (18) for central density ($DENSO$).

$$DENSO = A_0 + A_1 DENSG + A_2 GSDN + A_3 PRICEO + A_4 TPOP \quad (18)$$

Note that there are two density-related variables ($DENSG$ and $GSDN$) that help explain $DENSO$, the other density variable. The coefficients A_1 and A_2 (attached to the density variables) have expected a priori signs. Suppose, as in Figure 5.16a, we have two cities. If it is assumed that the gross population densities ($GSDN$) of the two cities are identical (i.e., we hold $GSDN$ constant), then the central density ($DENSO$) in Figure 5.16a will be higher, given a higher gradient $DENSG$; the gradient is given as $DENSG_1$ in Figure 5.16a. Thus, A_1 is positive. Conversely, if the gradients are held constant, then the higher the net population density, the higher will be the central density, as shown in Figure 5.16b. As a result, A_2 is positive.

Since the population density gradient is estimated on the basis of gross density, there are two possible explanations for the effect of central price ($PRICEO$) on central density. First, it is possible that the higher the central price, the more that residential locators will be driven to outlying areas. This would make central density lower. On the other hand, higher central prices might lead to a greater economizing of space with higher density being attained in the central parts of the city as a result (i.e., $A_3 > 0$). The coefficient for A_3, therefore, will be determined by which of these competing tendencies is stronger. In Eq. (22), where the empirical estimate of Eq. (18) is presented, A_3 is greater than zero. The coefficient attached to total population ($TPOP$) ought to be positive since the higher the total population of the city, the more people will be centrally located per unit of land. Thus, A_4 ought to be positive.

Now consider the next equation for the density gradient.

$$DENSG = B_0 + B_1 DENSO + B_2 GSDN + B_3 PRICEH + B_4 TPOP + B_5 AGCY \tag{19}$$

The coefficient of central density B_1 will be positive for the same reasoning that A_1 is greater than zero in Eq. (18). That is, if the gross densities for the two cities are held constant, then the higher the $DENSO$, the steeper will be the gradient. This is shown in Figure 5.16b. If, on the other hand, the central densities of the two cities are the same, then the higher the average density, the less steep will be the density gradient. Thus, B_2 will be negative; see Figure 5.16c.

As was the case of the influence of $PRICEO$ on $DENSO$, the coefficient attached to $PRICEH$, B_3, will depend on which of the two following tendencies is stronger. A steeper price gradient may force people to live further away from the city, thus making B_3 negative. On the other hand, it is possible that land will be economized upon, given higher prices, and thus more people will live on a unit of land at a given point in space. In the empirical estimates, given in Eq. (23), the effect of economizing on land is stronger and B_3 is positive. The coefficient for total population, B_4, should be negative as the larger the city, the more likely it will be that people will locate far from the center. Finally, the age of the city $(AGCY)$ should have a positive

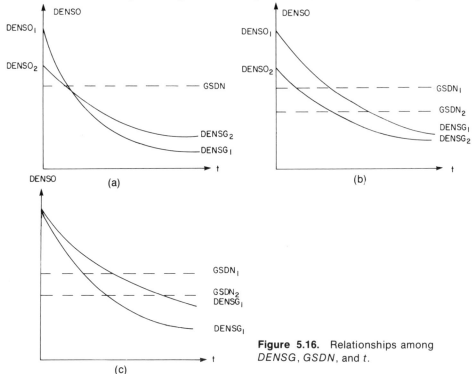

Figure 5.16. Relationships among $DENSG$, $GSDN$, and t.

coefficient since the older cities were developed around a tightly packed core and newer cities tend to be spread out and have better transportation and accessibility to the core; thus, newer cities would tend to have flatter density gradients. As a result, B_5 should be positive.

Equation (20) explain the value of the central price of land (*PRICEO*).

$$PRICEO = C_0 + C_1 \, PRICEH + C_2 \, AVLP + C_3 \, DENSO + C_4 \, TPOP \qquad (20)$$

The coefficients attached to *PRICEH* and *AVLP*, C_1 and C_2, respectively, can be explained by virtue of similar reasoning to the impact of *DENSG* and *GSDN* on *DENSO* in Eq. (18). The coefficient of *PRICEH* is positive because, given a level of *AVLP*, the higher the price gradient, the higher will be *PRICEO*. The higher the central density (*DENSO*), the higher will be the demand for centrally located land and thus *PRICEO* will be higher; as a result, C_3 should be positive. The coefficient attached to total population, C_4, would be positive since it also reflects a greater demand for land and thus a higher central price for land in the city.

The equation for the land price gradient (*PRICEH*) is

$$PRICEH = D_0 + PRICEO + D_2 AVLP + D_3 DENSG + D_4 TPOP + D_5 PAVRP \qquad (21)$$

For the price gradient equation, the coefficients attached to *PRICEO* and *AVLP* have the same a priori expectations as *DENSO* and *GSDN* in Eq. (19) for similar reasons. Thus, D_1 is positive and D_2 is negative. *DENSG*, the residential density gradient (D_3), should have a positive sign since a steep density gradient means that the demand for land decreases quickly as one moves from the city's center, and thus the price of land should also have a steep gradient. Total population should have a negative coefficient since it also represents the demand for land in a generalized way. In larger cities people will tend to live further from the core than in smaller cities, and thus demand for land in suburban areas will be relatively higher. Hence, D_4 is negative. I also enter on the right-hand side, the proportion of roads that are paved (*PAVRP*). This should influence *PRICEH* negatively since it implies greater accessibility of outlying land parcels to the core.

The OLS estimations of Eq. (18)–(21) are given in Eq. (22)–(25).

$$DENSO = 6.9867 + 2.9225 \, DENSG + .00010 \, GSDN + .1458 \, PRICEO \qquad (22)$$
$$(9.031) \qquad\qquad (4.377) \qquad\qquad (1.430)$$
$$+ .00002 \, TPOP$$
$$(6.024)$$
$$R^2 = .748 \quad SE = .335$$

$$DENSG = 1.4806 + .1992 \, DENSO - .00003 \, GSDN + 3.428 \, PRICEH \qquad (23)$$
$$(11.811) \qquad\qquad (5.249) \qquad\qquad (4.933)$$
$$- .00003 \, TPOP + .0010 \, AGCY$$
$$(5.356) \qquad\qquad (1.870)$$
$$R^2 = .762 \quad SE = .076$$

$$PRICEO = 2.0356 + 9.6366\,PRICEH + .0207\,AVLP + .0718\,DENSO \quad (24)$$
$$(6.407) \qquad (17.437) \qquad (1.658)$$
$$+ .0002\,TPOP$$
$$(1.532)$$
$$R^2 = .869 \qquad SE = .187$$

$$PRICEH = -.07192 + .03278\,PRICEO - .000077\,AVLP + .02846\,DENSG \quad (25)$$
$$(5.519) \qquad (5.645) \qquad (2.972)$$
$$-.00001\,TPOP - .00012\,PAVRP$$
$$(1.268) \qquad (1.705)$$
$$R^2 = .500 \qquad SE = .011$$

5.3.4 Block 3

Block 3 determines measures of the characteristics of urban residential activity. Here, I use the indices of density and land price given in Blocks 1 and 2 to estimate equations for the ratio of homes that are owner-occupied (*OWNHP*), and the size of dwellings as given by the number of *tatami* per capita (*TTMC*); a *tatami* is the standard measure of dwelling size and is equal to 1.65 m^2.

Equation (26) shows the estimated results for *OWNHP*.

$$OWNHP = 88.6917 - .0015\,GSDN - .0444\,AVLP - 4.1937\,DENSO \quad (26)$$
$$(2.961) \qquad (.868) \qquad (2.418)$$
$$+ 136.5827\,PRICEH + 13.1454\,DENSG$$
$$(2.348) \qquad (1.681)$$
$$R^2 = .601 \qquad SE = 6.172$$

Three variables have a negative effect on *OWNHP*. They are gross density, central density, and average land price. That is, when gross density (*GSDN*) is high it can be expected that home ownership rates will be low. This results from a characteristic of the Japanese land market in which rental housing generally consists of very small rooming-house-type dwellings. Higher population densities will be associated with small-scale housing, which is largely rental housing. Similarly, higher priced land, as proxied by *AVLP*, will be occupied by higher proportions of rental housing since expensive land will tend to have multiple dwelling (rental) units on it. The value of *DENSO* is negative since central locators tend to have small houses and are more often renters. Conversely, the gradients of population and price (*DENSG* and *PRICEH*) have positive signs because sharp decreases in land price and density as one moves from the core enables people to live in more spacious owner-occupied houses in outlying sections of the city.

For the equation for *tatami* per capita, we have

$$TTMC = 7.1301 - .0009\,GSDN - .1869\,DENSO - 0.3136\,PRICEO \quad (27)$$
$$(2.498) \qquad (1.668) \qquad (1.731)$$
$$+ 19.8340\,PRICEH + .0179\,INCM$$
$$(4.150) \qquad (1.821)$$
$$R^2 = .501 \qquad SE = .508$$

Here, the interpretations attached to *GSDN* and *DENSO* (which have negative signs) are similar to those in Eq. (26). *PRICEO* enters negatively since higher central land price will dictate that people will live in smaller dwellings. *PRICEH* is positive because a rapid decrease of price will allow people to reside in larger dwellings further from the core. *INCM* is positive since housing is a normal good; this sign is consistent with a priori expectations.

5.4   A Final Word about the Model

The model of land use constructed here explains the parameters of the population density and land price gradients of Sections 3 and 4, as well as a set of other variables that depict the workings of the urban land market. The model's statistical properties are good in that the relevant variables have appropriate signs and the equations have good explanatory power. This model can be used to explain the workings of the Japanese land market.

6   International Comparisons of Land Use

Having described and analyzed land use patterns in Japan, I now return to the comparative framework and view Japanese urban spatial structure to that of the United States, Great Britain, and West Germany.[19] Again, the negative exponential [Eq. (1)] model will be used for this purpose. Section 6.1 notes data sources for the three countries[20] and Section 6.2 presents the empirical results for those countries. The comparative analysis is the subject of Section 6.3 and some concluding remarks are given in Section 6.4.

6.1   Data Sources for the United States, Great Britain, and West Germany

6.1.1   Great Britain

The British sample consists of 23 cities in England and Wales for which density function were estimated for 1961 and 1971. The density data come from the *Census of Population, County Reports*. Straight-line distances were measured on 1 : 25,000 scale maps. For these estimations, the city subdivisions used were wards. On average there were 22 wards per city, all within the legal central city. All wards were included in the sample except the most central ward in each city.

---

[19] This section draws from Glickman and White (1978).

[20] The data for Japan are as in Section 3 of this chapter. The regressions have been converted from a kilometer to a mile basis to allow for comparability.

6.1.2 West Germany

The West German sample consists of 22 cities for which density functions were estimated for 1960 and 1970. Data for the German estimations come from annual yearbooks (*Statistiches Jahrbuchs*) published by the cities themselves.[21] Since data for several cities was unavailable for one of the years, the total German sample is 36 city-years. The German city areas also are legal subdivisions of the central cities called *bezirk;* on average there are 26 per city, of which all but the most central are included in the sample. *Bezirk* generally contain 5,000–15,000 people, but their size tends to increase as the city population increases. Since both the British and German data are for legal subdivisions, there was little variation between time periods in the size or boundaries of these areas. Thus, the comparability of the density functions for individual cities over time is good.

6.1.3 United States

Finally, density function estimates made by Barr (1970; Appendix 1) are reported for a sample of U.S. cities for 1960. Barr's study updates the results presented by Muth for 30 U.S. cities for 1950. Muth's estimates are based on a random sample of 25 census tracts for each city, all in the legal central city. The 1960 update uses the same census tracts for each city.[22]

6.2 Empirical Estimates of Density Functions

6.2.1 Great Britain

Table 5.12 presents the estimated density function parameters for the British cities. The results suggest that distance is a significant determinant of density levels at the 90% level in 39 of 46 cases (*t*-statistics are given for the G_1 values). On average, distance explains 38% of the variance in density in 1961 and 18% in 1971. For 1961, the average central density level is 27,000 people per square mile and the average gradient is .33. For 1971, these figures drop to 20,500 and .22, respectively. Thus, if the main effect of the passage of time is to raise incomes and/or lower travel costs, British urban structure changed in the way predicted by Section 2's model—the density gradients flattened and the intercepts fell. In particular, the average intercept fell 24% and the average gradient 33% over the period. These changes in urban form are shown in Figure 5.17, which plots the average density functions for both years for the British sample.

---

[21] Several of the German density functions were estimated for 1 year before or after 1960 or 1970, when the city yearbook for the desired year was unavailable.

[22] Unfortunately, to my knowledge, no one has updated the Muth study for 1970 data. Since many of the census tracts had different boundaries in 1970, retaining comparability would be a considerable task.

TABLE 5.12
British Urban Density Functions

	1961				1971			
	$D_{01}{}^a$	G_1	t	R^2	D_{01}	G_1	t	R^2
Birmingham	29.4	.19	4.67	.37	17.5	.07	2.22	.12
Bournemouth	14.9	.21	1.81	.20	14.3	.19	1.76	.19
Bradford	32.7	.59	6.01	.69	25.8	.48	4.48	.56
Bristol	26.5	.31	3.88	.38	21.2	.24	2.82	.24
Cardiff	29.0	.46	3.48	.45	19.5	.29	2.11	.23
Coventry	24.6	.41	3.49	.45	19.6	.27	2.53	.30
Derby	26.1	.61	3.75	.48	18.8	.43	2.41	.28
Kingston-on-Hull	34.2	.50	2.08	.19	16.8	.14	.88	.04
Leeds	35.3	.47	5.72	.55	24.9	.34	4.04	.37
Leicester	38.8	.62	4.51	.61	33.2	.54	3.73	.52
Liverpool	65.9	.37	8.15	.64	32.3	.21	4.85	.39
London	40.4	.13	5.90	.54	32.8	.11	5.39	.49
Luton	15.6	.30	2.18	.35	11.6	.05	.37	.02
Manchester	25.4	.13	2.42	.23	20.6	.10	2.10	.18
Newcastle-on-Tyne	29.5	.24	1.76	.15	15.9	.04	.33	.01
Nottingham	27.4	.36	3.03	.38	20.1	.24	2.22	.25
Oxford	9.7	.08	.45	.02	5.4	−.24	1.28	.12
Plymouth	27.9	.43	3.36	.48	21.6	.33	3.01	.43
Portsmouth	36.3	.41	3.94	.54	31.3	.37	3.43	.47
Sheffield	32.4	.40	6.14	.61	26.6	.34	5.44	.55
Southampton	17.0	.22	2.02	.21	12.4	.03	.25	.005
Wolverhampton	11.9	.08	.60	.02	12.6	.09	.81	.04
York	21.9	.52	3.07	.49	17.6	.37	2.29	.34
Average	27.0	.33		.38	20.5	.22		.18

^{a} In thousands per square mile.

6.2.2 West Germany

Table 5.13 gives the German results. Here, distance is a significant determinant of density in 34 of 36 cases. The density functions have an R^2 level of 39% in both 1960 and 1970. The fact that the model works as well in 1970 as in 1960 for the German data is contrary to a priori expectations—our discussion of the theoretical model in Section 2 led us to believe that increasing suburbanization of employment over time would impair the explanatory power of a monocentric model. Such is the case for the British and American results (see the following discussion) but not for the German situation. To further investigate the question of when the model works better or worse, I compared the R^2 for "independent cities," that is, those whose boundary does not touch that of another city, with the R^2 for cities in the Rhine–Ruhr conurbation.[23] For 1960, the explanatory power of the model is

[23] The Rhine–Ruhr cities in the sample are Bochum, Dortmund, Dusseldorf, Duisburg, Essen, and Oberhausen.

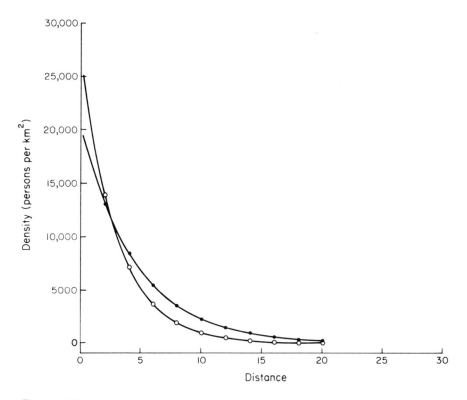

Figure 5.17.   Urban density functions for Great Britain, 1961 and 1971. ○: 1961; ●: 1971.

virtually the same for both groups of cities. For 1970, however, the model explains 42% of the variation in distance for the independent cities but only 29% for the Rhine–Ruhr cities. This difference may reflect the fact that for residents of any Rhine–Ruhr city, there are several employment centers within commuting distance. The distance from any one center therefore does not adequately measure accessibility to employment. My results suggest that over the decade the set of Rhine–Ruhr cities became more closely integrated.

German cities suburbanized rather little over the decade of the 1960s, as shown in Figure 5.18. For those cities having complete data, the average density intercept fell 9% from 32,400 to 29,500 people per square mile while the average gradient fell 15% from .55 to .47. These results suggest that British cities in 1970 were much more centralized than German cities. On average, the central density level in 1970 was 44% higher in German cities, and density fell off more than twice as fast with distance. Thus, the suburbanization process proceeded much less far in Germany than in Britain, in spite of the rapid rise in German income levels during the 1960s.

TABLE 5.13
German Urban Density Functions

	1960				1970			
	D^a_{01}	G_1	t	R^2	D_{01}	G_1	t	R^2
Augsburg	100.5	1.73	4.57	.45	88.2	1.60	4.35	.41
Berlin	79.2	.26	3.23	.54	66.3	.25	3.26	.54
Bielefeld	30.3	.84	3.93	.46	19.3	.56	2.56	.27
Bochum	12.9	.24	1.89	.19	12.0	.20	2.16	.24
Bremen	13.7	.21	3.99	.31	16.8	.26	3.23	.22
Cologne	21.6	.28	5.20	.38	47.8	.44	10.28	.69
Darmstadt	—	—	—	—	16.0	.63	3.10	.23
Dortmund	—	—	—	—	18.4	.39	3.11	.34
Dusseldorf	40.4	.44	4.87	.57	23.8	.22	2.50	.27
Duisburg	—	—	—	—	15.5	.22	2.70	.20
Essen	26.4	.38	4.61	.36	26.2	.33	4.40	.34
Frankfurt	21.9	.26	3.18	.24	17.3	.16	2.54	.17
Hamburg	24.9	.55	2.83	.25	17.1	.43	2.28	.18
Heilbronn	5.5	.52	1.83	.63	5.9	.41	2.77	.72
Karlsruhe	31.5	.92	6.21	.73	32.8	.85	6.56	.75
Munich	—	—	—	—	53.0	.38	9.88	.74
Oberhausen	24.8	.34	3.66	.40	20.3	.29	3.34	.35
Osnabruck	—	—	—	—	13.7	.53	1.62	.16
Saarbrucken	19.4	.69	2.44	.20	18.9	.63	2.69	.23
Stuttgart	—	—	—	—	20.3	.36	3.62	.31
Ulm	—	—	—	—	44.1	1.30	4.45	.74
Wiesbaden	7.5	.35	1.49	.07	—	—	—	—
Average	30.7	.53		.39	29.0	.50		.39
Average for cities with complete data	32.4	.55		.41	29.5	.47		.38

^{a} In thousands per square mile.

6.2.3   Japan

Table 5.14 and Figure 5.19 give the results for Japanese cities for 1970. For the 45 cities,[24] the mean central density level is 30,300 persons per square mile and the mean density gradient is .54. Distance alone explains 60% of the statistical variation in these regressions, a much higher goodness-of-fit than for any of the other samples. This suggests that there may be less employment suburbanization and less variation in income levels in Japanese cities than in the other samples. Comparing the Japanese and German results for 1970, we find that both the average central density levels and average density gradients are nearly the same. This is a somewhat

[24] All suburban cities have been eliminated from our original Japan sample in order to have strict comparability with the other countries. These cities are listed in Table 5.18.

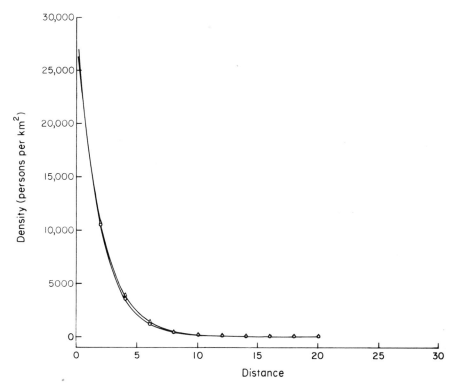

Figure 5.18. Urban density functions for West Germany, 1960 and 1970. ○: 1960; △: 1970.

surprising result considering the fact that German incomes (GNP per capita of \$4,218 in 1972) are a good deal higher than Japanese (GNP per capita of \$2,823).[25]

6.2.4 United States

Table 5.15 and Figure 5.20 give the American results. Density is a significant determinant of distance in 50 of 60 regressions. As in the British case, the model's explanatory power is lower for the later than the earlier

[25] Japanese houses are generally only two stories at maximum. High-rise or multifamily residential buildings are still uncommon because of the high cost required to make them earthquake resistant. German central cities typically are characterized by five- and six-story residential buildings. Mills and Otha (1976) note, however, that the Japanese increase central residential density levels by devoting less land to streets than is common in the United States or Europe. Average house size is also smaller in Japan.

TABLE 5.14

Japanese Urban Density Functions

	$D_{01}{}^a$	G_1	t	R^2
Akita	15.4	.35	2.89	.24
Aomori	38.7	.63	11.56	.83
Asahikawa	33.4	.79	14.86	.95
Fukui	26.8	.82	7.77	.80
Fukuoka	38.3	.30	3.66	.32
Fukushima	9.9	.48	9.51	.81
Fukuyama	13.9	.34	3.23	.30
Hachinoe	17.8	.60	4.33	.50
Hakodate	38.9	.27	2.34	.22
Hamamatsu	27.1	.50	11.38	.82
Himeji	16.8	.28	3.24	.27
Hiroshima	45.8	.52	4.45	.45
Kagoshima	37.4	.50	5.39	.51
Kanazawa	42.6	.71	9.14	.75
Kitakyushu	34.2	.26	3.75	.36
Kochi	39.0	.92	7.59	.79
Kofu	59.2	1.24	8.01	.77
Kooriyama	14.6	.47	9.57	.79
Kumamoto	31.8	.55	5.57	.53
Matsue	21.7	.79	6.96	.79
Matsuyama	32.9	.79	7.22	.65
Mito	19.1	.61	4.35	.61
Miyazaki	13.8	.48	5.80	.67
Morioka	29.6	.82	9.00	.76
Nagano	14.7	.41	8.61	.53
Nagasaki	51.2	.70	6.73	.62
Nagoya	64.9	.28	6.21	.47
Niigata	29.3	.36	8.23	.71
Oita	15.5	.43	6.37	.65
Okayama	24.6	.45	9.23	.75
Osaka	42.2	−.02	0.46	.004
Saga	21.3	.82	6.07	.77
Sapporo	76.5	.58	7.24	.65
Sasebo	25.1	.47	3.75	.52
Sendai	52.3	.66	5.38	.51
Takamatsu	29.6	.62	9.13	.76
Tokushima	22.9	.72	11.00	.86
Tokyo	45.3	.02	0.54	.003
Tottori	17.2	.76	6.45	.76
Toyama	24.5	.58	7.25	.68
Tsu	18.2	.68	4.11	.61
Utsunomiya	35.2	.72	8.56	.72
Wakayama	36.6	.60	9.82	.78
Yamagata	31.9	.87	14.46	.91
Yamaguchi	18.1	.25	2.48	.38
Average	30.3	.54		.60

^{a} In thousands per square mile.

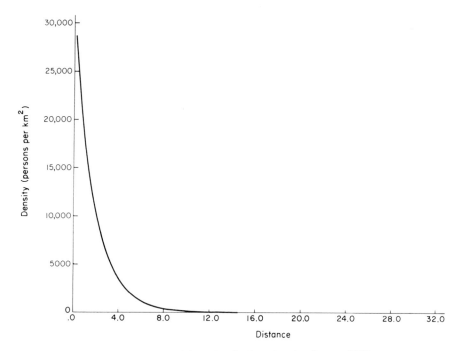

Figure 5.19. Urban density function for Japan, 1970.

year. Nine of the 10 regressions for which density is not significantly related to distance are for 1960, and on average the R^2 falls from .44 in 1950 to .24 in 1960. There is also considerable suburbanization over the decade. The average central density level falls by 33% from 30,000 to 20,000 people per square mile, and the average gradient falls by 35% from .43 to .28.

6.3   International Comparative Analysis

6.3.1   Introduction

This section brings together the results of Section 6.2 to consider how cities in different countries varied with respect to urban form. First, some overall comparisons are made and then density functions are observed by city size and by rates of change over time.

6.3.2   Comparisons among Countries: All Sample Cities

Several conclusions emerge from the presentation of individual country data in Section 3. First, we find that in 1960 the D_{01} levels for the United

TABLE 5.15
U.S. Urban Density Functions

	1950				1960			
	D^a_{01}	G_1	t	R^2	D_{01}	G_1	t	R^2
Akron	38.0	.84	7.63	.71	24.0	.61	6.10	.59
Atlanta	22.0	.48	4.36	.43	15.0	.30	2.00	.14
Baltimore	69.0	.52	5.20	.53	46.0	.39	4.88	.49
Birmingham	9.4	.20	3.33	.35	6.1	.092	1.31	.07
Boston	78.0	.30	3.75	.35	52.0	.22	2.75	.22
Buffalo	29.0	.19	2.11	.16	21.0	.10	1.11	.05
Chicago	56.0	.18	4.75	.53	49.0	.15	3.00	.31
Cincinnati	12.0	.69	6.90	.67	9.2	.59	5.90	.52
Cleveland	22.0	.13	1.08	.05	6.3	.18	1.29	.06
Columbus	10.0	.19	3.80	.43	6.7	.11	1.83	.10
Dallas	26.0	.48	4.80	.47	9.2	.21	2.63	.21
Dayton	18.0	.32	2.46	.22	17.0	.33	2.20	.19
Detroit	19.0	.098	3.26	.30	10.0	.005	0.21	.002
Los Angeles	14.0	.078	2.43	.20	12.0	.043	1.34	.07
Memphis	14.0	.22	4.40	.46	8.8	.10	2.00	.15
Miami	14.0	.24	2.40	.22	15.0	.19	1.72	.12
Milwaukee	61.0	.44	7.33	.70	48.0	.38	6.33	.64
New Haven	46.0	.99	8.25	.74	22.0	.59	3.93	.40
Oklahoma City	16.0	.43	6.14	.64	7.0	.10	1.43	.06
Providence	14.0	.41	4.55	.50	7.7	.23	3.29	.30
Richmond	41.0	.82	4.83	.49	29.0	.66	3.88	.40
Rochester	38.0	.52	3.71	.39	31.0	.41	2.93	.26
St. Louis	47.0	.28	3.11	.27	14.0	.02	0.17	.00
San Diego	18.0	.39	6.50	.62	11.0	.15	2.50	.20
Seattle	24.0	.31	5.17	.57	21.0	.24	4.80	.52
Spokane	5.9	.34	3.09	.31	2.9	.11	1.00	.03
Syracuse	48.0	.92	4.38	.45	32.0	.67	3.35	.34
Toledo	6.1	.20	4.00	.42	4.4	.14	2.80	.23
Utica	51.0	1.21	4.48	.46	42.0	1.02	3.42	.53
Washington, D.C.	20.0	.27	3.86	.43	5.8	.11	1.57	.035
Average	30.0	.43		.44	20.0	.28		.24

^{a} In thousands per square mile.

States and Germany were nearly identical, 30,000 and 30,700, respectively; both were somewhat higher than Britain's 27,000. By 1970, central density levels in Britain fell to 20,500, whereas, in Germany, they stayed relatively constant and close to the level in Japan for that year.

For G_1, the 1960 pattern shows the United States ($G_1 = .28$) and Great Britain ($G_1 = .33$) the most decentralized, with the German cities much less so ($G_1 = .53$). Between 1960 and 1970, British cities decentralized greatly; their average G_1 level was .22 by 1970. On the other hand, German cities experienced little suburbanization; their G_1 remained nearly constant during

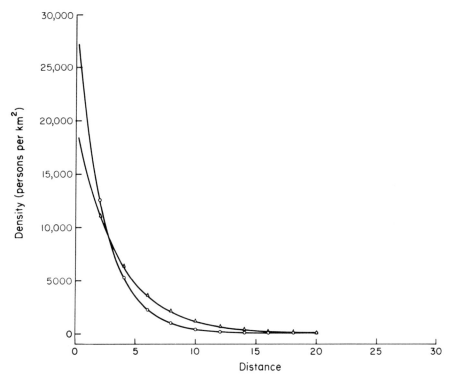

Figure 5.20. Urban density functions for the United States, 1950 and 1960. $\bigcirc$: 1950; $\triangle$: 1960.

the decade and the 1970 G_1 (.52) was very close to that of Japan (.54). Thus, Germany and Japan have nearly identical density functions in 1970 as shown in Figure 5.21 where the British (1971) and U.S. (1960) functions are also given.

6.3.3 Comparisons among Countries by City Size

Table 5.16 breaks down the results for each of the four data sets into four city size classes. Inspecting the table we can test the prediction of the "mixed" model that at a given time period, higher population in cities within a given country implies higher central density levels and lower density gradients. D_{01} in fact does rise consistently with city size for the British, German, and Japanese data sets; the U.S. pattern, particularly in 1950, is less clear. On average, central density levels are twice as high for cities of over 1 million people as for cities of less than .25 million. Density gradients also consistently fall as city size increases for all data sets. On average, cities of over 1 million people have a density gradient only one-third as great as

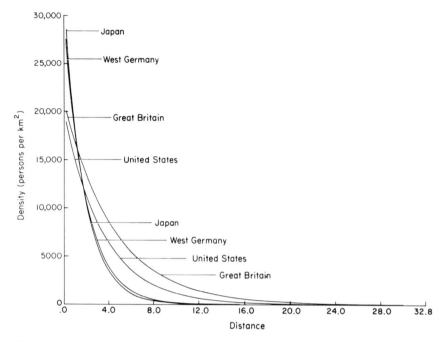

Figure 5.21. Urban density functions for the United States (1960), Great Britain (1971), West Germany (1970), and Japan (1970).

that of cities of less than .25 million. These large-city–small-city differentials seem to be increasing over time. Both of these results suggest confirmation of the general predictions of the simple urban model.

Table 5.17 gives 10-year rates of decline in the density function parameters for each city size class for the four samples. The British, German, and American data are calculated from Table 5.16. The Japanese data are derived from density function estimates made by Mills and Ohta (1976) for a sample of 22 Japanese cities for 1965 and 1970. The data do not show systematic trends by city size in the rate of decline of density function parameters. Large and small cities are decentralizing at about the same rate in Britain and the United States. The German cities likewise show no systematic pattern in terms of size, but the rates of decline are much slower in all cases. The Japanese cities show a pattern of greater suburbanization in large cities, except that the largest Japanese cities increased their central density levels while simultaneously flattening their density gradients rather rapidly. Suburbanization in the larger Japanese cities appeared to be proceeding more rapidly in the late 1960s than it did in the United States in the 1950s or in the English or German samples in the 1960s. This presumably reflects the very high rates of income growth occurring in Japan during the period

TABLE 5.16
Comparative Density Function Parameters

	1961		1971		
British cities' population	$D_0{}^a$	D_1	D_0	D_1	N^b
1,000,000 or more	34.9	.16	25.1	.09	2
500,000–1,000,000	31.8	.34	26.1	.25	4
250,000–500,000	28.3	.40	20.5	.26	9
250,000 or less	21.2	.35	13.9	.23	8
Average	27.0	.33	20.5	.22	23
	1960		1970		
German cities' population	D_0	D_1	D_0	D_1	N^c
1,000,000 or more	52.0	.41	45.5	.35	2,3
500,000–1,000,000	24.8	.31	24.4	.31	5,7
250,000–500,000	35.4	.72	25.7	.63	5,5
250,000 or less	18.4	.69	14.8	.55	3,5
Average	30.7	.53	29.0	.50	15,20
	1950		1960		
U.S. cities' population	D_0	D_1	D_0	D_1	N
1,000,000 or more	31.0	.12	24.0	.066	3
500,000–1,000,000	42.0	.35	25.0	.25	8
250,000–500,000	21.0	.40	14.0	.24	10
250,000 or less	28.0	.63	19.0	.43	9
Average	29.8	.43	19.5	.28	30
	1970				
Japanese cities' population	D_0	D_1			N
1,000,000 or more	52.6	.48			5
500,000–1,000,000	45.4	.49			3
250,000–500,000	29.3	.52			17
250,000 or less	23.4	.65			20
Average	30.3	.54			45

[a] In thousands per square mile.
[b] Number of cities.
[c] Number of cities in 1960 and 1970, respectively.

and the fact that Japan industrialized and urbanized later than the other countries under study here; therefore, one would expect the suburbanization process would lag as well, as has already been noted in Chapters 2 and 3.

Overall, Table 5.17 is quite remarkable in the consistent story it tells across wide ranges of city size and across several time periods and cultures. As the model predicts, the passage of time led to population suburbaniza-

TABLE 5.17
Ten-Year Average Rates of Decline in Density Function Parameters

Population	Britain 1961–1971		Germany 1960–1970		United States 1950–1960		Japan[a] 1965–1970	
	D_{01}	G_1	D_{01}	G_1	D_{01}	G_1	D_{01}	G_1
1,000,000 or more	.28	.44	.13	.15	.19	.45	−.093	.60
500,000–1,000,000	.18	.26	.02	.00	.40	.29	.65	.75
250,000–500,000	.28	.35	.27	.125	.33	.40	.35	.18
250,000 or less	.34	.34	.20	.20	.32	.32	.25	.23
Average	.24	.33	.06	.06	.35	.35	.30	.27

[a] Calculated from data given by Mills and Ohta (1976). The 10-year rate of decline is extrapolated from the actual rate of change between 1965 and 1970.

tion, that is, flatter density gradients, and to lower central density levels. This reflects rising average income levels in all cities over the period as well as declining transportation costs. The decreased transport costs are due mostly to more widespread availability of automobiles for commuting, better roads, and perhaps improved public transportation. In the United States in the 1950s, for example, urban freeways were just beginning to appear. In addition, the changes reflect the effects of employment suburbanization that acts to attract workers from the central areas to the suburbs, to increase residential densities near suburban subcenters, and to reduce them near the central business district. The consistency of results in Table 5.17 is yet more surprising when we recall that average land values are much higher in Britain and Germany than in the United States, and are yet higher in Japan. Similarly, the cost of gasoline is much higher in Britain, Germany, and Japan than in the United States. The data thus provide little support for the frequently voiced opinion that European tastes for housing and travel are different—that is, that Europeans regardless of their incomes "prefer" high-rise housing and commuting via public transportation.

Another prediction of the model—that the ratio of large city to small city density declines over time—is tested in Table 5.16. Section 2 argued that relative decreases in large cities' productivity advantage over small cities would lead to a decline in large city relative to small city G_1 levels. However, the comparison of G_1s for cities of greater than 1 million population to those of less than .25 million in Table 5.16 shows a mixed result. Britain, the United States, and Japan show lower ratios, thus confirming the model's prediction, but Germany's ratio increases slightly.

Finally, I look at goodness-of-fit over time for density functions. The model predicts that the R^2 should decline as suburbanization causes departures from the negative exponential. If one reviews Tables 5.12–5.16 and Mills and Ohta (Table 10.21), one sees sharp declines in the levels of average

R^2, especially for the United States, Britain, and Japan. For the United States, for example, the average R^2 fell from .44 to .24 between 1950 and 1960, reflecting a fall in R^2 for 28 of the 30 cities in the sample.

However, when the characteristics of similarly sized cities are compared at the same point in time in different countries, the results are less consistent with the model's predictions. We would expect cities in the higher income countries to have lower D_{01} and G_1 values. However, taking cities in the 250,000–500,000 size class in 1960, the density gradient was .21 for the U.S. cities, steeper for the British cities (.40), and still steeper for the German cities (.72). For 1970, Japan showed more compact smaller cities (i.e., $G_1 =$ .65) than Britain (.23) and Germany (.55). This is roughly consistent with a priori expectations.

6.4 Concluding Remarks concerning International Land Use Patterns

We have employed estimates of negative exponential density functions in order to compare land use patterns in four countries. In most cases, the predictions of the theoretical model are borne out by the data of our sample cities. We found, for instance, that the decentralization predicted by the theoretical model occurred in three of the four countries; Germany's density functions did not, on average, show much fall in G_1 during the 1960s. In looking at density functions by city size, we found that D_{01} is higher and G_1 is lower for the larger cities in most of our countries. Both results are predicted by the theoretical model. However, the model's predictions concerning the urban form of similar sized cities in different countries are not borne out. We expected lower values of D_{01} and G_1 in richer countries, but this did not occur: Germany had more compact and Japan more decentralized cities than we would expect on a priori grounds. Overall, though, Section 2's simple model seems to be a relatively good predictor of general urban land use patterns and a good tool for making international comparisons.

7 Conclusions

I have focused this chapter on land use patterns in Japan, using density functions as my principal measure. My review indicated that larger cities were much more spatially decentralized than smaller ones (as we have seen in Chapters 2 and 3) and that it is difficult to estimate such functions for suburban cities where there is interaction among competing employment centers. I also estimated regressions for the relationship between land price and distance from a city's core and an econometric model of land use that predicted several land market variables. Finally, I looked at land use in the United States, Great Britain, and West Germany and compared those countries to Japan. Most of the predictions of the theoretical model outlined in Section 2 were borne out by empirical studies of Sections 3 through 6. For example, central density falls and decentralization occurs with time, and larger cities have higher central densities and lower density gradients than smaller ones.

This chapter concludes the analysis of the Japanese urban system begun in Chapter 1. Chapters 2 and 3 looked at regional development patterns during the postwar period using the REC data set. Having seen general patterns in those chapters, more specific topics, such as migration in Chapter 4 and land use in this chapter, were examined. Having completed the observations on the nature and changing patterns of the Japanese urban system, I now turn my attention to governmental attempts to manage the urban system. The next chapter reviews regional planning efforts of the central government that were aimed at altering the spatial distribution of the population through public investment and tax incentive mechanisms. Then, in Chapter 7, intergovernmental relations and local finance are discussed in relation to regional development issues.

References

Alonso, W. (1964). *Location and Land Use*. Harvard University Press, Cambridge, Mass.

Barr, J. L. (1970). Transportation costs, rent and intraurban location, Discussion Paper. Department of Economics, Washington University, St. Louis, Missouri.

Brigham, E. F. (1964). *A Model of Residential Land Values*. Rand Corporation, Santa Monica, California.

Clark, C. (1951). Urban population densities. *Journal of the Royal Statistical Society, 114,* 375–386.

Glickman, N. J. and Y. Oguri (1978). Modeling the urban land market. *Journal of Urban Economics, 5,* (forthcoming).

Glickman, N. J. and M. J. White (1978). *Urban Land Use Patterns: An International Comparison. Environment and Planning A, 10*.

Hansen, W. (1959). How accessability shapes land use. *Journal of American Institute of Planners, 25,* 73–76.

Harris, B. (1966). *Notes on Accessability*. Mimeo, University of Pennsylvania, Philadelphia.

Japan Bureau of Statistics, Office of the Prime Minister (1972). *1970 Population Census of Japan, Volume 4, Census Tracts*. Bureau of Statistics, Office of the Prime Minister, Tokyo.

Japan Ministry of Construction (1973). *Public Notification of Land Price* (in Japanese). Ministry of Construction, Tokyo.

Japan National Land Agency (1975). *The National Land Use Policy in Japan*. Japan National Land Agency, Tokyo.

Japan National Land Agency (1976). *National Land Statistics Outline 1976* (in Japanese). Japan National Land Agency, Tokyo.

Kau, J. B. and C. F. Lee (1977). A random coefficient model to estimate a stochastic density gradient. *Regional Science and Urban Economics, 7,* 169–177.

McDonald, J. F. and H. W. Bowman (1976). Some tests of alternative urban population density functions. *Journal of Urban Economics, 3,* 242–252.

Mills, E. S. (1969). The value of urban land, in H. S. Perloff, ed., *The Quality of the Urban Environment*. Johns Hopkins Press, Baltimore. Pp. 231–253.

Mills, E. S. (1972a). *Studies in the Structure of the Urban Economy*. Johns Hopkins Press, Baltimore.

Mills, E. S. (1972b). *Urban Economics*. Scott Foresman, Glenview, Illinois.

Mills, E. S. and K. Ohta (1976). Urbanization and urban problems, in Patrick, H. and H. Rosovsky, eds., *Asia's New Giant: How the Japanese Economy Works*. The Brookings Institution, Washington, D.C. Pp. 673–751.

Muth, R. (1969). *Cities and Housing*. The University of Chicago Press, Chicago.

Newling, B. E. (1969). The spatial variation of urban population densities. *Geographical Review, 59*, 242–252.

Oguri, Y. (1974). *A Preliminary Study of A Metropolitan Residential Model: A Multi-Central Urban Population Density Model*. Mimeo.

Rickert, J. E. (1965). *The Present and Potential Role of State and Local Taxation in the Preservation or Development of Open Space in Urban Fringe Areas*. Urban Land Institute, Washington, D.C.

Schneider, M. (1959). Gravity models and trip distribution theory. *Papers and Proceedings of the Regional Science Association, 5*, 51–56.

Solow, R. (1973). On equilibrium models of urban location, in J. M. Parkin, ed., *Essays in Modern Economics*. Barnes and Noble, New York.

Wendt, P. F., and W. Goldner (1966). Land values and the dynamics of residential location, in *Essays in Urban Land Economics*. University of California, Berkeley, California.

White, M. J. (1976). Firm suburbanization and urban subcenters. *Journal of Urban Economics, 3*, 323–343.

Wilson, A. G. (1967). A statistical theory of spatial distribution models. *Transportation Research, 1*, 253–269.

Wilson, A. G. (1970). *Entropy in Urban and Regional Modelling*. Pion, Ltd., London.

The Management of the Japanese Urban System: Regional Development and Regional Planning in Postwar Japan

1   Introduction

In the postwar period, the Japanese economy experienced a very high level of economic growth as it recovered from the war and rebuilt its economy and its cities. This growth brought with it important structural change: a sharp reduction of the proportion of the population employed in primary industry and the migration of large numbers of people from rural to urban settings. These urban development and migration patterns have been discussed at greater length in Chapters 1 through 4 so that they need not be related again here.

Structural change had important ramifications for Japan's regions for three principle reasons. First, there occurred some depopulation of many rural areas. These regions, which include more than a third of the nation's municipalities, were seen by many analysts to be inefficient to support the remaining population that was largely old and engaged in low-productivity agriculture. Second, there was great overcrowding in Japan's large cities resulting in several well-known negative externalities such as pollution and congestion. Third, there was income gap between the richer cities and poorer rural centers, which many viewed as being too large.

The government, at various hierarchical levels, was asked to respond to these perceived problems and it did so in at least two ways. First, it formulated a series of regional plans—components of national plans—that were implemented during the postwar period. The experience of Japan in relation to national planning and regional development is the primary subject of this chapter. The second method used to attack regional problems was workings of the tax system in which revenues collected by the central government were allocated to local governments, in part on the basis of need. The system of intergovernmental relations and revenue sharing is the subject of Chapter 7 (and Gencer and Glickman, 1976). These two techniques should be viewed as complementary—regional planning and public investment in relation to local public finance—although, as I shall argue, it appears that the tax system was relatively more successful at accomplishing many of the goals of overall government policy toward regions.

This chapter has four additional sections. Section 2 reviews the experience of national economic development and planning so that the regional planning efforts can be placed in their proper perspective. Section 3 reviews the goals and strategies of regional planners, the implementation of plans, some of the experience with developing nodal "new" industrial cities, and the interlocking tax system. The planning experience of Japan with that of some other OECD countries, especially France, are compared in Section 4. Some conclusions are offered in Section 5.

2   The Management of Growth: Macroeconomic Policy and National Economic Planning[1]

2.1   General Themes

From the earliest postwar governments, the major goal configuration of economic policy can be described, following Ackley and Ishi (1976), as a "triad": growth, investment, and exports. Growth,[2] especially of exports and investment, was seen as both a means of recovery from the ravages of the war and, in later years, as the basis of national economic survival. This set of goals was proclaimed by Japan's ruling elite and was accepted and widely admired within Japanese society. And the goal of growth was supported by strategic government policy in the macroeconomic arena: fiscal and monetary policy and national economic planning.[3] Much less important were questions of equity. Relatively little in the way of income redistribution

---

[1] Useful references on economic planning and macroeconomic policy include Ackley and Ishi (1976), Fukui (1972), Komiya (1975), Okita (1974), Trezise and Suzuki (1976), and Watanabe (1970).

[2] The growth record and some of its consequences were discussed in Chapter 1.

[3] There were other government macroeconomic and microeconomic policies aimed at growth and development. These include industrial development policies that try to develop particular industries through tax and subsidy schemes. These plans are made by coordinating offices (called *genkyoku*) for particular industies within the government (particularly within the Ministry of International Trade and Industry) and with the private industry associations; on this subject see Komiya (especially pp. 13–17), and Tresize and Suzuki (pp. 792–797). Ackley and Ishi (pp. 236–239) also discuss the method of "administrative guidance" that the government gives to firms and individuals in order to influence their behavior.

programs were undertaken (either through taxes or transfers) that in any way interfered with the major goal of economic growth through greater economic efficiency. Although the policy of growth management was highly successful, "the benefits of growth have not been distributed evenly," say Patrick and Rosovsky (1976, p. 35).[4] We shall see in Section 3 that interregional equity was not an important policy goal in the regional planning process either.

2.2 Fiscal and Monetary Policy

Fiscal policy was used to encourage savings and investment as well as exports. Also, fiscal policy involved the government in direct investment in productive capital formation. Through most of the postwar period, fiscal policy served to restrain the economy: Largely through the conservative influence of the Ministry of Finance, the government's budget often showed a surplus until 1970. The surplus was used to provide credit for private investment. Monetary policy has been expansionary and has been employed to keep interest rates low and to make sure that credit was made available to the business community for the stimulation of capital-intensive, private investment; little in the way of investment funds were devoted, however, to social capital such as housing or consumer durables.

2.3 National Economic Planning

Economic planning was usefully employed to set economic goals for the society and to indicate the potential growth and distribution of the society's resources. As I shall argue, however, economic planning accomplished little that could not have been achieved by the confluence of monetary and fiscal policy, buoyant domestic aggregate demand, and the rapid growth of Japan's share of world trade.

[4] It is not clear how the income distribution has changed during the postwar period. Although Patrick and Rosovsky argue that wealth distribution has become more concentrated, they say that income distribution is probably more even than it was during the 1950s. However, their income distribution data do not include capital gains in the definition of income, thus confusing intertemporal comparisons. Data on the size distribution of income described by Sawyer (1976) show that there was some increase in income equality. The lowest quintile of families increased its share from 7.8 to 8.7% of income, while the upper quintile registered a declining share (from 40.2 to 38.2%) between 1962 and 1972. Although per capita income distribution figures are not available and international comparisons difficult, Japan (along with Sweden and Australia) had among the most egalitarian income distribution, as measured by Gini coefficients and other measures, of the 10 countries discussed by Sawyer. On the other hand, Denison and Chung (1976, pp. 86–87), show that the share of labor income in national income fell from 77.6% (1952–1959) to 72.7% (1960–1971). This might indicate a widening of the income distribution. Japan was the only country among 11 described by Denison and Chung in which the labor share fell over time, and Japan's labor share was the smallest among the 11. I shall discuss in more detail interregional income disparities in Section 3.5.3.

National economic planning began during the American occupation, and between 1949 and 1976, the Japanese government formulated 10 long- and medium-term plans.[5] Throughout, the emphasis was on the promotion of economic growth, although some consideration was given to the development of social welfare measures in later plans.[6] It is clear that economic planning, consistent with other governmental policy, aimed at trying to expand the private sector. For, as Okita (1974) points out in speaking of economic planning, "Japan's economic system is not a planned economy but a predominantly private enterprise economy [p. 1]."

Each plan[7] consists of a set of forecasts of the major sectors of the nation's economy (e.g., GNP, exports, investments, government spending) that have often been made using econometric techniques. In addition, especially in the later plans, there have been qualitative goals as well, although they often were quite vague and general. For instance, in the 1973 Basic Economic and Social Plan, goals for air pollution, water quality, and city parks are mentioned. The latest plan, The Economic Plan for the Second Half of the 1970's, was formulated in 1976[8] and focuses primarily on Japan's economic situation in a transition period from a high-growth to a lower-growth society. Lower growth is expected by Japanese planners because of the significant change in the terms of trade between resource-using and resource-consuming nations. Japan is facing serious problems because it must now pay much higher prices for the resources that it imports from abroad, especially oil. This has resulted in a slowing of the growth rate of the economy and considerable price inflation since 1973. Thus, the planners predict a growth rate of only 6% per year in real terms between 1976 and

---

[5] These were: "Economic Rehabilitation Plan" (1949), "Economic Self-Support Plan" (1951), "Five Year Plan for Economic Self-Support" (1955), "New Long-Range Economic Plan" (1957), "Plan for Doubling National Income" (1960), "Medium-Term Economic Plan" (1963), "Economic and Social Development Plan" (1967), "New Economic and Social Development Plan" (1970), "Basic Economic and Social Plan" (1973), and "Economic Plan for the Second Half of the 1970's" (1976).

[6] There were various stages in the economic planning. The first plans put emphasis on recovery from the war and industrial development through export and investment growth. Later, some attention was paid to (an ill-defined) "balanced growth" along with price stability and international cooperation. In still later stages, beginning in the late 1960s, social welfare, quality of life, and environmental considerations were alleged to be important. Okita (1974) has called these stages the "rehabilitation," "self-supporting," and "development" stages, respectively. On this subject, also see Komiya (1975).

[7] Plans have been constructed by a secretariat that primarily consisted of the staff of the Economic Planning Agency, with the participation of other elements in the Central Government bureaucracy. In addition, there was the constant interaction with the private sector, formally through the Economic Council (consisting of 30 members from the private sector) that had to approve plans, and informally through the day-to-day consultation with private industry that characterizes Japanese political economy. Final approval of each plan has been given by the Cabinet, which has never altered draft plans.

[8] Japan Economic Planning Agency (1976).

TABLE 6.1

Planned and Actual Growth of GNP under National Economic Plans

Plan	Planned growth	Actual growth
Five Year Plan for Economic Self-Support (1955)	5.0	9.1
New Long-Range Economic Plan (1957)	5.0	10.0
Plan for Doubling National Income (1960)	7.2	10.9
Medium-Term Economic Plan (1965)	8.1	10.8
Economic and Social Development Plan (1967)	8.2	9.9
New Economic and Social Development Plan (1970)	10.6	7.5
Basic Economic and Social Plan (1973)	9.4	2.4[a]
Economic Plan for the Second Half of the 1970's (1976)	6.0	NA

Source: Okita 1974, (Table 6), Japan Economic Planning Agency (1976), and OECD (1977).
[a] 1973–1976 growth.

1980. The plan also involves a large number of qualitative targets involving social policy, although in many cases the goals are not specific.

Scholars have paid considerable attention to the quantitative economic forecasts that have been made in connection with national planning. As is shown in Table 6.1, the long-term prospects of the Japanese economy have, at least until very recently, been grossly understated by planners. For example, the actual growth following the 1957 New Long-Range Plan was twice the predicted rate. During the National Income Doubling Plan (begun in 1960), the planned 1970 private investment level was reached in 1961. This constant underestimation of growth has made the plans quickly obsolete and has forced the government to make new plans often.[9] Thus, Watanabe (1970) has called Japanese plans "decorative" rather than "indicative."

Moreover, the plans and accompanying government statements are not binding on either private or public decision makers. As Komiya (1975) points out: "Nobody feels much obligation to observe its [the plan's] figures [p. 11]." Even the planners themselves say that the plans are not compulsory. In the introduction to the 1976 plan (Japan Economic Planning Agency, 1976) it is stated,

> Of course, it should also be noted that our system is based upon a market economy, and the economic plan is not intended to regulate minutely all sectors of the economy, nor is there anything compulsory about it. Rather, Japanese economic plans are attempts (*1*) to clarify preferable directions for economic and social development in view of the long-term domestic and international outlook, (*2*) to indicate basic policy orientations which

[9] Some observers have attributed this underestimation to poor forecasting procedures. Watanabe (1970) also attributes this to purposeful policy on the part of the government. Watanabe argues that the Ministry of Finance has been anxious to keep down the level of government spending, so that it makes bearish forecasts of the future growth of the economy. This allows the government's fiscal policy to be one of restraint as budget surpluses result. For examples of the uses of econometric analysis and models in Japan, see Kosobud and Minami (1977), Japan Economic Planning Agency (1967, 1973), and Glickman (1971).

> should be adopted by the government for achieving such development, and (3) to provide guidelines for personal and corporate behavior [p. 1].

Therefore, the plans are not followed by actors in the private sector, who are anxious to exploit economic advantage that they may see, whether or not there is a plan.

More surprisingly, plans are not even followed by public spending, since individual ministries determine their spending targets independently. By and large, government capital formation is determined through the annual budgetary process, which is often unrelated to the long-term considerations of the plans. Furthermore, the post-1960 plans all called for relative increases in social overhead capital. Yet, the ratio of public to private capital formation was virtually unchanged between 1961 and 1973.[10] Additionally, monetary and fiscal policy were determined outside the scope of the plans. It is especially clear that short-term monetary and fiscal policy targets dominated long-term considerations of the plans.

Although the plans set goals and targets for the private and public sectors in an effort to reduce economic uncertainty and to help private economic planning, many scholars argue that the plans had little to do with increasing growth. This is obvious since actual growth has nearly always exceeded planned growth. Plans may have helped to reduce potential bottlenecks within the economy by showing constraints (in an input–output format) that might exist under differing scenarios of growth. But, as Ackley and Ishi say, the plans' contribution was modest in this respect since (a) the plans became obsolete so quickly, (b) entrepreneurs acted independently of plans, and (c) the Ministry of International Trade and Industry (MITI) and other agencies had independent lines of communication with their private sector clients and did not need the plans' projections.

The major accomplishment of long-term economic planning at the national level seems to have been the exchange of information among the ministries of the government and between the private and public sectors. Thus, even though the plans have not been implemented in an optimal fashion, the planning process itself has been useful in that it has allowed the government to undertake internal discussion of policy and to signal the results of these discussions to the private sector. At the same time, the private sector participates in these deliberations and makes known its goals to the public bodies. But, it should be added, such signals could be made without formal planning. The government could merely set monetary and fiscal policy—as it has done anyway—and use these macroeconomic tools to guide the economy. The signals of the private sector to the public sector could be (and have been) made through the normal interaction between the two sectors, especially through the activities of the *genkyoku* of MITI and other ministries.

[10] See Trezise and Suzuki (1976, p. 791).

In sum, then, economic growth was accompanied by macroeconomic policy that helped set the stage for further growth. It seems clear that monetary and fiscal policy were used to manage growth and that national economic planning was much less important in this process. Planning lacked "teeth" to enforce the goals of planners, and private economic activity was unencumbered by planners' dictums. Also, even public sector decision makers did not follow the outlines of the plans in making decisions. Therefore, it cannot be said that economic planning had an important impact on the course of economic events in postwar Japan.

Before proceeding to a more detailed analysis of Japanese regional planning, it is important to make some comments about the nature of the planning process and the planners themselves. Although political scientists have discussed intergovernment relations and planning in more detail (for some references, see Chapter 7, particularly Footnote 5), I shall comment briefly on this subject here. First, planning activity became highly politicized with the interaction between the professional bureaucracy in the various ministries and politicians, especially those of the Liberal Democratic Party (LDP). The LDP has had its strongest support in rural areas and small cities. It is natural for LDP members to support measures to increase the economic viability of those regions, and the politicians have put great pressure on the bureaucrats to increase aid to their home districts. Second, the planners themselves (who were drawn from the ranks of top universities) seldom spoke with one voice. There were constant disagreements among professionals in different ministries and within the same ministries as well. So, when I speak of "the planners" and their actions in subsequent sections, I am talking about the result of both the politicization of the planning process and in-fighting within the planning establishment. The reader should keep in mind that I am focusing on the *outcomes* of these processes.

3 Postwar Regional Economic and Land Use Planning

3.1 Introduction

Regional economic planning is best viewed as a component of national economic planning and overall national economic policy. Historically, most of the national economic plans had parallel regional components that were augmented with specific regional planning laws to foster national goals. Therefore, it is difficult to comprehend regional planning in Japan without a full understanding of national planning and national policy. I hope that the review in Section 2 helped the reader in this regard.

During the postwar period, the major goal of regional policy was to make the spatial economy more efficient in order to foster economic growth.

Efficiency, especially in the 1950s, meant taking advantage of agglomeration economies within the private sector that were particularly strong in the Tokaido megalopolis. Therefore, public investment was spatially concentrated in that region and economic development was encouraged there, especially for heavy industry such as steel, petrochemicals, and shipbuilding. The spatial distribution of production made Japan more efficient in its drive for export-induced growth. Also, concentration along the Pacific belt allowed for more efficient trading with Japan's major trading partner, the United States.

However, several regional problems resulted from these policies. First, there was the tremendous overcrowing that occurred in Tokyo and in other large cities. Second, there was the need to develop backward areas such as Hokkaido, Kyushu, and Tohoku, which were drained of migrants to the metropolitan areas. Thus, there was a polarization of population into overcrowded cities, on the one hand, and depopulated rural areas on the other. Finally, there was a need perceived by policymakers to reduce interregional income disparities between the metropolitan regions and the more rural, less developed ones.

In this section, I shall discuss some of the techniques and instruments used to deal with these three principal regional problems. Government analysts believed that these problems required a policy of decentralization of jobs and population. The Japanese government has attempted to decentralize the economy and has had several approaches to regional development: nodal development of cities such as in the New Industrial Cities (NICs) and Special Areas (SAs), large-scale projects such as port development in Tohoku and elsewhere, infrastructure development through grants to local governments, direct investments by the central government, industrial relocation schemes through incentives to manufacturers, and "steering" policies in which the government advised businessmen on an informal basis as to where they should locate their plants. Additionally, the government has tried to foster decentralization and a more equal interregional income distribution through complicated tax and subsidy programs; this last technique is the primary subject of Chapter 7.

However, despite rhetoric to the contrary, the government has never had a very strong decentralization policy. Public investment remained heavily concentrated in regions central to the economy until the late 1960s and was not destined to be distributed to the more backward regions until later, as will be shown in Section 3.3.1. As with the case of national planning, the "equity-versus-efficiency" trade-off has been a difficult one and, in general, regional planning efforts have been used to increase the efficiency of the economy through spatially concentrated public investment at the expense of interregional and interpersonal equity. There have been some decreases in interregional income disparities, and, although there has been some decentralization of jobs and population (see Chapter 3), these phenomena have not been primarily the result of regional planning.

Section 3.2 offers some notes on regional economic planning and its relationship to national planning during the postwar period, observing the evolution of planning objectives. The implementation of regional planning with respect to public investment trends and evaluation of the NIC and SA programs are the major concerns of Section 3.3. The relationship between regional planning and the tax system is studied in Section 3.4. Some additional evidence and conclusions are offered in Section 3.5.

3.2 Regional Planning and National Economic Planning

3.2.1 Introduction

Regional planning in Japan is best viewed as an offshoot of national economic planning as it has reflected national goals and a style of planning used at a national level. Thus, regional planning has reflected the growth orientation of national plans in the early years and a somewhat more balanced approach and environmental concerns of the national planners in later years; this will be shown in Section 3.2.2. Additionally, regional planning was organized along "top-down" principles, with national goals and organizations[11] dominating those on the regional and local levels.

Finally, regional planning—like national planning—lacked the enforcement procedures necessary to significantly influence private decision makers to act in ways that planners desired. As in the case of national planning, private and public decision makers acted somewhat independently of plans.

3.2.2 Stages of Regional Development Planning[12]

As with national planning, there were various stages of thinking about regional problems and regional development policy. There have been five such stages within the postwar period.[13] This section will review these stages and indicate how the goals and methods of the planning process changed over time. Table 6.2 summarizes the major national and regional planning laws. I shall note the many goals set by regional planners (some of which

---

[11] See Miyasawa (1977) and Glickman (1972) on this issue. For analyses of Japanese organizational structures and decision-making processes in general, see Vogel (1975).

[12] For other discussions of regional planning, see Beika (1975) and OECD (1971, 1976).

[13] There was also considerable regional planning in the prewar period. In 1941, a Planning Committee (*Kikaku-in,* in Japanese) was established as part of the Great East Asian National Land Planning Act. There was a 15-year time horizon to deal with national defense, industrial development, food production, and transportation. There was an effort to have a "harmonious" relationship between urban and rural activity and a regional balance in industrial location. Here, however, strategic national defense was the main policy objective.

TABLE 6.2
Major Legislation concerning Regional Development

Period	Year	National comprehensive planning	Development acts	Regional development planning acts	Other comprehensive planning and development acts
(1) First Period 1945–1950	1946		Temporary Special City and Town planning Act (abolished 1954)		
(2) Second Period 1950–1955	1950		Comprehensive National Land Development Act; Port Act	Hokkaido Development Act; National Capital Construction Act	Establishment of Kyushu Electric Company
	1951		Amendment to River Act		
	1952		Electric Resources Development Promotion Act		
	1953		Port Ajustment Promoting Act; Cho, Son Annexation Promoting Act		
	1954		Land Reorganization Act		
(3) Third Period	1955	Five-Year Plan for Economic Self-Support		Aichi Irrigation Cooperation Act	
	1956		Principle Driveway Construction Act; Water Works for Industry Act; Airport Adjustment Act	National Capital Metropolitan Region Act	

Year			
1957	New Long-Range Economic Plan	New *Shi, Cho, Son* Construction Promoting Act National Highway Construction Act for National Land Development Specific Multi-Purpose Dam Act	Tohoku Development Act
1958	Five Year Street Adjustment Plan	Industrial Water Channel Construction Act Industrial Water Quality Protection Act	
1959		Industrial Development Control Act in the Already-Developed Areas of the National Capital Metropolitan Region Kyushu Development Act Special Measurements for Adjustment of Specific Facilities in Port and River Act	Establishment of National Capital Transportation Cooperation
(4) Fourth Period 1960	Ten Year Income Doubling Plan	Shikoku Development Act Hokuriku Development Act Chugoku Development Act Tokaido Trunk Highway Act	
1961	The Pacific Ocean Belt Plan	Emergency Measurement Act of Port Adjustment Expediting Industrial Development Act of Under-developed Areas	

TABLE 6.2 (*Continued*)

Period	Year	National comprehensive planning	Development acts	Regional development Planning acts	Other comprehensive planning and development acts
				Temporary Measurement Act for Promotion of Coal Mining Areas	
	1962	National Comprehensive Development Plan	Water Resources Development Promotion Act Water Resources Cooperation Act	New Industrial City Construction Expediting Act	Establishment of Water Resources Cooperation Establishment of Tokyo Bay Comprehensive Development Promotion Plan
	1963			Kinki Region Act	Report of Committee for Temporary Administrations
	1964		River Act	Special Areas for Industrial Consolidation Expediting Act	Japan Railroad Construction Cooperation
	1965	Medium-Term Economic Plan			Designation of New Industrial Cities

Year	Plans	Acts	Regional Development	Other
1966		National Trunk Highway Construction Act for National Land Development	Chubu Region Development Act	Establishment of New Tokyo International Airport Corporation
1967	Economic and Social Development Plan	Fundamental Act for Environmental Control		
1968		City Planning Act		General Principles for Urban Policy of the Liberal Democratic Party
(5) Fifth Period 1969	New Comprehensive National Development Plan	Urban Renewal Act		
1970	New Economic and Social Development Plan	National New Trunk Railway Adjustment Act		
1971		Induction of Industry to Agricultural Land Act		
1972	Tanaka Plan for Building a New Japan	Industrial Relocation Expediting Act		
1973	Basic Economic and Social Plan			
1974		National Land Use Planning Act		
1976	Economic Plan for the Second Half of the 1970's			

were mutually contradictory) and the relatively large number of regions over which development funds were to be spread.

The first regional planning stage was related to the problem of restoration of Japan from the war and occurred roughly between 1945 and 1950. The goals were to repair war damage, to employ the many repatriated Japanese returning from overseas, to increase food production sharply, and to reconstruct the industrial base and the cities.[14]

The second phase of Japanese regional planning took place in the first half of the 1950s, during the stage of economic reconstruction. In part, under the impetus of the supply activity connected with the U.S. involvement in the Korean war, Japan began to grow. And the goals of regional planning during the period 1950–1955 were to contribute to the growth process: to increase employment, to increase food production with the development of underdeveloped regions, to consolidate the rapidly growing areas (in this regard, areas with great growth potential were targeted for special development), and to undertake electric power and water resources development in an effort to increase industrial production.

The major piece of legislation during that period was the Comprehensive National Land Development Act (CNLDA),[15] which was passed in 1950. It was Japan's first nationwide regional development law and it had economic growth as its most important goal. It also indicated a "top-down" approach to regional development planning: National laws were to be passed to deal with regional problems. The aims of the CNLDA were to develop and to conserve the national land in a comprehensive manner, to have a more efficient spatial industrial distribution, to improve social welfare, to have comprehensive planning at each governmental level, to increase food production, and to develop power resources, especially water power. The planners set up 21 river basin districts[16] as special areas and attempted comprehensive planning for those regions. This was quite similar to the TVA model that had been implemented in the United States beginning in the 1930s.[17]

The next period of regional development planning took place between 1955 and 1960, with very vague and general plans made with respect to regions. There was a growing political realization that the overcrowding in the major metropolitan areas was in some way bad and that there was a need

---

[14] Laws were passed in this time period including the Livelihood Protection Law (1946), the Temporary Special City and Town Planning Act (1946), and the Employment Security Act (1947).

[15] In Japanese, *Kokudo Sogo Kaihatsu Ho.*

[16] Originally 42 of Japan's 47 prefectures were selected as special areas for development under the CNLDA. This was regarded as a situation in which resources were being spread too thinly and, as a political compromise, the 21 river basins were chosen. This was still a large number of regions for a then-poor country.

[17] Most observers argue that the CNLDA did not succeed because of administrative problems; on this subject see Beika (1975).

for more efficient land utilization, implying the necessity to decentralize the economy spatially. However, the goal of having a more balanced distribution and a more equitable interregional distribution of income came into conflict with the goal of growth during this period of high growth for the Japanese economy. In terms of regional planning, there was an emphasis on heavy and chemical industries along the Pacific coast, and there was much public works investment for industrial development near the large cities, but little in poor, remote regions.[18] As a result, economic efficiency goals dominated those of interregional equity.

The period from 1960 to 1969 constituted the fourth stage of regional planning in Japan. This was the era of the Income Doubling Plan in which high national growth was forecasted and attained. On the regional level, planners formulated more specific policies with respect to regions (in contrast to the more general notions of regional development in a previous period), and growth pole development was initiated. In general, the major goals of planning during the 1960s, in addition to growth pole development, was for "big project" regional development of ports and other infrastructure, the establishment of national transportation networks (especially the Shinkansen high-speed railroad), the promotion of rural areas, the continuing need to decentralize population from metropolitan areas, and the reduction of income disparities among regions. However, for reasons of economic efficiency, planners also continued to support the development of heavy and chemical industries along the Pacific belt. As noted in Table 6.2, several laws were passed during that period, including the Comprehensive National Development Plan (1962) and two laws that were passed in connection with it: the New Industrial City Construction Act (1962)[19] and the Act for Promotion of Special Areas for Industrial Development (1964).[20]

The 1962 CNDP sought to reduce overconcentration in the major metropolitan areas and to help develop rural ones: Thus, "balanced growth" in an interregional sense was the key element here. Few new organizational structures were instituted under the plan, but there was a reshuffling of old ones for purposes of better coordination. Importantly, the notion of nodal or growth pole development was initiated as the major format for regional development. The plan conceptualized some fairly large growth centers away from Tokyo and the other large regions and some smaller centers that were related to the larger ones through transportation and communication links; central management functions were to be concentrated in the larger growth centers.

The CNDP divided the nation into three areas. The first was for those of

---

[18] During this period there were regional planning acts passed for the National Capital Region (1956) and those for underdeveloped regions such as Kyushu (1959), Tohoku (1959), and Shikoku (1960); see Japan National Capital Region Development Commission (1971).

[19] *Shin Sangyo Toshi-Sokushin Ho.*

[20] *Kogyo Seibi Tokubetsu Chiiki Kogyo Kaihatsu Sokushin Ho.*

the "excessive concentration" (the large cities) where measures were instituted in order to restrain further growth. These included restrictions on
industrial development and assistance to factories seeking to relocate.[21] The
second category of land use was for cities outside of the large cities known as
"areas of adjustment." Here, the effort was to establish suburban growth
centers—thus expediting metropolitan decentralization—and to induce industrial development there. The third set of areas, the "development
areas," were the targets of large-scale regional development efforts. It was
here that the 16 New Industrial Cities (NICs) and five Special Areas (SAs)
were designated in efforts to further deconcentrate the major cities and to
attract industry in order to stem the flow of migration away from agricultural
land. These three interrelated area-specific programs were aimed at the goal
of furthering economic growth by more efficiently using land in a decentralized manner.

The final stage in postwar regional planning began in the late 1960s and
manifested itself in part as to a reaction to the high growth of the 1960s, to
environmental disruption, and to high and rising land prices. The goals of
this period were to have more effective utilization of land and better land
planning, a more comfortable environment, the promotion of small cities, a
more effective allocation of social overhead capital, a better balance between large cities and small cities on an interregional basis, better interregional transportation systems, an emphasis on "knowledge-intensive"
industries rather than heavy and chemical industries, and the promotion of
industrial parks. This era began with the 1969 New Comprehensive National
Development Plan that sought to develop regional policy to 1985. The 1969
plan was necessary because of inability of the 1962 plan (i.e., the CNDP) and
related measures to carry out regional development in the face of continued
rapid economic growth. The key problems of the early 1960s—over-
crowdedness and sparsely populated rural areas—continued to plague
Japanese planners and Japanese society. Also, the increased political con-
sciousness of citizens forced planners to pay more attention to citizens'
preferences with respect to environmental conservation, pollution, and congestion.

The 1969 plan divided Japan into seven major regions,[22] with emphasis
on large-scale projects and extensions of the nodal development efforts of
earlier periods. There was an effort to have more comprehensive planning
and to synthesize the overall development of the national economy. Here,

---

[21] Among the "push" factors which restricted development in large cities were prohibitions
of factories that used more than 500 m² or schools that used more than 1,500 m² of land.
According to many government officials, these prohibitions have not been strictly enforced.

[22] The regions were Hokkaido, Tohoku, the capital region, Chubu, Kinki, Chu-Shikoku,
and Kyushu.

there were attempts to integrate central management functions of government and industry, to establish better transportation systems for provincial regions, to decentralize footloose industries, and to improve metropolitan region transportation systems. The most notable impact of the 1969 plan was to place a strong emphasis on communications and transportation systems; this involved the construction of high-speed trunk railroads (such as the extensions of the Shinkansen), highways, telephone systems, and tunnels. Furthermore, the New Comprehensive National Development Plan aimed at the construction of entirely new cities; this is in contradistinction to the 1962 plan in which existing cities were used.

The 1969 plan was followed in a nonlegislative way in 1972 by the so-called Tanaka plan (Tanaka, 1972). The Tanaka plan, set forth during Kakuei Tanaka's campaign for the Prime Minister's position, contained several elements for changing the shape of the Japanese archipelago with regard to regional development. First, Tanaka envisioned the development of much larger superexpress train and highway networks. Second, Tanaka proposed a large amount of industrial relocation to deal with the problems of overcrowding in the major cities and with the underpopulation of some of the local areas. His plan was to relocate industries from metropolitan areas to those in areas with low density of development. There would be considerable tax exemptions for relocating industry from congested to noncongested areas. Third, it was proposed that there would be large-scale development for cities with population of approximately 250,000 persons. These were growth poles in the spirit of the NICs of the 1960s. The plan was never implemented, but it did have a substantial impact on land values in cities that were designated for rapid growth.[23]

In an effort to come to grips with the problem of slow growth and rapidly rising land prices, the National Land Use Planning Act was passed in 1974. This act instituted the National Land Agency (NLA) that was organized to administer overall land use policy for Japan and consisted of elements of the central government bureaucracy formerly in the Economic Planning Agency (EPA) and elsewhere; see Japan National Land Agency (1974, 1975a). The NLA was empowered to take an active role in transactions involving land and with implementing regional development policies under both the CNLDL and the National Land Utilization Law of 1974. Here, the NLA undertakes measures to try to develop the poorly developed regions in Japan through integrated planning and to disperse development that already has taken place in and around the three major cities.[24]

---

[23] For example, in Tsuyama in Okayama prefecture, one of the cities designated for development under the Tanaka plan, the land cost in the central area of the city went from about $.65 per m² to nearly $28.00 per m² within 2 years following the announcement of Tanaka's plan.

[24] See Japan National Land Agency (1975a).

3.3   The Implementation of Regional
Development Policy

3.3.1   Trends in Central Government Public Investment

As noted in the discussion of national planning in Section 3.2, the planning process and planning mechanisms were influenced heavily by the activities of the individual ministries within the national government. Although the regional plans, however vague, called for significant amounts of decentralization of public investment within the Japanese urban system, the actual distribution of public and private investment continued to be relatively centralized until the late 1960s. Patterns of the distribution of public investments by major region can be seen in Tables 6.3 and 6.4.

Table 6.3 shows total public investment for each of the major regions. Observe that in 1958 the coastal part of the Tokyo metropolitan region (Coastal Kanto) had 19.3% of total public investment by the central government in that year. This proportion increased during the 1960s, reaching a maximum of 24.4% in 1970 and then declining between 1970 and 1973. Similarly, the Osaka region (Coastal Kinki), increased its share of total public investment from 11.9 to 15.1% in 1965; the share going to the Nagoya (Tokai) region also increased between 1958 and 1960, although it has declined since then. Overall, then, the share going to the major metropolitan regions increased from 44.0% of total public investment in 1958 to a maximum of 50.2% in 1965 before declining to 46.7% in 1973;[25] the peripheral (suburban) regions increased their share slightly over the period so that the nonmetropolitan, nonsuburban cities—those that were supposed to be receiving significantly more investment through the various planning programs—had an actual decline in total public investment shares, from 45.6% (1958) to 42.3% (1973).

Table 6.4 shows public investment by the central government on a per capita basis by region and by type of investment. Once again, the major metropolitan areas, at least through the 1960s, were still getting more public investment per capita than many of the poorer regions, although the gap was narrowing. Exceptions are the cases of Hokkaido and Shikoku, which showed increasing shares of per capita public investment during the period. For industry-related investment, the picture is one in which there is a relative increase in the amounts going to nonmetropolitan regions. Thus, Tohoku increased its index (the Japan average was 1.00) of per capita public investment for industry from .98 (1959–1961) to 1.36 (1973), and Shikoku went from .91 to 1.08 over the same time span. At the same time, Coastal Tokyo went from 1.07 to .63; however, the move toward suburbanization is shown in the data for Inland Kanto (suburban Tokyo) where the index went from .62 to 1.08. Life-related (i.e., social welfare) investment continued to

---

[25] Miyasawa (1977) has discussed this point as well.

TABLE 6.3
Share of Total Central Government Investment by Major Region, 1958–1973

	1958	1960	1965	1970	1971	1972	1973
Japan	100.0	100.0	100.0	100.0	100.0	100.0	100.0
Hokkaido	7.3	6.6	6.8	7.2	7.3	6.5	6.8
Tohoku	11.8	10.9	10.7	10.4	10.0	10.5	10.6
Inland Kanto	6.5	6.7	6.0	7.2	6.8	7.1	7.2
Coastal Kanto	19.3	20.9	24.1	24.4	24.3	23.3	23.1
Tokai	12.7	15.5	11.0	10.9	10.4	10.7	10.5
Hokuriku	3.4	3.3	3.3	3.0	3.0	3.4	3.3
Inland Kinki	3.9	4.5	3.4	3.3	3.2	3.5	3.8
Coastal Kinki	11.9	11.8	15.1	14.0	14.4	13.2	13.1
Chugoku	7.0	6.4	6.2	6.0	6.5	7.0	6.5
Shikoku	4.2	3.4	3.6	3.9	3.9	3.9	3.1
Kyushu	11.9	10.0	9.7	9.9	10.3	10.9	11.4
Metropolitan	44.0	48.2	50.2	49.2	49.1	47.2	46.7
Peripheral	10.4	11.2	9.4	10.5	10.0	10.6	11.0
Others	45.6	40.6	40.3	40.3	40.9	42.3	42.3

Source: Japan Economic Planning Agency (1975).

be concentrated in the major metropolitan areas such as Tokyo (1.36 index in 1973) and Osaka (1.30 index in 1973). The other regions seemed to be relatively neglected in terms of life-related public investment.

Overall, then, the pattern of public investment by region continues to be relatively concentrated in the major metropolitan areas, although less so than in the 1950s. During the period of major economic growth (the 1960s), investment was highly concentrated in the more central regions despite public rhetoric that indicated that public investment should and would be decentralized. Not until the late 1960s and early 1970s did the pattern of public investment change spatially. Then, there was a considerable amount of investment in nonmetropolitan regions, most of it industry related.

3.3.2 The New Industrial Cities and Special Areas Programs

3.3.2.1 Nature of New Industrial Cities and Special Areas

This section reviews two related regional development programs that were devised in the early 1960s: New Industrial Cities (NICs) and Special Areas (SAs). Both were aimed at solving the principal regional problems of that era and were implemented under the 1962 National Comprehensive Development Plan. Both involved the use of growth poles as the basis for development.

The New Industrial Cities Construction Expediting Act was passed in

TABLE 6.4
Index of Public Investment per Capita by Major Regions by Type of Investment, 1959–1973

	Total public investment				Industry-related				Life-related			
	1959–1961	1964–1966	1969–1971	1973	1959–1961	1964–1966	1969–1971	1973	1959–1961	1964–1966	1969–1971	1973
Japan	1.00	1.00	1.00	1.00	1.00	1.00	1.00	1.00	1.00	1.00	1.00	1.00
Hokkaido	1.26	1.30	1.42	1.42	1.83	1.68	1.34	1.85	.87	.81	.80	.88
Tohoku	.87	.92	.94	1.01	.98	.98	1.12	1.36	.66	.66	.60	.63
Inland Kanto	.81	.78	.88	.94	.62	.70	.99	1.08	.64	.64	.65	.74
Coastal Kanto	1.08	1.08	1.04	.97	1.07	.99	.78	.63	1.60	1.59	1.47	1.36
Tokai	1.32	1.05	.93	.92	1.25	1.31	.95	.94	1.13	.92	.91	.94
Hokuriku	1.13	1.18	1.11	1.27	1.03	1.04	1.33	1.65	.83	.82	.67	.73
Inland Kinki	1.13	.89	.87	.95	1.05	.76	.69	.68	.85	1.03	1.08	1.25
Coastal Kinki	1.11	1.22	1.12	1.02	1.06	1.10	1.01	.84	1.45	1.38	1.42	1.30
Chugoku (Sanin)	1.06	1.21	1.08	1.25	1.00	1.21	1.31	1.42	.63	.64	.69	.75
Chugoku (Sanyo)	.83	.82	.89	.94	.91	.77	.93	1.02	.76	.70	.76	.72
Shikoku	.80	.90	1.00	1.00	.91	1.03	1.18	1.08	.57	.63	.63	.78
Northern Kyushu	.76	.76	.86	.93	.78	.65	.90	1.00	.72	.71	.78	.83
Southern Kyushu	.70	.79	.86	.93	.75	.81	1.05	1.21	.55	.56	.51	.56
Okinawa	—	—	—	1.33	—	—	—	2.00	—	—	—	1.05

Source: Japan Economic Planning Agency (1975).

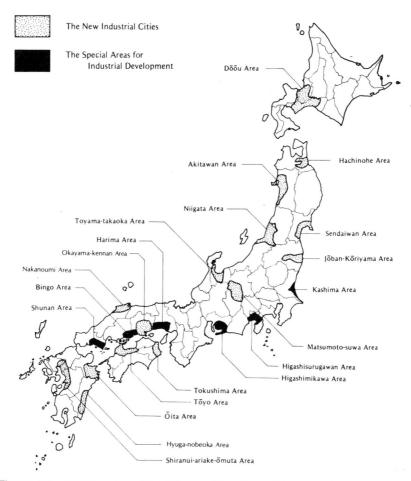

Figure 6.1. The New Industrial Cities and the Special Areas for Industrial Development.

1962, and 13 areas were designated as NICs[26] the following year; 2 more regions were added later (see Figure 6.1 for the location of NICs). The purpose of the act was to alleviate overconcentration of population and industry in the metropolitan areas and to increase employment in smaller

---

[26] Each New Industrial City in fact consisted of several cities, towns, and villages within a region. In all, there were 94 cities and 288 towns and villages designated under this act. Therefore, these were not "new towns" in the commonly understood meaning of the term, but clusters of existing municipalities. Although there was a delicate political compromise in the selection of the 15 cities, several criteria were used in selecting them. Among them, the city-region had to be relatively undeveloped, and second, the NIC had to have some established infrastructure and considerable available land and water.

ones. The idea was to promote new "local" (nonmetropolitan) cities as the development cores of regions and to have a balanced utilization of economic development. Targets were set for each nodal city with respect to industrial development, labor supply and demand, and other elements such as land use and the construction of industrial facilities. The target years of the plan were 1975 for industrial development and 1980 for population growth. Provisions of the law allowed for specially financed loans and grants to local governments for public facilities, housing, harbors, and related facilities; these consisted of low-interest loans to local governments for infrastructure extensions and prefectural low-interest loans for similar types of activities. There were provisions with respect to the NCDP to coordinate the activities of several ministries with respect to the NICs. In the NICs in Hokkaido and Tohoku there were special development loans as well. The planning for the NICs was also partly under the supervision of private industry, through the Ministry of International Trade and Industry (MITI), with supervisory committees for each NIC.

The other major growth-pole law was the Special Areas for Industrial Consolidation Expediting Act of 1964. Six SAs (see Figure 6.1) were designated under this act, most of them in the Pacific Belt between the major metropolitan areas. These SAs could be used to locate industry that was decentralizing from cores of the major metropolitan areas, thus increasing overall economic efficiency. As with the NICs, the SAs had targets for the consolidation of factories, industrial facilities plans, and for population size.

3.3.2.2 Public Investment Patterns in New Industrial Cities and Special Areas

Given the designation of the NICs and SAs in the early 1960s, what was the pattern of public investment in these regions and what was the resulting rate of economic and social development? Investment plans formulated in 1965 called for approximately 4,655 trillion *yen* (about $15.5 billion) in investments for the NICs and 2,118 trillion *yen* (about $7.1 billion) for the SAs between 1965 and 1975. The actual cumulative investment to 1974 for the NICs was 5,959 billion *yen* and 2,644 trillion *yen* for the SAs. As shown in Table 6.5, the NICs and SAs accomplished 128.0 and 106.1% of their plans, respectively. However, when one accounts for the effects of inflation that occurred between 1965 and 1975 and measures investment in real terms, it is shown that the NICs achieved only 92.1% of planned investment by 1974 and the SAs only 76.6% of investment. Furthermore, with the exception of Do-ou, Sendai-wan, and Niigata, none of the individual NICs or SAs achieved planned investment targets. Some, such as Toyo (56.8% of planned investment) and Shunan (56.6%), showed relatively little accomplishment of planned goals.

In addition to the fact that the planned level investment by authorities was not reached, if one looks at public investment per capita for the NICs

TABLE 6.5

Planned and Actual Public Investment in New Industrial Cities and Special Areas 1965–1974[a]

	Amount of the basic plan		1974 Cumulative total		Percentage of achievement of the basic plan	
	Current value	Real value	Current value	Real value	Current value	Real value
New Industrial Cities						
Do-ou	722	760	1,449	1,071	201	141
Hachinohe	167	175	197	149	118	85
Sendai-wan	360	379	499	381	138	101
Akita-wan	157	165	189	143	120	87
Joban–Koriyama	330	347	369	272	112	78
Niigata	332	350	459	352	138	100
Matsumoto-Suwa	224	236	265	200	118	85
Toyama–Takaoka	324	341	359	280	111	82
Nakonoumi	190	200	239	182	126	91
Okayama–Kennan	589	620	579	445	98	72
Tokushima	228	240	287	219	126	91
Toyo	211	222	163	126	77	57
Oita	241	253	279	213	116	84
Hyuga–Nobeoka	140	148	140	106	100	72
Shiranui-Ariake-Omuta	439	462	488	371	111	80
Total	4,655	4,900	5,959	4,511	128	92
Special Areas						
Kashima	189	199	258	194	136	97
Higashi-suruga wan	377	397	303	238	80	60
Higashi-mikawa	286	301	280	213	98	71
Harima	688	724	812	609	118	84
Bingo	331	349	406	307	123	88
Shunan	247	260	189	147	77	57
Total	2,118	2,230	2,248	1,709	106	77

Source: Japan National Land Agency (1975b).

[a] Real figures in 1965 billions of yen.

TABLE 6.6

Public Investment Index per Capita by Major Regions,
New Industrial Cities and Special Areas

Area	1965	1970	1973
All Japan	100.0	100.0	100.0
Hokkaido	129.0	143.8	140.5
Tohoku	91.4	94.4	101.2
Inland Kanto	74.5	92.1	93.7
Coastal Kanto	112.9	104.8	96.9
Tokai	99.2	95.7	92.1
Hokuriku	117.3	112.0	125.2
Inland Kinki	89.7	84.1	96.7
Coastal Kinki	123.5	108.7	101.9
Chugoku	89.3	89.4	98.7
Shikoku	87.8	102.3	100.0
Kyushu	77.3	84.8	94.9
New Industrial Cities			
Do-ou [a]	101.2	115.8	188.6
Hachinohe [b]	92.6	79.4	89.9
Sendai-wan [b]	98.8	82.2	87.8
Akita-wan [b]	91.6	111.3	94.6
Joban–Koriyama [b]	59.8	61.8	84.3
Niigata [b]	78.2	98.4	78.6
Matsumoto-Suwa [c]	76.8	74.7	72.0
Toyama-Takaoka [d]	87.0	84.4	62.2
Nakanoumi [e]	64.8	67.1	69.9
Okayama-Kennan [e]	81.8	92.9	81.9
Tokushima [f]	75.7	124.3	88.4
Toyo [f]	50.7	76.3	38.5
Oita [g]	120.6	65.2	70.3
Hyuga-Nobeoka [g]	124.5	85.4	93.7
Shiranui-Ariake-Omuta [g]	52.7	50.1	53.9
All New Industrial Cities	81.0	85.1	93.5
Special Areas			
Kashima [c]	122.2	321.9	162.2
Higashi-suruga wan [h]	57.4	73.8	42.4
Higashi-mikawa [h]	64.0	98.9	78.5
Harima [i]	75.0	82.3	124.0
Bingo [e]	58.6	92.2	79.7
Shunan [e]	93.7	88.6	70.8
All Special Areas	71.0	98.1	89.2

Source: Japan Economic Planning Agency (1975) and Japan National Land Agency (1975b).

[a] Hokkaido region.
[b] Tohoku region.
[c] Inland Kanto.
[d] Hokuriku region.
[e] Chugoku region.
[f] Shikoku region.
[g] Kyushu region.
[h] Tokai region.
[i] Inland Kinki region.

and SAs, Japan's lack of a fundamental industrial decentralization policy becomes even more clear. Table 6.6 presents an index of public investment per capita for all of the NICs and SAs as well as for the major regions in Japan for 1965, 1970, and 1973. This index (the average per capita level for Japan is 100.0) shows that the level of per capita investment for all the NICs for 1965 was 81.0, increasing to 93.5 by 1973; for the SAs, the index went from 71.0 to 89.2. This means that even though the central government claimed that it was investing heavily in these underdeveloped areas, the per capita investment index shows that this is not the case: Levels of public investment per capita were much lower in the NICs and SAs than in all of Japan. Furthermore, if one compares individual NICs and SAs with the major regions in which they are located, one sees that the level of public investment per capita in the NICs is even lower than in the larger regions in most cases. For instance, all five NICs in Tohoku have indexes for 1973 well below the average for that region.

3.3.2.3 Population and Output Growth

The NICs failed to achieve their target levels of population growth as shown in Table 6.7. Planners wanted to have 12.3 million people in 1970 and 13.4 million people in 1975 within the NICs. However, according to available data[27] the population of the NICs reached only 11.2 million people in 1970 and 11.8 million people in 1975, or 89.9 and 88.0% of planned population, respectively. None of the individual NICs achieved their planned growth by 1975, only a few of the NICs (Sendai-wan, Do-ou, and Nakanoumi) coming close. Many others lagged significantly from planned totals, however. In relation to the nation, the share of population in the NICs increased by only .1% between 1965 and 1975 and, therefore, no clear trend toward decentralization toward NICs from other regions can be observed.

Furthermore, interesting patterns can be seen in the spatial development within the NICs. My data (see Table 6.8) indicate that of the population growth that did occur within the NICs, 77.7% took place within the large cities. The NICs' rural portions either had little population growth or declined absolutely. The latter is the case in Akita-wan, Joban-Koriyama, and Nakanoumi. Thus, in some cases, depopulation of nearby areas occurred within the NICs' clusters. It also can be shown that the NICs often grew more slowly than most of the cities in Table 6.9 where comparisons are made between 1970–1975 population growth of the NICs, the prefectures in which they are located, and all cities in those prefectures. Although the NICs grew faster than their predominantly rural prefectures in most cases, there was faster growth among the other cities in the prefectures for 7 of the 15 NICs.

Another question was whether or not the NICs were growing faster than other cities of similar characteristics that were not specially designated

[27] See sources to Table 6.7.

TABLE 6.7
Planned and Actual Population[a] of New Industrial Cities, 1960–1975

New Industrial Cities	Actual population				Planned population	
	1960	1965	1970	1975	1970	1975
Do-ou	1,292	1,558	1,804	2,057	1,841	2,069
Hachinohe	325	344	359	372	390	440
Sendai-wan	800	866	957	1,015	950	1,050
Akita-wan	298	306	322	347	383	430
Joban-Koriyama	823	810	811	831	971	1,011
Niigata	697	720	746	779	840	900
Matsumoto-Suwa	526	537	554	579	604	670
Toyama-Takaoka	750	750	764	802	887	917
Nakanoumi	540	536	543	656	562	611
Okayama-Kennan	896	942	1,052	1,176	1,266	1,385
Tokushima	454	460	471	514	537	619
Toyo	486	477	477	497	579	638
Oita	446	466	497	551	560	640
Hyuga-Nobeoka	214	220	233	239	323	359
Shiranui-Ariake-Omuta	1,514	1,455	1,437	1,463	1,560	1,662
Total	10,060	10,448	11,016	11,787	12,262	13,401

Source: Japanese *Population Census* for 1960, 1965, 1970, and 1975, and Japan Ministry of Home Affairs (1975b) and Japan National Land Agency (1975).
[a] In thousands.

for development. It could be argued, for instance, that since public investment was not heavily concentrated in the NICs, there would be no particular reason for them to grow faster than other cities. Thus 19 cities of similar size and population characteristics to the NICs were compared to the NIC core cities for 1960–1975. The characteristics used for selecting the cities to be paired with the NICs were as follows:

1. The selected cities should have population sizes similar to the NIC core cities.
2. The cities should be in the same prefecture or same major region as the NIC (this was to help select cities with similar socioeconomic characteristics).
3. The compared cities should have similar access to major markets as measured by distance and travel time to Tokyo or Osaka.
4. The cities should have similar historical and cultural characteristics.[28]

The results of the calculations are given in Table 6.10, where the distribution

[28] For detailed discussion of these cities, see Tanifuji and Nozu (1977).

TABLE 6.8
Population Growth of Major Cities within
New Industrial Cities, 1965–1975

New Industrial City	Major city	Increase in population, 1965–1975 (in thousands)		Percentage increase of population accounted for by major city
		New Industrial City	Major city	
Do-ou	Sapporo	574.0	445.7	77.5
Hachinohe	Hachinohe	41.5	34.8	83.9
Sendai-wan	Sendai	192.9	134.6	79.6
Akita-wan	Akita	40.7	44.7	109.6
Joban-Koriyama	Iwaki and Koriyama	8.0	37.7	471.3
Niigata	Niigata	95.4	66.9	70.1
Matsumoto-Suwa	Matsumoto	45.8	31.5	68.8
Toyama-Takaoka	Toyama	52.8	34.2	64.8
Okayama-Kennan	Okayama	278.5	221.7	79.6
Tokushima	Tokushima	81.2	26.0	32.0
Toyo	Niihama	18.1	6.5	35.9
Oita	Oita	96.7	93.8	97.0
Hyuga-Nobeoka	Nobeoka	13.2	10.5	79.5
Shiranui-Ariake-Omuta	Kumamoto	106.0	81.0	76.4
Nakanoumi	Yonago and Matsue	29.4	31.2	106.1
All New Industrial Cities		1,674.2	1,300.8	77.7

Source: Japanese *Population Census* for 1965, 1970 and 1975.

of comparisons of growth rates between pairs of cities is tabulated. Although the NICs showed more rapid growth in the 1965–1970 period in 11 of 19 comparisons, between 1970 and 1975 the NICs grew faster than their comparative pair in only 8 cases. The other cities grew faster in 8 cases and little difference could be seen in the remaining 3. Since the effects of a public investment program should be felt with some lag, it would have been expected that, if the NIC program were effective, NIC relative growth rates would be greater during the later period. This was not the case. In sum, the evidence indicates that the NICs did not grow any faster than cities of similar characteristics between 1960 and 1975.

Table 6.11 shows the growth of output of the NICs since their inception. Industrial shipments grew from about 23.9 billion *yen* to 122.5 billion *yen* between 1965 and 1974, that is, 17.8% per year; the SAs' growth rate was 18.0%. This represents a faster rate of growth than the average for Japan

TABLE 6.9

Comparison of Population Growth Rates between New Industrial Cities
and Their Prefectures, 1970–1975

New Industrial City	Percentage change	Prefecture	Percentage change	
			Cities in prefecture	Entire prefecture
Do-ou	16.8	Hokkaido	8.2	3.0
Hachinohe	5.8	Aomori	7.2	2.9
Sendai-wan	10.7	Miyagi	13.4	7.5
Akita-wan	7.5	Akita	3.2	−.7
Joban–Koriyama	.9	Fukushima	4.8	1.3
Niigata	6.2	Niigata	4.0	1.3
Matsumato-Suwa	5.3	Nagano	5.2	3.1
Toyama-Tokaoka	5.1	Toyama	4.8	4.0
Nakanoumi	4.1	Tottori and Shimane	4.8	.6
Okayama–Kennan	12.9	Okayama	8.5	6.3
Tokushima	6.5	Tokushima	5.4	1.8
Toyo	3.8	Ehime	6.6	3.3
Oita	13.3	Oita	8.4	3.0
Hyuga Nobeoka	4.6	Miyazaki	6.0	3.2
Shiranui-Ariake and Omuta	2.3	Fukuoka and Kumamoto	6.3	4.9

Source: 1975 Japanese Population Census.

(15.8% per year), and therefore the share of the NICs' and SAs' development as a percentage of Japan increased from 14.1 to 16.9%.[29]

Most of the industrial development in the NICs and SAs was in the heavy and chemical industries as shown in Table 6.12. The percentage of all industrial production in those industries was 54.2% in 1960, increasing to 61.6% by 1974. During that same period the percentage of manufacturing in heavy and chemical industries for all of Japan remained relatively constant. Moreover, since this production took place in heavily capital-intensive industry, employment increased relatively little during the period relative to output. This is one of the reasons that population did not grow very quickly during the period under study. The NICs and SAs did not produce new jobs commensurate with their output levels. Often, new employees were not recruited locally. The lack of buoyant employment growth was one reason for public complaints about these programs during recent years. Citizens felt that they had gained relatively little from the NIC- and SA-related factories in their communities. Problems of air and water pollution created by these factories were another reason for much public dissatisfaction.

[29] However, there was a large (unexplained) jump in this share in the last year of the period, 1974, which accounts for a large share of this increase.

TABLE 6.10

Comparison between Population Growth Rates of New Industrial Cities
and Other Cities of Similar Characteristics, 1960–1975

	1960–1965	1965–1970	1970–1975
New Industrial City grew faster[a]	7	11	8
Non-New-Industrial-City grew faster[a]	6	4	8
Little difference in growth rates[b]	6	4	3

Source: Tanifuji and Nozu (1977).

[a] The city that grew at least 1% faster (over the 5-year period) was considered faster growing.

[b] Neither city grew more than 1% faster than the other.

3.4 Summary Evaluation of New Industrial Cities and Special Areas Programs

It should be clear from this analysis that little in the way of realization of public goals with regard to regional policy was accomplished by these programs. The central government has not had a strong decentralization policy with respect to public investment in general and has not invested heavily in these particular city-regions either. Public investment did not reach planned levels in real terms, and there was less invested on a per capita basis there than the average for all of Japan. Low public investment was accompanied by the failure to meet population goals. This was, in part, due to the low employment intensity of investment. Although output in the NICs and SAs increased more rapidly than for the nation as a whole, it did not increase employment opportunities in regions away from the metropolitan centers sufficiently to induce very much migration.

Yet some of the NICs and SAs did grow significantly. What were the characteristics of successful growth poles? An example is given by Lo (1975) in his study of Okayama–Kennan whose major city is Mizushima. He shows that Mizushima had several characteristics that made for a favorable growth environment. First, there was considerable economic development activity prior to its designation as a NIC that was locally determined and planned. Second, the prefectural government allowed significant subsidies to new plants locating in Mizushima.[30] Third, there was the active cooperation of a

---

[30] The question of proper incentives to encourage location of plants is an important one here. According to an EPA (1975) survey, the major reasons for firms locating in NICs are as follows: availability of land (16.4% of those interviewed), availability of labor (11.5%), and closeness to markets (9.3%). For the SAs, 20.9% considered land availability the most important factor, followed by proximity to related factories (either owned by the same company or a trading partner) and nearness to markets. Tax incentives, often noted as important inducements to firms locating in the NICs and SAs, were relatively unimportant according to the survey: This factor was rated the eleventh most important locating factor among NIC firms and sixteenth among SA companies. In the case of Mizushima, however, the subsidies were far more than for the average growth pole.

TABLE 6.11

Share of Industrial Shipments of New Industrial Cities and Special Areas in Relation to All Japan, 1965–1974

		New Industrial Cities		Special Areas		
	Value of industrial shipment in Japan	Value of shipments	Percentage of Japan	Value of shipments	Percentage of Japan	Percentage of share of New Industrial Cities and Special Areas
1965	294,889	23,888	8.1	17,780	6.0	14.1
1966	342,019	28,227	8.2	20,459	6.0	14.2
1967	411,622	33,580	8.1	25,443	6.2	14.3
1968	482,785	39,146	8.1	29,680	6.2	14.3
1969	581,068	47,141	8.1	36,681	6.3	14.4
1970	690,348	57,304	8.3	45,332	6.6	14.9
1971	728,951	62,004	8.5	49,660	6.8	15.3
1972	809,619	68,829	8.5	54,630	6.7	15.2
1973	1,037,286	90,746	8.7	70,340	6.8	15.5
1974	1,275,746	122,499	9.6	93,107	7.3	16.9

Source: Japan National Land Agency (1975b).

TABLE 6.12

Percentage of Heavy and Chemical Industries in All Manufacturing
for New Industrial Cities, Special Areas and All Japan,1960–1974

Industry	1960	1965	1970	1974
New industrial cities				
Chemical and Allied	17.9	16.4	13.3	12.8
Petroleum and Coal	3.2	5.1	5.3	10.2
Iron and Steel	9.2	7.5	10.7	11.3
Nonferrous Metals	7.1	5.7	6.9	6.2
Machinery	13.2	14.6	17.8	15.9
Total	50.5	49.2	53.9	56.4
Special areas				
Chemical and Allied	12.2	13.1	13.7	12.5
Petroleum and Coal	7.4	4.9	2.6	7.2
Iron and Steel	15.9	14.9	19.2	21.8
Nonferrous Metals	2.7	3.2	3.4	2.8
Machinery	20.8	23.9	26.8	23.9
Total	59.0	60.0	65.8	68.4
New industrial cities and special areas				
Chemical and Allied	15.4	15.0	13.5	12.7
Petroleum and Coal	5.0	5.0	4.1	8.9
Iron and Steel	12.1	10.7	14.4	15.8
Nonferrous Metals	5.2	4.6	5.4	4.7
Machinery	16.5	18.6	21.8	19.4
Total	54.2	53.8	59.1	61.6
All Japan				
Chemical and Allied	NA	9.3	9.2	9.1
Petroleum and Coal	NA	2.9	3.0	6.0
Iron and Steel	NA	9.5	10.8	1.4
Nonferrous Metals	NA	4.1	4.9	4.4
Machinery	NA	27.5	35.3	33.1
Total	NA	53.3	63.2	54.0

Source: Japan National Land Agency (1975b).

few very large corporations who wanted to locate there anyway. Fourth,
there was good transportation access to major markets. These ingredients
were simply not present in many of the other NICs and SAs.

3.5 Regional Developing Policy and Changes in the Interregional Distribution of Population and Income

3.5.1 Introduction

We have discussed Japanese regional development policy and seen
several underlying themes, strategies, and assumptions. In the mid-1950s

many policymakers concluded that big cities were too big and that a deconcentration policy was essential. Deconcentration was also beneficial with regard to reducing income differentials between rich and poor regions. Therefore, the policies reviewed in this section were put into effect: growth poles, decentralized public investment, and regulations constraining new factories within Tokyo and other large cities. In the 1960s population began to decentralize and income differences among regions decreased. A simplistic view of these phenomena would hold that regional policy "worked." In fact, this may not be true. Not only was the policy ineffective, as I have argued, but many of its underlying assumptions might have been wrong. The assumptions, the phenomena, and the policies will be reviewed in the following sections.

3.5.2 Some Assumptions Underlying Japanese Regional Development Policy

First, planners assumed that cities were too big and needed deconcentration. Although the Tokyo region has grown to its present size of nearly 25 million (see Chapter 3), in what sense can it and other regions be said to be "too" big? For instance, Kabaya (1971) argues for both theoretical and empirical reasons that Japanese cities may not have been too big from the standpoint of economic efficency. Kabaya says that although the costs of per capita public services rise with city size, production per worker increases faster. For 1965, Kabaya shows that mean per capita income rises smoothly and nearly doubles as one goes from the least dense to the most dense prefecture. At the same time, the curve showing per capita government expenditure is U-shaped, but shallow. Therefore, according to Kabaya, the difference between income and expenditure increases " in a clearly progressive way with population density [p. 29]." Therefore, the denser prefectures are in this sense more efficient. Although these results are not completely conclusive, they certainly question the commonly held view that Japanese cities were too big.

Of course there are important negative externalities in the large cities (e.g., pollution and congestion), and they are a source of concern for planners and the public. But the "cities-are-too-big" argument needs to be reconsidered on the grounds of possible greater efficiency of larger centers. Such a reconsideration might still lead analysts to say that Tokyo is too big, but further study of this issue should be undertaken. It seems not to have been seriously considered by the politicians and planners in the late 1950s and early 1960s when deconcentration policies were begun.[31]

A second assumption is that by developing underdeveloped regions,

---

[31] This issue has been hotly debated in academic circles. See for instance, the exchange between Mera (1973, 1975) and Borukhov (1975). See also Alonso (1971), Hirsch (1968), Neutze (1967), Thompson (1968), and Wingo (1972).

interregional and, therefore, interpersonal income differentials would be reduced. That is, Japanese planners assumed that "place" equity (i.e., the development of poor regions relative to rich regions) implied "people" equity (i.e., reductions of income differences among individuals). This assumption is not necessarily true either. For if people from poor regions are able to migrate to richer regions and thereby better themselves, interpersonal equity could, under certain circumstances, be attained without any change in interregional, that is, place, equity. This, too, has occurred in postwar Japan as Kabaya has pointed out. The real question is whether the development of lagging regions will be more effective in helping residents than encouraging out-migration to richer, more productive regions. The empirical evidence for Japan is not conclusive on this point. Kabaya (1971, pp. 19–21) shows that during the early 1960s many lagging regions that had out-migration also had high growth rates of per capita income and that prefectures with net in-migration had lower rates of income growth. He does not postulate a causal relationship between migration and regional income growth, however.

In the senses noted here, it is unclear that either of the major assumptions underlying regional planning efforts were well founded. Even in the terms of the planners, which meant emphasis on the promotion of greater economywide efficiency, encouraging out-migration to more productive, that is, denser, regions might have made the economy more efficient. This, in turn, would have permitted the resulting extra income to be redistributed to poorer people producing greater interpersonal equity. Social costs—both the negative externalities in the big cities and those of the migrants—would remain, but microeconomic policy could have been used to reduce the interpersonal effects. This was never done, nor is there evidence that it was ever seriously considered. Here, pressures from LDP politicians with rural constituencies probably influenced the bureaucrats' thinking. The point here is that other approaches to policy could have been followed that were based on other assumptions about equity, efficiency, and externalities.

3.5.3 The Evidence concerning the Effects of Regional Policy on Population and Income Distribution

To what extent has regional policy been successful? The evidence advanced in Sections 3.3 and 3.4 concluded that the growth pole policy of Japan in the 1960s—which stressed "place" prosperity over "people" prosperity—failed to help in any meaningful way to decentralize population and employment. Similarly, I have shown that regional investment policy in general did little to influence the spatial distribution of economic activity. Until the late 1960s, there was relatively little public investment in lagging regions.

Yet, some population deconcentration was taking place during that time period. As was shown in Chapter 3,[32] there was a sharp decline in out-migration from lagging regions in the 1960s. In fact, the peak year of in-migration to the three largest metropolitan areas was 1962. Mera (1976) shows that the number of rapidly depopulating prefectures fell from 36 in 1953 to 28 in 1965 to only 3 in 1974. It is important to understand that this trend to population deconcentration began *prior* to the time when most of the central government's deconcentration efforts were put into effect. We have noted this in Chapter 3, Figure 3.2. Therefore, it is difficult to argue that it was government policy that produced this change in migration patterns.

A second phenomenon—one related to population deconcentration—has been declining interregional income inequality over time. Mera (1976) indicates that one index of income disparity (the difference between the highest and lowest indices of prefectural per capita income) fell by 30% between 1962 and 1972. This, he argues, has reduced the propensity for people in poor regions to migrate to richer ones. This, then, is another reason for relative deconcentration. Again, greater equity in cross-regional incomes predated most government policy.

One interesting question involves the reason for this decline in income disparities across Japanese regions. Was it because of income redistribution programs of the government? Or, as some have argued, has it occurred because of the decentralization of industry? Sakashita (1976) helps answer these questions. He calculates the coefficient of variation (the standard deviation divided by the mean) for three types of prefectural-based income data. First, there is prefectural income per capita, a measure that includes wages and salaries as well as the returns from capital and transfer income from the government; this is given by the term v_x in Table 6.13. His second measure is per capita personal income that excludes returns from capital investments (v_q). Third, he measures production income per employee, the sum of value added divided by the number of workers (v_y). Sakashita notes that all three measures of income inequality have decreased over time, but that the personal income disparity, as measured by v_q, is decreasing the fastest.

Most important for the analysis here is that v_y (production income) has decreased relatively little—from .28 to .26 from 1960 to 1971. Therefore, it is not through the decentralization of jobs (which would produce more income in outlying areas and reduce the size of v_y) that income differentials have decreased. As can be seen from Table 6.13, before 1970, v_x was greater than v_y; that is, the disparity of prefectural income was greater than the disparity in production income. But the opposite was true after 1970: There has been the unchanging relative productivity per worker interregionally, while there has been a rapid decrease in the disparity of individual incomes. The reduc-

---

[32] See also Vining (1977), Vining and Kontuly (1976, 1977), Kuroda (1969, 1977), Unno (1975), and Mera (1976).

TABLE 6.13
Changing Interregional Income Disparities, 1956–1972[a]

Year	Prefectural Income per Capita (v_x)	Personal Income per Capita (v_q)	Production income per employee (v_y)
1956	.3276	.2704	NA
1960	.3440	.2648	.2832
1965	.2815	.2268	.2580
1971	.2542	.1921	.2654
1972	.2499	.1869	NA
Percentage decline 1960–1971	23.71	30.88	6.29

Source: Sakashita (1976).
[a] Coefficients of variation.

tion in income differentials, which is shown by the large fall in v_x and v_q (23.7 and 30.9%, respectively, for 1960–1971), can better be explained by the tax redistribution policies of the central government, in which poorer regions are aided. The government redistribution program can be seen in two steps, according to Sakashita. First, there is the redistribution from rich to poor regions through subsidies and tax programs. Second, there is redistribution within regions by subsidies from prefectural to local government.

The importance of tax and subsidy programs in reducing interregional fiscal disparities is shown in Chapter 7. There, detailed analyses of intergovernmental revenue flows are undertaken, and the subsidization of relatively poor cities by the relatively rich is demonstrated. For instance, the Ministry of Home Affairs calculates "standard" financial needs and revenues for localities that favor the poorer cities in the distribution of funds. In general poorer cities were favored by the central government with regard to the disbursement of nonearmarked revenues, treasury disbursements, and prefectural disbursements. To the extent that relative advances in local government finance helped individuals (for instance, through a smaller local tax burden), then the goal of interpersonal equity was advanced.

The analysis in Chapter 7 also shows the effects of intergovernmental transfers on special development programs such as the NICs and SAs. For instance, a regression that explains the level of central government treasury disbursement to large cities in 1965–1970 includes a positive coefficient for a "dummy" variable for those cities that were either NICs or SAs. That is, cities so designated received relatively more treasury disbursements. The special district dummy variable is also an independent variable in explaining the level of bonds that a municipality may issue.

These results, coupled with those of Sakashita, indicate another method of reducing interregional income disparities: the intergovernmental revenue system that tends to favor the poorer regions.

TABLE 6.14
Share Quotients for Revenue Sources for New Industrial Cities, 1970

	Local taxes	Local bonds	Treasury disbursements	Prefectural disbursements	Nonearmarked revenues
Sapporo	.71	1.85	1.60	1.14	1.43
Sendai	1.12	1.82	1.08	.62	.91
Akita	1.13	.49	.89	.86	2.06
Koriyama	.68	2.22	.79	.89	3.34
Niigata	1.18	1.24	.86	.55	.92
Toyama	1.08	1.47	.70	1.08	.56
Takaoka	1.22	.77	.90	1.28	1.23
Matsumoto	1.05	1.17	.83	1.12	1.21
Yonago	.81	.62	.19	1.34	2.37
Matsue	.85	.81	1.15	1.49	2.13
Okayama	1.10	1.17	1.22	.69	1.21
Niihama	1.42	1.17	1.16	1.03	.15
Kumamoto	.85	.56	1.68	.55	1.86
Oita	.98	.89	1.66	.95	1.32
Nobeoka	.96	1.11	1.40	.89	1.77

Source: Gencer and Glickman (1976, Appendix III, Table 5).

However, my analysis also indicates that the NICs were not over-whelming recipients of central government revenues within the inter-governmental transfers system. This is shown in Table 6.14, which presents share quotients for the NIC central cities. A share quotient gives the relative level of revenues for each category compared to the level for all cities in our sample; therefore, a share quotient of greater than unity indicates a greater than average share of a particular revenue item. The major items that were used to redistribute revenues to poorer cities were treasury disbursements and nonearmarked revenues. For the NICs in Table 6.14, the picture for treasury disbursements is mixed. Seven of the 15 cities had share quotients of less than 1, indicating less than average levels of that revenue category. New Industrial Cities got relatively more nonearmarked revenues in 11 cases, on the other hand; however, there are some very low quotients for Toyama and Niihama. Additionally, 8 of 15 cities were forced to collect more than average amounts of taxes from local sources. This, too, shows the relative lack of the underwriting of the NICs' development.[33]

Tentative conclusions to be drawn from these discussions are as follows:

1. There was some effect on government tax and subsidy programs on poorer regions in general.
2. These programs were not well-focused on the NICs.

---

[33] Note that these conclusions are for the NICs' main cities and may not hold for the smaller ones. However, since the large ones dominate the NIC regions, their impact is probably the most important compared to other municipalities.

The effect on personal income inequality was probably small but tending toward greater equity.

Another way in which income disparities have been narrowed was a relative increase in the demand for labor in industrialized regions, which has pulled workers out of poorer regions into richer ones through the migration process. There was a significant increase in labor demand[34] that has drawn workers away from poor regions to those areas with abundant jobs. The migration option is one that increasing numbers of Japanese took during the 1950s and 1960s. Out-migration from poor regions has two principal advantages with respect to interregional equity. It reduces the level of unemployment in poor regions and tends to increase the level of wages, if labor demand is assumed to be constant. Out-migration will increase the capital–output ratio and, therefore, the marginal productivity of labor. In Japan, the decline of income inequality was directly associated with out-migration. As Kabaya shows, every prefecture for which population decreased during the 1960s had a higher than average growth rate of personal per capita income during that period.

According to the analysis here, there is very little evidence that government policy had any direct effect on migration behavior. Therefore, to the extent that deconcentration occurred, little can be attributed to government policy with respect to migration. Migration occurred principally because of greater job opportunity in industrialized regions and because of reduced income differentials between rich and poor regions. As the income differentials decreased, migration (in some cases, the "U-turn" phenomenon) took place.

What has caused the phenomenon we have observed? The arguments about government investment policy are not very persuasive. Population deconcentration and reductions in interregional income disparities preceded government policy. Since government policy *followed* these events, it did not and could not have been a principal cause. The "concentration-then-deconcentration" phenomenon apparent in Japan, and even more strongly in countries such as the United States, may have been the product of other forces, some not well understood. As Vining (1977) argues, and as stated in Chapter 3, there may have been some structural changes that affected Japanese and other industrialized societies in the late 1960s and 1970s. These changes may be having important effects on the spatial distribution of population. Some have argued that the major contributing factor to decentralization has been the slower national economic growth that has occurred since 1973; see, for instance, Mera (1976) for this argument. However, the slowdown of in-migration from rural areas began long before 1973 as was noted previously. Other reasons, such as environmental conditions and

---

[34] There also has been a relative increase in the demand for labor for those remaining in agriculture through governmental subsidies in rice production.

changing cultural values, may have had some influence on living patterns in Japan, but these cannot supply complete explanations of the phenomena observed.

I return now to one fundamental issue in understanding Japanese regional policy: efficiency of the economy. Throughout most of the period under study, it was the major goal of planners at the national level to increase output and exports at the national level and, to do this, investment was concentrated in the Tokaido megalopolis. Interregional equity was not a very important goal when compared to that of economywide efficiency. The resulting concentrated public investment patterns, outlined in Secion 3.3.1, were the product of this policy. According to Mera (1976) the deconcentration of public investment in the late 1960s "followed rather than preceded the change in the trend [toward deconcentration] of population concentration [p.17]." This is essentially correct as already noted. For various reasons, people and employers began to find large metropolitan regions less attractive and began to look for other locations for homes and jobs. Public investment was made later in smaller and poorer regions. It was, as in the case of planning at the national level, a situation in which private decisions and efficiency dominated public decisions and equity. Deconcentration has taken place, but this phenomenon is much more a product of private decision-making and, possibly, of structural change, than of public planning. It appears that the decentralization sought by the planners would have occurred largely without planning. Planning and the intergovernmental tax system certainly contributed to this process, but other elements appeared to have been at least as important.

4 Regional Development Policies in Other Developed Countries[35]

4.1 Goals and Problems in Regional Development Efforts

What regional problems are perceived and what are the goals of regional planning and policy in other developed, liberal capitalist countries, particularly in Europe? How may problems and goals there be compared to the situation in Japan? This section reviews these issues.

[35] There are numerous studies of regional economic policy and planning in European and other Western developed countries that provide far more detail than can be presented here. The interested reader may consult Allen and MacLennan (1970), Andersson (1974), Beika (1975), Brown (1972), Cameron (1974, 1977), Cao-Pinna (1974), Chapman (1976), Clawson and Hall (1973), Emanuel (1973), Grémion and Worms (1975), Hansen (1968, 1974a, 1974b), Kalk (1971), Liggins (1975), OECD (1969, 1974, 1976), and Sundquist (1975).

One interesting aspect of this brief, comparative analysis is the relative uniformity of reasons that countries have undertaken regional development policies. These reasons are similar to those given by Japanese planners. First, there is the problem of "distressed" areas, especially those that have had large proportions of their working populations employed in the primary sector. This goal has important political support from legislators of these areas. Thus, "place" prosperity has been one of the major purposes for undertaking regional development efforts. A second and related issue involves the attempt to reduce interregional income disparities. Large differences in income among regions have been examined and deemed intolerable. Third, there is the goal of making the economy efficient with respect to production and exports. By reducing unemployment in backward areas, it is hoped that the economy will be more efficient and will have increased growth rates of GNP. As Cameron (1970, as quoted in Hansen, 1974a) points out: "although political pressures give regional policy its main justification and its ever-changing vitality, efficiency arguments are never far below the surface [p. 16]." Cameron perceives efficiency in two senses: first, in terms of increasing the growth rate of national income and, second, in relation to the effective use of public funds for regional development purposes.

Related to the questions of distressed regions, interregional income inequality, and efficiency, are two additional issues that have been discussed by policy makers. One is the question of city size. The arguments are similar to those given by Japanese planners, that is, that the major cities are too large. This is particularly true of the experience of French regional planning where great efforts have been made to reduce the growth rate of Paris, but this has been true in other countries as well. The problem of controlling the size of large cities has been seen as complementary to that of developing the rural, backward regions.

The various countries also view the ramifications of regional imbalance similarly. The major problems involve demographic selectivity in migration choice (the younger, better educated workers tend to leave poor regions), downward multiplier effects on local gross regional product as marginal firms and those oriented toward the market close down, and the loss of efficiency in the delivery of public services in the face of population loss and a declining tax base.

The phenomena are also similar. The British worried about the "drift to the South" resulting in out-migration from the English Northeast, South Wales, and Scotland and the heavy concentration around London. The French concerned themselves with the decline of the West, parts of the North, and the *Midi* (South) simultaneously with the buildup of the Paris basin. In Italy, the long-term problems of the *Mezzogiorno* (the South) were under attack by regional planners. Declining agriculture and mining, out-migration from poor regions, and the alleged overdevelopment of main centers are phenomena common to many European countries. As the review of the Japanese situation in Section 3 indicated, similar problems have been seen there.

4.2   Strategies of Regional Development

The strategies undertaken by Western countries with regard to regional development are, as in Japan, dominated by considerations of place prosperity. One can see that in the attempts to develop the *Mezzogiorno* or the eight French *métropoles d'équilibre*. The use of growth centers as a regional development strategy is also important, as in the case of the French *métropoles*. The purpose, as with other growth center efforts, has been to generate further economic expansion of regions that had growth potential and to divert economic activity and population away from largest cities. As noted in Chapter 2 (Section 5.2.2), Paris dominates France to a greater degree than the largest metropolis dominates any other city system in a developed country; see also, Prud'homme (1974), Sundquist (1975, pp. 91–141), and Gravier (1947). The use of growth centers was seen by the French as a way of lessening the domination of Paris with regard to the rest of the city system. In the case of France, the situation was different from that of Japan. Where Japan tried to develop relatively small cities in remote regions, the French *métropoles* (Lyon, Marseille, Lille, Bordeaux, Toulouse, Nantes, Metz-Nancy, and Strasbourg), which form a ring around Paris, are larger on average than the NICs and are much less geographically remote.

Regional planners also have discussed the advantages of decentralizing public investment and thus building up public infrastructure in lagging regions in line with regional development policy. In some cases this has not occurred, however. Prud'homme concludes that, for France, "the spatial distribution of public investments do not follow regional policy prescriptions [p. 48]." In general, we find that, as in Japan, regional planners control relatively small budgets for the effectuation of regional policy.[36] Most of the central government spending that has a direct or indirect effect on regional matters remains in the control of traditional agencies that are often not concerned with regional problems.

Governments have used several other tools for regional planning purposes. The OECD (1974) has catalogued them for member countries and their tally is shown in Table 6.15. These other procedures principally involve tax and subsidy schemes to encourage capital to move to lagging regions: investment grants, public funds for building plants, loan programs, and fiscal

---

[36] For instance, DATAR, the French agency that is in charge of regional development policy spent only $60 million in 1971, down from $70 million the previous year; see Sundquist (p. 120). OECD (1976, p. 21) says that total French regional development spending varied between 200 million and 500 million *francs* in the 1960s and early 1970s. For further discussion of French planning, see DATAR (1976b).

TABLE 6.15

Regional Development Incentives to Industry for OECD Countries[a]

Incentives	Austria	Belgium	Canada	Denmark	Finland	France	Germany (F.R.)	Greece	Ireland
I. Investment grants									
On industrial building		A[c]	A	A		A	A		A
On plant and machinery			A	A`		A	A		A
II. Provision of factory buildings and sites at low cost			A	A	A				A
III. Loans									
At market rates					A				
At subsidized rates	A	A	A	A	A	A	A[e]		A
guaranteed	A	A		A	C		A		A
IV. Fiscal concessions									
On investment	A[b]	A			A	A	A[f]	A	A
On profits					A	A		A	A
On revenue from State aid			A						
On State charges, local taxes, license fees, etc.	A	A			A	A		A	A
V. Grants toward labor costs								A[g]	
VI. Assistance for working costs				A[d]					
VII. Labor training aids	A	A	C	A	A	A	A	C	A
VIII. Assistance for netting-in costs					A				
IX. Grants for moving costs				A		A			
X. Financial aids to worker mobility away from designated areas	A	C			C				
XI. Financial aids to worker mobility into designated areas	A	C		A	C	A			
XII. Shareholding		A			A	A			
XIII. Transport and other public service concessions	A					A	A[f]		A
XIV. Preferential treatment in the award of Government contracts							A[f]	A	

TABLE 6.15 (Continued)

Incentives	Italy	Japan	Netherlands	Norway	Portugal	Spain	Swedan	Switzerland	Turkey	United Kingdom
I. Investment grants										
On industrial building	A		A	A		A	A			A
On plant and machinery	A		A	A		A	A^b			A
II. Provision of factory buildings and sites at low cost	B	A		A						A
III. Loans										
At market rates				A						A
At subsidized rates	A	A	B			A	A		A	A
Guaranteed			A	A			A			
IV. Fiscal concessions										
On investment	A	A	A	A	A	A	A	—^i	A	
On profits	A				A	A	A	—^i	A	A
On revenue from State aid						A			A	
On State charges, local taxes, licence fees, etc.	A^h	A						—^i	A	
V. Grants toward labor costs	A^h					A	A			A

VI. Assistance for working costs	C	C			A	A	C	A	A
VII. Labour training aids	C	B		A	C	A			A
VIII. Assistance for netting-in costs	B			A		A			A
IX. Grants for moving costs			A	A			A		A
X. Financial aids to 'worker mobility away from designated areas	B	B		B		B			A
XI. Financial aids to worker mobility into designated areas	A	A	B		B		B	A	A
XII. Shareholding	A	A	B		B		B		A
XIII. Transport and other public service concessions	B		A	A		A		A	
XIV. Preferential treatment in the award of Government contracts	A	B	A	B	B		A	A	A

Source: OECD (1974).

[a] Symbols: A—available; B—available, but not particularly important; C—available throughout the country.

[b] Terminated at the end of 1973.

[c] Interest subsidies are the normal form of aid, but a capital bonus equivalent in value may be taken as an alternative.

[d] Available to firms facing exceptional difficulty.

[e] Firms may opt for this form of aid, but in such cases the amount of interest subsidy is deducted from the gain.

[f] In the Eastern border areas only.

[g] Exemption from employees' social security contributions.

[h] Reduction of employees' social security contributions.

[i] Various fiscal concessions are applied by the Cantonal Governments.

concessions, among them. We can see from Table 6.15 that Japan provided relatively few of such grants; the United Kingdom seemed to provide the most variety of grants and subsidies.[37] Also, technical assistance to relocating firms is available. Usually, these grants and subsidies are differentiated according to the severity of the regional problem.

Less often used, but to some observers (such as Andersson, 1974) possibly effective, are grants to employers to subsidize the hiring of workers. The British, for instance, subsidized wages (to the amount of $5.25 per week in distressed areas in 1967) with some success.

Both the British and the French also have employed various measures to prohibit factory construction in the London and Paris regions. For instance, construction of manufacturing plants in the Paris region with net floor area of more than 1,500 m^2 and office space of more than 1,000 m^2 is subject to a tax that varies according to location; see Sundquist (1975, pp. 130–131). Japan has tried similar controls for Tokyo and other large cities.

4.3   Problems with Regional Development Planning

Despite the multiplicity of efforts by the different governments in Europe and elsewhere, many observers argue that regional economic planning has not done very much to alter the spatial distribution of economic activity. There appear to be several reasons for this. First, the goals are often contradictory and confused. Second, plans lack enforcement power, and financial backing from the central governments has not been forthcoming to the extent necessary to make structural change take place in backward regions or to prohibit growth in highly populated ones. That, after more than 30 years of effort in the *Mezzogiorno,* Scotland, and the *Massif Central,* these regions are not much better off relative to other regions in those countries is testimony to the lack of success of planning relative to need. One of the problems has been the fact that development funds have been spread too thinly. This has been true in Japan; it is also true in France where help to the eight *métropoles* has been superceded by aid to a larger number of small- and medium-sized cities. There simply has not been enough money to make much difference to regions in serious need of development funds.

A major problem is the lack of governmental power relative to the power of the market. If firms are able to locate where profit is highest, as they are in the countries being discussed here, then spatial policy faces the dilemma outlined in this chapter. This is particularly true with respect to the internationalization of capital over the postwar period. Controls on foreign capital with regard to location are more difficult to enforce than controls on

---

[37] Sundquist (pp. 37–90) discusses some of these schemes available in the United Kingdom. DATAR (1975, 1976a, 1976c) provides additional information on subsidies and grants available in France.

domestic capital. Although this has not been a major problem in Japan, where there is relatively little foreign capital, it is a significant factor in countries such as France where foreign capital's penetration in the national and regional economies is important.[38]

An additional problem in several countries has been the lack of control over the location of the service sector. This comes in part from the heavy emphasis on controlling location of manufacturing. Controls on office building in Paris and London have not been very effective in stemming speculative building that has occurred there. As a result, the centralization of the service sector in the postindustrial age has gone untouched by most regional planning efforts; on this, see Sundquist (1975, pp. 111–115).

There are many other problems involved in regional planning, but space does not permit a fuller explication of them. The conclusion that can be arrived at is that, in most instances, the goals and strategies of planners have not overcome the power of profit-maximizing entrepreneurs. Therefore, most of the regional problems that faced planners in the 1950s and 1960s persist to some degree. As the OECD (1974) concludes, "We cannot point to any country that has been able, despite determined and considerable effort over long periods, to achieve the objectives it has set for itself [p. 138]."

Yet, some changes in the regional economies, alluded to in Sections 3 and 4 of Chapter 3, have begun to occur. There have been signs of deconcentration in many countries. The London region lost population absolutely during the 1961–1971 period. Paris, while still growing faster than most other regions in France, is not growing as fast as it was previously. The more peripheral regions in some countries are not losing population as quickly as formerly; some are now experiencing net in-migration for the first time in many years. It was argued in Section 3 that these phenomena are not the result of planning, at least in the Japanese context. Here I argue (somewhat less forcibly, because of the more limited review) that planning was probably not responsible for much of this change in migration patterns. This is true since not much emphasis has been placed on migration incentives (or human capital approaches to planning, in general) in these countries and because out-migration from urban regions has been occurring in countries that have little or no planning at all. The United States is a case in point; there, declines in the Northeast and North Central states and increased in-migration to the South and Southwest have occurred since the end of the

---

[38] There is considerable controversy over this point. Some French planners argue that considerable spatially decentralized investment has been undertaken by foreign firms. This is so because agencies such as DATAR provide assistance in getting through the bureaucratic red tape and financial assistance for plant locations in designated regions. Additionally, foreign investors may be less prejudiced against provincial locations than French entrepreneurs. On the other hand, some argue that much of the foreign investment is in low-wage, low-technology industry that would indicate a non-Paris location anyway. They further indicate that such investments do not provide the basis for permanent, self-sustaining local economic development and result in a dependency relationship to foreign investors on the part of these regions.

1960s. Few would argue that planning had anything to do with these trends in the United States.

5 Concluding Remarks

This chapter has attempted to catalogue the development of Japanese regional planning and to evaluate its effects. National economic planning was discussed, and it was argued that the rapid national economic development that occurred in the 1950s and 1960s was probably not the result of national planning; more traditional Keynesian tools were at least as effective. Regional components of national plans and strictly regional plans were then analyzed. The experience of the New Industrial Cities and Special Areas was reviewed and it was concluded that these programs did little to alter the spatial pattern of development. Furthermore, the place prosperity programs may have been based upon wrong premises: Migration policies might have accomplished the goals of interpersonal income equity more easily. Of course, place-oriented programs have great political appeal (not only in Japan but in other countries), especially to legislators from the lagging regions. Thus, these programs have been pushed vigorously by various Japanese governments. Interregional income redistribution was taking place through the tax and subsidy system of the various ministries, especially the Ministry of Home Affairs; this element of Japanese political economy will be discussed in much more detail in Chapter 7. Finally, the Japanese experience was compared to that of other countries and it was shown that many of the same problems were perceived, similar goals set, and tools employed to counter the twin problems of depopulation of lagging regions and overcrowding of prosperous ones. Planning appeared to have little to do with spatial change in France, Britain, and other countries. There has been a trend toward disurbanization (see Berry, 1976) in many Western developed countries. The reasons for this phenomenon are not well understood, but it seems that planning, as currently practiced, has not been responsible for it. More likely, factors like slower economic growth, cultural, and other factors have caused these changes in living patterns in much of the developed world.

References

Ackley, G. and H. Ishi (1976). Fiscal, monetary, and related policies, in H. Patrick and H. Rosovsky, eds., *Asia's New Giant: How the Japanese Economy Works*. The Brookings Institution, Washington, D.C. Pp. 153–247.

Allen, K. and M. C. MacLennan (1970). *Regional Problems and Policies in Italy and France.* Allen and Unwin, London.

Alonso, W. (1971). The economics of urban size. *Papers of Regional Science Association, 26,* 67–84.

Andersson, A. (1974). Regional economic policy: Problems, analysis and political experiments in Sweden, in N. M. Hansen, ed., *Public Policy and Regional Economic Development: The Experience of Nine Western Countries.* Ballinger, Cambridge, Mass. Pp. 199–233.

Beika, M. (1975). Regional development policies of Japan in recent quarter of the twentieth century. *Kobe Economic and Business Review, 21,* 1–22.

Berry, B. J. L. (1976). *The Counterurbanization Process: How General?* Mimeo.

Borukhov, E. (1975). On the urban agglomeration and economic efficiency: Comment. *Economic Development and Cultural Change, 24,* 199–205.

Brown, A. J. (1972). *The Framework of Regional Economies in the United Kingdom.* Cambridge University Press, London.

Cameron, G. C. (1970). Growth areas, growth centres and regional conversion. *Scottish Journal of Political Economy, 17,* 19–38.

Cameron, G. C. (1974). Regional economic policy in the United Kingdom, in M. M. Hansen, ed., *Public Policy and Regional Economic Development: The Experience of Nine Western Countries.* Ballinger, Cambridge, Mass. Pp. 65–102.

Cameron, G. C. (1977). Constraining the growth of primate cities: A study of methods, in T. Bendixson, ed., *The Management of Urban Growth.* OECD, Paris.

Cao-Pinna, V. (1974). Regional policy in Italy, in N. M. Hansen, ed., *Public Policy and Regional Economic Development: The Experience of Nine Western Countries.* Ballinger, Cambridge, Mass. Pp. 137–179.

Chapman, G. (1976). *Development and Underdevelopment in Southern Italy.* University of Reading Department of Geography, Geographical Papers, *41,* University of Reading, Reading, England.

Clawson, M. and P. Hall (1973). *Planning and Urban Growth: An Anglo-American Comparison.* Johns Hopkins University Press, Baltimore.

Datar (1975). *France: A New Investment Climate.* DATAR, Paris.

Datar (1976a). *Aides au Développement Régional* (in French). DATAR, Paris.

Datar (1976b). *Aménagement du Territoire: Rapport d'Activité, 1976* (in French). DATAR, Paris.

Datar (1976c). *Investment Incentives in France.* DATAR, Paris.

Denison, E. F. and W. H. Chung (1976). Economic growth and its sources, in H. Patrick and H. Rosovsky, eds., *Asia's New Giant: How the Japanese Economy Works.* The Brookings Institution, Washington, D.C. Pp. 63–151.

Emanuel, A. (1973). *Issues of Regional Policies.* OECD, Paris.

Fukui, H. (1972). Economic planning in postwar Japan: A case study in policy making. *Asian Survey, 12,* 327–348.

Gencer, E. and N. J. Glickman (1976). *An Empirical Analysis of the Japanese Urban Public Finance System.* Mimeo.

Glickman, N. J. (1971). *Regional Econometric Models: The Japanese and American Experience.* University of Pennsylvania Institute for Environmental Studies, Philadelphia, Pennsylvania.

Glickman, N. J. (1972). Conflict over public facility location in Japan. *Area Development in Japan, 6,* 20–43.

Gravier, J. F. (1947). *Paris and the French Desert* (in French). Editions to the Portulan, Paris.

Grémion, P. and J. P. Worms (1975). The French regional planning experiments, in J. Howard and M. Watson, eds., *Planning Politics and Public Policy: The British, French and Italian Experiences.* Cambridge University Press, London. Pp. 217–236.

Hansen, N. M. (1968). *French Regional Planning.* Indiana University Press, Bloomington, Indiana.

Hansen, N. M. (1974a). Preliminary overview, in N. M. Hansen, ed., *Public Policy and Regional Economic Development: The Experience of Nine Western Countries.* Ballinger, Cambridge, Mass.

Hansen, N. M. (1974b). *Public Policy and Regional Economic Development: The Experience of Nine Western Countries.* Ballinger, Cambridge, Mass.

Hirsch, W. C. (1968). The Supply of Urban Public Services, in H. S. Perloff and L. Wingo, eds., *Issues in Urban Economics.* Johns Hopkins University Press, Baltimore. Pp. 477–526.

Japan Bureau of Statistics, Office of the Prime Minister (1976). *Japan Statistical Yearbook 1976.* Japan Bureau of Statistics Office of the Prime Minister, Tokyo.

Japan Economic Planning Agency (1967). *Study of Japan's Nationwide Regional Econometric Model.* Japan Economic Planning Agency, Tokyo.

Japan Economic Planning Agency (1972). *The New Comprehensive National Development Plan (Summary) and Its Implementation.* Japan Economic Planning Agency, Tokyo.

Japan Economic Planning Agency (1973). *Econometric Models for Basic Economic and Social Plan, 1973–1977.* Japan Economic Planning Agency, Tokyo.

Japan Economic Planning Agency (1975). *Reference Data for an Observation of Regional Structure* (in Japanese). Japan Economic Planning Agency, Tokyo.

Japan Economic Planning Agency (1976). *Economic Plan for the Second Half of the 1970s: Towards a Stable Society.* Japan Economic Planning Agency, Tokyo.

Japan Ministry of Home Affairs (1975). *Basic Resident's Registration* (in Japanese). Japan Ministry of Home Affairs, Tokyo.

Japan National Capital Region Development Commission (1971). *Outline of National Capital Region Development.* Japan National Capital Region Development Commission, Tokyo.

Japan National Land Agency (1974). *The Outline of the National Land Agency.* Japan National Land Agency, Tokyo.

Japan National Land Agency (1975a). *The National Land Use Policy of Japan.* Japan National Land Agency, Tokyo.

Japan National Land Agency (1975b). *Present Situation of the New Industrial Cities and Special Areas* (in Japanese). Japan National Land Agency, Tokyo.

Kabaya, R. (1971). *Development of Poor Regions: General Considerations and the Case of Japan.* Mimeo, University of California, Berkeley, California.

Kalk, E., ed. (1971). *Regional Planning and Regional Government in Europe.* International Union of Local Authorities, The Hague, The Netherlands.

Komiya, R. (1975). Economic planning in Japan. *Challenge, 8,* 9–20.

Kosobud, R. and R. Minami, eds. (1977). *Econometric Studies of Japan.* University of Illinois Press, Urbana, Ill.

Kuroda, T. (1969). *A New Dimension of Internal Migration in Japan.* Institute of Population Problems, Japan Ministry of Health and Welfare, Tokyo.

Kuroda, T. (1977). *Migration, Distribution of Population and Development in Japan.* Mimeo.

Liggins, D. (1975). *National Economic Planning in France.* Saxon House, D. C. Heath Ltd., Westmead, England.

Lo, F.-C. (1975). *The Growth Pole Approach to Regional Development: A Case Study of Mizushima Industrial Complex.* United Nations Centre for Regional Development, Nagoya, Japan.

Mera, K. (1973). On the urban agglomeration and economic efficiency. *Economic Development and Cultural Change, 21,* 309–324.

Mera, K. (1975). On the urban agglomeration and economic efficiency: reply. *Economic Development and Cultural Change, 24,* 207–210.

Mera, K. (1976). *The Changing Pattern of Population Distribution in Japan and Its Implications for Developing Countries.* International Development Center, Tokyo.

Miyasawa, K. (1977). *Comprehensive National Development Plans in Japan: Their Logic and*

Realities. Paper presented at a conference on the Shinkansen project at the International Institute for Applied Systems Analysis, Laxenburg, Austria.

Neutze, G. M. (1967). *Economic Policy and the Size of Cities*. A. M. Kelley, New York.

Okita, S. (1974). *The Experience of Economic Planning in Japan*. Japan Economic Research Center, Tokyo.

Organization for Economic Cooperation and Development (1969). *Multidisciplinary Aspects of Regional Development*. OECD, Paris.

Organization for Economic Cooperation and Development (1971). *Salient Features of Regional Development Policy in Japan*. OECD, Paris.

Organization for Economic Cooperation and Development (1974). *Re-Appraisal of Regional Policies in OECD Countries*. OECD, Paris.

Organization for Economic Cooperation and Development (1976). *Regional Problems and Policies in OECD Countries*. OECD, Paris.

Organization for Economic Cooperation and Development (1977). *Main Economic Indicators*. OECD, Paris.

Patrick, H. and H. Rosovsky (1976). Japan's economic performance: An overview, in H. Patrick and H. Rosovsky, eds., *Asia's New Giant: How the Japanese Economy Works*. The Brookings Institution, Washington, D.C. Pp. 1–62.

Prud'homme, R. (1974). Regional economic policy in France, 1962–1972, in N. M. Hansen, ed. *Public Policy and Regional Economic Development: The Experience of Nine Western Countries*. Ballinger, Cambridge, Mass. Pp. 33–63.

Sakashita, N. (1976). *Methods of Regional Economic Analysis* (in Japanese). Japan Economic Planning Agency, Tokyo.

Sawyer, M. (1976). Income distribution in OECD Countries. *OECD Economic Outlook Occasional Studies*. OECD, Paris. Pp. 2–36.

Sundquist, J. L. (1975). *Dispersing Population: What America Can Learn from Europe*. The Brookings Institution, Washington, D.C.

Tanaka, K. (1972). *Building a New Japan: A Plan for Remodeling the Japanese Archipelago*. Simul Press, Tokyo.

Tanifuji M. and T. Nozu (1977). *A Case Study of Regional Planning in Japan: Policy and Development of New Industrial Cities*. Mimeo.

Thompson, W. R. (1968). Internal and external factors in the development of urban economies, in H. S. Perloff and L. Wingo, eds., *Issues in Urban Economics*. John Hopkins University Press, Baltimore. Pp. 43–80.

Trezise, P. H. and Y. Suzuki (1976). Politics, government, and economic growth in Japan, in H. Patrick and H. Rosovsky, eds., *Asia's New Giant: How the Japanese Economy Works*. The Brookings Institution, Washington, D.C. Pp. 753–811.

Unno, T. (1975). Problems of overpopulation and depopulation. *Japanese Economic Studies, 3*, 59–87.

Vining, D. R., Jr. (1977). Book review of "Post-Industrial America: Metropolitan Decline and Interregional Job Shifts" by G. Sternlieb and J. W. Hughes. *Journal of Regional Science, 17*, 141–146.

Vining, D. R., Jr. and T. Kontuly (1976). *Population Dispersal from Metropolitan Regions— A Review of Three Current Hypotheses*. Mimeo.

Vining, D. R., Jr. and T. Kontuly (1977). Increasing returns to city size in the face of an impending decline in the sizes of large cities: Which is the bogus fact? *Environment and Planning A, 9*, 59–62.

Vogel, E. F. (1975). *Modern Japanese Organization and Decision-Making*. University of California Press, Berkeley, California.

Watanabe, T. (1970). National planning and economic development: A critical review of the Japanese experience. *Economics of Planning, 10*, 21–51.

Wingo, L. (1972). Issues in a national urban development strategy. *Urban Studies, 9*, 3–27.

7

Financing the Japanese Urban System: Local Public Finance and Intergovernmental Revenues

1 Introduction

Chapter 6 covered Japan's regional planning system and its attempts to redistribute population and reduce interregional income inequalities.[1] It was concluded that the planning system had little to do with the relative decline in in-migration to the large cities that began in the early 1960s. Additionally, since the spatial distribution of central government investment was relatively centralized, it was argued that public spending patterns did little to reduce income differences among regions. A further conclusion was that most of the decentralization could be attributed to the normal workings of the market place: Firms sought locations where land prices were relatively low and where labor was cheap and available; families sought housing where jobs were located and where the environment was more congenial. Increasingly, this meant that people and firms were locating away from the three main metropolitan centers, primarily in middle-sized regions.[2] Evidence was also presented that a reduction in interregional income differentials has lowered the propensity of families to migrate to the richer urban centers. However, not all of the narrowing differences could be accounted for by the decentralization of industry to poorer regions. Sakashita (1976) indicated that government tax and subsidy programs were responsible for some of the

[1] This chapter is an extension of Gencer and Glickman (1976).

[2] I have discussed these trends in Chapters 2 and 3 and have shown that the metropolitan areas that form the Regional Economic Clusters grew more quickly than nonmetropolitan areas, principally because of higher birth rates in the cities, and that there was evidence of lower levels of in-migration to the major metropolitan centers beginning in the late 1960s.

increased incomes of both the people and the local governments in poorer regions.

To understand better the Japanese method of income redistribution among regions, this chapter analyzes the revenue structure of the local governments. The two major questions addressed are

1. What are the revenue sources available to local government?
2. What socioeconomic and political factors determine the amount of local revenue from each source?

The first question leads to a study of the institutional framework of the local governments (hereafter, LG) and the fiscal relations among various governmental levels. The second question requires finding socioeconomic variables that explain the amount of revenues coming from the various sources.

There are five additional parts to this chapter. Section 2 outlines the institutional structure of the Japanese government and the fiscal relations of its several layers. Sections 3 and 4 are devoted to quantitative analysis of the revenue structure of municipal governments and form the major contribution of this chapter. Section 5 briefly discusses the role of prefectural governments, and Section 6 presents some conclusions.

2 The Structure of Local Government in Japan

2.1 A Brief History of Local Government

The opposing themes of centralization and decentralization figure prominently in the development of local government in Japan. Decentralized systems of governance of the feudal era were replaced with centralized government institutions with the rise of mercantilist and, later, industrial forces. The Meiji constitution was the first movement toward centralization; on this subject, see Steiner (1965). Japan is now politically subdivided into 47 prefectures (including Okinawa), which were first established following the Meiji restoration and the abolition of feudal fiefdoms in the 1870s. The Meiji Constitution and the Law concerning the Organization of Urban and Rural Prefectures (1890) established a unitary system rather than a federal type of government such as that of the United States. The governor (*chiji*) of each prefecture was appointed by the emperor on recommendation of the minister of home affairs. The governor had the power to override decisions of the prefectural legislature, the ability to formulate prefectural budgets, and considerable control over the budgets of villages, towns, and cities.

As noted by McNelly (1972), centralization and bureaucracy rather than local autonomy were the prevailing principles of local government in prewar Japan. During the American occupation period, a decentralized government system, which emphasized local home rule, was superimposed on the highly centralized and bureaucratic ruling heritage of Japan. After the war, localities were granted more home rule than they had in prewar days. However, no precise functions and powers are enunciated in the constitution, so that, despite the newly promulgated principle of local autonomy, local governments were able principally to exercise powers delegated to them by the Diet and, to a lesser extent, carry out their own affairs according to local law.

The three echelons of government in Japan are the *central (national) government, prefectural government*, and *municipal government*. Postwar legislation has encouraged the amalgamation of municipalities, and, for reasons of economy and efficiency, many chose to merge. This was particularly true during the 1950s.[3]

2.2　Functions of Local Governments

The major institutional functions of LGs in Japan are as follows: (*a*) to carry out certain central government (hereafter, CG) legislation and projects and (*b*) to enact and enforce the legislation of the LGs themselves. In performing the former group of functions, the LG agencies are supervised by the relevant ministries of the CG, especially the Ministries of Home Affairs, Finance, Education, and Welfare. The powers of the local governments are sometimes delegated by legislation passed by the Diet. According to the Local Autonomy Law, the LGs have authority concerning general police work, social security and welfare, establishment and maintenance of urban infrastructure, urban planning, education, and levying and collecting taxes. The CG also may deal with these matters when it wishes.[4] Governors of prefectures and mayors of municipalities are elected by the voters of their respective units for terms of 4 years, subject to recall by the voters. The

---

[3] To date, the amalgamation movement, so important at the municipal level, has not resulted in the merger of any of the prefectures that have the same boundaries as they had before World War II. Much more radical are the proposals to abolish the prefectures completely and to replace them with 7–9 districts or states. A controversial modification of the former proposition is that of interposing administrative units of the central government between the present prefectures and the central government. Most of such ideas are opposed by prefectural governors, who insist that the rights and the interests of the people in the prefectures must be preserved, and by the opposition parties, who accuse the Liberal Democratic Party (LDP) advocates of these schemes of plotting to destroy the principle of local autonomy in favor of a centralized regime run by the conservatives. As McNelly (1972) notes, opportunities for socialists to win prefectural governorships and assembly seats would be reduced by the proposals for amalgamations of prefectures.

[4] The overlapping of functional relationships among the three levels of the government hierarchy concerning local problems may create organizational inefficiency and may render it quite difficult for a concerned citizen to pinpoint where government-related problems originate. The muddle of the functions makes it easy to pass the buck, and government, even at the local level, too often seems bureaucratic and unresponsive, according to many observers.

Local Autonomy Law provides that local executives should carry out national laws and cabinet orders and 80% of all work handled by local government units consists of administrative affairs entrusted to them by agencies of the central government. Thus, local mayors and governors must serve two masters since they function as agents of the CG in national matters and officers of their local governments in local affairs. Under present laws, 70% of the taxes are collected by the CG with 30% retained by the local administrations.[5] However, about 60% of the taxes assigned to the CG are subsequently returned to the local governments in various ways. As a result, only some 30% of all taxes are directly spent by the CG, whereas the rest is spent by the local governments. The professed policy is to collect the maximum revenue from the wealthier localities and to redistribute it to local entities with insufficient financial ability relative to need, according to the Ministry of Home Affairs (1972). As will be shown, a large proportion of the CG disbursements are problem- or project-specific (i.e., earmarked), leaving little initiative to the LG toward financial policies.

3 Local Government Revenue Sources

3.1 The Local Finance System of Japan

The remainder of this chapter will concentrate on analyzing the methods of financing urban development through the complex system of intergovernmental relations. First the various revenue sources to LGs will be described (Sections 3.1.1 to 3.1.6). The data base will then be examined (Section 3.2) and LG revenue sources categorized (Section 3.3). This section provides background for the empirical analysis of Section 4, where the relationship between the CG and the LGs will be detailed.

3.1.1 Local Taxes

Local taxes are levied by the municipality in accordance with the Local Tax Law enacted by the Diet in 1950. The same law "provides the taxes to be levied by the local public entities and describes the basis of tax computation and methods of collection of respective taxes"; see Ministry of Home Affairs (1972). The Local Tax Law provides standard tax rates and assessment methods. However, local governments may levy taxes at rates higher than the standard ones when they consider it necessary, but not at rates exceeding the limit set forth by the law.

There are two types of local taxes: (*a*) Ordinary (or "standard") taxes such as the Municipal Inhabitant, Fixed Assets, Electricity and Gas, and the

---

[5] See Steiner on this subject. For other treatments of Japanese local government and politics see Aqua (1977), Ide (1965), Ike (1957), Mukherjee (1966), Tsuneishi (1966), and Ward and Rustow (1964).

Mineral Product Tax; and (*b*) Special Purpose taxes such as the Spa, City Planning, Water Utility, and Land Profit Tax. The latter levies are determined by the locality according to its assessment of its needs.

3.1.2 Local Transferred Taxes

The CG levies and collects local transferred taxes on goods relating to transportation and related consumption. They are transferred to municipalities and prefectures on the basis of decisions by the CG when transportation and related facilities are located within the municipality. The basic forms of such taxes are local road, special tonnage, liquified petroleum gas, aviation fuel, and motor vehicle tonnage taxes.

3.1.3 Local Allocation Taxes

Local allocation taxes comprise the revenue-sharing system under which 32% of the sum of the three basic national taxes (corporation tax, liquor tax, and income tax) is collected by the CG and then allocated to LGs; Aqua (1977) calls these taxes "equalization grants." The local allocation tax is divided into two parts, ordinary and special. The ordinary allocation tax is given by the CG to local public authorities in accordance with the calculated difference between the amount of standard financial needs and the standard financial revenues as computed by the CG, through a rather rigid, complicated formula. Distribution of the special allocation tax is designated by the CG and the funds can be spent at the discretion of the LG without much monitoring by the CG.

3.1.4 Treasury Disbursements

Treasury disbursements are earmarked by the CG for specific purposes, and programs (often for capital construction projects) and are then allocated to the LGs. There are three components to the treasury disbursements:

1. Programs in which the LGs share financial responsibility with the CG. In this case, the share of the CG is governed by the Local Finance Act.
2. Expenses related to projects for which only the CG is financially responsible and execution of which is entrusted to the LG. For instance, the election of Diet members and the collection of national statistics are included in this category, which is known as "money in trust."
3. Treasury subsidies and grants-in-aids are allocated by the CG (*i*) to subsidize special financial needs of the LGs concerning local or public corporations located in the municipality, (*ii*) to encourage special projects, usually for stimulating economic growth, and (*iii*) as grants-in-aid for municipalities where national institutions are located.

3.1.5 Prefectural Disbursements

Prefectural disbursements are allocated by prefectural governments to municipalities. This type of revenue has two components: (a) those funds that accompany treasury disbursements of the CG and are earmarked for special projects to which the municipalities contribute as well; and (b) those that are allocated by the prefecture alone, again earmarked by use category, but for which the prefectural government alone is financially responsible.

3.1.6 Local Bonds

Every fiscal year LGs sell local bonds. However, the control over the total value of the local bonds that can be issued by a LG, and the amount of those bonds bought by the CG, rests with the Ministry of Home Affairs. Of all local bonds issued each year, 65% are purchased by CG agencies, and the rest are bought by private individuals and various financial institutions. Local bonds are issued for financing public housing, compulsory education, acquisition of public land, public and quasi-public corporations, and welfare projects.

Table 7.1 shows the relative importance of each revenue item to local government finance. Note that the largest item, local taxes, is still only 33% of all LG revenues. The rest comes from either the central government or from prefectural governments. Figure 7.1 indicates the revenue structure of local government.

3.2 The Data Base Used in the Analysis of the Japanese Local Public Finance System

A data bank has been organized for 336 cities for 1960, 1965, and 1970, which will be called the "City Data Bank." It consists of a set of data that are constant through time, such as a city's distance from Tokyo or whether or not it is a prefectural capital; these are in File 1, as listed in Appendix 1. There are four remaining data files having over 100 other variables for

TABLE 7.1

Level and Percentage Distribution of Revenues for Cities, Towns, and Villages, 1970

	Billions of Yen	Percentage
Total revenue	4,535	100.0
Local taxes	1,485	32.74
Transferred tax for local government	14	.30
Local allocation tax	835	18.41
Treasury disbursements	529	11.67
Prefectural disbursements	245	5.41
Local bonds	431	9.51
Rents, fees, and charges	169	3.73
Miscellaneous	827	18.24

Source: Japan Bureau of Statistics, Office of the Prime Minister (1973).

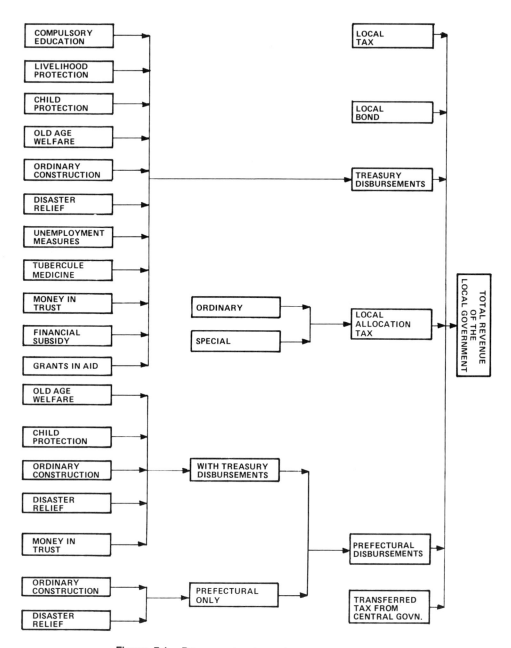

Figure 7.1. Revenue structure of a local government.

demographic, social, economic, political and governmental, and environmental characteristics. These variables were used in this study and in Chapter 4 to supplement the "Regional Data Bank" outlined in Appendix 2 of Chapter 2.

3.3 Identification of the Types of Revenues

The discussion of the LG revenue structure suggests three decision points for revenue allocations. National and prefectural policies directed to specific problems and programs are the first category of decision points. There, certain funds are earmarked for use by the CG; hence, they are dictated by the CG's perception of the locality's needs and the city's relative position in the national economic structure. Prefectural disbursements are another type of earmarked revenue, reflecting prefectural governmental priorities. For nonearmarked CG disbursements—the second category—it is claimed by the CG that such funds are directed at establishing vertical financial equity between the poor and wealthy cities, that is, reducing interregional income disparities. This category includes the local allocation tax and local transferred taxes. The third category—locally based revenues—depends on the political and socioeconomic structure of the city itself, in that its components (local taxes and local bonds) are determined by the characteristics of the locality and the decisions of their administrators, subject to dictums of the centralized hierarchic system.

To see whether the data would support such a grouping of revenue sources and to test this initial set of hypotheses, correlation matrices for eight revenue items were obtained for three different formulations: (*a*) 1970 revenues (in million *yen*), (*b*) percentage change in revenues between 1965–1970, and (*c*) percentage share of the revenue items in total revenue in 1970. By looking at the correlation coefficients, it became clear that formulation *a* had high coefficients, whereas the other two formulations showed no statistically significant relationships. The correlation matrix of *a* is given in Table 7.2.

TABLE 7.2
Correlation Coefficients of the Eight Revenue Items for All Cities, 1970

	LTX	LTT	LAT1	LAT2	TRD	PRD1	PRD2	LB
LTX	1.000	.687	.560	.601	.894	.747	.768	.749
LTT	.687	1.000	.831	.882	.754	.313	.139	.789
LAT1	.560	.831	1.000	.901	.725	.438	.080	.761
LAT2	.601	.882	.901	1.000	.762	.353	.082	.779
TRD	.894	.754	.725	.762	1.000	.667	.521	.870
PRD1	.747	.313	.438	.353	.667	1.000	.744	.450
PRD2	.768	.139	.080	.082	.521	.744	1.000	.247
LB	.749	.789	.761	.779	.870	.450	.247	1.000

Using the linkage method of factor analysis, the following groupings of the revenue items were obtained:

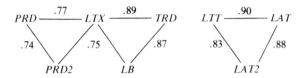

where

LTX = local taxes;
LTT = local transferred taxes;
$LAT1$ = local allocated taxes (ordinary);
$LAT2$ = local allocated taxes (special);
TRD = treasury disbursements;
$PRD1$ = prefectural disbursements (with TRD);
$PRD2$ = prefectural disbursements only;
LB = local bonds.

The figures give the correlation coefficients between the variables. The linkage method verifies our selection of a second group, nonearmarked revenues ($NEMR$). On the other hand, it shows that the local and the earmarked revenues (EMR) vary together to a considerable degree. Prefectural disbursements, despite their division into two items—those accompanying EMR and those allocated by the prefectural alone—show a positive correlation with the direction of variation local taxes.

Another interesting observation is that local bonds vary positively with treasury disbursements. Recall that 65% of local bonds issued by the LGs are purchased by the CG in order to finance public corporations and debt. It appears that local bond purchases by the CG are not used as a substitute for treasury disbursements, but as a complement to it. Concerning the relation of $NEMR$ to other revenue types, it can be seen that $NEMR$ is highly correlated to both treasury disbursements (on average, $r \cong .74$), and to local bonds ($r \cong .77$). Having made these observations, I decided to keep my initial revenue groupings and proceeded to analyze what factors affect the amounts of revenue in each category, using regression analysis.

Even though the R^2s were high, the results of these preliminary regressions gave little insight into the question of how urbanization was financed, owing to the aggregate nature of the analysis. Therefore, I decided to make a more disaggregated analysis. Since the Liberal Democratic Party (LDP) and its conservative power is most significant in rural areas and small towns, whereas more liberal bodies tend to be elected to LGs in larger localities with relatively developed economies, I decided to study revenue structures in two subgroups of cities. One subgroup contains cities that are small and less developed in terms of the secondary sector of the economy; the other contains larger, more developed urban areas.[6]

In working with the set of small cities, the three categories of revenues (local revenues, nonearmarked revenues, and earmarked revenues) were retained because they gave better statistical estimations than more disaggregated categories. However, a more detailed revenue classification was made for the large cities. First, local revenues are divided between local taxes and local bonds, since local taxes are determined by the characteristics of the locality, whereas local bonds are affected primarily by the purchase plans of the CG. Second, earmarked revenues were divided into two components, treasury and prefectural disbursements. It was hoped that this would help in tracing the role of CG in relation to the municipalities more clearly.

4 Empirical Analysis of the Local Government Finance System

4.1 Introduction

A regression analysis of local government finance was undertaken in order to try to explain how local revenues, nonearmarked revenues, and earmarked revenues are determined within the Japanese local public finance system. Section 4.2 examines the behavior of the set of small cities. The large cities are examined in Section 4.3 with a more detailed analysis, first in a descriptive mode and then using regressions.

4.2 Regression Analysis of the Set of Small Cities

The best regression estimates were obtained with three revenue categories, estimated for two time periods, 1960–1965 and 1965–1970. In each time period there are three equations, (a) local revenues (local taxes and local bonds), (b) nonearmarked revenues (local transferred taxes and local allocation taxes), and (c) earmarked revenues (treasury and prefectural

---

[6] There were two criteria for dividing the data set: (a) the mean population of all cities, and (b) overall mean value added (VA) per worker in the manufacturing sector. We observed that the set of cities with populations less than the national average corresponded to cities with VA/worker lower than the national average, and the same relation exists for the set of large and developed cities. The correspondence between the cities divided according to the two criteria was 93.4%. Since the set of large cities thus obtained closely corresponds with the central cities of the Regional Economic Clusters (RECs) outlined in Chapter 2, we delineated 65 cities as "large" according to the two criteria just mentioned; these 65 cities are all included in the 80 RECs. Therefore, to ensure consistency and continuity with the related research, we decided to adopt the central cities of the 80 RECs as the set of "large cities" and the rest as the set of "small cities," and to pursue research on two different sets of data.

disbursements). The dependent variable is expressed in millions of *yen* at the end of the period, and all independent variables that are not expressed in percentage change terms are calculated for the end of the time period.

Table 7.3 lists and describes the variables used in these regressions (these variables are also used in the analysis of large cities in Section 4.3) Table 7.4 presents the results of the best fitting regressions for the two time periods, where each cell contains the sign of the regression coefficient if the respective independent variables were significant at the 95% confidence level.

4.2.1 Local Revenues (*LR*)

Local revenues (*LR*) are positively related to socioeconomic variables showing growth and development; that is, cities with high productivity and greater percentage of employment in manufacturing, a high percentage of population at adult age and college graduates, a high index of infrastructure development, and more population all show higher local revenue levels.[7] The relationships seem quite stable over the two time periods.

4.2.2 Nonearmarked Revenues (*NEMR*)

Low R^2s are found for both periods. Nonearmarked revenues are negatively related to the socioeconomic variables that were positively related to local revenues. In fact, local taxes and nonearmarked revenues are negatively correlated within the set of small cities. Obviously, in the calculation of the standard financial needs and revenues, the CG considers the more populated small cities (i.e., 100,000–175,000 population group) better able to handle their own financial needs. Since many of these cities are NICs (Ministry of Home Affairs, 1969), labor productivity is high, resulting in a less skewed income distribution with high wages, and, thus, a richer local tax base. This reduces their need for *NEMR*.

4.2.3 Earmarked Revenues (*EMR*)

This category gives satisfactory R^2s in both time periods. *EMR* varies directly with *NEMR* in cities that are more populated, having relatively little manufacturing employment, and with low rates of total employment growth;

---

[7] Interestingly, the independent variables *SALES* (wholesale plus retail sales) is negatively related in both periods with high levels of confidence, even though its simple correlation to local revenues is positive (+.66). This paradox can best be understood when the positive correlation between population (*POP*) and wholesale and retail sales (*SALES*) is considered. Since, in the first period, *POP* enters the regression equation with a positive sign, the positive covariance of *SALES* with the dependent variables is taken care of, and only the negative contribution of *SALES* remains. A similar effect comes from the rather strong positive relation of inmigration (*INMGR*) to local revenues in the second period. In both time periods, the R^2s are high, approximately .96.

TABLE 7.3
Description of the Independent Variables Used in Regression Analysis

MFPRD	Value added per worker in the secondary sector.
SALES	Total retail and wholesale sales (millions of *yen*).
INMGR	Ratio of daytime to nighttime population.
DEPR	Ratio of population to employed persons.
ΔPOP	Percentage of change in population.
ADULT	Percentage of population between the ages 15–64.
INFRA	Index of infrastructure and social overhead capital:

$$\sum_n \frac{X_{in}}{X_n} \text{ where } X_i \text{ is a vector of } n \text{ infrastructure variables in city } i:$$

X_{i1} = *Tatami* per household member where one *Tatami* = 1.65 m²
X_{i2} = telephones per 1,000 persons;
X_{i3} = percentage of households with water supply;
X_{i4} = number of books in municipal libraries;
X_{i5} = number of households living in dwelling units; and $\bar{X}_n$ is the mean of nth
variable for the 80 central cities.

LDPV	Percentage of total votes received by LDP candidates.
COLGE	Percentage of population with college degrees.
INC	Average monthly family income.
REMP	Ratio of the employment in mining, fishing, construction, and secondary sectors to employment in tertiary and government sectors.
SPDIST	Dummy variable, assigning value 1 if the city is part of a New Industrial City or other development district and a 0 if the city is not an NIC.
POP	Total nighttime population of the city.
CTYAGE	Age index of cities, where the year 1868 is equal to 1.
ΔTEMP	Percentage of change in the total employment.
ΔSRVE	Percentage of change in tertiary and government sector employment.
ΔSECE	Percentage of change in the secondary sector employment.

it is also higher in regional centers in the less developed regions (Kyushu and Shikoku, for instance), with high population and low industrial growth. Also, a positive relation of *EMR* to local revenues occurs in cities with a high volume of business activity.

4.2.4   Summary of Analysis of Small Cities

Overall, the behavior of the system of small cities does not change significantly over the two time periods, as shown by stable regression equations. In short, local revenues are higher in economically well-established cities with growth potential; *NEMR*, owing to the manner by which it is calculated by the CG, goes to cities with low local revenue bases, independent of population size. Earmarked revenues play an intermediary role between *LR* and *NEMR*, in that they favor poor, highly populated cities with little growth in less developed regions, and also help to stimulate further growth in cities that are relatively well-to-do.

TABLE 7.4
Regression Estimates for the Set of Small Cities, 1960–1965 and 1965–1970

1965–1970			1960–1965			
Earmarked revenues	Non-earmarked revenues	Local revenues	Earmarked revenues	Non-earmarked revenues	Local revenues	
.85	.40	.96	.77	.53	.97	R^2
102.0 sign	12.0 sign	491.0 sign	86.0 sign	25.0 sign	5.98 sign	F-value
+	−			−	+	MFPRD
	+	−		+	−	SALES
+		+	+		+	INMGR
+	+					DEPR
						ΔPOP
	−	+		−		ADULT
					+	INFRA
						LDPV
−				−	+	COLGE
	−	+				INC
−	−		−	−	+	REMP
						SPDIST
			+		+	POP
		−				CTYAGE
			−	−		ΔTEMP
						ΔSRVE
−			+	+		ΔSECE

4.3   The Set of Large Cities: A Descriptive and Regression Analysis of the Geographic Distribution of Local Government Revenues

4.3.1   Introduction

The data for the set of large cities are more interesting because, at this level of urbanization, the agglomeration effects and externalities offered by urban areas are apparent. Such externalities are positive in terms of more vibrant economic development and negative with respect to congestion and pollution. Two levels of analysis are used in this section. The spatial distribution of LG revenues to the large cities and their patterns of change are described first. Second, a statistical association is attempted between the revenues of a LG and factors that summarize its relative status in terms of social, economic, and physical aspects.

4.3.2   Descriptive Analysis of the Financial System in Large Cities

4.3.2.1   Measures for Descriptive Analysis

Five measures are used in the descriptive analysis of the spatial distribution of revenues.

a. *Percentage Distribution of Total Revenues to Cities.* Here, the percentage shares of the cities in national[8] totals are given. The shares are computed over three points in time (1960, 1965, and 1970) for five revenue categories and total revenues of the locality; see Gencer and Glickman (1976, Appendix III, Table I) for detailed data for individual cities.

b. *Per Capita Revenues.* The percentage share of cities in national totals (as in *a*) should be correlated with the size of the urban areas. It is also important to know which areas are being stimulated for growth by the CG or where growth can be locally supported. One measure used to discern these effects is per capita revenues. Later in this section, measures *a* and *b* are used to observe whether larger tax bases also enabled higher per capita revenues (i.e., polarization of tax bases in which richer cities receive revenues at the expense of poorer cities) or if there is an explicit CG intervention toward vertical equity in revenue sharing as commonly hypothesized. Per capita revenues are also calculated over the three time periods and five revenue items plus total revenues; see Gencer and Glickman (1976, Appendix III, Table II) for detailed data.

c. *Percentage Change in Per Capita Revenue.* The percentage change in the five revenue items and total revenues is computed for the time periods 1960–1965 and 1965–1970. The direction and the magnitude of changes

---

[8] By "national" in Section 4, I mean the total for all cities in the data bank.

indicates whether the system of revenue sharing is moving toward vertical equity, growth stimulation through polarization, or some other relationship. Gencer and Glickman (1976, Appendix III, Table II) give detailed data for individual cities.

    d. *Shift Index.* This measure was devised in order to understand changes in the shares of cities in the five revenue items. The index is computed as

$$SI_{i,k} = \frac{R^0_{ik}/R^0_{.k}}{R^1_{ik}/R^1_{.k}} = \frac{\text{(Share of city } i \text{ at time 0)}}{\text{(Share of city } i \text{ at time 1)}}$$

where

    $R^0_{ik}, R^1_{.k}$ = Revenue of type k (in millions of *yen*) in city i, for the beginning and end of the time period, respectively:

$$R^0_{.k} = \sum_{i=1}^{80} R^0_{ik}$$

$$R^1_{.k} = \sum_{i=1}^{80} R^1_{ik}$$

Thus, if

    $SI_{ik} > 1$, city i has decreased its share in revenue k;
    $SI_{ik} \cong 1$, no change in city i's share in revenue k;
    $SI_{ik} < 1$, city i has increased its share in revenue k.

See Gencer and Glickman (1976, Appendix III, Table IV) for calculations of shift indices for individual cities.

    e. *Share Quotients.* The purpose of share quotients is to measure whether municipality i has a relative advantage over others in revenue sharing in terms of a specific revenue type, say, k. In other words, we want to account for the size—that is, population—of the municipality (which affects the magnitude of its revenues), as well as the economic importance of that municipality vis-à-vis the national system, in order to see if the city is being favored in terms of a revenue type by the CG. Two possible formulations for this are

$$\frac{\text{Percentage share of revenue } k \text{ in total revenues of city } i}{\text{Percentage share of revenue } k \text{ in total national revenue}}$$

or

$$\frac{\text{Percentage share of city } i \text{ in national total revenue } k}{\text{Percentage share of city } i \text{ in national total for total revenues}}$$

These formulations are, in fact, two interpretations of the same thing and we define share quotients as

$$SH_{ik} = \frac{R_{ik}/R_{.k}}{R_{i.}/R_{..}}$$

where each dot represents summation over that subscript; see Gencer and Glickman (1976, Appendix III, Table V) for each city's share quotient. Share quotients are used with per capita revenues and percentage share of cities in looking at the geographic distribution, both in terms of regional and metro-politan versus nonmetropolitan cities. Also, percentage changes in revenues and shift indices will help us trace the patterns of change in these distri-butions.

4.3.2.2 Descriptive Analysis of the Spatial Distribution of Revenues of Large Cities

The percentage share of cities in total revenues is mapped in Figure 7.2 for 1970. As one would expect, total revenues are highest in large metropoli-tan centers. One can also observe that the suburban cities in a major metropolitan region or Standard Consolidated Area (the SCA is a region of three or more contiguous RECs, as noted in Chapter 2) have percentage shares far below the mean share of the 80 cities. This contrast between the suburban cities and the central cities in a SCA does not change significantly when we speak of revenues in per capita terms; this is shown in Figures 7.3 and 7.4. With the exception of Tokyo for 1960 and 1970, central cities in all SCAs have higher per capita revenues than suburban cities. When per capita revenues for non-SCA cities are examined vis-à-vis the cities within the SCAs, it is evident that the former have per capita revenues near or below the mean per capita revenue of the SCA cities (with the exception of the four Hokkaido cities in the data bank). These observations suggest that per capita revenue, an important indicator of vertical equity in revenue sharing sys-tems, is higher in the larger metropolitan areas (the SCAs) and in central cities of the RECs.

The distribution in terms of the contrast among the SCAs can also be examined. Table 7.5 contains the percentage shares of the eight SCAs in total revenues. The Tokyo, Osaka, and Nagoya SCAs taken together domi-nate the others in the northwest and southeast parts of Japan with respect to shares of per capita revenues. The Tokyo SCA, however, has different characteristics from the rest of the metropolitan regions in terms of revenue sharing: The central city, the Tokyo *ku* area, has less per capita revenue than its surrounding cities (as shown by Gencer and Glickman, 1976), and the SCA as a whole has a remarkably low per capita revenue when compared to the other SCAs.[9] Since the Tokyo region is relatively older and more de-

---

[9] Note that Table 7.5 gives data for the total share of revenues. If these data are calculated on a per capita basis, Tokyo's share is low.

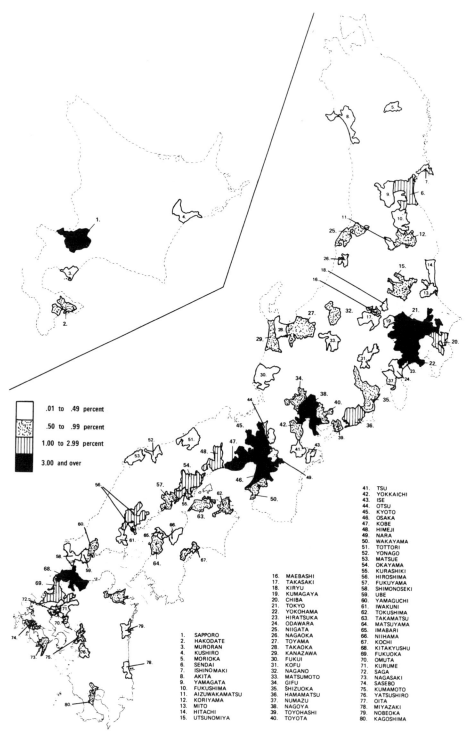

Figure 7.2. Percentage of share of total revenue, 1970.

Legend:

☐	.01 to .49 percent
░	.50 to .99 percent
▥	1.00 to 2.99 percent
■	3.00 and over

1. SAPPORO
2. HAKODATE
3. MURORAN
4. KUSHIRO
5. MORIOKA
6. SENDAI
7. ISHINOMAKI
8. AKITA
9. YAMAGATA
10. FUKUSHIMA
11. AIZUWAKAMATSU
12. KORIYAMA
13. MITO
14. HITACHI
15. UTSUNOMIYA
16. MAEBASHI
17. TAKASAKI
18. KIRYU
19. KUMAGAYA
20. CHIBA
21. TOKYO
22. YOKOHAMA
23. HIRATSUKA
24. ODAWARA
25. NIIGATA
26. NAGAOKA
27. TOYAMA
28. TAKAOKA
29. KANAZAWA
30. FUKUI
31. KOFU
32. NAGANO
33. MATSUMOTO
34. GIFU
35. SHIZUOKA
36. HAMAMATSU
37. NUMAZU
38. NAGOYA
39. TOYOHASHI
40. TOYOTA
41. TSU
42. YOKKAICHI
43. ISE
44. OTSU
45. KYOTO
46. OSAKA
47. KOBE
48. HIMEJI
49. NARA
50. WAKAYAMA
51. TOTTORI
52. YONAGO
53. MATSUE
54. OKAYAMA
55. KURASHIKI
56. HIROSHIMA
57. FUKUYAMA
58. SHIMONOSEKI
59. UBE
60. YAMAGUCHI
61. IWAKUNI
62. TOKUSHIMA
63. TAKAMATSU
64. MATSUYAMA
65. IMABARI
66. NIIHAMA
67. KOCHI
68. KITAKYUSHU
69. FUKUOKA
70. OMUTA
71. KURUME
72. SAGA
73. NAGASAKI
74. SASEBO
75. KUMAMOTO
76. YATSUSHIRO
77. OITA
78. MIYAZAKI
79. NOBEOKA
80. KAGOSHIMA

307

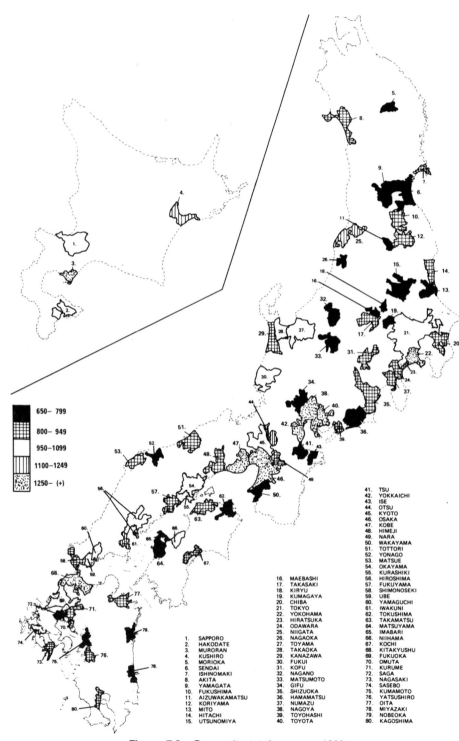

650– 799		
800– 949		
950–1099		
1100–1249		
1250– (+)		

		16.	MAEBASHI	41.	TSU	
		17.	TAKASAKI	42.	YOKKAICHI	
		18.	KIRYU	43.	ISE	
		19.	KUMAGAYA	44.	OTSU	
		20.	CHIBA	45.	KYOTO	
		21.	TOKYO	46.	OSAKA	
		22.	YOKOHAMA	47.	KOBE	
		23.	HIRATSUKA	48.	HIMEJI	
		24.	ODAWARA	49.	NARA	
		25.	NIIGATA	50.	WAKAYAMA	
1.	SAPPORO	26.	NAGAOKA	51.	TOTTORI	
2.	HAKODATE	27.	TOYAMA	52.	YONAGO	
3.	MURORAN	28.	TAKAOKA	53.	MATSUE	
4.	KUSHIRO	29.	KANAZAWA	54.	OKAYAMA	
5.	MORIOKA	30.	FUKUI	55.	KURASHIKI	
6.	SENDAI	31.	KOFU	56.	HIROSHIMA	
7.	ISHINOMAKI	32.	NAGANO	57.	FUKUYAMA	
8.	AKITA	33.	MATSUMOTO	58.	SHIMONOSEKI	
9.	YAMAGATA	34.	GIFU	59.	UBE	
10.	FUKUSHIMA	35.	SHIZUOKA	60.	YAMAGUCHI	
11.	AIZUWAKAMATSU	36.	HAMAMATSU	61.	IWAKUNI	
12.	KORIYAMA	37.	NUMAZU	62.	TOKUSHIMA	
13.	MITO	38.	NAGOYA	63.	TAKAMATSU	
14.	HITACHI	39.	TOYOHASHI	64.	MATSUYAMA	
15.	UTSUNOMIYA	40.	TOYOTA	65.	IMABARI	
				66.	NIIHAMA	
				67.	KOCHI	
				68.	KITAKYUSHU	
				69.	FUKUOKA	
				70.	OMUTA	
				71.	KURUME	
				72.	SAGA	
				73.	NAGASAKI	
				74.	SASEBO	
				75.	KUMAMOTO	
				76.	YATSUSHIRO	
				77.	OITA	
				78.	MIYAZAKI	
				79.	NOBEOKA	
				80.	KAGOSHIMA	

Figure 7.3. Per capita total revenue, 1960.

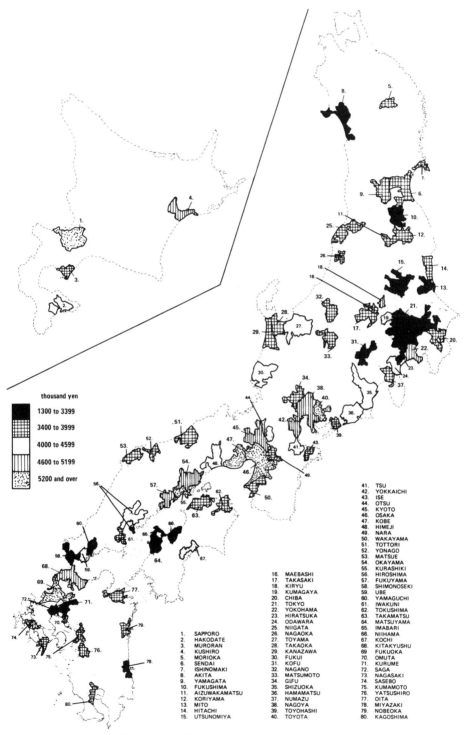

thousand yen

- ■ 1300 to 3399
- ▦ 3400 to 3999
- □ 4000 to 4599
- ▥ 4600 to 5199
- ▨ 5200 and over

1.	SAPPORO	41.	TSU
2.	HAKODATE	42.	YOKKAICHI
3.	MURORAN	43.	ISE
4.	KUSHIRO	44.	OTSU
5.	MORIOKA	45.	KYOTO
6.	SENDAI	46.	OSAKA
7.	ISHINOMAKI	47.	KOBE
8.	AKITA	48.	HIMEJI
9.	YAMAGATA	49.	NARA
10.	FUKUSHIMA	50.	WAKAYAMA
11.	AIZUWAKAMATSU	51.	TOTTORI
12.	KORIYAMA	52.	YONAGO
13.	MITO	53.	MATSUE
14.	HITACHI	54.	OKAYAMA
15.	UTSUNOMIYA	55.	KURASHIKI
16.	MAEBASHI	56.	HIROSHIMA
17.	TAKASAKI	57.	FUKUYAMA
18.	KIRYU	58.	SHIMONOSEKI
19.	KUMAGAYA	59.	UBE
20.	CHIBA	60.	YAMAGUCHI
21.	TOKYO	61.	IWAKUNI
22.	YOKOHAMA	62.	TOKUSHIMA
23.	HIRATSUKA	63.	TAKAMATSU
24.	ODAWARA	64.	MATSUYAMA
25.	NIIGATA	65.	IMABARI
26.	NAGAOKA	66.	NIIHAMA
27.	TOYAMA	67.	KOCHI
28.	TAKAOKA	68.	KITAKYUSHU
29.	KANAZAWA	69.	FUKUOKA
30.	FUKUI	70.	OMUTA
31.	KOFU	71.	KURUME
32.	NAGANO	72.	SAGA
33.	MATSUMOTO	73.	NAGASAKI
34.	GIFU	74.	SASEBO
35.	SHIZUOKA	75.	KUMAMOTO
36.	HAMAMATSU	76.	YATSUSHIRO
37.	NUMAZU	77.	OITA
38.	NAGOYA	78.	MIYAZAKI
39.	TOYOHASHI	79.	NOBEOKA
40.	TOYOTA	80.	KAGOSHIMA

Figure 7.4. Per capita total revenue, 1970.

309

TABLE 7.5
Percentage Share of National Total Revenues for SCAs, 1960–1970

	1960	1965	1970
Sendai	2.32	2.52	2.80
Tokyo	23.28	23.82	23.97
Kanazawa	2.16	1.76	1.79
Nagoya	10.69	8.71	9.39
Osaka	28.04	24.35	26.62
Okayama	1.74	1.50	2.97
Fukuoka	2.34	5.59	7.08
Matsuyama	1.33	1.03	1.10

veloped, the metropolitan decentralization process has set in (like in U.S. metropolitan areas), whereas the other metropolises showed less decentralization (this has been shown in Chapters 2 and 5); political considerations (i.e., socialist LG in Tokyo facing a conservative LDP CG) may be another possible cause for the lower per capita revenues. The difference between the Tokyo SCA and the other SCAs is also observable when the changes in percentage shares are considered in Table 7.5. Although all SCAs have declining shares in the 1965–1970 period, the Tokyo SCA increases its share in both periods.

To get a more comprehensive idea of revenue sharing, the manner by which individual revenue items are distributed was examined. However, the analysis was to be in relative terms. Thus, the share quotient, a measure that expresses the relative advantage of a city in receiving a specific type of revenue, was used.

First, let us look at local taxes. In this category there is great uniformity in the relative ability of cities to raise local taxes, as most of the indices are close to 1.0[10] This is consistent with the expectations because local taxes are regulated by Diet laws and standards. Levying a local tax higher than the national standard rates requires special action from the CG.

Local bonds are considered in Figure 7.5, which maps share quotients for 1965. Two patterns are evident from examining share quotients for local bonds in all three points in time. First, almost all metropolitan cities outside the SCAs have indices of 1.05 or greater. That is, their revenue sharing relies heavily on local bonds purchased by the CG. In fact, the Ministry of Home Affairs allows NICs to issue local bonds at higher than standard levels. Since some of the non-SCA cities in the data set are designated as industrial and growth areas, they issue relatively more bonds. Second, in the highly developed municipalities within the Tokyo, Nagoya, and Fukuoka SCAs, relatively small amounts of local bonds were issued.

---

[10] This is also consistent with my regression analyses of local taxes where the variables relating to the size of the city and its economic activities explain the variations in local taxes at a magnitude of $R^2 = .97$, as noted in Section 4.3.3.

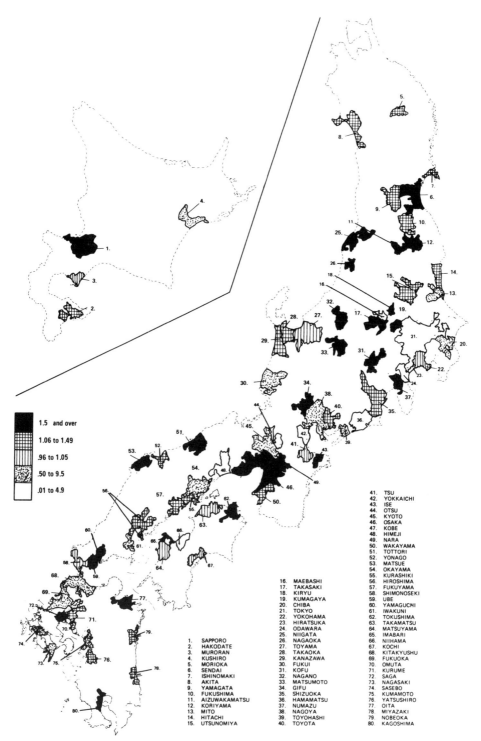

1.5 and over				
1.06 to 1.49				
.96 to 1.05				
.50 to 9.5				
.01 to 4.9				

41.	TSU	
42.	YOKKAICHI	
43.	ISE	
44.	OTSU	
45.	KYOTO	
46.	OSAKA	
47.	KOBE	
48.	HIMEJI	
49.	NARA	
50.	WAKAYAMA	
51.	TOTTORI	
52.	YONAGO	
53.	MATSUE	
54.	OKAYAMA	
55.	KURASHIKI	
56.	HIROSHIMA	
57.	FUKUYAMA	
58.	SHIMONOSEKI	
59.	UBE	
60.	YAMAGUCHI	
61.	IWAKUNI	
62.	TOKUSHIMA	
63.	TAKAMATSU	
64.	MATSUYAMA	
65.	IMABARI	
66.	NIIHAMA	
67.	KOCHI	
68.	KITAKYUSHU	
69.	FUKUOKA	
70.	OMUTA	
71.	KURUME	
72.	SAGA	
73.	NAGASAKI	
74.	SASEBO	
75.	KUMAMOTO	
76.	YATSUSHIRO	
77.	OITA	
78.	MIYAZAKI	
79.	NOBEOKA	
80.	KAGOSHIMA	

16.	MAEBASHI	
17.	TAKASAKI	
18.	KIRYU	
19.	KUMAGAYA	
20.	CHIBA	
21.	TOKYO	
22.	YOKOHAMA	
23.	HIRATSUKA	
24.	ODAWARA	
25.	NIIGATA	
26.	NAGAOKA	
27.	TOYAMA	
28.	TAKAOKA	
29.	KANAZAWA	
30.	FUKUI	
31.	KOFU	
32.	NAGANO	
33.	MATSUMOTO	
34.	GIFU	
35.	SHIZUOKA	
36.	HAMAMATSU	
37.	NUMAZU	
38.	NAGOYA	
39.	TOYOHASHI	
40.	TOYOTA	

1.	SAPPORO	
2.	HAKODATE	
3.	MURORAN	
4.	KUSHIRO	
5.	MORIOKA	
6.	SENDAI	
7.	ISHINOMAKI	
8.	AKITA	
9.	YAMAGATA	
10.	FUKUSHIMA	
11.	AIZUWAKAMATSU	
12.	KORIYAMA	
13.	MITO	
14.	HITACHI	
15.	UTSUNOMIYA	

Figure 7.5. Share quotients for local bonds, 1965.

The third revenue item is treasury disbursements. As discussed in Section 3.1, these disbursements are earmarked by the CG for specific projects. The share quotients for treasury disbursements for 1965 are given in Figure 7.6. The share quotients for treasury disbursements show a changing pattern between 1960 and the years 1965 and 1970. There was a shift from a priority for subsidizing already developed cities in 1960 to one favoring the development of urban areas in less developed regions in 1965–1970. This change in the priority of distributing treasury disbursements is consistent with the change in national policies toward promoting national economic growth through developing the lagging regions. This has been discussed in Chapter 6 and in the Japan Ministry of Home Affairs (1969).

Finally, let us examine the share pattern for the *NEMR* in Figure 7.7. The distribution of *NEMR* revenues is relatively simple to interpret if we recall that a city's local allocation tax (the largest component of *NEMR*) is computed by the CG as the difference between the former's standard financial needs and standard revenues. In general, three elements seem to affect the priority given to a city in receiving *NEMR* revenues: first, the national and/or regional growth policies for urban areas (which roughly determine the magnitude of necessary expenditures); second, the ability of the locality to issue local bonds; and third, the proportion local needs met by treasury allocations. In other words, in cities designated for growth and development by national policies (even though such areas have priority in receiving treasury disbursements and in issuing local bonds), *NEMR* share quotients are higher than the average. Cases in point are cities in the Kyushu and the Hokkaido regions. In such areas *NEMR* should have high positive correlations with both local bonds and treasury disbursements. A positive correlation between treasury disbursements and *NEM* revenues also can be observed in well-developed urban areas, such as the metropolitan regions of Tokyo, Nagoya, and Osaka, where both revenue types have low scores. These were fast-growing areas both in terms of population and economic activities during the 1960s (see Chapter 2) and they had less priority for treasury disbursements and less need for *NEMR*. In Fukuoka and the Tohoku region in general, however, a negative relation holds between these two types of revenues. Although these areas had low priority for treasury disbursements, they received higher *NEMR* to meet their financial needs because they were slow-growing and often targeted by regional planners as we have seen in Chapter 6.

4.3.2.3   Changes in the Spatial Patterns of Revenue
          Sharing

This section describes general changes in revenue sharing and then offers some detail, particularly observing these changes in spatial terms. I first compare percentage changes in per capita total revenues and then percentage changes in total revenues (see Figures 7.8 and 7.9). In general, there is a

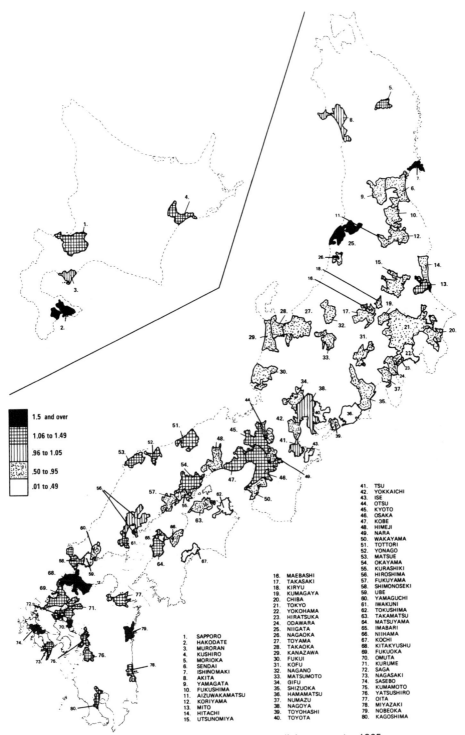

Figure 7.6. Share quotient for treasury disbursements, 1965.

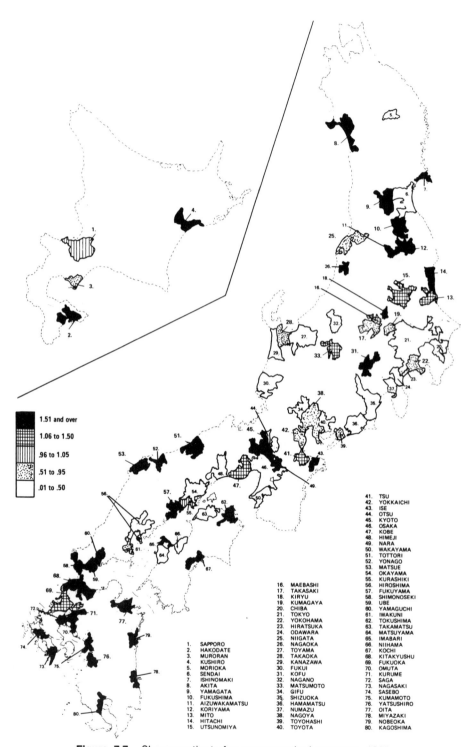

1.51 and over				
1.06 to 1.50				
.96 to 1.05				
.51 to .95				
.01 to .50				

16.	MAEBASHI	41.	TSU
17.	TAKASAKI	42.	YOKKAICHI
18.	KIRYU	43.	ISE
19.	KUMAGAYA	44.	OTSU
20.	CHIBA	45.	KYOTO
21.	TOKYO	46.	OSAKA
22.	YOKOHAMA	47.	KOBE
23.	HIRATSUKA	48.	HIMEJI
24.	ODAWARA	49.	NARA
25.	NIIGATA	50.	WAKAYAMA
26.	NAGAOKA	51.	TOTTORI
27.	TOYAMA	52.	YONAGO
28.	TAKAOKA	53.	MATSUE
29.	KANAZAWA	54.	OKAYAMA
30.	FUKUI	55.	KURASHIKI
1.	SAPPORO	31.	KOFU	56.	HIROSHIMA
2.	HAKODATE	32.	NAGANO	57.	FUKUYAMA
3.	MURORAN	33.	MATSUMOTO	58.	SHIMONOSEKI
4.	KUSHIRO	34.	GIFU	59.	UBE
5.	MORIOKA	35.	SHIZUOKA	60.	YAMAGUCHI
6.	SENDAI	36.	HAMAMATSU	61.	IWAKUNI
7.	ISHINOMAKI	37.	NUMAZU	62.	TOKUSHIMA
8.	AKITA	38.	NAGOYA	63.	TAKAMATSU
9.	YAMAGATA	39.	TOYOHASHI	64.	MATSUYAMA
10.	FUKUSHIMA	40.	TOYOTA	65.	IMABARI
11.	AIZUWAKAMATSU			66.	NIIHAMA
12.	KORIYAMA			67.	KOCHI
13.	MITO			68.	KITAKYUSHU
14.	HITACHI			69.	FUKUOKA
15.	UTSUNOMIYA			70.	OMUTA
				71.	KURUME
				72.	SAGA
				73.	NAGASAKI
				74.	SASEBO
				75.	KUMAMOTO
				76.	YATSUSHIRO
				77.	OITA
				78.	MIYAZAKI
				79.	NOBEOKA
				80.	KAGOSHIMA

Figure 7.7. Share quotients for nonearmarked revenues, 1965.

314

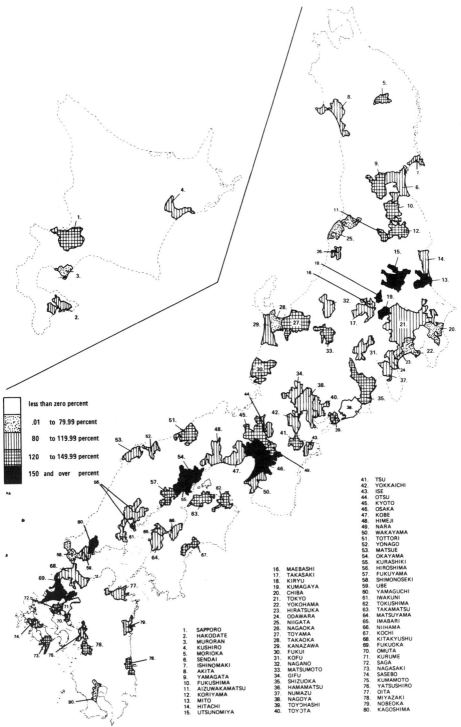

Figure 7.8. Percentage change in per capita total revenues, 1965–1970.

less than zero percent

.01 to 79.99 percent

80 to 119.99 percent

120 to 149.99 percent

150 and over percent

1. SAPPORO
2. HAKODATE
3. MURORAN
4. KUSHIRO
5. MORIOKA
6. SENDAI
7. ISHINOMAKI
8. AKITA
9. YAMAGATA
10. FUKUSHIMA
11. AIZUWAKAMATSU
12. KORIYAMA
13. MITO
14. HITACHI
15. UTSUNOMIYA
16. MAEBASHI
17. TAKASAKI
18. KIRYU
19. KUMAGAYA
20. CHIBA
21. TOKYO
22. YOKOHAMA
23. HIRATSUKA
24. ODAWARA
25. NIIGATA
26. NAGAOKA
27. TOYAMA
28. TAKAOKA
29. KANAZAWA
30. FUKUI
31. KOFU
32. NAGANO
33. MATSUMOTO
34. GIFU
35. SHIZUOKA
36. HAMAMATSU
37. NUMAZU
38. NAGOYA
39. TOYOHASHI
40. TOYOTA
41. TSU
42. YOKKAICHI
43. ISE
44. OTSU
45. KYOTO
46. OSAKA
47. KOBE
48. HIMEJI
49. NARA
50. WAKAYAMA
51. TOTTORI
52. YONAGO
53. MATSUE
54. OKAYAMA
55. KURASHIKI
56. HIROSHIMA
57. FUKUYAMA
58. SHIMONOSEKI
59. UBE
60. YAMAGUCHI
61. IWAKUNI
62. YOKUSHIMA
63. TAKAMATSU
64. MATSUYAMA
65. IMABARI
66. NIIHAMA
67. KOCHI
68. KITAKYUSHU
69. FUKUOKA
70. OMUTA
71. KURUME
72. SAGA
73. NAGASAKI
74. SASEBO
75. KUMAMOTO
76. YATSUSHIRO
77. OITA
78. MIYAZAKI
79. NOBEOKA
80. KAGOSHIMA

315

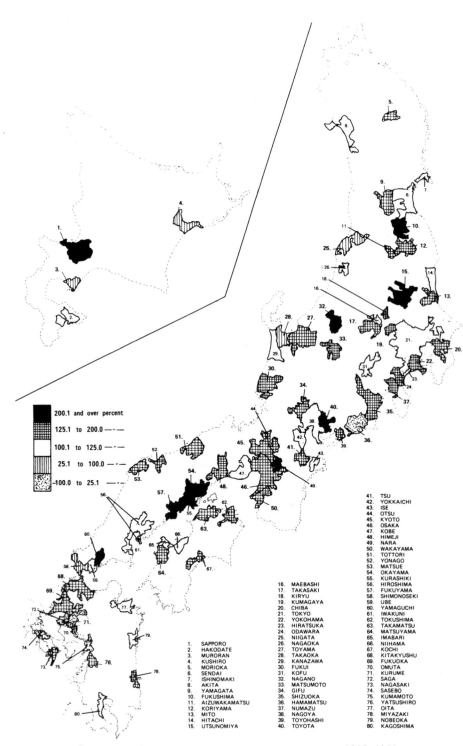

41.	TSU
42.	YOKKAICHI
43.	ISE
44.	OTSU
45.	KYOTO
46.	OSAKA
47.	KOBE
48.	HIMEJI
49.	NARA
50.	WAKAYAMA
51.	TOTTORI
52.	YONAGO
53.	MATSUE
54.	OKAYAMA
55.	KURASHIKI
56.	HIROSHIMA
57.	FUKUYAMA
58.	SHIMONOSEKI
59.	UBE
60.	YAMAGUCHI
61.	IWAKUNI
62.	TOKUSHIMA
63.	TAKAMATSU
64.	MATSUYAMA
65.	NIIHAMA
66.	IMABARI
67.	KOCHI
68.	KITAKYUSHU
69.	FUKUOKA
70.	OMUTA
71.	KURUME
72.	SAGA
73.	NAGASAKI
74.	SASEBO
75.	KUMAMOTO
76.	YATSUSHIRO
77.	OITA
78.	MIYAZAKI
79.	NOBEOKA
80.	KAGOSHIMA

16.	MAEBASHI
17.	TAKASAKI
18.	KIRYU
19.	KUMAGAYA
20.	CHIBA
21.	TOKYO
22.	YOKOHAMA
23.	HIRATSUKA
24.	ODAWARA
25.	NIIGATA
26.	NAGAOKA
27.	TOYAMA
28.	TAKAOKA
29.	KANAZAWA
30.	FUKUI
31.	KOFU
32.	NAGANO
33.	MATSUMOTO
34.	GIFU
35.	SHIZUOKA
36.	HAMAMATSU
37.	NUMAZU
38.	NAGOYA
39.	TOYOHASHI
40.	TOYOTA

1.	SAPPORO
2.	HAKODATE
3.	MURORAN
4.	KUSHIRO
5.	MORIOKA
6.	SENDAI
7.	ISHINOMAKI
8.	AKITA
9.	YAMAGATA
10.	FUKUSHIMA
11.	AIZUWAKAMATSU
12.	KORIYAMA
13.	MITO
14.	HITACHI
15.	UTSUNOMIYA

Legend:

- ■ 200.1 and over percent
- ▦ 125.1 to 200.0 —"—
- ☐ 100.1 to 125.0 —"—
- ▥ 25.1 to 100.0 —"—
- ▒ -100.0 to 25.1 —"—

Figure 7.9. Percentage of change in total revenues, 1965–1970.

316

high correlation between the two measures of total revenue changes. The corollary to this observation, then, is that there is a positive correlation between changes in population and changes in revenues. In fact, population becomes one of the major independent variables in forecasting the revenues in the regression analysis reported in Section 4.3.3.

I also offer several observations about percentage changes of both per capita revenues and absolute revenues. Increases in both absolute and per capita revenues were substantial, averaging about 100–150% for the 1960–1965 and 1965–1970 time periods.[11] This reflects the growth of the Japanese economy (as noted in Chapter 1) and the fact that expenditures (both in absolute and per capita terms) were increasing in urban areas. This can be attributed to somewhat more emphasis on social welfare and to coping with problems arising from congestion and high-density development in urban areas. As the GNP per person rose, public spending could be afforded more easily.

In the first period, changes in local bonds were highly skewed: there were increases of more than 500% for 23 of the 80 cities, whereas 9 cities declined. A similar picture, although with smaller magnitudes, held for treasury disbursements. Also, during the first period, total local bonds and total treasury disbursements were higher than those in the latter period. These changes can be interpreted as responses to smaller increases in the local taxes in the first period. First, the larger amounts of local bonds and treasury disbursements were allocated by the CG to compensate for the lower than expected levels of locally raised revenues and nonearmarked revenues. This is discussed in the following paragraph. Second, the rather uneven distribution observed for local bonds and treasury disbursements in the first period can be explained as increasing the revenue levels of those cities involved in special development programs, such as those noted in Chapter 6.

Regarding *NEMR*, the 1960–1965 period witnessed a general fall in the amount of per capita *NEMR* distributed. The conservative policies of the Ministry of Finance in setting tax policy led to a relatively small volume of national taxes collected; this, in turn, decreased the *NEMR* allocated. Again, in the first period, the distribution was highly skewed. The cutbacks fell upon suburban cities of the SCAs and fast-growing non-SCA cities of Honshu. Great increases, on the other hand, were seen in the SCAs' central cities and in regions designated for development.

The second period (1965–1970) showed a less skewed distribution. Actually, one can compare 1960 and 1970 total revenue shares and observe the striking correspondence between them, whereas the 1965 shares were

---

[11] During the first period, local taxes increased more in SCAs than in the non-SCA cities, reflecting greater SCA economic growth. In the second period, both non-SCA cities and SCAs had large increases. The total local tax increase in the first period was much smaller than that in the period of 1965 to 1970.

different. However, one cannot establish whether the 1960 distribution was more equitable than that of 1965. Descriptively, the polarization observed in percentage change during the period 1960–1965 did not continue into the second period. Local taxes showed uniform increases for all cities, and the total increases were higher than the first period. Local bonds, however, showed a decline in the rate of increase in the second period: 9 cities show negative changes. Treasury disbursements also displayed a smaller increase, and the peaks and troughs of the early period were smoothed out. *NEMR*, on the other hand, more than doubled for 65 of the 80 cities.

Next, we observe the shift indices in order to trace the patterns of change. The shift indices confirm the interpretations made previously (see Figures 7.10 and 7.11 for the maps of shift indices for the two time periods). Given the percentage change trends as described in the preceding paragraphs, we can look at the shifts in shares of cities in the national total. The 1960–1965 shift scores for local taxes for many cities are quite low. The areas that did badly were non-SCA cities in less developed regions and the metropolitan centers (except for Tokyo and Sendai).

To offset these declines, two mechanisms were employed by the CG: local bond purchasing and treasury disbursements. The shift analysis (see Gencer and Glickman, 1976, Appendix IV, Table IV) indicates large increases in local bonds and treasury disbursements for certain urban areas with heavy losses for others. First, there was the redistribution from urban areas in the SCAs and old urban areas on Honshu to non-SCA cities in developing regions. Second, there was a shift from suburban to central cities within the SCAs. The reasons are (*a*) SCA metropolitan centers (and some non-SCA cities) had low levels of local tax revenues and (*b*) cities in designated development areas were consciously being subsidized by the CG. In both cases, local taxes fell short of expected expenditures. Even though *NEM* revenues were limited, their distribution followed a similar pattern to that of local bonds and treasury disbursements. That is, the reductions occurred in urban areas on Honshu, whereas the increases were observed in SCA metropolitan centers as well as the Kyushu and Hokkaido regions.

Despite the efforts by the CG to offset the relative decrease in local taxes in older and well-developed urban areas, metropolitan regions (SCAs) lost some of their share to non-SCA cities, especially to those in Kyushu and Hokkaido. Between 1965 and 1970, however, we see a reversal of the situation. Local taxes and *NEMR* increased at the national level as the Japanese economy grew more rapidly. As these revenues increased, fewer local bonds were purchased; this is particularly true in the Kyushu and Chugoku regions, where cities were more likely to be financed through treasury disbursements and prefectural disbursements. Those areas that were supported by local bonds were the SCAs, so that they could reattain their 1960 levels in their share of the national revenues.

Overall, the second period is governed by two tendencies. First, re-

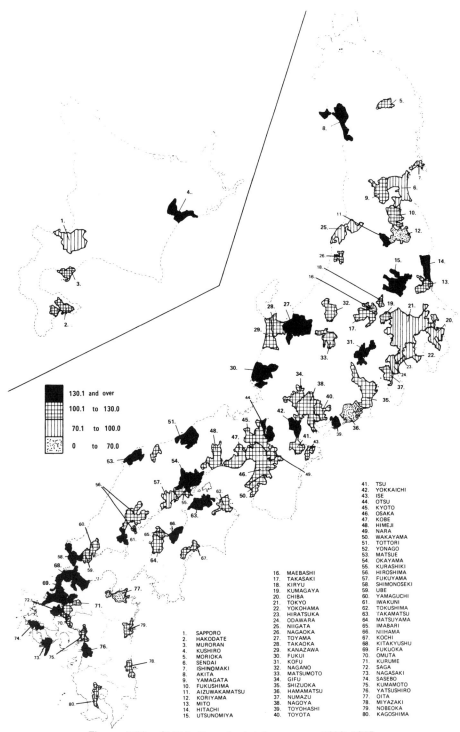

Figure 7.10. Shift indices for total revenues, 1960–1965.

130.1 and over
100.1 to 130.0
70.1 to 100.0
0 to 70.0

1.	SAPPORO
2.	HAKODATE
3.	MURORAN
4.	KUSHIRO
5.	MORIOKA
6.	SENDAI
7.	ISHINOMAKI
8.	AKITA
9.	YAMAGATA
10.	FUKUSHIMA
11.	AIZUWAKAMATSU
12.	KORIYAMA
13.	MITO
14.	HITACHI
15.	UTSUNOMIYA

16.	MAEBASHI
17.	TAKASAKI
18.	KIRYU
19.	KUMAGAYA
20.	CHIBA
21.	TOKYO
22.	YOKOHAMA
23.	HIRATSUKA
24.	ODAWARA
25.	NIIGATA
26.	NAGAOKA
27.	TOYAMA
28.	TAKAOKA
29.	KANAZAWA
30.	FUKUI
31.	KOFU
32.	NAGANO
33.	MATSUMOTO
34.	GIFU
35.	SHIZUOKA
36.	HAMAMATSU
37.	NUMAZU
38.	NAGOYA
39.	TOYOHASHI
40.	TOYOTA

41.	TSU
42.	YOKKAICHI
43.	ISE
44.	OTSU
45.	KYOTO
46.	OSAKA
47.	KOBE
48.	HIMEJI
49.	NARA
50.	WAKAYAMA
51.	TOTTORI
52.	YONAGO
53.	MATSUE
54.	OKAYAMA
55.	KURASHIKI
56.	HIROSHIMA
57.	FUKUYAMA
58.	SHIMONOSEKI
59.	UBE
60.	YAMAGUCHI
61.	IWAKUNI
62.	TOKUSHIMA
63.	TAKAMATSU
64.	MATSUYAMA
65.	IMABARI
66.	NIIHAMA
67.	KOCHI
68.	KITAKYUSHU
69.	FUKUOKA
70.	OMUTA
71.	KURUME
72.	SAGA
73.	NAGASAKI
74.	SASEBO
75.	KUMAMOTO
76.	YATSUSHIRO
77.	OITA
78.	MIYAZAKI
79.	NOBEOKA
80.	KAGOSHIMA

319

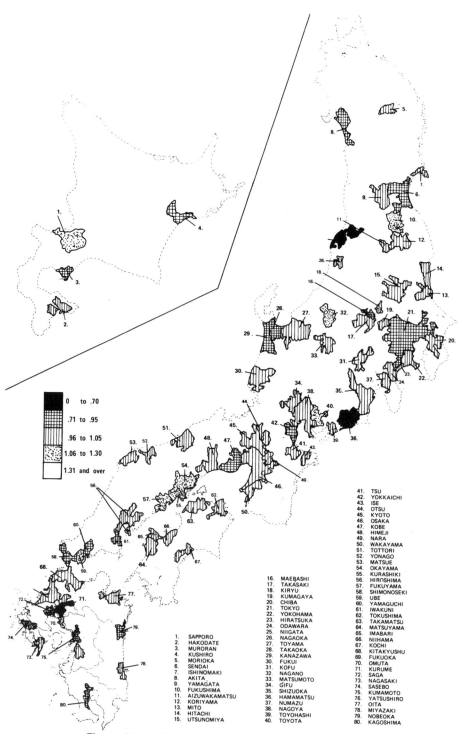

0 to .70	
.71 to .95	
.96 to 1.05	
1.06 to 1.30	
1.31 and over	

16.	MAEBASHI
17.	TAKASAKI
18.	KIRYU
19.	KUMAGAYA
20.	CHIBA
21.	TOKYO
22.	YOKOHAMA
23.	HIRATSUKA
24.	ODAWARA
25.	NIIGATA
26.	NAGAOKA
27.	TOYAMA
28.	TAKAOKA
29.	KANAZAWA
30.	FUKUI
31.	KOFU
32.	NAGANO
33.	MATSUMOTO
34.	GIFU
35.	SHIZUOKA
36.	HAMAMATSU
37.	NUMAZU
38.	NAGOYA
39.	TOYOHASHI
40.	TOYOTA

1.	SAPPORO
2.	HAKODATE
3.	MURORAN
4.	KUSHIRO
5.	MORIOKA
6.	SENDAI
7.	ISHINOMAKI
8.	AKITA
9.	YAMAGATA
10.	FUKUSHIMA
11.	AIZUWAKAMATSU
12.	KORIYAMA
13.	MITO
14.	HITACHI
15.	UTSUNOMIYA

41.	TSU
42.	YOKKAICHI
43.	ISE
44.	OTSU
45.	KYOTO
46.	OSAKA
47.	KOBE
48.	HIMEJI
49.	NARA
50.	WAKAYAMA
51.	TOTTORI
52.	YONAGO
53.	MATSUE
54.	OKAYAMA
55.	KURASHIKI
56.	HIROSHIMA
57.	FUKUYAMA
58.	SHIMONOSEKI
59.	UBE
60.	YAMAGUCHI
61.	IWAKUNI
62.	TOKUSHIMA
63.	TAKAMATSU
64.	MATSUYAMA
65.	IMABARI
66.	NIIHAMA
67.	KOCHI
68.	KITAKYUSHU
69.	FUKUOKA
70.	OMUTA
71.	KURUME
72.	SAGA
73.	NAGASAKI
74.	SASEBO
75.	KUMAMOTO
76.	YATSUSHIRO
77.	OITA
78.	MIYAZAKI
79.	NOBEOKA
80.	KAGOSHIMA

Figure 7.11. Shift indices for total revenues, 1965–1970.

gional development, particularly for Kyushu and Hokkaido regions, and second, increasing SCA cities to their 1960 shares. Both these tendencies were helped by the increase in local taxes and an enormous increment in *NEMR* coupled with a steady and uniform increase in treasury disbursements.

4.3.3   Multilinear Regression Analysis of the Large Cities

4.3.3.1   Introduction

This section summarizes the multilinear regression analysis undertaken to further the understanding of the spatial distribution of revenues and changes in this distribution over time, in an attempt to associate local revenues with social, economic, and poltical aspects of urban areas. There are five regression equations, each corresponding to one of the five revenue types.[12] The dependent variables are the revenue categories and the independent variables are the same as used in the previous regressions (see Table 7.3 for variable definitions).[13] In the regressions, summarized in Sections 4.3.3.2–4.3.3.6, each independent variable and the R^2 is significant at a 95% confidence level.

4.3.3.2   Local Bonds (*LB*)

The regression equations for local bonds in the two time periods are:

$$
\begin{aligned}
LB\ (1965) = {}& -371.700 + .05 SALES + 146.50 INFRA \\
& - 1{,}028.30 LDPV + 248.50 SPDIST \\
& + 5.34 CTYAGE \qquad R^2 = .80
\end{aligned}
\tag{1}
$$

$$
\begin{aligned}
LB\ (1970) = {}& -3{,}086.10 + .12 SALES + 346.90 INFRA \\
& - 1{,}798.10 LPDV + 1{,}022.20 SPDIST + 2{,}313.80\ \Delta TEMP \\
& \qquad R^2 = .93
\end{aligned}
\tag{2}
$$

Clearly, the equations do not change significantly between periods. Two points can be made about Eqs. (1) and (2). First, in both periods, the variables in Group I of Appendix 2 (*SALES, INFRA,* and *LDPV*) account for most of the explained variance with expected signs. This suggests that revenues from local bonds are higher in big metropolitan centers. Also, the remaining variance in the dependent variables is explained by variables

[12] To repeat, these are local bonds, local taxes, treasury disbursements, nonearmarked revenues, and prefectural disbursements.

[13] Appendix 2 examines the interrelationships among the independent variables. This was necessitated by the high multicollinearities observed among the variables. Keeping in mind the interrelationships among the independent variables that are explained in Appendix 2 will be helpful in analyzing the results of the regressions in the following discussion. In Appendix 2 I show certain groups of interrelated variables that I refer to in the text in Sections 4.3.3.2 to 4.3.3.6.

relating to designated growth areas. *SPDST* is a dummy variable showing either a NIC or SA. Note the large change in the coefficient attached to *SPDIST*, from 248.5 to 1,022.2, indicating the increasing importance of the government's regional development programs in the late 1960s. The positive sign on *CTYAGE* (which shows how recently the city was constituted) also conforms with this assertion. In the second period, the positive sign on $\Delta TEMP$ also indicates that a portion of local bonds go to cities that were growing quickly in the 1965–1970 period. These two inferences are consistent with the descriptive analysis of Section 4.3.2 where it was observed that the revenues from local bonds were relatively higher in the non-SCA cities of Kyushu, Hokkaido, and Chigoku major regions, in fast-growing metropolitan centers in 1965, and in all metropolitan centers in 1970.

4.3.3.3   Local Taxes (*LTX*)

The regression equations for local taxes are as follows:

$$
\begin{aligned}
LTX\ (1965) = {} & 14{,}519.00 + .20SALES + 880.80INFRA \\
& - 19{,}429.00ADULT + 39{,}556.00COLGE \\
& - 9.10INMGR + 7{,}866.00REMP \\
& + 79.90MFPRD \qquad R^2 = .98
\end{aligned}
\tag{3}
$$

$$
\begin{aligned}
LTX\ (1970) = {} & 33{,}415.00 + .07SALES + 358.30INFRA \\
& - 48{,}909.00ADULT - 2{,}624.00DEPR \\
& + 2.20INMGR + 1{,}498.00REMP \\
& + 96.10MFPRD \qquad R^2 = .99
\end{aligned}
\tag{4}
$$

The basic change between the two years is the change of sign and explanatory power of *INMGR*. But this is expected because we have seen that *INMGR* enters into Group I of the independent variables, those variables relating to general economic activity. As with the local bonds equations, the major part of the explanation is given by Group I variables (*SALES, INFRA,* and *INMGR* in 1970). This is so since larger metropolitan areas (with high population and labor force levels, large local markets, and well-developed public facilities) were able to levy a multiplicity of local taxes and increase their tax revenues. It is also interesting to see the positive relationship of Group IV variables (*REMP* in 1965 and *MFPRD*) to *LTX*. This suggests that cities with heavy concentrations of secondary industrial production with high value added per worker raise more local taxes. It has been suggested that such cities are small, with flat income distributions (owing to the occupation structures of such cities, i.e., heavy concentration in blue-collar jobs), so that the income-related tax revenues are high. The negative sign with *ADULT*, which seems contradictory at first glance, can be explained by the fact that smaller cities that are slow-growing tended to have older work forces. Such economically stagnant areas also were less capable of raising local taxes; these cities are found in underdeveloped regions of Japan. The positive sign on *COLGE* is expected, and the minus sign on *DEPR* indicates that the higher the dependency rate of population of the employed labor force, the less revenue from local taxes. This, too, is plausible on a priori grounds.

4.3.3.4 Treasury Disbursements (*TRD*)

We have estimated the following equations.

$$
\begin{aligned}
TRD\ (1965) = &- 9{,}999.00 + .09SALES + .33POP \\
&+ 5{,}054.00DEPR + 28{,}967.00ADULT \\
&- 37{,}610.00\ COLGE - 53.40MFPRD \qquad R^2 = .83 \quad (5) \\
TRD\ (1970) = &- 2{,}509.00 + .19SALES + 632.20INFRA \\
&- 3{,}286.00LDPV + 2{,}715.00DEPR - 8.00INC \\
&+ 633.90SPDIST + 2{,}569.00\Delta TEMP \qquad R^2 = .96 \quad (6)
\end{aligned}
$$

Here, the Group I variables (i.e., *SALES, POP, LDPV, INFRA*) explain most of the variation in 1970, whereas their contribution in 1965 is less important. In the 1965 period, treasury disbursements vary positively with Group I and negatively with Group II variables. The first group indicates that *TRD* was higher in cities with high population and volume of market transactions; the second component suggests lower *TRD* allocations in urban areas where the population was highly educated and where there was a high ratio of value added to employment in the secondary sector. The latter two inverse relations suggest that growing, high-production urban areas and big metropolitan centers received less *TRD*. These interpretations are consistent with the analysis of the previous section where we found that in the first period metropolitan areas and non-SCA cities of lesser developed regions on the one hand, and Northern Honshu metropolitan areas on the other, had priority in receiving *TRD*. This is also consistent with governmental policy, which did, in general, seek to stimulate such regions, as noted in Chapter 6.

In 1970, Group I variables dominate and the R^2 of the regression increases as well. However, the negative relation to *INC* and positive relation to *SPDIST* and $\Delta TEMP$ are consistent with the continuing national policy of stimulating and sustaining growth in lesser developed regions of Japan. Thus, cities with lower average incomes received more treasury disbursements. We reinforce this conclusion in Section 5.2.

4.3.3.5 Nonearmarked Revenues (*NEMR*)

This set of regressions yielded quite different regression equations from those of the three preceding revenue types.

$$
\begin{aligned}
NEMR\ (1965) = &- 1{,}808.00 - .04SALES + .21POP \\
&+ 992.00DEPR - 6{,}588.00COLGE \\
&+ 3.10CTYAGE - 24.70MFPRD \qquad R^2 = .74 \quad (7)
\end{aligned}
$$

$$
\begin{aligned}
NEMR\ (1970) = {} & - 5{,}224.00 - .04 SALES + .33 POP \\
& + 506.00 INFRA + 3{,}146.00 DEPR \\
& + 15{,}963.00 COLGE - 5.31 INC \\
& - 2{,}450.00 REMP + 2{,}759.00 \Delta SECE \qquad R^2 = .95
\end{aligned}
$$

$$(8)$$

First, observe the inconsistency between the signs of *SALES* and *POP* (and *INFRA* in 1970) and those of *REMP* and *ΔSECE* in 1970. In both cases, one would expect the signs to be the same because the simple correlation coefficients (with regard to *NEMR*) in each group are positive and greater than .75. However, it must be remembered that *NEMR* is calculated as a residual of the estimated financial needs after the estimates of local taxes are subtracted. Also, the financial need of a LG is very sensitive to national or local public projects that the LG must participate in financially. Therefore, in cities located in designated development regions, the tax base could be high, a large amount of *TRD* could be received and *LB* floated, but still a substantial residual could remain due to national growth policies and their consequent financial resource demands.

Nonearmarked revenues increase their correlation with *LB* and *LTX* from first period to the second; therefore, it can be better explained by the attributes of the urban areas. This is reflected in the higher R^2 of the latter time period.

4.3.3.6 Prefectural Disbursements (*PRD*)

We have the following regression equations.

$$
\begin{aligned}
PRD\ (1965) = {} & - 161.00 + .01 SALES + 33.10 INFRA \\
& + 194.80 REMP \qquad R^2 = .88
\end{aligned}
$$

$$(9)$$

$$
\begin{aligned}
PRD\ (1970) = {} & - 2{,}547.00 + .38 POP - 110.90 INFRA \\
& - .18 INMGR + 4{,}689.00 ADULT \\
& - 5{,}401.00 COLGE + .97 INC \\
& - 611.70 \Delta TEMP \qquad R^2 = .87
\end{aligned}
$$

$$(10)$$

The equation for 1965 is dominated by *INFRA* and *SALES; REMP* is also positively related, although not as strongly. In this period, there was a relatively small amount of *PRD* to be distributed, and most RECs received very little from this source; however, cities in the metropolitan regions of Tokyo, Kanazawa, Osaka, and Nagoya were exceptions, that is, they received substantial amounts of *PRD*. Thus, we have the dominance of *SALES* and *INFRA*. The distribution of *PRD* changed significantly by 1970. There was a much more uniform distribution with a larger amount of total *PRD* to be allocated. However, population size was still a significant determinant in the amount of *PRD* as far as the cities in the developed regions are concerned. In the other regions (Kyushu, Hokkaido, Shikoku, and Tohoku), population is an important determining factor, but also cities where prefectural governments and the initiated public projects had greater shares of *PRD*. Thus, the negative signs on *INFRA, INMGR,* and *COLGE* and the positive sign of *POP* and *INC* can be attributed to the continuing *PRD* flow into metropolitan areas in the Tokaido region where both population and average family income are higher.

5   Further Evidence concerning the Role of Intergovernmental Relations in Reducing Interregional Income Inequality

5.1   Introduction

Section 4 presented analyses for data sets of large and small cities from the city data bank, and indicated that redistribution of government revenues from rich to poor cities was being carried out during the 1960s. This section presents further evidence of this phenomenon, employing more aggregative data on a prefectural basis for 1970.

5.2   Redistribution as Indicated by Prefectural Data

Data from the Japan Bureau of Statistics, Office of the Prime Minister (1973) for 1970 confirm the evaluation of the redistribution mechanisms outlined in Section 4. First, in order to see the extent that prefectural governments (hereafter, PGs) with below average incomes receive more (or possibly less) revenue from the CG, I calculated the variable *PTS*, the percentage of a *PG's* total revenues accounted for by CG treasury disbursements. This variable should show how these percentages vary across the 46 prefectures.[14] Table 7.6, shows that *PTS* accounts for only 12.8% of Tokyo's total revenue in 1970, the lowest percentage of all prefectures. The highest percentage was in Kagoshima, 38.3%.

How does *PTS* vary with the index of prefectural personal income (*Y*), which is also given in Table 7.6? A regression relating the two variables was computed that yielded the following results:

$$PTS = 61.01179 - .35039Y \quad R^2 = .744 \quad F = 128.046 \quad (11)$$
$$(11.31575)$$

The figure in parentheses below the regression coefficient is the *t*-statistic, which is significant at a 95% confidence interval, and the *F* is the *F*-statistic, that measures the goodness-of-fit of the regression. It is significant at a 1% confidence interval. Equation (11) shows that for every unit increase in income there will be a .35 unit decrease in the proportion of total revenues of a PG received from the central government. This is also seen in Figure 7.12

---

[14] Okinawa was not included.

TABLE 7.6
Intergovernmental Transfers as Seen from Prefectural Data, 1970

	Treasury and prefectural disbursements as a percentage of cities' total revenue (CTPS)	Treasury disbursements as a percentage of prefectures' total revenues (PTS)	Treasury and prefectural disbursements as a percentage of cities' total revenues (DEP)	Index of per capita personal income (Japan = 100.0) (Y)
Hokkaido	22.9	36.9	79.3	94.8
Aomori	23.3	35.2	86.8	77.7
Iwate	21.7	32.8	80.1	76.7
Miyagi	16.8	28.3	41.1	86.7
Akita	17.8	33.3	54.2	79.6
Yamagata	15.4	34.7	46.3	83.5
Fukushima	17.0	31.8	58.5	79.8
Ibaraki	13.8	25.2	35.4	83.5
Tochigi	14.6	25.1	36.3	88.1
Gumma	14.4	26.2	39.9	91.6
Saitama	9.9	21.9	27.0	108.5
Chiba	12.2	26.4	28.7	102.9
Tokyo	17.5	12.8	17.5	142.7
Kanagawa	12.5	15.5	25.7	120.0
Niigata	16.9	37.6	36.3	84.6
Toyama	16.6	32.0	40.2	91.9
Ishikawa	18.6	26.6	47.6	95.2
Fukui	15.2	29.5	39.4	88.9
Yamanashi	18.5	29.4	59.9	86.7
Nagano	15.4	31.5	44.3	85.4
Gifu	13.9	27.0	37.3	94.0
Shizuoka	12.6	25.7	28.2	98.5
Aichi	13.1	17.8	27.9	112.7

where the two variables and the regression line are plotted. Figure 7.12 shows the strong negative correlation between *PTS* and *Y*. Therefore, there is clearly a redistribution of government revenues between rich and poor prefectures through the central government's allocations to prefectural governments.

A second type of redistribution—the combined effects of CG and PG redistribution to cities—can be seen in Eqs. (12) and (13). Two measures of the relationship between LGs and the higher governmental units were constructed. *CTPS* (Table 7.6) is the percentage of the cities' revenues coming from combined prefectural and treasury disbursements; the lowest was in Saitama (9.9%) and the highest was Kochi (28.7%). Equation (12) relates *CTPS* to *Y* in an effort to see if the hypothesis that cities in poorer regions are subsidized through treasury and prefecture disbursements is confirmed.

$$CTPS = 32.21341 - .15143Y \quad R^2 = .231 \quad F = 13.252 \quad (12)$$
$$(3.64037)$$

TABLE 7.6 *(Continued)*

	Treasury and prefectural disbursements as a percentage of cities total revenue (CTPS)	Treasury disbursements as a percentage of prefectures' total revenues (PTS)	Treasury and prefectural disbursements as a percentage of cities' total revenues (DEP)	Index of per capita personal income (Japan = 100.0) (Y)
Mie	17.2	28.3	46.3	95.4
Shiga	15.1	24.7	37.7	93.5
Kyoto	17.7	21.7	46.7	110.0
Osaka	15.9	14.9	41.5	123.5
Hyogo	15.4	23.2	42.1	106.0
Nara	15.7	27.2	49.4	85.8
Wakayama	18.8	29.4	43.1	93.1
Tottori	21.1	30.5	67.6	83.5
Shimane	17.7	32.6	68.3	74.0
Okayama	15.1	28.3	36.0	99.4
Hiroshima	17.3	27.9	36.8	102.1
Yamaguchi	19.5	29.0	46.7	92.1
Tokushima	18.6	31.1	63.4	92.3
Kagawa	16.4	27.2	44.4	92.7
Ehime	20.4	30.2	53.7	91.2
Kochi	28.7	34.5	133.1	93.1
Fukuoka	25.2	31.9	82.7	97.3
Saga	26.3	33.3	115.7	80.4
Nagasaki	27.5	34.0	109.2	78.5
Kumamoto	25.7	33.4	93.1	73.7
Oita	24.5	34.7	84.7	75.6
Miyasaki	26.0	36.1	97.4	74.6
Kagoshima	25.4	38.3	113.4	64.8

The negative sign attached to Y indicates that this hypothesis is correct. The lower (higher) the prefectures income, the more (less) its cities get from these revenue sources. Figure 7.13 shows this graphically. However, the relationship is much weaker than that given in Eq. (11), as shown by the lower F- and t-statistics, although both are still highly significant.

Equation (13) relates prefectural income to another (and related) measure of the relationship between LGs and higher governmental levels, called the "dependency ratio" (*DEP*): the ratio of the cities' treasury and prefectural disbursements to local taxes. It measures the extent to which LGs are "dependent" upon the CG and the PGs and is also a gauge of local "tax effort."

$$DEP = 153.48419 - 1.12747Y \qquad R^2 = .360 \qquad F = 24.771 \qquad (13)$$
$$(4.97705)$$

This also confirms the general argument that poorer cities are aided by other

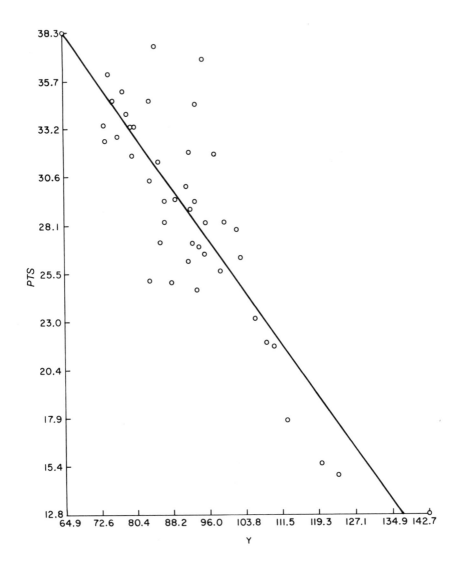

NUMBER OF OBS. = 46
INTERCEPT = 61.01179
REGR. COEFF. = −.35039
ST. ERR. OF REG. = .03096
VALUE OF RR = .74425
VALUE OF T = −11.31575
VALUE OF F = 128.04622

Figure 7.12. Relationship between *PTS* and *Y*, 1970.

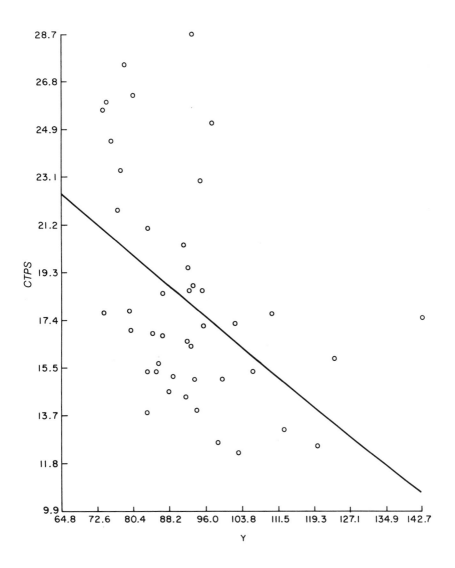

NUMBER OF OBS. = 46
INTERCEPT = 32.21341
REGR. COEFF. = −.15143
ST. ERR. OF REG. = .04160
VALUE OF RR = .23148
VALUE OF T = −3.64037
VALUE OF F = 13.25231

Figure 7.13. Relationship between *CTPS* and *Y*, 1970.

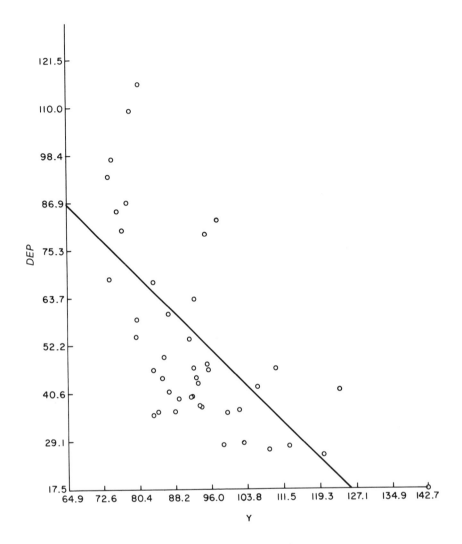

NUMBER OF OBS. = 46
INTERCEPT = 159.48416
REGR. COEFF. = −1.12747
ST. ERR. OF REG. = .22653
VALUE OF RR = .36019
VALUE OF T = −4.97705
VALUE OF F = 24.77100

Figure 7.14. Relationship between *DEP* and *Y*, 1970.

governments since, again, the coefficient is negative and significant: LGs in poorer prefectures, therefore, get more exogenously determined funds relative to locally raised revenues than LGs in richer prefectures. This relationship is also shown in Figure 7.14, which graphs DEP and Y.

One final relation, given in Eq. (14), shows the extent to which prefectures "pass through" revenues received from the CG to LGs and to some degree, the joint effects of CG and PG efforts toward cities. Thus, DEP and PTS were related.

$$DEP = -34.94318 + 3.15200PTS \qquad R^2 = .464 \qquad F = 38.147 \quad (14)$$

Equation (14) and Figure 7.15 indicate that the relationship is strongly positive: The more a prefecture gets from the CG, the more it and the CG give to its cities.

The results of Section 5 underline those of Sections 3 and 4 as they indicate the redistributive nature of the Japanese urban public finance system in yet another way. It was seen that (a) low-income prefectural governments got relatively more treasury disbursements and (b) cities in low-income prefectures got relatively more funds from the CG and their respective PGs (both in relation to total revenues and in relation to local taxes) than did cities in richer prefectures.

6 Conclusions

The major purpose of this chapter was to investigate the trends and patterns of intergovernmental fiscal relations within the Japanese urban system. After undertaking a brief description of the system itself (Section 2), the empirical analysis of fiscal relations among the levels of government for the 1960s was conducted (Sections 4 and 5). The empirical part of this study was largely done on a data base consisting of city-specific data.

The major question posed in this study involved the degree to which vertical redistribution of financial revenues took place within the financial system and how this was related to the level of economic development in individual regions. Vertical equity was the stated goal of Japanese policymakers and, to a degree, movements toward equity were achieved. Poorer regions were clearly seen to be benefiting from the tax and subsidy programs carried out during the 1960s, especially with respect to EMR. This was particularly true in the less developed regions such as Kyushu, Shikoku, and Hokkaido. The less elaborate analysis of prefectural data (Section 5) confirms these findings.

These patterns of fiscal behavior are important not only in isolation but in relation to the overall regional planning system discussed in Chapter 6. There, we saw that even though the central government planners who were involved in regional development efforts claimed to be redistributing resources and people away from the richer, more densely populated agglom-

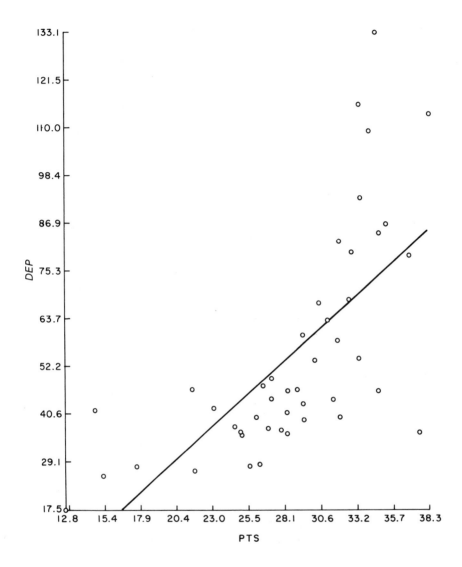

NUMBER OF OBS. = 46
INTERCEPT = −34.94318
REG. COEFF. = 3.15200
ST. ERR. OF REG. = .51033
VALUE OF RR = .46437
VALUE OF T = 6.17635
VALUE OF F = 38.14725

Figure 7.15. Relationship between *DEP* and *PTS*, 1970.

erations, this was not the case. Central government investment remained highly concentrated in the Tokaido megalopolis until late in the 1960s. The governmental efforts to create NICs and SAs as growth poles were not backed by sufficient public investment. Moreover, the plans lacked enforcement powers to encourage plants to locate away from the metropolitan core. The redistribution of population and, to a lesser degree, of jobs that occurred in the late 1960s was seen to be more of a result of market-oriented forces than of planning. The redistribution of income from rich to poor regions was probably not a result of formal planning.

But, this chapter indicates that there were other forces at work in the attempt to redistribute income. The intergovernmental fiscal system was responsible for some of the decline in income disparities noted by Mera (1976) and Sakashita (1976) and reviewed in Chapter 6. By reducing the relative tax burden of people in poorer regions and by making tax subsidies available to LGs in those regions, the income gap between rich and poor was somewhat reduced. Obviously, this program was not the only factor, as I have argued in Chapter 6, but it certainly made a contribution.

Appendix 1. Variables in the City Data Bank

File 1 contains the following items:

1. Prefectural Government (Dummy)
2. New Industrial City (Dummy)
3. Special Area (Dummy)
4. Distance from Tokyo
5. Distance to the Nearest City
6. Comprehensive Growth Index
7. Comprehensive Inhabitant Power Index
8. Age of City (1968 = 1)

Each of the remaining three files is composed of the following data:

General

1. Index of Financial Power
2. City Planning Area
3. Number of Terms of the Mayor's Election
4. Mayor's Affiliation (LDP = 1)
5. Japan Housing Corporation Units
6. Number of Eligible Voters
7. Number of Voters
8. Number of Voters Obtained by LDP Candidates
9. Telephones per 1,000 population
10. Percentage of Population with Water Supply
11. Number of Books in Libraries
12. Ordinary Households Living in Dwelling Houses
13. Owned Houses
14. Tatami per Household Member
15. DID Ordinary Households Living in Dwelling Houses

16. DID Owned Houses
17. DID Tatami per
    Household Member

18. Cars Owned
19. New Housing, Total
20. New Housing, Owned House

Demographic

21. Total Population
22. Area
23. Population Growth Rate
24. Number of Persons per
    Household
25. Ordinary Household
26. Age Distribution,
    percentage 15–64
27. Age Distribution,
    percentage 65+
28. Average Age of
    Residents
29. Education, percentage
    completing primary
    school
30. Education, percentage of
    high school graduates
31. Education, percentage of
    college graduates
32. In-migration

33. Ratio·of Daytime
    population to Nighttime
    population
34. Male/Female Ratio
35. DID Population (not
    adjusted)
36. DID Population Growth
    Rate
37. DID Area (not adjusted)
38. DID Population Density
    (not adjusted)
39. DID Population (adjusted)
40. DID Ordinary Household
    (not adjusted)
41. Ordinary Household
    (adjusted)
42. DID Ordinary
    Households (adjusted)
43. Population of the nearest
    city (adjusted)

Family Income and Expenditures

44. Receipts
45. Income (monthly)
46. Wage and Salaries
47. Receipts Other Than Income
48. Carry over from Previous
    Month
49. Living
50. Food
51. Housing
52. Fuel and Light
53. Clothing
54. Miscellaneous
55. Transportation and
    Communication

56. Private Transportation
57. Nonliving Expenditures
58. Earned Income Tax
59. Other tax
60. Savings Flow
61. Amount of Savings (stock)
62. Yearly Income
63. Wholesale Sales
64. Retail Sales
65. Bank Deposits
66. Bank Loans
67. Value added by
    manufacturing

Economy

By municipality, by place of residence

68. Percentage of white-collar workers
69. Employment, All Industry
70. Employment, Primary Industry
71. Employment, Secondary Industry
72. Employment, Manufacturing
73. Employment, Tertiary Industry
74. Employment, Wholesale and Retail
75. Employment, Finance and insurance
76. Employment, Transportation and Communication
77. Employment, Service
78. Employment, Government

By Densely Inhabited District (DID)

79. Employment, All Industries
80. Employment, Primary Industry
81. Employment, Secondary Industry
82. Employment, Manufacturing
83. Employment, Tertiary Industry
84. Employment, Wholesale and Retail
85. Employment, Finance and Insurance
86. Employment, Transportation and Communication
87. Employment, Services
88. Employment, Government

By Municipality, by place of work

89. Total labor force
90. Participation Rate
91. Employment, Total
92. Employment, Primary
93. Employment, Secondary and Tertiary
94. Employment, Mining
95. Employment, Construction
96. Employment, Manufacturing
97. Employment, Wholesale and Retail
98. Employment, Finance and Insurance
99. Employment, Transportation and Communication
100. Employment, Service

101. Total labor force
102. Value Added per Worker in Manufacturing
103. DID Employee Total
104. DID Primary Employment
105. DID Secondary and Tertiary Employment
106. DID Mining Employment
107. DID Construction Employment
108. DID Manufacturing Employment
109. DID Wholesale and Retail Employment
110. DID Finance and Insurance Employment
111. DID Transportation and Communication Employment
112. DID Service Employment

Appendix 2. Interrelationships of the Independent
Variables Used in the Study

Most of the independent variables that were constructed for this study
are highly correlated. Analyzing these relations will help understanding the
results of the regression analysis. In Tables A.1 and A.2 of this appendix,
correlation matrices of the independent variables are given for 1965 and
1970, respectively. An examination of these matrices reveals two patterns:
First, certain variables have very high interrelations and, second, the correlation coefficients change significantly from first time point to the second for
certain sets of variables. I searched for families of variables by using the
linkage method of factor analysis (a rather approximate method, but
sufficient when the objective is solely the description of families of factors).
Figure A.1 on page 339 contains the groupings of the variables both for
1965 and 1970.

In 1965 the outstanding family of variables is Group I that consists of (*a*)
SALES: volume of retail and wholesale sales, (*b*) *POP:* population, and
(*c*) *INFRA:* the index of physical and social infrastructural development of
the urban area. The fourth member—the percentage of LDP votes
(*LDPV*)—is negatively related to the other variables in this group, while the
first three are highly positively related. Group II displays high positive
relations among its members as well, all of which are rate-of-change variables: (*a*) total employment ($\Delta TEMP$), (*b*) total population (ΔPOP), (*c*)
secondary sector employment ($\Delta SECE$), and (*d*) service sector employment ($\Delta SRVE$). Interestingly, $\Delta TEMP$ plays the central role, that is, the
other three variables relate to each other via $\Delta TEMP$ rather than directly.

The third group relates *ADULT* (percentage of population at adult age)
positively to *COLGE* (percentage of population with college degrees) and
INC (average family income), while negatively to *DEPR*, which shows the
ratio of population to total employment (dependency ratio). Finally, in the
fourth group, we have *CTYAGE* (index the age of the city) and *MFPRD*
(manufacturing value added per worker), which are related positively, but
very weakly, to *REMP* (the ratio of the employees in the producing sectors
to that of service sectors of the urban economy).

These four groups have relatively low correlations with each other,
none of them exceeding $r = .25$. This means good statistical separation, a
sound basis for any interpretation to follow. The first group of variables are
indicators of a metropolitan area: large volume business transactions, high
population, and a significantly developed physical urban layout and social
overhead capital, which urbanists expect to occur simultaneously in big
metropolitan areas. This hypothesis is further supported by the negative
relation of *LDPV* to the preceding three variables, that is, LDP support
comes mostly from smaller urban areas.

TABLE A.1

Correlation Coefficients for the Independent Variables for the Set of Large Cities, 1965.

	MFPROD	SALES	INMG	DEPR	ΔPOP	ADULT	INFRA	LDPV	COLGE	INC	REMP	SPDIST	POP	CTYAGE	ΔTEMP	ΔSRVE	ΔSECE
MFPROD	1.																
SALES	−.01	1.															
INMG	−.17	.40	1.														
DEPR	.16	−.15	−.22	1.													
ΔPOP	.21	−.02	−.17	−.20	1.												
ADULT	.03	.37	.13	−.52	.10	1.											
INFRA	−.05	.88	.23	−.16	.01	.55	1.										
LDPV	−.16	−.29	.17	−.19	−.16	−.27	−.40	1.									
COLGE	−.10	.20	−.05	.10	.15	.52	.43	−.33	1.								
INC	.10	.32	−.05	−.24	.04	.56	.50	−.15	.48	1.							
REMP	.39	−.01	−.06	−.40	.18	.11	−.11	.01	−.43	.01	1.						
SPDIST	.07	−.23	−.14	.14	.06	−.13	−.25	.04	.00	−.05	−.12	1.					
POP	.03	.88	.17	−.12	.04	.50	.97	−.43	.41	.48	−.01	−.28	1.				
CTYAGE	.24	.08	−.10	−.09	.07	.15	.11	.03	−.04	.00	.20	−.14	.12	1.			
ΔTEMP	.18	−.14	−.11	−.24	.76	.10	−.16	.02	.11	−.02	.18	.05	−.14	−.03	1.		
ΔSRVE	.10	−.06	−.08	−.19	.62	.14	−.07	.01	.16	.00	.10	.01	−.05	.04	.81	1.	
ΔSECE	.07	−.19	−.12	−.16	.62	−.03	−.22	.10	.05	−.13	.07	.00	−.21	−.01	.91	.76	1.

TABLE A.2
Correlation Coefficients for the Independent Variables for the Set of Large Cities, 1970

	MFPROD	SALES	INMG	DEPR	ΔPOP	ADULT	INFRA	LDPV	COLGE	INC	REMP	SPDIST	POP	CTYAGE	ΔTEMP	ΔSRVE	ΔSECE
MFPROD	1.																
SALES	-.04	1.															
INMG	-.01	.91	1.														
DEPR	.10	-.04	.01	1.													
ΔPOP	.15	-.12	-.05	-.24	1.												
ADULT	.04	.41	.53	-.24	.06	1.											
INFRA	-.01	.78	.93	-.04	-.06	.53	1.										
LDPV	-.17	-.32	-.46	-.34	-.15	-.33	-.39	1.									
COLGE	-.12	.20	.45	-.08	.02	.64	.44	.33	1.								
INC	.39	.13	.25	.08	.11	.26	.28	-.24	.22	1.							
REMP	.21	-.05	-.05	-.20	.71	-.12	.01	.03	-.25	.11	1.						
SPDIST	.06	-.27	-.30	.80	.18	-.15	-.21	.12	-.09	-.16	.13	1.					
POP	.00	.84	.99	.02	-.02	.54	.94	-.48	.51	.29	-.05	-.31	1.				
CTYAGE	.25	.10	.11	-.06	.08	.04	.12	-.14	-.11	.08	.09	-.19	.11	1.			
ΔTEMP	.09	.05	.07	-.15	.16	.02	-.04	-.12	.03	.14	-.39	-.16	.08	.18	1.		
ΔSRVE	.17	.01	.06	.23	.90	.01	.03	-.20	-.04	.15	.81	.16	.07	.13	.04	1.	
ΔSECE	-.01	-.04	-.02	-.26	.87	-.07	-.04	-.03	-.05	.03	.75	.20	-.02	.08	.01	.84	1.

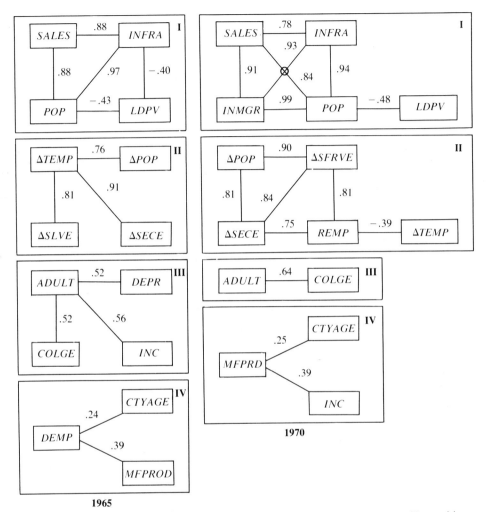

Figure A.1. Groups of independent variables in two points in time for the set of large cities (figures show correlation coefficients).

The second family of variables is associated with urban areas experiencing rapid growth. Such areas would usually be in the newer metropolitan regions, or, in individual RECs in regions designated for growth. Thus, the Sendai metropolis has very low rates of change but high scores in Group I, while Osaka has high rates of change associated with high scores in Group I. This example illustrates that the rate of change of employment and population does not correlate with the size and levels of development of the urban area. (The correlation coefficient between Group I and Group II is, on average, .11.)

The internal relations among the other two families are not as strong and not as interesting. Group III suggests that urban areas with high ratios of college graduates and work force earn more, which is neither astonishing nor very revealing. Group IV, on the other hand, shows that newer urban areas with high manufacturing value added per worker covaries with a higher ratio of secondary to total employment. However, this assertion should not be taken as anything more than plausible because the correlation coefficients are quite low in this group.

Observing Figure A.1 of Appendix 2, we can see whether any changes have occurred in these families of variables from 1965 to 1970. Generally, the interpretation of the groups does not change greatly but some variables change groups, and some new ones enter. The first group stays relatively constant, except now a new variable, *IMMGR* (daytime/nighttime population, showing the relative commuting for work to the city) establishes a very strong positive relation with the first three variables of the group. Group II gains a new variable as well, *REMP*. However, the significant change is not in this new addition of a member, but rather that the variable Δ*TEMP* loses the significant relationship to other change variables in the group to be replaced in this role by *REMP*. The third group reduces to *ADULT* and *COLGE*, the correlation among which increases in 1970. Group IV is very loosely bound, so much so that one cannot make much of the new membership of *INC* into this group, while *REMP* drops out.

References

Aqua, R. (1977), *Central Aid and Local Choice in Japan.* Mimeo.

Gencer, E., and N. J. Glickman (1976). *An Empirical Analysis of the Japanese Urban Public Finance System.* Mimeo.

Glickman, N. J. and W. W. McHone (1977). Intercity migration and employment growth in the Japanese urban economy. *Regional Studies, 11,* 165–181.

Ide, Y. (1965). *Changing Dimensions of Local Administration in Japan; Three Cases on Town-Village Amalgamation, Urbanization and Popular Participation in Local Government.* Mimeo, East-West Center, Translation Series No. 7, Honolulu.

Ike, N. (1957). *Japanese Politics: An Introductory Survey.* Knopf, New York.

Japan Bureau of Statistics, Office of the Prime Minister (1973). *Japan Statistical Yearbook, 1972.* Bureau of Statistics Office of the Prime Minister, Tokyo.

Japan Ministry of Home Affairs (1969). *Systems for Development of Underdeveloped Areas in Japan.* Ministry of Home Affairs, Tokyo.

Japan Ministry of Home Affairs (1972). *An Outline of Japanese Local Tax System.* Ministry of Home Affairs, Tokyo.

McNelly, T. (1972). *Politics and Government in Japan,* second edition. Houghton Mifflin Co., Boston.

Mera, K. (1976). *The Changing Pattern of Population Distribution in Japan and Its Implications for Developing Countries.* International Development Center of Japan, Tokyo.

Mukherjee, A. K. (1966). *The Japanese Political System.* World Press Private, Calcutta.

Sakashita, N. (1976). *Methods of Regional Economic Analysis* (in Japanese). Japan Economic Planning Agency, Tokyo.

Steiner, K. (1965). *Local Government in Japan.* Stanford University Press, Stanford.

Tsuneishi, W. M. (1966). *Japanese Political Style: An Introduction to the Government and Politics in Modern Japan.* Harper and Row, New York.

Ward, R. E. and D. A. Rustow (1964). *Political Modernization in Japan and Turkey.* Princeton University Press, Princeton.

The Growth and Management of
the Japanese Urban System

1 Introduction

This chapter brings together the strands of several arguments made in previous chapters concerning regional development and regional economic policy in postwar Japan. I shall concentrate primarily on the work in Chapters 2, 3, 6, and 7, which are central to these subjects. Section 2 highlights and extends some of the important elements of previous chapters on the subject of regional development trends. Public policy toward regional development is noted in Section 3, and perspectives on the future of Japanese cities concludes this volume in Section 4.

2 Urbanization and Regional Development in Postwar Japan

2.1 The Growth of the Japanese Urban System

The level of urbanization—as measured by conventional data sources (see Chapter 1) or by RECs (as in Chapters 2 and 3)—has increased significantly. Therefore, Japanese society has continued to transform itself from an agrarian to a largely urban society. Some of Japan's urban dimensions are noted in Table 8.1. Clearly, the RECs dominate the urban scene. The number of residents in the RECs increased by more than 31 million persons between 1950 and 1975 (compared to a 28.7-million increase in the total national population); over the same period, the SCAs grew by 26 million, from 31.7 to 57.9 million. As can be seen in Figure 8.1, the RECs increased

TABLE 8.1

Regional Development in Postwar Japan

	1950	1955	1960	1965	1970	1975
REC population (thousands)	45,492	51,407	56,651	63,593	70,269	76,571
SCA population (thousands)	31,663	35,724	41,120	47,258	53,267	57,910
Percentage change of REC population for 5-year period	—	13.0	10.2	12.3	10.5	9.0
Percentage change of SCA population for 5-year period	—	12.8	15.1	14.9	12.7	8.7
Percentage change of Japanese population for 5-year period	—	7.3	4.6	5.2	5.5	7.9
REC population as a percentage of Japanese population	54.7	57.6	60.6	64.7	67.3	68.4
SCA population as a percentage of Japanese population	38.1	40.0	44.0	48.1	50.9	51.7

their shares of total population greatly as Japanese left rural regions and moved to metropolitan areas in large numbers. Whereas only 54.7% of the population lived in the RECs in 1950, nearly 70% lived in them 25 years later. So, by the principal measure of urbanization, there was increasing concentration in relatively few city-regions over time. Japanese urbanization, as was shown in Section 5.2 of Chapter 2, has been more rapid than many other large countries[1] during the period that I have studied.

2.2 Growth of Individual Regions, 1950–1975

Table 8.2 displays some basic data for the 80 RECs between 1950 and 1975 including: (*a*) total population and the percentage change in population for 5-year intervals, (*b*) the average annual population growth for 1950–1960, 1960–1970, and 1970–1975, (*c*) 1950–1975 percentage growth, and (*d*) the shift index (as defined in Chapters 2 and 3) for 1950–1975. Several conclusions can be drawn from Table 8.2 and the analyses in Chapters 2 and 3.

First, there was considerable centralization of the urban system during the 1950s and 1960s as the major metropolitan regions in the Tokaido megalopolis grew rapidly at the expense of peripheral urban regions and non-metropolitan areas. Second, large regions grew more rapidly than smaller regions, and there was relatively little metropolitan decentralization. Third, there were some changes in patterns after 1970 as there was considerably less growth of the big regions. Then, growth was centered in middle-sized

[1] See, for instance, Tables 2.21 and 2.22. Remember also that postwar urbanization was a continuation of prewar trends; see Chapter 1.

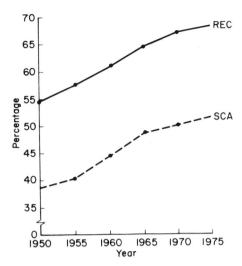

Figure 8.1. REC and SCA population as a percentage of total population.

regions—most of them either suburbs of the largest regions or independent centers away from the system's core. Fourth, the 1970s saw more suburbanization of the major metropolises such as Tokyo, although the smaller regions continued to centralize. Many RECs showed spatial centralization, as their central cities grew faster than their suburbs; this was particularly true of the smaller RECs. These and some other trends are spelled out in the following subsections.

2.2.1 Region Size and Region Growth

There was a changing relationship between region size and region growth over time. During the 1950s, in particular, the larger a region, the more likely it would be to grow more rapidly than smaller regions. This propensity for large region development clearly declined with time, however. To understand the relationship, I regressed regional growth on region size for 1950–1960, 1960–1970, and 1970–1975 according to Eq. (1):

$$AAG = B_0 + B_1 POP \qquad (1)$$

where

AAG　= average annual growth rate of population of a REC;
POP　= REC population at the beginning of the time period;
B_0, B_1 = parameters estimated by OLS regressions.

The results of those regressions are summarized in Table 8.3 and Figure 8.2.

For the 1950s, there is a strong positive relationship: both the R^2 and the regression coefficient b are statistically significant as can be seen from Table 8.3; the regression line is displayed in Figure 8.2, and it runs from its intercept in a northeasterly direction. However, the statistical relationship

TABLE 8.2
Regional Economic Clusters, 1950–1975

1	2	3	4	5	6	7	8	9	10	11	12	13	14	15	16	17	18
1	626	743	878	1,093	1,108	1,543	18.59	18.20	24.49	1.37	39.26	146.35	1.463	3.437	4.002	.833	3.672
2	287	303	312	322	334	353	5.69	3.02	3.21	3.73	5.69	23.18	.732	.870	.670	1.132	6.837
3	155	173	201	227	238	243	11.83	16.15	12.94	4.85	2.10	57.04	.933	2.660	1.699	.402	1.622
4	110	137	171	192	207	222	24.42	24.68	12.28	7.81	7.25	101.40	1.196	4.513	1.927	1.333	2.840
5	142	158	172	192	212	238	10.90	9.18	11.63	10.42	12.26	67.53	.995	1.921	2.156	2.247	2.286
6	705	751	794	859	957	1,113	6.55	5.76	8.19	11.41	16.30	57.97	.938	1.211	1.874	2.680	1.846
7	126	129	132	136	145	154	1.89	2.46	3.03	6.62	6.21	21.79	.723	.447	.883	1.266	.792
8	339	351	361	368	383	408	3.64	2.87	1.94	4.08	6.53	20.50	.716	.647	.594	1.287	.749
9	381	382	383	382	391	410	.22	.38	-.26	2.36	4.86	7.69	.640	.062	.213	.938	.297
10	284	307	307	314	327	347	7.97	.06	2.28	4.14	6.12	22.10	.725	.775	.635	1.208	.802
11	114	118	119	120	121	124	4.10	.65	.84	.83	2.48	9.18	.648	.489	.116	.622	.352
12	288	359	309	316	333	357	24.55	-13.85	2.27	5.38	7.21	23.96	.736	.714	.734	1.397	.863
13	327	347	359	380	414	459	6.17	3.43	5.85	8.95	10.87	40.40	.834	.932	1.432	2.095	1.367
14	269	287	318	331	335	348	6.56	10.88	4.09	1.21	3.88	29.30	.768	1.686	.523	.776	1.033
15	509	518	519	541	583	651	1.76	.21	4.24	7.76	11.66	27.92	.760	1.910	1.183	2.198	.930
16	253	264	266	283	305	327	4.18	.85	6.39	7.77	7.21	29.16	.767	.488	1.401	1.338	1.029
17	335	344	353	369	391	425	2.64	2.57	4.53	5.96	8.70	26.76	.753	.524	1.030	1.651	.953
18	146	150	149	155	162	169	2.28	-.36	4.03	4.52	4.32	15.59	.687	2.17	.831	2.824	.581
19	258	262	260	270	290	296	1.59	-.82	3.85	7.41	2.07	14.70	.686	.059	1.098	1.894	.550
20	451	479	520	621	816	1,052	6.25	8.57	19.42	31.40	28.92	133.36	1.386	1.431	4.617	5.211	3.448
21	8,857	10,958	13,099	15,578	17,712	18,504	23.72	19.53	18.93	13.70	4.47	108.91	1.241	3.991	3.062	.879	2.491
22	1,527	1,789	2,077	2,667	3,324	3,931	17.15	16.12	28.41	24.63	18.26	157.47	1.529	3.125	4.815	3.413	3.855
23	129	146	156	191	234	279	13.32	6.97	22.44	22.51	19.23	116.81	1.288	1.926	4.175	3.544	3.144
24	201	218	234	263	284	303	8.60	7.11	12.39	7.98	6.69	50.62	.895	1.505	1.965	1.292	1.652
25	588	639	634	662	692	741	8.60	-.76	4.42	4.53	7.08	25.96	.748	.757	.867	1.384	.928
26	195	205	213	218	224	233	4.92	4.09	2.35	2.75	4.02	19.46	.709	.874	.520	.782	.714
27	440	473	478	480	494	522	7.50	1.03	.42	2.92	5.67	18.60	.704	.824	.324	1.146	.685
28	363	380	368	363	364	376	4.72	-3.19	-1.36	.28	3.30	3.58	.615	.125	-.094	.656	.141
29	438	446	483	508	540	565	1.82	8.18	5.18	6.30	4.63	28.85	.765	.969	1.130	.896	1.219
30	472	477	485	494	500	533	1.15	1.68	1.86	1.21	6.60	13.03	.671	.284	.294	1.291	.491
31	346	364	360	364	378	402	5.30	-1.20	1.11	3.85	6.35	16.17	.690	.408	.475	1.234	.681
32	363	380	382	394	412	444	4.74	.46	3.14	4.57	7.77	22.29	.726	.521	.739	1.518	.808
33	268	269	274	280	294	316	.33	1.94	2.19	5.00	7.48	17.95	.701	.227	.712	1.414	.663

1	2	3	4	5	6	7	8	9	10	11	12	13	14	15	16	17	18
34	531	584	621	688	750	822	9.99	6.27	10.79	9.01	9.60	54.71	.919	1.567	1.905	1.849	1.761
35	660	735	794	858	928	993	11.49	7.98	8.06	8.16	7.00	50.56	.894	1.871	1.569	1.380	1.652
36	621	717	744	779	827	892	15.41	3.75	4.70	6.16	7.86	43.55	.853	1.813	1.072	1.515	1.457
37	281	305	331	375	422	469	8.42	8.55	13.29	12.53	11.14	66.76	.990	1.639	2.451	2.137	2.067
38	2,462	2,746	3,268	3,780	4,123	4,642	11.53	19.02	15.67	9.07	12.59	88.55	1.120	2.872	2.351	2.400	2.569
39	347	368	381	415	375	490	6.20	3.45	8.92	-9.64	30.67	41.29	.839	.945	-.153	1.877	1.392
40	239	284	311	364	445	526	18.61	9.64	17.04	22.25	18.20	119.95	1.306	2.607	3.645	3.392	3.203
41	282	293	291	299	312	339	3.77	-.52	2.75	4.35	8.65	20.25	.714	.319	.701	1.667	.740
42	346	365	384	421	453	500	5.44	5.22	9.64	7.60	10.38	44.46	.858	1.053	1.665	1.984	1.482
43	169	173	174	178	179	184	2.47	.29	2.30	.56	2.79	8.68	.645	.274	.262	.564	.333
44	285	294	302	322	356	424	3.42	2.58	6.62	10.56	19.10	48.95	.885	.601	1.656	3.572	1.627
45	1,312	1,433	1,511	1,645	1,809	1,985	9.17	5.45	8.87	9.97	9.73	51.24	.898	1.419	1.818	1.868	1.669

TABLE 8.2 (Continued)

1	2	3	4	5	6	7	8	9	10	11	12	13	14	15	16	17	18
46	4,784	5,762	6,781	8,272	9,495	10,252	20.42	17.69	21.99	14.78	7.97	114.28	1.273	3.549	3.424	1.546	3.095
47	1,127	1,316	1,442	1,588	1,741	1,908	16.70	9.61	10.12	9.63	9.59	69.26	1.005	2.491	1.904	1.859	2.127
48	643	658	682	733	783	839	2.37	3.64	7.48	6.82	7.15	30.51	.775	.597	1.382	1.389	1.071
49	189	201	205	235	285	341	6.28	1.90	14.63	21.28	19.65	80.14	1.070	.801	3.336	3.693	2.382
50	436	468	482	525	563	589	7.27	3.00	8.92	7.24	4.62	35.01	.802	1.004	1.564	.907	1.208
51	282	332	337	355	418	480	17.70	1.37	5.34	17.75	14.83	69.95	1.009	1.785	2.185	2.789	2.144
52	201	210	205	200	199	205	4.34	-2.20	-2.44	-.50	3.02	2.04	.606	.190	-.283	.596	.781
53	174	183	182	183	186	198	5.18	-.51	.55	1.64	6.45	13.84	.676	.431	.256	1.235	.520
54	218	227	226	224	228	237	4.00	-.39	-.88	1.79	3.95	8.63	.645	.361	.075	.761	.332
55	534	564	578	600	642	720	5.69	2.48	3.81	7.00	12.15	34.93	.801	.826	1.048	2.323	1.225
56	620	694	767	894	1,026	1,196	12.00	10.48	16.56	14.77	16.57	92.94	1.146	2.154	2.949	3.122	2.664
57	458	468	476	491	545	605	2.09	1.76	3.15	11.00	11.01	32.04	.784	.379	1.364	2.115	1.118
58	293	323	332	332	329	337	10.18	2.79	0.00	-.90	2.43	14.96	.683	1.249	-.095	.482	.559
59	223	237	242	220	211	222	6.08	2.10	-9.09	-4.09	5.21	-.65	.590	.810	-1.355	.984	-.026
60	109	114	117	114	117	123	4.60	2.42	-2.56	2.63	5.13	12.62	.669	.715	-.015	1.037	.476
61	144	159	168	166	174	182	10.62	5.57	-1.19	4.82	4.60	26.51	.751	1.567	.372	.801	.945
62	402	428	429	434	445	473	6.42	.21	1.17	2.53	6.29	17.58	.698	.649	.363	1.215	.650
63	574	584	580	582	603	648	1.77	-.71	.34	3.61	7.46	12.89	.670	.102	.390	1.444	.686
64	328	351	369	394	429	483	7.18	5.03	6.78	8.88	12.59	47.36	.875	1.188	1.511	2.402	1.563
65	160	163	164	166	171	182	1.72	.75	1.22	3.01	6.43	13.74	.676	.244	.433	1.242	.516
66	190	195	197	195	193	201	3.10	.81	-1.02	-1.03	4.15	6.05	.630	.401	-.207	.765	.235
67	295	311	320	339	362	399	5.65	2.81	5.94	6.78	10.22	35.43	.804	.838	1.226	1.993	1.221
68	1,246	1,414	1,518	1,516	1,502	1,554	13.44	7.39	-.13	-.92	3.46	24.71	.741	1.996	-.112	2.692	.887
69	867	979	1,064	1,173	1,324	1,541	12.87	8.74	10.24	12.87	16.39	77.75	1.056	.066	2.217	3.069	2.328
70	295	308	308	290	263	258	4.33	.01	-5.84	-9.31	-1.90	-12.60	.519	.410	-1.542	-.375	-.537
71	423	455	449	440	443	453	7.58	-1.26	-2.00	-.68	2.26	7.17	.637	.607	-.127	.443	.277
72	252	268	267	259	256	263	6.32	-.51	-3.00	-1.16	2.73	4.20	.619	.562	-.411	.533	.165
73	423	471	507	524	545	592	11.44	7.64	3.35	4.01	8.62	40.06	.832	1.847	.742	1.653	1.357
74	264	300	297	274	272	276	13.54	-.85	-7.74	-.73	1.47	4.62	.621	1.195	-.868	.241	.181
75	374	430	453	483	516	569	14.87	5.45	6.62	6.83	10.27	52.14	.904	1.934	1.316	1.952	1.693
76	141	151	152	146	141	140	6.55	.84	-3.95	-3.42	-.71	-1.04	.588	.726	-.768	-.312	-.242
77	351	378	386	412	447	514	7.62	2.16	6.74	8.50	14.99	46.41	.870	.957	1.472	2.845	1.537
78	163	178	186	201	223	257	8.62	4.73	8.06	10.95	15.25	57.19	.934	1.290	1.821	2.916	1.826
79	120	133	138	139	144	151	11.16	3.69	0.72	3.60	4.86	26.12	.749	1.452	.394	1.009	.933
80	344	391	405	437	469	529	13.47	3.65	7.90	7.32	12.79	53.63	.912	1.636	1.486	2.370	1.732

TABLE 8.3

Relationship between Regional Population Growth and Regional Population Size, 1950–1975

	Values of coefficients of regression equations relating population growth during period and population size in base year		
	R^2	B_1	t
1950–1960	.26884	.00044	5.35542
1960–1970	.10734	.00025	3.06250
1970–1975	.00032	.00001	.15918

deteriorates with time. During the 1960s, the values of B_1 and R^2 fall, although both are still statistically significant. The regression line rotates in a clockwise manner from the 1950s' situation. By the 1970s the relationship becomes statistically insignificant, as we also see in Figure 8.2: Growth and regional size became unrelated. Therefore, there was a dramatic change in the relationship between growth and region size in two decades.[2] Large regions clearly lost their growth preeminence by the 1970s. Middle-sized

[2] This analysis was extended in the following manner to investigate the growth–size relationship more fully. First, I recalculated AAG in Eq. (1) to convert it to a continuously compounded form and estimated

$$\log P_{t+1} = B_0 + B_1 \log P_t$$

which converts to

$$P_{t+1} = B_0' P_t$$

or

$$P_{t+1}/P_t = B_0' P_t^{B_1-1}$$

and

$$\log(P_{t+1}/P_t) = B_0 + (B_1 - 1) \log P_t$$

which is the regression estimated. A value of $B_1 > 1$ means that large RECs are growing faster than small RECs, and the regressions show that B_1 is greater than 1 for each year from 1950–1955 to 1970–1975. However, B_1 increases, reaching a peak in 1960–1965 and then sharply declines. This indicates that the relationship between growth and size was positive in each year, but was very weak by 1970–1975. This is consistent with, but less clear than, the analysis in the text.

Another element here is the importance of the largest RECs in these regressions. It may be argued that these ''outlyers'' may heavily influence the overall regression results. As we know, their growth rates declined significantly over time. To view their impact, I reestimated the regressions, but omitted the four largest RECs. The results indicate that the relationship still holds (i.e., $B_1 > 1$) but is insignificant (as measured by the t test) for some years. Interestingly, B_1 is greatest for 1970–1975 showing the rapid growth of medium-to-large regions in that time period.

These additional results modify but do not contradict the results noted in the text.

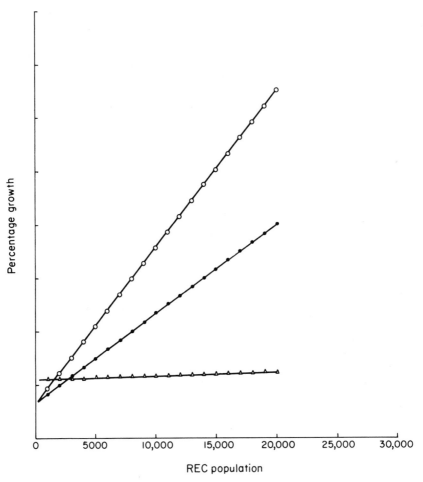

Figure 8.2.   Growth and REC size, 1950–1975. (○)—1950–1960; (●)—1960–1970; (△)—1970–1975.

regions—those in the suburban portions of metropolitan areas and independent centers as well—became the prime beneficiaries of Japan's urban growth.[3]

[3] The growth of middle-sized cities (in addition to middle-sized RECs) at the expense of larger ones can be seen from 1975 Census. For instance, the Tokyo *ku* area and Osaka *shi* lost population on an absolute basis between 1970 and 1975; the loss in Tokyo *ku* was 198,000 (2.2%) while Osaka *shi*'s loss was 201,000 (6.8%). At the same time, there was significant growth in the cities of Chiba (36.7%), Sakai (26.3%), Matsudo (35.9%), and other medium-sized cities, that is, those with populations of between 300,000 and 700,000. Only Amagasaki, a heavily industrial city near Osaka, lost population between 1970 and 1975 in the group of cities above 200,000 beside Tokyo and Osaka. All others grew, many of them rapidly.

Additionally, if one compared the average annual population growth of randomly selected

There also has been a decline of large metropolitan centers in other industrialized countries. In the United States, for instance, the relative decline of such regions during the 1960s became an absolute decline for many in the 1970s. As argued earlier, Japan's urban development has lagged behind that of the United States historically. In view of the possibility of continued out-migration from the major metropolitan regions[4] and a declining birth rate, Japan could very well see some of the same phenomena that have occurred in the United States in the mid-1970s. I shall return to this theme in Section 4.

2.2.2 Centralization of the Urban System

The system centralized rapidly between 1950 and 1970, as was shown in Chapter 2. But the 1970s' experience indicates that this situation may be changing. Although the RECs still grew faster than non-REC areas (and the SCAs grew even more rapidly), the *difference* in growth rates has declined. This can be seen in Table 8.1 where these growth rates are compared over time. Both the RECs and SCAs grew more than twice as fast as the nation as a whole for most of 1950–1970, but between 1970 and 1975 the urban regions grew less quickly relative to all Japan. Furthermore, although the non-REC regions declined throughout most of 1950–1970 (losing over 11% of their population), they grew by 5.7% between 1970 and 1975. Thus, the absolute decline of the nonmetropolitan areas was reversed in the 1970s.[5] So, while population continued to centralize, it did so far less dramatically in the 1970s than previously.

A second aspect of the decentralization process concerns the evening of interregional population growth rates. In general, the large central regions had their highest growth rates during the 1950s; this is true for Tokyo, Osaka, Nagoya, Kobe, Shizuoka, and Kitakyushu, as indicated in Table 8.4. As one can see from Columns 15–17 of Table 8.2 as well as Table 8.4, the growth rates of these regions declined thereafter. The 5-year growth rates for the three largest regions is shown in Figure 8.3, and this trend is particularly strong for Tokyo and Osaka. On the other hand, 50 RECs had their highest growth rates during the 1970s. These regions consist of a mixture of suburban RECs (a subject that will be discussed further in Section 2.2.3), middle-sized independent centers (most not far from the Tokaido megalopolis, such as Sendai), and some smaller peripheral regions. In the 1970s, outer suburbs of the major metropolises grew at their fastest rates. Table 8.4 lists some of these RECs at the outskirts of major regions that grew fastest during the 1970s; these include Kumagaya, Chiba, and Takasaki (near

---

middle-sized cities for 1970–1975 with (a) the 10 largest cities and (b) the 10 smallest cities, the results are as follows. The middle-sized group had higher growth rates than the other groups. Therefore, the preeminence of the middle-sized group is once again shown.

[4] See Table 3.7 and Vining and Kontuly (1977).

[5] An event that also occurred in the United States at the same time.

TABLE 8.4
Period during Which Average Annual Growth Rate Was Greatest for Regional Economic Clusters, 1950–1975

1950–1960	1960–1970	1970–1975	
Muroran	Maebashi	Sapporo	Yokkaichi
Kushiro	Kiryu	Hakodate	Ise
Hitachi	Yokohama	Morioka	Otsu
Tokyo	Hiratsuka	Sendai	Kyoto
Nagasaki	Odawara	Ishinomaki	Himeji
Shizuoka	Kanazawa	Akita	Nara
Hamamatsu	Gifu	Yamagata	Tottori
Nagoya	Numazu	Fukushima	Yonago
Osaka	Toyota	Aizuwakamatsu	Matsue
Kobe	Wakayama	Koriyama	Okayama
Shimonoseki		Mito	Kurashiki
Iwakuni		Utsunomiya	Hiroshima
Kitakyushu		Takasaki	Fukuyama
Omuta		Kumagaya	Ube
Kurume		Chiba	Yamaguchi
Saga		Niigata	Tokushima
Nagasaki		Toyama	Takamatsu
Sasebo		Takaoka	Matsuyama
Yatsushiro		Fukui	Imabari
Nobeoka		Kofu	Niihama
		Nagano	Kochi
		Matsumoto	Fukuoka
		Toyohashi	Kumamoto
		Tsu	Oita
		Nagaoka	Miyazaki

Tokyo), Tsu, Yokkaichi, and Ise (south of Nagoya), Himeji and Nara (near Osaka). This growth is essentially a spillover from the central RECs and is a manifestation of metropolitan sprawl.

Another important set of fast-growing regions in the 1970s were independent centers, most of which were middle-sized and formerly slow-growing. These include Sendai, Niigata, and Akita; Sapporo is also in this group, but it grew rapidly throughout the postwar period.

The third set of regions growing at their fastest rates during the 1970s consists of those that were previously not included in the urban growth process to any substantial degree: geographically isolated regions such as Kochi, Miyazaki, and Hakodate, which had previously grown slowly or declined. There appears to be a clear change in pattern as the 1970s witnessed buoyant growth in some of them. It should be noted, however, that many other remote regions continued to grow slowly or decline (Omuta and Yatsushiro lost population) in the 1970s. Some of the polarization between fast- and slow-growing so evident in the 1950s and 1960s continued into the

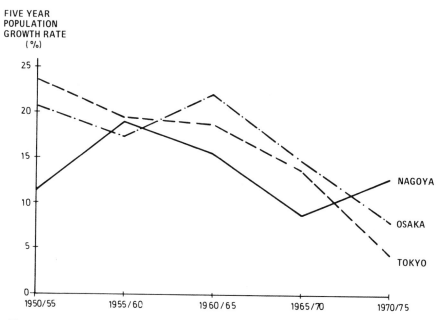

Figure 8.3. Five-year population growth rates of Toyko, Osaka, and Nagoya RECs, 1950–1955 to 1970–1975.

1970s. However, this phenomenon was clearly less pronounced in the later years.

Overall, Tables 8.2 and 8.4 indicate an evening of the growth rates, as formerly slow-growing, spatially peripheral regions began to catch up with larger regions that exhibited less exuberant population increases over time. As I have noted in Chapter 3, these changes are built upon significant alterations of migration patterns. We see, then, the beginnings of decentralization of Japanese urban system in the 1970s as greater growth occurred down the urban hierarchy. We may see more of this in the late 1970s and 1980s.

Another view of changes in the urban system can be had by calculating some "rank–size" relationships among the RECs and comparing them over time.[6] Under this rule, the populations of urban regions can be ranked in decreasing order of size (with the largest region given rank 1, the second largest given rank 2, etc.), and it may be found that a hierarchy of regions can be defined. If we plot the log of the population of a city on the ordinate

---

[6] This regularity among cities has been analyzed by Stewart (1947), Zipf (1949), and others, including Berry (1964, 1967), Berry and Horton (1970), Mills (1972), Nourse (1968), Parr and Suzuki (1973), and Vining (1977).

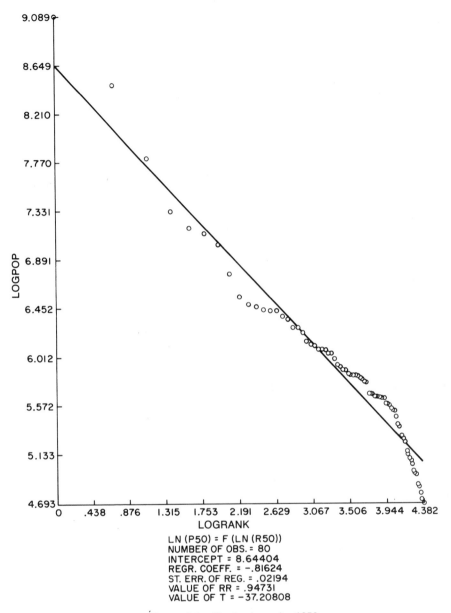

LN (P50) = F (LN (R50))
NUMBER OF OBS. = 80
INTERCEPT = 8.64404
REGR. COEFF. = −.81624
ST. ERR. OF REG. = .02194
VALUE OF RR = .94731
VALUE OF T = −37.20808

Figure 8.4. Rank–size rule, 1950.

and the log of the city's rank on the abscissa on log–log paper, we obtain an approximation of a straight line. The rank–size rule is written in Eq. (2).

$$PR_B = P_1 \tag{2}$$

where

P = the population of a given city;
R = the rank of that city among cities in the urban system;
P_1 = the population of the largest city;
B = a parameter.

Converting Eq. (2) to logarithmic form yields Eq. (3).

$$\log P = \log P_1 - B \log R \tag{3}$$

Therefore, we shall have a line with slope B that, according to several studies, should be close to -1. A corollary of the rank–size rule is that if one multiplies the population of each city by its rank, the result is a constant. That is,

$$P_1 \times R_1 = P_2 \times R_2 = P_3 \times R_3 = \cdots = R_r \times r = \text{const.} \tag{4}$$

in an r city system.

The REC data was used to calculate rank–size relationships for 5-year periods from 1950 to 1975, as shown in Figures 8.4–8.9. We see the individual data points and the estimated OLS regression line in each figure. Note that the largest deviations from the trend line are at the extreme ends of the distribution; this has been shown to be true for other countries in other studies as well. Table 8.5 lists the regression coefficients. Note that B decreases in value over time, going from $-.816$ in 1950 to $-.956$ in 1975; $\log P_1$ increases and the R^2 also goes up. Figure 8.10 shows the trends in the regression lines estimated for each year. There is a clockwise rotation through time as B approaches -1.0. However, the rank–size rule is not borne out for Japan: The level of B for 1975 ($-.956$) is more than $2SD$ (the standard deviation is .021) so that on statistical grounds we can conclude that B is statistically different from -1.0.

The rank–size rule is of interest in viewing the centralization of the urban system. The movement toward -1 from more than -1 (i.e., from $-.816$ to $-.956$) indicates a centralization of the urban system: Large RECs are growing faster than smaller ones. However, if one peruses Column 4 of Table 8.5, one sees that this rate of centralization is lessening. The *rate of change* of B increases from 1950–1955 to 1960–1965, but increases less rapidly thereafter. This means that the system continues to centralize but less rapidly than previously. The findings of Chapter 3 and earlier in the present chapter, and the rank–size analysis confirms those conclusions.

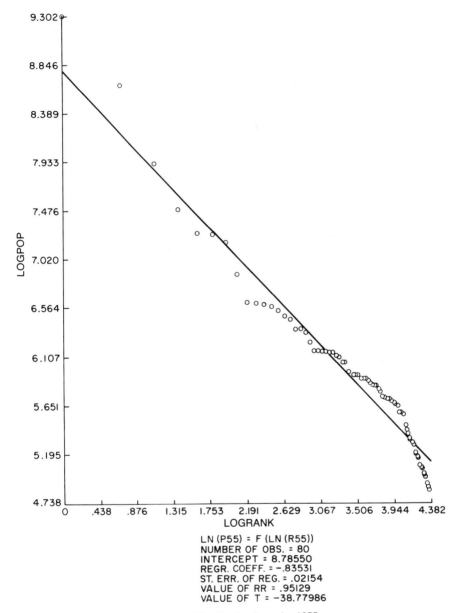

Figure 8.5. Rank–size rule, 1955.

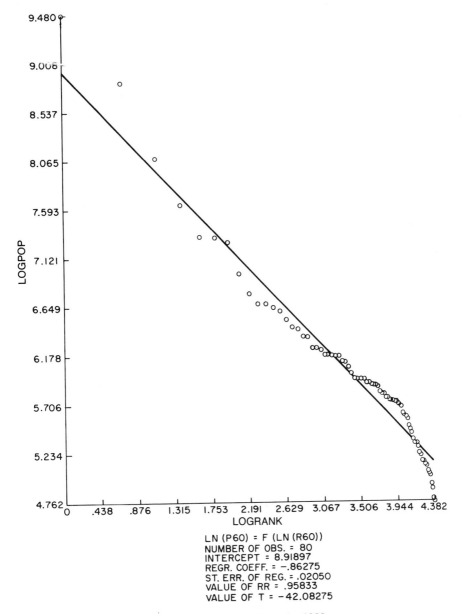

LN (P60) = F (LN (R60))
NUMBER OF OBS. = 80
INTERCEPT = 8.91897
REGR. COEFF. = −.86275
ST. ERR. OF REG. = .02050
VALUE OF RR = .95833
VALUE OF T = −42.08275

Figure 8.6. Rank–size rule, 1960.

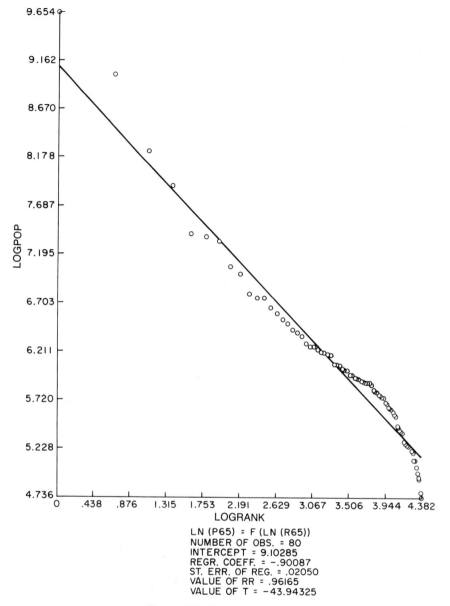

LN (P65) = F (LN (R65))
NUMBER OF OBS. = 80
INTERCEPT = 9.10285
REGR. COEFF. = −.90087
ST. ERR. OF REG. = .02050
VALUE OF RR = .96165
VALUE OF T = −43.94325

Figure 8.7. Rank–size rule, 1965.

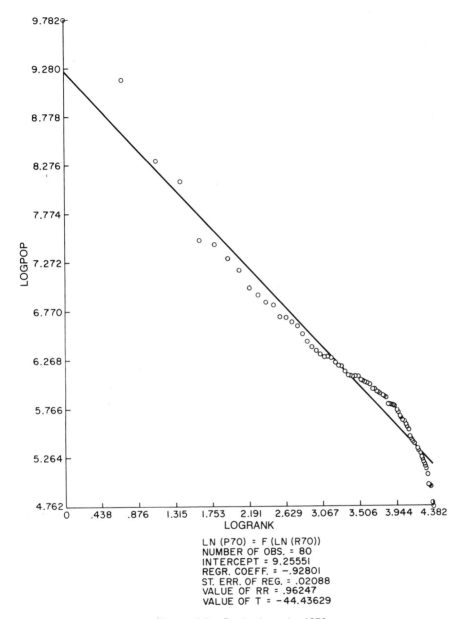

LN (P70) = F (LN (R70))
NUMBER OF OBS. = 80
INTERCEPT = 9.25551
REGR. COEFF. = −.92801
ST. ERR. OF REG. = .02088
VALUE OF RR = .96247
VALUE OF T = −44.43629

Figure 8.8. Rank–size rule, 1970.

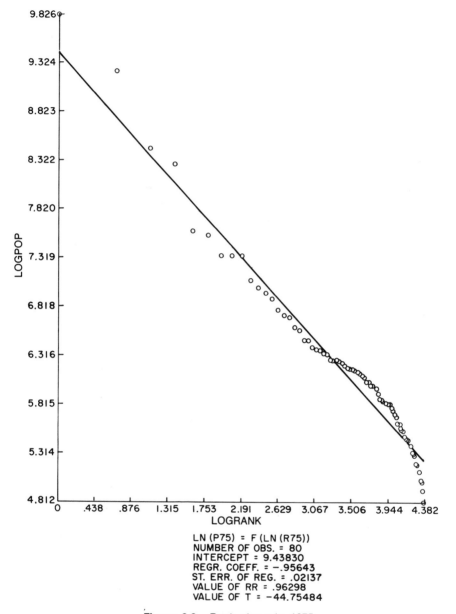

LN (P75) = F (LN (R75))
NUMBER OF OBS. = 80
INTERCEPT = 9.43830
REGR. COEFF. = −.95643
ST. ERR. OF REG. = .02137
VALUE OF RR = .96298
VALUE OF T = −44.75484

Figure 8.9. Rank–size rule, 1975.

TABLE 8.5
Rank–Size Coefficients, 1950–1975

Year	Value of regression coefficients			
	$\log P_1$	B	R^2	$\% \Delta B$
1950	8.644	−.816	.947	—
1955	8.786	−.835	.951	2.336
1960	8.919	−.863	.958	3.285
1965	9.103	−.901	.962	4.418
1970	9.256	−.928	.962	3.013
1975	9.438	−.956	.963	3.062

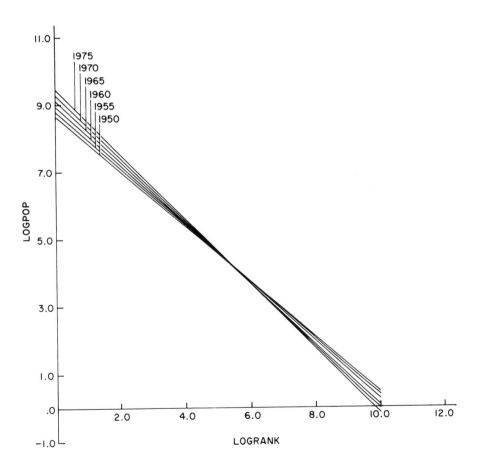

Figure 8.10. Rank–size relationships, 1950–1975.

2.2.3   Metropolitan Spatial Structure

The movement of population from central cities to suburban subregions proceeded in a different manner in Japan than in other industrialized countries during the same time period. As was shown in Chapter 5, Japanese central cities are more spatially compact than those of the United States, the United Kingdom, and West Germany. Using density functions as a measure of population dispersion, higher central densities and higher density gradients for Japan were found than for these other countries. Looking beyond central cities to the experience of metropolitan regions, Chapters 2 and 3 showed that there were greater population increases in central cities than the suburbs in the 1950s—denoting relative metropolitan centralization— followed by some suburbanization in later years. This is also shown in Figure 8.11. However, suburbanization was occurring mainly in the large metropolitan regions: 63 of 80 RECs—almost all smaller ones—were still centralizing in the 1970s as rural people were attracted to jobs in rural-region central cities. In comparison to other countries, Japan is not highly suburbanized. For instance, 54.8% of the REC population was in central cities in 1970, while in comparable functional urban regions for countries such as the United States and West Germany, the proportions were much lower.

As in other countries, suburbanization occurred in stages. A perusal of Table 8.2 will reveal that the inner suburbs of the large urban centers grew fastest during earlier time periods than did the more distant suburbs. Figure 8.12 charts the 5-year growth rates of three suburbs (Chiba, Toyota, and Nara). It can be seen that their peak growth years were from 1965 to 1970. In the 1970s, even more outlying cities experienced their sharpest population influxes.

Table 8.6 shows growth of suburban subregions within the eight SCAs—showing the period in which each component REC had its highest average annual population growth rate. For the Tokyo SCA, the Tokyo REC grew at its fastest rate in the 1950s; the suburban movement to the southwest is indicated by maximum growth rates for Yokohama and its neighbors in the 1960s. Finally, Chiba and Kumagaya grew quickly in the 1970s. This pattern emerges in the Nagoya and Osaka SCAs as well, as the central RECs reach maximum growth rates in the 1950s.[7]

These data indicate that metropolitan decentralization patterns were somewhat different in Japan than in countries such as the United States. Japanese regions are much more spatially compact (i.e., a smaller percentage of the population of the RECs live in the suburbs and the population density functions are more steep), and only the larger metropolitan areas are

---

[7] Table 8.6 also highlights the diffusion of growth down the urban hierarchy. We see the largest SCAs' central RECs growing fastest in the 1950s. However, the maximum growth rates for the central RECs (and the suburban RECs as well) for the smaller and less central SCAs (such as Sendai, Okayama, and Matsuyama) peaked later.

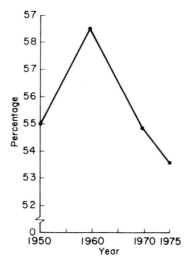

Figure 8.11. Central city population as a percentage of REC population, 1950–1975.

having significant suburbanization trends. This may change in future years if Japan's regions follow the patterns of other developed countries.

3 Regional Planning and Regional Economic Policy

3.1 Introduction

The discussions in Chapters 6 and 7 involved the interplay of two sets of policies that affected regional development. The first group was macro-economic (monetary and fiscal) policy at the national level that sought to stimulate investment, exports and, as a result, GNP. Related to such macro-policy was national indicative planning and its regional planning components. Regional planning, it was argued, attempted to induce investment in peripheral areas of Japan and to help disperse population. Section 3.2 reviews the findings on regional planning. Coupled with macropolicy and planning was a second set of policies, to be discussed in Section 3.3: the complex of tax and subsidy schemes contained in Japan's intergovernmental relations. Through differential levies on LGs, the CG hoped to create more interregional equity.

3.2 Regional Planning in Postwar Japan

Regional planners adopted a "place" prosperity strategy and attempted to build up lagging regions. This was due in part to intense pressure from rural-based elements of the Liberal Democratic Party. In theory, the CG was

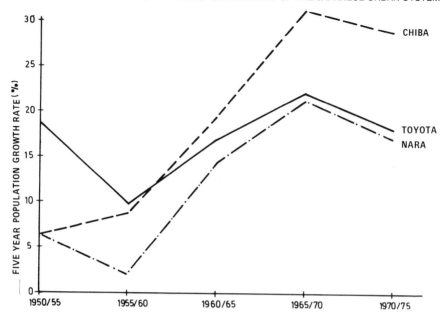

Figure 8.12. Five-year population growth rates of Chiba, Toyota, and Nara, 1950–1955 to 1970–1975.

to make infrastructure and other investments in poor areas such as Kyushu and Tohoku. To some extent, this occurred, as was shown in Table 6.6. Per capita public investment did increase in some poor regions, but not until the late 1960s and early 1970s. Even then, many poor regions lagged in their shares of government spending. For instance, Kyushu had a per capita CG investment level of only 77% of the nation in 1965 (years after the decentralization policy was supposed to have begun); although Kyushu had 95% of the national average by 1973, it still lagged Coastal Kanto (nearly 97%). Therefore, the reality of spatially deconcentrated investment did not follow the rhetoric of the CG. During the 1960s when economic growth was most rapid, investment was highly concentrated in the more prosperous and central prefectures in the Tokaido region. This helped to make the economy spatially efficient and to increase GNP. Equity considerations were not paramount then. Later when population began to disperse, public investment followed. Clearly, from our look at migration phenomena in Chapter 3 combined with our view of public investment patterns in Chapter 6, population dispersal *preceded* public investment decentration. Therefore, the major forces that explain these population movements must be found elsewhere than in regional investment planning. Public investment deconcentration cannot "explain" population deconcentration.

Chapter 6 also contained an analysis of two specific "place"-oriented policies: the NICs and the SA development programs. These regions were

TABLE 8.6

Period in Which REC Components of SCAs Reached Maximum Average Annual Growth Rates of Population[a]

Sendai SCA		Osaka SCA	
Sendai	3	Osaka	1
Yamagata	3	Kyoto	3
Fukushima	3	Kobe	1
Koriyama	3	Himeji	3
		Wakayama	2
Tokyo SCA		Otsu	3
Tokyo	1	Nara	3
Yokohama	2		
Chiba	3	Okayama SCA	
Kumagaya	3	Okayama	3
Hiratsuka	2	Kurashiki	3
Odawara	2	Fukuyama	3
Numazu	2		
		Matsuyama SCA	
Kanazawa SCA		Matsuyama	3
Kanazawa	2	Imabari	3
Takaoka	3	Niihama	3
Toyama	3		
		Kitakyushu SCA	
Nagoya SCA		Kitakyushu	1
Nagoya	1	Fukuoka	3
Toyota	2	Kurume	1
Gifu	2		
Tsu	3		
Yokkaichi	3		

[a] 1 = 1950–1960; 2 = 1960–1970; 3= 1970–1975.

amalgamations of existing cities that were to receive special development funds and other subsidies so that new employment opportunities could be attracted there. However, public investment in real terms was much less than targeted by the regional planners; there was more than 400 billion *yen* (about $2 billion) less spent than proposed for the NICs and about an equal deficit for the SAs. Only three NICs and none of the SAs reached targeted investment levels by 1974. Moreover, the NICs and SAs often did not reach the relatively low levels of investment channeled to their respective prefectures or major regions.

The lack of concentrated public investment in these regions, and the fact that most industries attracted were capital intensive, has meant that employment has not increased very much and, therefore, population goals were not met. Clearly, people were not leaving overcrowded metropolitan regions[8] to live in the NICs, at least to any great extent, because of increased

---

[8] There were "push" policies formulated by various governmental level that we also discussed in Chapter 6. These policies involved restrictions on new factories in large metropoli-

employment opportunities. I compared the NICs to non-NICs cities with similar characteristics and found that NICs did not consistently grow faster than the other group. This reinforced my contention that whatever population movements that occurred to small and medium-sized cities were the product of market and other forces that made such locations better for firms and households. Additionally, there was less net migration to the major regions because income differentials among regions was declining. That is, there was less reason for people to leave the poorer, more remote regions because the returns to migration investment were falling. It is important to note that these declines in income differentials preceded most of the regional planning efforts. Again, planning cannot be credited with reducing migration propensities or income differences.

3.3 Local Government Finance

Although regional planning probably did not reduce interregional income differentials, the system of intergovernmental relations contributed to this phenomenon. I have shown in Chapter 7 that the LGs in the poorer regions were net beneficiaries of intergovernmental grants and subsidies from the CGs and prefectural governments (PGs). Aqua (1977) also has indicated this in his study.

My analysis, undertaken on two data sets (for large and small cities), showed that relatively more funds went to cities with low levels of industrial development. This was particularly true of nonearmarked revenues and treasury disbursements. I found that cities in Kyushu, Hokkaido, and Chugoku were important recipients of such funds. The discussion of prefectural data in Section 5 of Chapter 7 confirmed the conclusion that the system of intergovernmental transfers tended toward vertical equity.

Seen in relation to the decline in migration to rich regions and the fall in income differentials, the tendency for vertical equity in the tax system is important, supplying a partial explanation for those phenomena. Therefore, the fact that local tax burdens in poor cities were reduced, coupled with private market location decisions, helps me to explain the changing pattern of urban growth that I summarized in Section 2 of this chapter.

Therefore, it is important to view the policies reviewed in Chapters 6 (regional planning) and 7 (intergovernmental fiscal relations) as complementary and somewhat reinforcing. Although we have seen that regional plan-

---

tan areas. Inoue (1977) argues that they became more important in later years. Such measures included the Industrial Relocation Law (1972) that divided the nation into three classifications according to future industrial concentration. The law instituted the Industrial Redistribution Corporation that was to help, with the aid of a $100 million yearly budget, expand industrial production into "industrial inducement" areas. Industrial decentralization is also fostered, indirectly at least, by environmental laws such as the Public Nuisance Countermeasures Basic Law (1967) and its successors. Often, industries in large cities found it difficult to meet the requirements of such acts.

ning efforts were relatively weak, the attempts to decentralize jobs and population were genuine. The tax system helped this by making the local costs of government less expensive in poorer cities.

4 Concluding Remarks

There were some important changes in settlement patterns beginning in the late 1960s. Big city living became less favored and there was an increasing propensity to locate in medium-sized cities, both in suburban subregions and in independent growth centers.

An important question—and one not directly answerable by this study—involves the continuing evolution of the Japanese urban system during what many believe will be a period of relatively slow economic growth: What will be the future shape of the system?[9] The answer to this question involves a set of subsidiary questions that are difficult to answer at this point in urban history. I shall make some speculation about Japan's urban future subsequently after raising a set of interrelated questions.

We know that Japan's urban system centralized during the high economic growth period of the 1950s and 1960s, but how will it change if growth slackens? Will there be more out-migration from the metropolitan RECs to smaller ones? Will jobs decentralize under the stress of relative economic stagnation? Or, on the other hand, will slow growth make large cities more attractive for jobs and housing and will the economic slowdown inhibit new investment in smaller cities?

And what of the role of the public sector in determining land use policy? Although there has been a conscious decentralization policy since the early 1960s as I have shown in Chapter 6, it has not been very strong and effective. What directions will the government follow regarding settlement policies?

Also, how will sharply higher energy prices affect the shape of the urban system and individual cities? Will this tend to centralize the urban system as many have argued?

Additionally, what of the social and cultural factors that have appeared to make small-town living more attractive to the Japanese in the last 10 years? Under the pressure of slow economic growth and higher energy costs, will the "U-turners" again begin to favor large-city living? How will the cultural homogenization, which has come with mass communications in Japan, affect living patterns in the future?

It is only with the answers to this set of interrelated questions that the future shape of the Japanese urban system can be predicted. What seems

---

[9] And the urban systems of other developed countries that face similar economic conditions.

probable is an extension of the urbanized Tokaido megalopolis south and west from Osaka toward Kitakyushu and north from Tokyo to Southern Tohoku and Hokuriku; Kornhauser (1977) has indicated a belief in this future as well. Second, there may be some development in Southern Hokkaido based on natural resource development and manufacturing attracted by lower priced land and the new port facilities at Tomakomai. Third, suburban growth, especially near the large cities, should continue and the suburbanization phenomenon should spread to middle-sized regions.

This all spells a continuing relative decline of the major cities and even their surrounding regions as the migration data indicate continued out-migration[10] from the core prefectures. My sense of urban economic history tells me that Japan will likely follow the patterns of other developed countries where rural depopulation accompanied high concentration in large cities; then, suburbanization and movements to smaller regions constituted a later stage of urban development. This has been seen in the United States, for instance, and the decline of big cities has been associated with fiscal problems and accompanying social service level declines and physical deterioration.[11] Therefore, Tokyo's fiscal problems in early 1978 come as no great surprise. Other large and old Japanese cities may see similar problems in the future. Should Japan follow the lead of these countries in the near future, it will be doing so by greatly speeding up the course of urban change. Where the U.S. urban system took nearly 100 years to go from the stage of urban concentration to the deconcentration era, Japan seems to be doing it in, at most, 40 years. It will be interesting to see how the Japanese adjust to this "telescoping" of the urban growth process.

References

Aqua, R. (1977). *Central Aid and Local Choice in Japan*. Mimeo.

Alonso, W. (1977). *The Current Halt in the Metropolitan Phenomenon*. Mimeo.

Berry, B. J. L. (1964). Cities as systems within systems of cities. *Papers of the Regional Science Association, 13*, 147–164.

Berry, B. J. L. (1967). *Geography of Market Centers and Retail Distributions*. Prentice-Hall, Englewood Cliffs, N.J.

Berry, B. J. L. and F. E. Horton (1970). *Geographic Perspectives on Urban Systems*. Prentice-Hall, Englewood Cliffs, N.J.

Edel, M. (1976). The New York crisis as economic history, in R. E. Alcaly and D. Mermelstein, eds., *The Fiscal Crisis of American Cities*. New York, Vintage Books. Pp. 228–245.

Gordon, D. M. (1976). Capitalism and the roots of urban crisis, in R. E. Alcaly and

---

[10] According to a 1977 article in the English-language *Mainichi Times*, the rural-to-urban migration pattern has ended. Forty-six of Japan's 47 prefectures gained population in 1976. Only Tokyo-*to* lost population. The article also notes continuing suburban growth.

[11] See the sources given in Footnote 18 of Chapter 3 as well as Alonso (1977), Morrison (1977), Jusenius and Ledebur (1976), Gordon (1976), and Edel (1976).

D. Mermelstein, eds., *The Fiscal Crisis of American Cities*. New York, Vintage Books. Pp. 82–112.

Inuoe, S. (1977). *Factors in the Retardation of Metropolitan Growth Rates in Japan*. Mimeo.

Jusenius, C. L. and L. C. Dedebur (1976). *A Myth in the Making: The Southern Economic Decline*. U.S. Department of Commerce Economic Development Administration, Washington, D.C.

Kornhauser, D. H. (1977). *Some Comments on Urban Viability in Japan*. Mimeo.

Mills, E. S. (1972). *Urban Economics*. Scott, Foresman, Glenview, Ill.

Morrison, P. A. (1977). *Emerging Public Concerns Over U.S. Population Movements In An Era of Slowing Growth*. Paper P-5873, RAND Corp., Santa Monica, California.

Nourse, H. O. (1968). *Regional Economics*. New York, McGraw-Hill.

Parr, J. and K. Suzuki (1973). Settlement populations and the lognormal distribution. *Urban Studies, 10*, 335–352.

Stewart, J. Q. (1947). Empirical mathematical rules concerning the distribution and equilibrium of population. *The Geographical Review, 37*, 461–485.

Vining, D. R., Jr. (1977). The rank-size rule in the absence of growth. *Journal of Urban Economics, 4*, 15–29.

Vining, D. R., Jr. and T. Kontuly (1977). *Population Dispersal From Major Metropolitan Regions: An International Comparison*, Paper No. 100, RSRI, Regional Science Research Institute Discussion, Philadelphia.

Zipf, G. K. (1949). *Human Behavior and the Principle of Least Effort*. Addison-Wesley, Cambridge, Mass.

Index